The Boy
Who Saved
Billy Bremner

**A Novel By
Nicholas J Dean**

Produced by Softwood Books, Suffolk, UK

Text © Nik Dean

Cover design @Nik Dean

All rights reserved. Without limiting the rights under copyright reserved above, no part of this publication may be reproduced, stored, or introduced into a retrieval system, or transmitted, in any form or by any means (electronic, mechanical, photocopying, recording or otherwise) without the prior written permission of both the copyright owners and the publisher of this book.

First Edition

Paperback ISBN 978-1-3999-8939-8

www.softwoodbooks.com

In Memory of Mum
Jacqueline Lavinia Nott

Chapter 1

One could be forgiven for thinking that a fourteen year old boy, waking up on the first morning of the summer holidays, would have a heart bursting at the seams with joy and a mind that was buzzing with anticipation of what lay ahead over the next six or seven weeks. He would also be smiling contently at the thought of not having to do any homework, not having to go to detention and not having to face the prospect of thin wispy strips of cane crashing down from a great height, stinging his open sweaty palms, as punishment for not turning up to the detention he had received for failing to do his homework.

As we get older, we foolishly and naively create a narrative that believes every boy spends endless summer days wrapped up in an equally endless supply of euphoria, each moment being spent as if it had just leapt from the pages of a Famous Five adventure story, each day occupied with the pursuit of pirates and the discovery of hidden caves full of lost treasure, before handing the crooks over to the proper authorities and then jumping back on his bicycle and frantically peddling home in time for tea and a succulent slice of Victoria sponge.

For young Philip Knott however, as he lay in his bed and stared up at the ceiling on that particular July morning in the summer of 1973, all was not wonderful, bright and shimmering with excitement. This is not to say that it was all as bleak as mid-winter either. There were certain pockets of hope and tingles of excitement upon the horizon.

Would this summer be the summer that he experienced his first proper kiss with Lesley Bennett? They had held hands on numerous occasions since they had become boyfriend and girlfriend a few months earlier and they had also kissed, more than once. However, up to now these kisses could only be described as tentative pecks with mouths firmly closed and with lips only connecting for the briefest of moments. In fact, these connections had been so brief that Philip was often unsure whether they had actually happened at all. He longed for something more, something that he would have a better than average chance of remembering. He longed to experience some form snogging or heavy petting for himself. Up to now, he had only been an observer of a young teenage couple at the bus stop or on the back seat of the upper deck. He had watched out of the corner of his eye and wondered when it would be his turn to experience such emotions, as he headed into town on his way to the swimming baths.

Along with his desire to finally view the world of romance from the other side of first base, swimming was very important to Philip. Not just because it was something that he enjoyed immensely, it was also a very good reason for staying out of the house and this above all else was a good thing. Thankfully for Philip and his friends, as they were growing up on their neglected and forgotten council estate on the outskirts of the city, going swimming was relatively cheap. The bus fare into town cost two pence, admission into the swimming baths, where you could swim all day cost two pence. A cone of chips from Fishy Moore's chip shop afterwards cost two pence and the bus back home again was another two pence. A whole days' worth of escape and change out of a ten pence piece.

His paper round, which paid him sixty pence a week for seven mornings and six evenings, included the dreaded Sunday morning, when each paper was as thick as his maths textbook. Thus, resulting in him having to drag the paper-bag along the pavement, until he had successfully delivered papers to approximately a dozen houses, but it meant he was at least able to go swimming every weekend, and as often as he liked in the holidays. He could even afford to pay for one or two of his mates to go when they had no money of their own. This was rather a regular occurrence as money was always in short supply amongst his friends' families as well as his own.

Another cloud which sported a lining of polished glimmering silver was the fact that before he returned to school the new football season would have begun. For Philip football was the passion that sat undisputed at the top of the pile, or to put it another way, the top of the table. This included reading about it, watching it and playing it. He purchased the 'Tiger' comic every week out of his paper round wages due to its main feature and character strip 'Roy of the Rovers', and if the chance presented itself he would slip a copy of 'Shoot' magazine into his paper bag when the owner of the newsagents wasn't looking. Except for the week at the start of the season when the magazine had the free league table ladders inside. On that particular occasion he and every other schoolboy worth his salt was more than happy to pay the asking price, as missing out on the league ladders was a price not worth paying.

Two separate thoughts suddenly and simultaneously popped into Philip's head as he lay in his bed on that bright and shimmering first Saturday of the holidays. One was the fact that he was going to be late for his paper round and the other was the fact that the forthcoming season's fixtures had been released and would be in the paper that morning. With this, he threw back the blanket and climbed down from the top bunk without disturbing his younger brother who was still sleeping in the bottom bunk. He stretched, scratched a certain part of his anatomy and removed something unpleasant but interesting to a fourteen-year-old boy from inside his nose. Once this had been dealt with, he proceeded to remove his cotton pyjamas. He picked his clothes up off the floor, got dressed, threw his pyjamas onto his bunk and headed downstairs in search of some breakfast.

The aroma of gently frying bacon met Philip approximately halfway between his bedroom and the kitchen, at the bottom of the stairs to be precise. The sound of the bacon popping and sizzling in the pan was only a few paces behind the aroma and was clearly audible as he pushed open the kitchen door. Upon entering the kitchen Philip immediately saw his father standing directly in front of him but facing the cooker. He had a spatula in his hand and was busily manoeuvring four thick cut rashers of bacon around inside a frying pan. Philip let the door slowly close behind him as he walked past his father and headed for the fridge at the opposite end of the long narrow kitchen. He opened the fridge door and took out a pint of milk. His dad momentarily took his attention off his bacon and looked down the kitchen at Philip.

"Pour us a glass, son," he said, before focusing once again on his breakfast.

Philip placed the bottle on a small table that was pushed up against the side of the fridge before reaching above it and taking two coloured plastic beakers from the cupboard.

"Do you want a bacon sandwich, son?" His dad asked as Philip poured out two glasses of milk.

"No, thanks."

Philip finished pouring out the milk and returned the near empty bottle to the fridge. His dad switched off the cooker and walked over to the table, firmly gripping the handle of the frying pan as he did so. Waiting on the table and resting upon a plate, were four slices of freshly cut bread, each slice thickly buttered and covered in tomato ketchup. Philip's dad began lifting the bacon from the pan, laying them out onto his waiting bread.

"Do you want to dip some bread in the fat, son?"

Philip looked up from his glass of milk and smiled. He reached for the crusty uncut loaf sat on the cutting board with one hand and grabbed the bread knife that lay next to it with the other. He cut off a thick slice as his dad placed the frying pan on the table. Philip dipped his freshly cut slice of bread into the warm glistening fat and gently pressed it down with his fingers. He lifted it out again and whilst his dad returned the pan to the cooker, he took a big bite. His dad then reacquainted himself with his bacon sandwich and they both sat and ate their breakfasts.

They ate in silence for the next few minutes before Philip's dad asked, "I thought the fixtures came out today?"

Philip just nodded as he ate.

"So, how come you weren't standing outside the newsagents waiting for it to open at first light?"

"No rush, doesn't matter what time I get there, it's not going to change the fixtures."

"No, I suppose not, so who do you want on the opening day?"

"I don't mind, as long as it isn't Man Utd and as long as we're at home."

"So, you do mind?" Philip's dad replied.

With a puzzled expression on his face, Philip wiped the bacon fat from his lips with the back of his hand before reaching for his glass of milk.

"You do mind," his dad repeated.

"I suppose so," Philip replied, with a mouthful of bread and milk before he reached for the loaf again and cut off another slightly more modest slice. He went back to the pan and placed the bread in the still translucent fat. He pushed it around a little and gave it a quick press before lifting it out and returning to his seat.

Philip's dad finished his sandwiches and reached for the top pocket of his works overalls. He undid the button, lifted the lapel, and removed a packet of Senior Service cigarettes and a box of matches. He placed them on the table, before washing down his final mouthful of sandwich with his final mouthful of milk.

"What are you plans for the day?" he asked Philip as he extracted a cigarette from the packet. "I don't want you hanging around the house making noise, I need my sleep."

"I'm probably going swimming if the others want to go", Philip replied as he also washed down the last of his bread with a final gulp of milk.

"Good, make sure you take your brother with you."

As his dad spoke, he simultaneously lit his cigarette, got up from the table, and left the kitchen in the direction of the living room. Philip got up and headed in the opposite direction. He exited through the door that connected the kitchen to the scullery. He weaved his way through the cluttered room, gathered his paperbag from the row of hooks by the side door and left the house.

Chapter 2

Although it was still relatively early when Philip began the ten-minute walk from his home to the newsagents, the sun was already shining brightly and the temperature was already in the mid-teens. A gentle breeze accompanied Philip as he made his way along the quiet and deserted street. The silence was only broken as he got closer and closer to the main road that ran along the bottom of the street and where the newsagents was also located.

As Philip entered the newsagents, he was taking random wild guesses under his breath regarding who the opening game would be against. He walked towards the counter where the newsagent, Mr Underwood, was waiting. Mr Underwood was deliberately looking at his wristwatch as Philip approached, but Philip didn't notice. Just to the left of the counter was a decorators pasting table that was placed there every morning by Mr Underwood, and currently resting on top of it were two stacks of morning papers, one of which were Philip's. Philip picked up the paper from the top of his pile, the 'Daily Mirror', and began scanning the front cover.

"I don't pay you to read them lad, I pay you to deliver them and you're late."

"Yeah, yeah," Philip replied, with eyebrows suitably raised as he turned the paper over and scanned the back page, immediately spotting a red banner at the top of the page, which read 'Full Fixture List Inside- Four Page Pull-out'. An impatient Philip quickly began turning pages in search of the four-page pull-out. An equally impatient Mr Underwood had come from behind his counter, taken Philip's bag from his shoulder and filled it with the remaining papers for Philips customers. He then ushered Philip towards the door.

"Charlie hasn't got here yet, so, when you're finished call back in, I may have an extra round for you to do," He said, as he pushed Philip out onto the street. Mr Underwood placed Philip's bag by his side, and then went back inside the shop and closed the door.

As the door clicked shut behind him, Philip finally located the four-page pull-out. He headed straight to the 'First Division' fixture list. They were listed alphabetically, a final minor delay before he found the team he was searching for, Leeds United.

"Everton," he muttered to himself before adding. "Well at least it's at home." It was at this point that he noticed the next two fixtures. His eyebrows rose, his eyes bulged, and his hands gripped the pull-out a little more tightly.

"Arsenal away, then Spurs away! I know everybody hates us, but that is a harsh start to anybody's season." Philip put the pull-out back inside the Daily Mirror and rather forcefully shoved the paper back inside the bag. He slung the bag over his rather disgruntled shoulder before removing a bar of 'Old Jamaica' chocolate that he had carefully concealed inside the newspaper whilst he was inside the shop. He then set off to deliver his papers.

How Philip Knott came to be a Leeds United supporter is a story in itself and began five years earlier in 1968. Philip was not born in Leeds, nor was any other member of his family. The first time he actually went to Leeds was to see them play during the 1968-69 season. This was his first visit to Elland Road once he had decided that Leeds United were indeed the team for him. It was the 1st of February 1969 and a young Philip stood on the terraces next to his dad and witnessed a 3-0 victory over Coventry City. The only negative of an otherwise glorious day was that he had to watch the game in the away end with the Coventry City supporters.

Philip was born in Coventry but was the first member of his family to be born there and, as a result, he did not have any sense of history connecting him to the city. His parents and older sister had moved to the city in 1958 for employment reasons, so there wasn't a long line of family ancestry going back to the early days of Coventry City Football Club. There was no grandfather telling him of great days past, no uncle that never missed a game. His mother's side of the family were from Worcestershire and although he very rarely saw his mother's relatives, none of them were football fans, as far as he could recall.

His dad however was a very different proposition. He was from a small seaside town called Seaton Carew, near Hartlepool and he was very much a passionate Hartlepool United F.C supporter. His dad still spoke about the greatest game of football ever played. It took place on January 5th, 1957, between Hartlepool United F.C and Manchester United who at the time were managed by the legendary Matt Busby. It was an F.A.Cup third round tie and it was played in front of over 17,000 fans. Philip's dad was amongst the crowd that day. He was twenty-six at the time. Despite an almighty performance by the home side they eventually lost the game 4-3. Matt Busby later in his life was to describe the game as the most exciting match he had ever watched. Philip also felt that he had been there as he had heard so much about it due to his dad's constant reminiscences of the day's events.

Despite this knowledge of the greatest day in Hartlepool United's history, Philip himself felt as little of a connection to Hartlepool as he did to Worcester or Coventry. However, his dad was more working class than a pigeon whose best friend was a whippet and as he said to Philip's mother back in 1968 'He has to have a team to support, all boys his age have to have a team to support, if you don't have a team to support, people think there is something wrong with you.' Philip didn't have a problem with needing to support a team and he felt that under the circumstances, as he had no obligations or allegiances, he was free to choose any team he liked. He shared his dad's passion for football from a very early age and

13

by the age of eight he had already grasped the importance of different players performing different roles within a team and the fact that not everybody could be the superstar striker.

As Philip's dad had decided that the time had come for him to choose a team to support, he took Philip off to Highfield Road, the home of Coventry City, to watch a few games. Philip's dad would rather had been watching his beloved Hartlepool or failing that Middlesbrough but they lived too far away and the money they would save on the gate, they would ultimately lose in petrol and food costs. Philip was more than happy to accompany his dad to the games, and not just because he enjoyed watching football. He also enjoyed the opportunity to spend time with his father. The two of them spending time together rarely happened. As far as his dad was concerned, there were clearly defined roles within a household, it was the woman's job to raise children and his job to provide for them, and spending time together was not that high on his list of priorities. This was not to say it never happened, it just didn't happen as often as Philip would have liked. They went to some good games, although nothing in the world class league of Hartlepool United versus Manchester United, as his dad constantly reminded him.

"You can support a team all your life Philip, never miss a game, home and away, season after season, rain or shine, and never see a game like that one. Only the very fortunate ones are lucky enough to see a game as good as that one".

Philip saw Chelsea win 1-0, Spurs win 2-1, Wolverhampton Wanderers win 2-1 and a couple of 1-1 draws against Manchester City and Southampton. Though none of these teams were disliked in any particular way, none of them really appealed either. None of them grabbed hold of him or lit a fuse.

However, all this changed on the 16th of November 1968 when Coventry City played host to Leeds United. It certainly wasn't the greatest game of football ever to be played. In fact, for all but one in the crowd that day it was a game that would live short in the memory and be forgotten by the time the rolled-up match day programme was shoved inside the coat pocket. It would have been described in the match report as 'a dogged, resilient performance by the away side', who managed to carve out a 1-0 victory, thanks to a goal scored by Paul Madeley.

The goal itself was a well-worked team effort, one that any manager would be satisfied with. Nothing spectacular, but it all began with a player that mesmerised Philip all afternoon. It was this particular player's performance that sealed the deal for Philip and, as he made his way home after the game on that cold November evening, he knew that he was and would always be a Leeds United supporter. The player in question was Billy Bremner, and it wasn't just the way that he played the game that caught young Philip's eye, but the way he 'played' the game. Every time he got clobbered and was sent sprawling to the ground, which was quite often, he didn't complain. Even when a free kick wasn't awarded, he didn't complain, he just got up, wiped himself down and got on with the game. He played a very simple game. He tended not to move much. He spent the majority of the game in an area of the pitch between the edge of his penalty area and the halfway line. He rarely ventured into the opposing half. His job was straightforward, and he made it look straightforward, nothing flash and nothing unnecessary. He would break up the opposition's attack with a precisely timed tackle, and then set his own team on the offensive with a simple, no frills pass. He was small but solid, feisty in nature, and aggressive in the tackle. When it came to reading the game, he was a genius. He knew exactly where he needed to be and exactly what was going on around him at all times. This was no more evident than in the creation of the game's only goal. An excellently timed tackle from Bremner just outside his own penalty box broke up a promising Coventry City attack. This was immediately followed by a few quick short strides forward before he released the ball with a direct and simple pass over the halfway line, a pass that instantly put his team on the front foot and, three or four passes later a cross from the right wing was met by Paul Madeley and that was that, 1-0 to Leeds United.

Five years later Philip was still a passionate Leeds United supporter and an equally passionate Billy Bremner supporter, so when he entered a 'Roy of the Rovers' competition located within the pages of his 'Tiger' comic strip, where you had to describe your favourite player in no more than one hundred words, there was only ever one player that Philip was going to write about.

Chapter 3

"Run!"

All of a sudden, a small group of boys, who moments before were casually walking and talking without a care in the world, burst into life and began to sprint as fast as they could. As they had rounded the corner they'd caught sight of the number 21 bus sitting at the terminus opposite the 'Live and Let Live' public house. It could pull out and begin its journey into town at any moment, and they did not want to wait twenty minutes or more for the next one. In an instant, the group of boys became nothing more than a blur, all running as fast as they could, their brightly coloured tank tops and wide-collared flowered shirts leaving a trail behind them like a roman candle firework in the evening sky on bonfire night. Flared trousers and cut off denim jackets were flapping uncontrollably in the morning breeze, as they bounded towards the bus in their plastic training shoes or cheap pumps, each one of them carrying their respective swimming paraphernalia in an assortment of bags, or just rolled up inside their towels and wedged tight under their arms.

Craig Swinburn was the first of the group to reach the bus. He was the oldest amongst them, at fifteen, and was by some margin the quickest runner. He wasn't exceptionally tall, but he was a thin, wiry lad who the rest of the group tended to look up to. Craig was the one who could blow the best smoke rings. He was also the best footballer, and he had got to third base with Claire Chase on more than one occasion, or at least this is what he claimed. This alleged successful arrival at third base had usually happened when Claire had been babysitting her younger brother, Thomas. The claim, although not proven, was good enough for the rest of the group as they struggled to reach third base even when they added all their bases up together. Their eagerness to accept Craig's story also allowed them to believe that one day they too could reach this particular milestone for themselves.

It was a dead heat for second place, with Philip and his closest friend, Michael Robinson, reaching the bus at the same time. They were closely followed by Paul Jones, Philip's brother James, and finally Martin Matthews. Martin was a rather chubby lad who had a tendency to snack between snacks, never mind between meals, but it still seemed to have little impact on his appetite.

Once aboard the group headed upstairs and immediately made their way to the back of the bus. No sooner had they all sat down before Martin Matthews rummaged around inside his bag and pulled out a packet of crisps. Craig Swinburn flipped open the top pocket of his cut off denim waistcoat and took out a ten packet of No 6 cigarettes and a box of matches.

"I'm telling you, "He said as he took a cigarette from the packet and lit it. He took a long drag of the cigarette and blew out six perfectly formed smoke rings, watching as they drifted away, before he continued.

"Friday night, it's going to happen on Friday night, her mum will be in the Livvy getting plastered as usual." He motioned towards the pub across the road as he spoke. "All I need to do is turn up with a nice gift and fourth base will be as good as in the bag."

"No home run yet then?" Phillip asked.

"Not yet, but I bet you I've shagged her before the end of the summer holidays. She wants to do it, she's just a bit nervous." Craig continued to smoke his cigarette with a confident, cocksure expression upon his face before passing the smaller half to Paul Jones, just as the bus pulled out of the terminus and set off for the town centre.

"So what gift are you going to get her?" Martin Matthews enquired, with a mouthful of cheese and onion crisps.

"I don't know yet. It depends on what I can pinch this afternoon after swimming. Maybe you should nick something for Lesley," Craig said, whilst looking over at Philip. "Once you get them a gift, they owe you something in return" he added.

Stealing the correct gift was crucial to Craig's ultimate success on Friday night, and he knew this only too well. The problem in itself was quite a simple one. The better the gift he was able to steal, the higher the chances of him getting caught whilst attempting to steal it. The shops and, therefore, the opportunities that presented themselves all had degrees of difficulty attached to them on a sliding scale. Right at the top of the pile was the Owen Owen department store. There were certain sections of this particular department store that were easier to steal from than others but, unfortunately for Craig, these sections did not offer anything that would be on a fifteen year old girl's wish list when it came to gifts. It was all well and good if he wanted to turn up on Friday night clutching a set of bathroom scales or a thermos flask. But items such as these were not going to cut much ice with Claire Chase, or loosen her underwear in any way, or allow her knees to move in opposite directions.

The items of real worth were to be located in the jewellery and perfume departments. However, these items were heavily guarded by ferocious looking, forty something, female shop assistants. They would prowl up and down behind their counters, scanning the terrain in front of them, a sickly-sweet scent filling the air around them. Their hair would be lacquered stiffer than a retired army colonel's upper lip, and accompanied by false eyelashes, a more than generous application of foundation and bright red shimmering lipstick. You needed to be alert and on your toes if you were going to steal from under the noses of these ladies. The biggest problem was that somebody like Craig would be spotted as soon as he came within five feet of their precious domain. He had to keep a safe distance and remain unnoticed, whilst at the same time waiting and watching for an opportunity to present itself. This was always going to be tricky, as he also needed to keep on the move to avoid the attention of the floor walkers. In a department store such as Owen Owen, he stuck out like a bottle of lime cordial in an alcoholic's drinks cabinet.

Coming down the sliding scale, both in respect of completing the mission and the quality of the gifts available, was Woolworths. The pick 'n' mix section alone was regularly visited by young shoplifters from all over the city. However, Craig knew that fourth base required a lot more than a stripy paper bag with a few chocolates inside. Away from the soft centre of the pick 'n' mix counter, the rest of the store presented more difficult challenges. Admittedly, the counter staff were not as eagle eyed and vulture-like as the ladies of Owen Owen, but they were no slouches either. Many an error of judgement had been made in Woolworths, and many a teenager had found his collar being felt by a member of the store's security team, as they briskly attempted to exit the store with their stolen goods concealed.

Coming further down the sliding scale would find you entering the indoor market. Obviously, the majority of the stalls inside were of no use what-so-ever, unless you were stealing something for your grandmother, that is. Under those circumstances the pickings were indeed rich and on a busy and bustling Saturday afternoon there were also opportunities a plenty. However, in between the stalls selling balls of wool, knitting patterns, and breakfast cereal in bags, there were a few retailers with more to offer.

At the bottom of the pile both in terms of likelihood of getting caught and the suitability of the gift was the Coventry Cathedral Gift Shop. It was only a small shop, so choice was limited. This was coupled with the fact that the majority of the gifts on display were of little interest to a fifteen year old girl growing up on a rundown council estate. However, if you looked beyond the Lord's Prayer bookmarks, potpourri, and glass angel figures, you would find some nice necklaces, rings, and soft toys. Also, because of the size of the shop, the layout, and the fact that it was usually staffed by two little old ladies, once five or six teenage boys entered, there were blind spots aplenty and the lifting of items became extremely fruitful.

As the bus pulled into the city centre bus station, Craig was still thinking about the possible outcome of Friday night. The rest of the group, apart from Martin Matthews were making their way down the bus towards the stairs. As for Martin, he was busy trying to finish off a 'bar six' before the bus came to a complete stop.

"Come on, you fat twat," Craig muttered, as he scampered past Martin and caught up with the rest of the group, who were now climbing down the stairs.

Once out of the bus station, it was a short walk to the swimming baths. Unfortunately, the queue for the main pool wasn't that short, but eventually they were heading down the stairs and towards the changing rooms. Once inside, and after everybody had collected a basket for their clothes, Martin disappeared into a private cubicle, whilst the rest of the group headed for the communal changing space at the far end of the changing room.

"Last one in the pool is it," Paul Jones called out, as soon as he felt sure that it wasn't going to be him.

At Coventry baths in 1973, once you had changed, you took your basket with your belongings inside to the changing room attendants. They would take it from you and hang it up. In return, you would receive a large safety pin with a small, coloured metal disc attached to it. Upon the metal disc was a stamped number. Once you had securely pinned the disc to your trunks, you would head up a different flight of stairs, through the shower, and out into the pool itself. Paul was the first one out, Phillip's brother came next, then Philip, Craig, and Michael Robinson. Martin Matthews was last.

Chapter 4

The swimming pools at the Coventry Baths and Sports Centre Complex were located on the first floor. There was a fifty metre Olympic standard swimming pool, toddlers' pool, and a third, not so spacious, pool just beyond the toddlers' pool. On the one side of the main pool there was a raised spectators seating area for when the swimming club held competitions. The whole area was encased in large glass windows, including the diving area which had five diving boards of varying height. The summer sunlight poured through the gleaming clear panes and down onto the surface of the cool blue water. A shimmering golden glow danced and bounced across the top of the pool.

The pool was full of the sounds of children playing, splashing, and shouting but, as Philip stood at the water's edge with his toes dangling above its surface, he could hear nothing at all. He looked down at the water, bent his legs a little, pushed himself forward, and dived in. Coming to the surface, moments later, he swam effortlessly across to the other side of the pool.

If you were to ask Philip Knott where his ability to swim came from, he would just look back at you with a blank expression, as if you had just asked him the square root of four thousand four hundred and forty-four. He would then follow this with a simple shrug of his shoulders and eventually he would utter the words, "I dunno". The funny thing is, he would be telling the truth because he genuinely did not know. All he could tell you about his swimming was the following. He took to swimming like a duck to water and was already swimming unaided by the age of three. The other thing he could tell you was how he felt when he was swimming. When he was in the water, nothing else mattered. Life at home, problems at school, his mother's illness, his father's drinking, the mood swings, the arguments, the shouting, all of this seemed to float away like an oil spill on the surface of the water from which Philip just swam in the opposite direction. No matter how crowded or noisy it was, the minute he burst through the surface of the pool and became submerged beneath the water, he felt happily alone and, above all else, he felt free. He was able to separate himself from everything else in his life, as he knew deep down that this was the one thing that he was good at.

Craig Swinburn may have been the best footballer, a promising shoplifter, and the best runner (which came in handy on the occasions when the shoplifting hadn't gone to plan). However, Paul Jones would argue that he was the best footballer, not counting a couple of the older boys that lived on the estate. Surprisingly, for such a young age, Philip's brother was regarded as one of the best forgers of parents' signatures. If you had wagged school for a day or just wanted to get out of a maths test or P.E lesson in the dead of winter, the young James Knott was one of the best people that you could turn to, for a small fee, of course. However, when it came to swimming, Philip was not just the best in the group, he was just the best, full stop. He could give the rest of the group a fifteen-metre head start, twenty for Martin, and over fifty metres he would still beat them. Whilst they thrashed about in the water, ironically, like a fish on a river bank, Philip would effortlessly and gracefully glide by. Philip swam with freedom and finesse, stroke after smooth perfect stroke propelling him across the surface of the water. He couldn't explain how he felt, as he did not have the ability or the vocabulary to do himself justice; he just knew that, for him, swimming was something special, and when he swam, for the briefest of time, he felt special.

"Phil! Philip! Oi Phil!"

At first, Philip was slightly disorientated and he couldn't work out where the sound was coming from. Then, standing across the other side of the pool, he caught sight of Michael and Paul, who were both frantically waving their arms at him. Once they were sure that Philip had spotted them, they both started to point over at the diving boards. Philip turned and pushed himself away from the edge a little, so that he could get a clearer view of the diving boards. There were five boards' altogether, two springboards and three higher, fixed platforms. As Philip scanned the boards to see what his friends were pointing at, they climbed back into the water and swam over to join him.

"Up there, look," Paul said, as he grabbed Philip's shoulder with one hand and pointed up at the fourth and fifth boards with the other.

The fourth and fifth boards, or highest and second highest, depending on how you looked at it, were located on one side of the diving area and the other three boards were located on the opposite side. You had to get permission from the pool attendants to use either of these two boards, and when you were ready to dive the attendant would blow a whistle and clear the diving area. This action also resulted in the rest of the pool stopping and looking at you as you dived. Philip looked up at the fourth board, just as Craig climbed the last few steps.

"What's he doing?" Philip asked. "Has he forgotten that he's afraid of heights?"

"He's tryin' to impress that girl over there," Paul replied, as he shifted his pointing finger in the direction of two girls who were standing at the edge of the diving area, opposite the two high boards. "Not the skinny one with all the teeth, but her chubby mate with the big tits."

Craig slowly walked towards the edge of the diving platform and peered down at the cool, dark blue water below, before looking over at the two young girls. First, he looked over to check that they were still there, and second to look at the larger girl's breasts, as he was in need of a reminder as to why he had climbed up there in the first place. For a moment, he wasn't sure which was bigger, the girl's breasts or the lump in his throat. The attendant looked up, and then blew his whistle. That was that there was no backing out now. No turning and climbing back down again because the sound of the whistle had put paid to any possible retreat. With virtually the whole pool watching, Craig raised his arms above his head, leaned forward a little, and pushed himself off the platform. Unfortunately, his nerves got the better of him and he pushed off a little too vigorously. Instead of the motion picture dive off a rugged and rocky coastline that he had planned out in his head, he did a complete turn in mid-air. By the time he collided with the water below, he was in an almost seated position. His arms were still in the air above his head and hit the water last. However, his legs were almost straight out in front of him with his feet breaking the surface of the water first, a fraction before his arse.

When he popped back to the surface, a few seconds later, there was now an empty space where the two girls had been standing only moments before. Just to the right of the empty space was a pool attendant with tears of laughter streaming down his cheeks. He was still laughing and wiping away the tears with one hand as he helped Craig out of the pool with the other.

"Are you all right, lad?" he just about managed to ask, before adding, "That was one of the best dives I've ever seen. It must have taken you years of practice."

Craig just stood and stared at the attendant, waiting for the laughter to subside. Quickly realising that this might take a while, he walked off in search of his friends.

"If you want another go just let me know," the attendant called after him, before climbing back into his chair.

On spotting his friends, Craig sat down at the edge of the pool and dangled his feet in the water. Philip, Michael, and Paul swam over to him.

"You all right?" they asked.

"Yeah, I'm fine," Craig replied.

"What did you do that for, you spaz?" Paul said.

"Piss off, I ain't no spaz, and anyway that fat girl we were talking to said she would show me her tits if I dived off one of the high boards."

"You didn't have to do that. Fat birds will always show you their tits. It's the only way anybody will look at them," Paul muttered.

"Yeah, like you've seen loads," Craig quickly replied.

"You should go and find her and get her to show you her tits," Philip remarked. "I mean, you did as she asked, you dived off the high board. It wasn't a very good dive, but you still dived."

Craig elected to ignore this suggestion. "Are we swimming or not?" he asked, as he flopped off the side of the pool and back into the water.

After a few more hours swimming, ogling girls, and generally messing about in the water, the calling of the cone of chips became too great and it was almost time to get out of the pool. But before then, this meant that it was time for the traditional final game. The rules were very simple; you had to break the pool rules until you were caught by an attendant and the last one to get evicted from the pool was the winner. However, you weren't allowed to simply sit back and wait for your competitors to be evicted from the pool and then declare yourself the winner. At all times, you had to be making a conscious attempt to flout the rules and run the risk of being caught. Michael was the first to be evicted, caught dive bombing off the first diving board. James was another dive-bombing victim, shortly after. Craig was the next to go and, to be honest, it was a very soft eviction indeed. He was caught running as he prepared to dive bomb, but the whistle blew before he was able to complete his mission. Martin Matthews went in a far more impressive style when he was caught belly flopping into a group of young girls. It was a dead heat for first place between Philip and Paul. Even though the attendant's whistle only blew the once, when they both came to the surface after their synchronised illegal dives off boards two and three, the attendant pointed to both of them, before pointing to the changing rooms. Philip had opted for a dive bomb off the second springboard, whilst Paul had gone for his trademark Scooby-do off the first of the fixed platforms. For those not in the know, a Scooby-do is when you run off the board and continue the running action for as long as possible before hitting the water. It is a dive that is guaranteed to get you thrown out.

Chapter 5

Sitting in the lounge of the Bell Inn public house on a busy Saturday afternoon was Phillip Knott's dad, Francis. He was at a table next to a set of open French doors that led out into the beer garden. On the table, in front of him was a half-consumed pint of bitter, a packet of Senior Service cigarettes and a Dunhill Rollagas lighter. Beneath the lighter was a betting slip. Sat in the centre of the table was an ash tray that was being used for a different purpose than the one intended, currently housing the kitty for the card game that was in progress. Francis and three associates were in the middle of a game of seven card brag and the three associates were waiting patiently for Francis to deal. A short, stocky, balding man who was sitting directly opposite Francis very quickly ran out of patience.

"Come on, Frankie, are you dealing those bloody cards or what?"

However, Francis's attention was firmly fixed upon the television, which was on the wall just a few feet away from where the group were sat, and the recently dispatched request for him to start dealing the cards failed in its attempt to register. The request was instantly re-dispatched for a second time and, on this occasion, was accompanied with a couple of knocks on the table for good measure.

"Frankie, man, deal the bloody cards."

This time around the request did reach its intended target. "Yes, yes," Francis replied, without taking his eyes off the television screen, before adding, "I'm on for a soddin' treble here, Jack."

On the television screen, and just about to start entering the stalls, were the runners and riders for the third leg of the 'ITV Seven' on 'World of Sport'.

Around the corner from the Bell Inn was a small independent bookmaker. Francis was a regular customer most Saturdays on route to the pub for his equally regular Saturday lunchtime drinking session. On this particular visit, one of the bets he had placed was a ten-shilling treble. His first horse 'Red Alert' had won the 1.30 at Chester at a price of three to one. This meant he had two pounds going on to his second horse 'Paddington the Bear'. Paddington had duly obliged at a price of six to one. This resulted in Francis having fourteen pounds riding on his third and final horse, 'Boots Green'. Boots Green was currently priced up at four to one and was just about to enter the stalls for the 2.05 at Newcastle.

Moments later, the nine runners and riders exited the stalls and set out on their one mile four-furlong trip. No sooner had the field jostled for a good early pitch and settled into their stride, than an extremely anxious expression had appeared upon Francis's face. He lifted up his betting slip from beneath his lighter and stood up, pushing his head through the layer of smoke that filled the room, in the belief that this would somehow improve his and his horse's chances. Accepting that play had been temporarily suspended, his three associates turned to watch the screen. Despite the clinking sound of glasses and the constant soft rumbling of chatter coming from all areas of the room, the only voice that Francis could hear was the commentator on the television.

'They complete the first two furlongs with Admiral Bobby taking them along at a fair old clip, and he pushes a few lengths in front of the chasing pack. Get More Fun is next in the field, with Peak Times on his outside, and Atlantic Crossing making a line of three. Boots Green is against the rail, showing just ahead of Favourite Tune on his outside, and closely followed by The Works Do. Splash of Colour comes next. Chile is out the back and, rather ironically, is finding this early pace a bit too hot.'

Without taking his eyes of the television screen, Francis reached for his drink and raised it to his lips. He took a large gulp, before placing it back down on the table again. He then proceeded to fumble about some more, before gathering up his cigarettes and lighter.

'As they pass the mile pole there's little change in the order. Admiral Bobby is still holding a two length lead over the rest of the field. The favourite, Get More Fun, still shows up in second. Both Splash of Colour and Chile are still out the back, but the rest of the field appear to be happy to let Admiral Bobby stride along in front as we approach the seven furlong pole.'

"Come on Boots," Francis called out, before lighting his cigarette and taking an extra-large drag. He inhaled deeply and held the smoke in his lungs for a moment, before slowly releasing it through his nostrils.

'They approach the last half mile and the Admiral is trying to wind it up from the front, and goes three lengths clear of the chasing pack. Get More Fun goes off in pursuit, with Peak Times on his outside. Boots Green is still penned in on the rail and has nowhere to go. Favourite Tune is on his outside, and widest of all is The Works Do. These six are beginning to forge clear from the rest.

"Get out Boots, get out," Francis cried at the television screen.

'Admiral Bobby is coming back to the field. Get More Fun is cutting him down with every stride. The Works Do is making eye catching ground on the outside. Boots Green is fourth but needs a gap to appear on the rails. Peak Times has nothing more to give, and the rest look like beaten horses at this stage.'

Francis stood rigid with his pint glass in one hand, his betting slip tightly gripped in the other, and his cigarette hanging from his lips.

'They fly past the furlong pole with long-time leader Admiral Bobby giving way. Get More Fun and The Works Do are stride for stride. Boots Green finally has a gap, but he has two lengths to find. Get More Fun and The Works Do are having a ding dong battle up front, with The Works Do just getting on top, but here comes Boots Green flying up the inside rail.'

Francis stared with his mouth open wide and his half-smoked cigarette attached to his bottom lip.

'Will the finish line come in time for The Works Do? Boots Green is getting there with every stride. They're neck and neck as they approach the finish line. They flash past together. That's one for the judge. Get More Fun is a half-length back in third, with the long-time leader Admiral Bobby finishing in fourth.'

Francis's body suddenly resembled the consistency of a raspberry jelly and he flopped back into his seat. He wore an expression on his face similar to that of a small boy sitting in a dentist's waiting room and regretting the fact that he had eaten far too many sweets. He watched the replay like a lioness stalking her prey, as he waited for the result of the photo finish to be called. He swallowed what was left of his pint, before taking one final drag of his cigarette and stubbing it out in the correct ashtray. "What's taking so long?" he muttered to nobody in particular, whilst staring up at the television screen and again listening to the commentator.

'This one must be desperately close. I must say if Boots Green has lost, then he is a very unlucky loser as he was certainly ahead a stride after the line. It is certainly on the nod. Hang on, I believe the result is coming through now.' The commentator paused and listened as the course announcer called out the number of the wining horse. 'Boots Green is the winner. He wasn't in front at any other stage of the race, but he got his nose across the line first'.

Francis sat motionless and stared intently at his betting slip before he released a rather loud "Get in."

"Congratulations, Frankie, how much have you won?" asked the friend sitting to his left.

"Not sure, depends what price he was, but it must be close to seventy pounds."

Boots Green had returned at a price of nine to two, which meant that Francis's original ten-shilling stake was now worth seventy seven pounds exactly.

"Good for you, Frankie, you should be able to get your car fixed now. So, can we get back to this bloody card game, or what?"

Francis happily obliged by finally picking up the cards. He gave them a shuffle and tapped them on the table. "Kitty, gentlemen," he said, before dealing out seven cards to each player.

It took another three rounds before somebody won both hands and, in turn, the ever-growing kitty. Francis didn't win a single kitty all game, but it didn't seem to matter one bit. After a few more pints and just after last orders was called, a slightly vague-around-the- edges Francis picked up his cigarettes and lighter and made his way out of the French doors. He weaved his way between the tables and chairs in the beer garden and out onto the high street, before walking the short distance to the bookmakers to collect his winnings.

Within a few short minutes of entering A.G.Richards turf accountants, Francis exited again with his seventy seven pounds safely tucked inside his jacket pocket. As he stood for a moment on the high street, enjoying the glow from within, he pondered what to do with his winnings. When he had entered the bookies to collect his money, he had every intention of going home and using the proceeds to get the family car fixed. He drove a dark green 1965 Ford Corsair V4 and, for the last three and a half weeks, due to a dodgy gearbox, he had been driving it as little as possible. On the odd occasion he had driven it, he was only able to use first and fourth gear. However, as he stood on the corner of the street and basked in that warm glow of victory, he found himself being drawn to the travel agents directly opposite.

Before he could utter the words 'the wife will go spare', he was sitting in a chair and patiently waiting for the young lady on the other side of the desk to finish her telephone call.

"Sorry to keep you waiting," the young lady said, as she put down the receiver. "I'm Amanda and how can I help you today?"

"Could you tell me how much a week at Butlins will cost for a family of four?"

"When would you like to go?"

"As soon as possible," Francis replied.

"I'll just check," Amanda said, "but I am pretty sure that Butlins weeks run from Saturday to Saturday".

"Then I'd like to go next Saturday," Francis said, as Amanda got up from behind her desk and collected a Butlins brochure from the rack, before returning to her seat.

Amanda began flicking through the brochure. "Which camp?" she asked.

"Does the price vary from camp to camp?" Francis asked.

"It depends on availability. Let's see what we can find."

As Amanda continued to flick through the brochure, she would occasionally pause and jot a few numbers down on a pad that was lying on the desk in front of her. Once the pad had several numbers scrawled upon it, Amanda closed the brochure and picked up the telephone. She looked across at Francis and smiled, tapping her teeth with her pen as she patiently waited for the person on the other end to answer. Sure enough, it did not take long.

"Afternoon again," she began. "It's Amanda here from Wainwrights Worldwide, agency number 676. I'm looking for a week at Butlin's arriving next Saturday, for a family of four. Don't mind which camp, depends on what you have available." Amanda paused for a moment, before looking across at Francis. "Self-catering, or all in? " she asked.

"It all depends on the price," Francis replied.

Amanda continued to listen to the person on the other end of the phone, whilst also continuing to tap her teeth with her biro. Meanwhile, Francis was desperately trying to look at anything other than Amanda's breasts, which were pressed against the thin, shimmering blue material of her blouse, but he found himself continually being drawn back to her firm, young, ample bosom. After a few more minutes of discussion and note taking, Amanda thanked the person on the other end of the phone, put down the receiver, and looked once more at Francis. Thankfully, he had just enough time to avert his gaze.

"Right, let's see. We have a week at Ayr, but that is not until the Saturday after next, all in for fifty nine pounds. However, we do have a choice for this Saturday coming. We have Ayr again, Clacton on Sea, Filey, or Minehead, all with availability and all in, once again for fifty nine pounds."

"Fifty nine pounds," Francis replied.

Francis knew that at this point he should have got up from his seat, thanked Amanda for her time, and left. In fact, he knew that he should never have walked into the shop in the first place. Exactly eight minutes and forty seven seconds later, and with one final glance at Amanda's breasts, Francis did exit the shop. However, he was minus fifty nine of his seventy seven pounds, but clutching the documentation confirming his holiday booking, for a family of four in two chalets, for a week all in at Butlin's, Clacton on Sea, arrival date next Saturday.

Chapter 6

When they heard the news about their forthcoming holiday, Philip and his younger brother almost popped with excitement. They both cheered in unison when their dad confirmed the news by showing them the booking details. However, their father was unable to hear the cheers. This was due to the fact that his ears were still ringing from the tongue lashing he had received from his wife for booking the holiday in the first place, and from his daughter for assuming that she would not want to go. He was right, his daughter did not want to go, but that was beside the point, as it was not his place to decide for her.

"She's got her Saturday job at Sketchley's, and her three afternoons a week in Woolworths. On top of that she hates me and she dislikes her brothers to a lesser extent," Francis pointed out to his wife, shortly after their daughter had stormed out of the house, and just before his sons had returned home from swimming. His final word on the matter was to tell his wife that if she did not feel well enough to go, then their daughter could go in her place. But, come next Saturday, he and the boys were getting in the car and heading for Clacton-on-Sea, in fourth gear all the way.

Due to the obvious tension in the house later that evening, Philip and James opted to go to bed early, shortly after watching a repeat episode of 'The Persuaders'. Their heads were still crammed full of thoughts about the holiday that lay ahead as they clambered into bed. However, as Philip lay on his bunk, watching the room become steadily darker, his excitement was steadily pushed aside by the increasing volume of the argument that was now taking place downstairs. As the room disappeared slowly beneath the ever-growing darkness, the ferocity of his parents' row appeared to be making its way up the stairs, across the landing, and seeping under the bedroom door. No sooner had it arrived in the room, than it made the short journey across the floor, and proceeded to pin Philip down in his bed. It felt like he was trying to fall asleep encased inside an extremely tight-fitting wet suit. The force of each insult thrown by his parents tossed his head from side to side, as he remained trapped in his bed. There was no escape, and all he could do was hang on in there and wait for the storm to pass. Eventually, after one final, hysterical bout of insults from both sides had crashed head on, Philip heard the front door slam shut and all fell silent, for a moment.

The slamming of the door had awoken James from his sleep. "What was that?" he asked, as he rubbed his eyes in an attempt to pick something recognisable out of the darkness.

"Nothing," Philip replied. "Go back to sleep."

Their dad leaving the house meant that the pubs were still open, and Philip guessed that he would soon be propping up the bar of the 'Live and Let Live'. It was a pub his dad rarely used, claiming that it was full of unemployed scroungers and drunken Irishmen. Philip was still fearful that the situation had the capacity to escalate upon his dad's return. However, on this occasion the rest of the night was thankfully event and noise free. It wasn't that long before the tension that had been created by his parents' war of words began to ebb away and loosen its grip. Philip slowly began to feel a little more comfortable. After a while, he felt relaxed enough to turn his thoughts back to his holiday and despite being conscious of being able to hear the faint sound of his mother sobbing, he decided that it would be best to stay in his bed, and he slowly drifted off to sleep.

Sunday morning arrived a lot quicker, and with a lot less fuss, than Saturday night. However, it only took a few seconds, once Philip was awake, for him to realise what Sunday morning meant. For most people,

Sunday morning meant an opportunity for some peace and quiet, a lie in, a time to relax. But when you are a skinny fourteen year old boy with a paper round, Sunday morning meant something very different. Every boy that had ever taken on the responsibility of a paper round knew that Sunday morning was by far the worst round of the week. Each paper was thicker than any newspaper had a right to be, and each one contained at least one supporting Sunday supplement. Some of them had as many as three supplements: one for travel, another for food and drink, and another one for fashion. This resulted in a paper bag that was bursting at the seams and remaining in contact with the pavement, until at least half a dozen or more papers had been delivered. Up and down the country, on a Sunday morning, paper boys could be seen dragging their paper bags along the street like deranged serial killers dragging the lifeless corpse of their latest victim into the undergrowth.

After discovering his dad asleep on the living room sofa, Philip quietly made his way into the kitchen. He buttered two slices of bread, and attempting to make as little noise as possible, took a packet of ready salted crisps from the cupboard and opened it. He placed a handful of crisps onto one of the slices of bread. After placing the other slice on top, he gently pushed it down with the palm of his hand, listening to the crisps crunch. Once his sandwich was complete and he had taken a large drink of milk from the bottle in the fridge, he headed out the side door and through the scullery, collecting his paper-bag as he went.

Twenty minutes later, Philip dragged the same paper bag out of the newsagents and along the street. Once he had delivered enough papers to lift the bag off the ground and onto his reluctant shoulder, he delved inside and retrieved his bar of chocolate, before continuing on his way.

Once he had completed his paper round, Philip opted against going straight home. It wasn't that he didn't enjoy Sundays at home. As a rule, most of the gang would be out, usually having a game of football on the field or heading over to 'The Wreck' on their bikes. On the odd occasion, a few of the boys would go fishing on the canal and, in the past, before he began to struggle with his health, there was always a very good chance of Philip's granddad (on his mother's side) turning up in the afternoon. This would mean a bag of sweets, a shiny ten pence piece, and some wonderful stories of days gone by. However, on this particular Sunday, Philip thought it best to stay away from the house for as much of the day as possible.

He took his empty bag back to the newsagents before catching the bus into town. The town centre was virtually deserted when he arrived and quite the opposite of the hectic hustle and bustle of the previous day. Upon alighting the bus, he headed along the deserted street and into the swimming baths. Once inside the building he made his way upstairs and to the spectators seating area overlooking the main pool. Just like the streets outside, the pool was virtually deserted. As Philip sat and read his stolen copy of Shoot magazine the seating area around him slowly filed up and the noise levels rose. He and everybody else had come to watch a West Midlands league meet between three local clubs. Coventry Godiva were playing host to their closest and fiercest rivals Nuneaton & Bedworth and Leamington Spa.

Despite the ever increasing noise levels, once the meet began Philip couldn't hear a sound from the crowd. The cheers, whistles and rattles faded away as he watched each race unfold. He watched each swimmer as they cut their way through the water. He watched how many strokes they took, what distance they covered between each stroke; he watched them turn, and how they finished, and he clocked the all-important times of the race winners. It was a comfortable win for the home team, and deep down he felt that he was a good enough swimmer to make the team.

As Philip made his way home that afternoon, it was his head that was doing the swimming. His thoughts were uncontrollably bobbing around like a buoy in a storm. One minute he was thinking about winning the hundred meters butterfly to seal a victory at an important meet, the next minute he was on holiday at Butlins, getting lost in the funfair, before he found himself lying under the covers in his bed while his parents argued long into the night.

When it came to arriving home Philip could not have timed it worse. He was like a comedian delivering his punch line thirty minutes after the audience had left the building. As he opened the side door and headed through the scullery, all he could hear were his parents shouting at each other, without bothering to pause in order to hear what each of them were actually shouting.

As he entered the kitchen, Philip was immediately greeted by the comforting aroma of the Sunday roast and a pan of rich dark gravy gently simmering on the cooker. However, this joyous scene was short lived as the intensity of the raised voices coming from the living room soon overpowered his brief moment of pleasure. Philip carefully and silently opened the door that led into the living room, just a little, and peered through the gap. He was unable to see anybody, but he was able to hear every word.

"So you are bleedin well telling me I can't take my family on holiday now."

"No, I'm not saying that, all I'm saying is that the money could have been better spent."

"So, on what exactly should I have spent the money?"

"Getting the car fixed, paying off the rest of the provy money that we borrowed at Christmas. The settee is on its last legs, the kids' beds need blankets for the winter, or shall we just use coats again to keep them warm. But you decided to spend sixty pounds on a holiday".

"Yes, I did. I decided to take my family on holiday and all I've got for my troubles is a pile of shit. Maybe I thought it would help you with this so-called depression of yours."

"What do you mean by that? You make it sound like I bought it from a shop! It's not so-called depression, it is depression."

"That's all I hear these days, bloody depression. You're not depressed you are just unhappy, the same as every other sod around here. I've got news for you, I'm unhappy, the scrounger next door is unhappy, if we had a dog the dog would be unhappy, but we don't all make a bloody song and dance about it or go rushing off to our beds. We just soddin' well get on with it."

With this, Philip's mum just froze for a moment, looking directly into her husband's cold staring eyes. She stood with a large metal spoon in one hand and a half-filled dinner plate in the other. Her eyes began to fill up, her bottom lip began to tremble, and the spoon in her hand began to shake.

"Oh, here we go," Francis muttered.

As his comment fell from his lips, the spoon fell from his wife's hand and clattered on the table, sending several small peas sprawling across the surface. She turned away, just as her eyes overflowed and the tears began to tumble down her cheeks. The dinner plate in her hand crashed onto the table and she bolted out of the room and raced up the stairs.

Francis's daughter, who had been sitting at one end of the table throughout this latest exchange, stood up and glared at her father, feeling both angry and brave in equal measure, and shouted, "Nice one, dad. That will certainly have helped," before she quickly exited the room through the same door as her mother.

Francis just stood for a moment, looking down at his now discarded Sunday dinner, before the frustration of the situation and his feeling of powerlessness to control it triumphantly got the better of him. He picked up his dinner plate and sent it crashing into the living room wall. No sooner had the China fragments and roast dinner ceased tumbling to the ground, than Francis had collected his jacket from the hallway and left, slamming the front door behind him as he did so.

All fell instantly quiet as if somebody had just flicked a switch. Philip waited for a moment, just to be sure, before he left the relative safety of the kitchen and walked into the living room. He looked at the table with the half-served dinners, before looking over at the marks on the opposite wall where the plate of food had connected moments earlier.

As he was busy picking up the pieces of food and broken plate, his brother entered the living room. Philip could see that James had been crying and was still gently sobbing as he closed the door behind him.

"Are you hungry?" Philip asked.

His brother just nodded as he wiped his nose with the sleeve of his shirt and sat down at the table. Philip carried the broken plate and discarded dinner into the kitchen before returning with the pan of gravy. Soon, both boys were sitting at the table and eating their roast dinners.

"What's wrong with mum?" Philip's brother asked, as they ate.

"I don't know," Philip replied.

"But she will get well again, won't she?"

"I don't know."

"Why can't the doctor make mum well again?"

"I don't know," Philip replied again, with a certain amount of annoyance in his voice. This was partly because of the questions, but also because he was frustrated by not knowing the answers. "Just eat your dinner, mum will be fine. Everything will be okay, just wait and see."

Chapter 7

The rest of the week passed by relatively trouble free. The only incident of note occurred on Thursday morning when Philip received a letter in the post. The letter was swiftly followed by both a sense of inevitability and a sense of disappointment. Philip was not sure as to the order in which these senses arrived, he only knew that they both arrived shortly after the letter. On reading the letter and in an attempt to make up for the disappointment, Philip's dad offered to take Philip along when he went to work that evening.

The letter itself was from the publishers of the 'Roy of the Rovers' comic strip and it was very much of the standard variety. It informed Philip that he had been unsuccessful in his attempt to win one of their recent competitions. The letter thanked him for entering and hoped that he would continue to enjoy reading about the adventures of Roy and the rest of the Rovers every week in the 'Tiger' comic. The letter did however finish with a small silver lining as it informed Philip that all the entries into the competition would be forwarded on to the footballers who been nominated.

The competition itself gave the lucky winner the opportunity to attend a first division match at the home ground of their favourite team and to also meet their favourite player. The competition had been in two parts; the first required the entrant to answer three questions. So as not to discourage people from entering all of the answers could be found in that particular issue's 'Roy of the Rovers' adventure. The second part of the competition had been to nominate your favourite player and in no more than one hundred words state why they were your favourite player. His dad had suggested that he should choose Peter Lorimer or Alan 'Sniffer' Clarke, both excellent players in Philip's eyes and in their own right. However, there was only going to be one player that Philip was going to write about and that player was Billy Bremner.

Philip wrote as follows. 'My favourite player is Leeds United's captain Billy Bremner. He is my favourite player because he tries his best and he always works hard for the team. Even when the team is losing, he doesn't give up. He always plays fair and never complains if he thinks the referee has made the wrong decision. At the end of the game, no matter what the score is, he always shakes the hands of the other team's players. He is a great captain and never blames his teammates if they make a mistake. This is why Billy Bremner is my favourite player'. Just for the record Philip's entry was one hundred words exactly.

Thankfully his dad's invitation, coupled with the fact that the forthcoming holiday was now within touching distance, managed to take most of the sting out of the initial disappointment Philip felt upon opening and reading the letter.

Before long Thursday evening had crept into view, and Philip had been given the task of making the sandwiches and the flasks for the night ahead on account of his mother not feeling well enough to get out of bed.

He made cheese sandwiches for his dad, cheese and onion sandwiches for himself. After placing the sandwiches into two plastic lunchboxes he added a packet of crisps to each box. Finally he placed a banana into his dad's lunchbox and a chocolate Wagon Wheel into his. Once that task was completed he started on the flasks, a large one of very sweet tea for his dad and a smaller one of not so sweet tea for himself.

Philip loved going to work with his dad. He loved being in the cab, being up all night. He loved eating his sandwiches with the other drivers at the depot at one o' clock in the morning and listening to their conversations. He also loved the virtually deserted motorway on the return journey and watching as the sun rose on the horizon. Above all however, above all else he simply loved being in the cab with his dad. This was because when he was in the cab travelling along the smooth grey tarmac, Philip saw in him a person that he didn't recognise at any other time. Philip couldn't put his finger on it but the moment that his dad put the key in the ignition of his cab and started the engine he appeared to become a very different man. The more familiar mixture of anger, frustration, impatience and vulnerability of life outside of the cab would simply ebb away from him as he put the lorry into gear, removed the handbrake and pulled out of the yard. These emotions were replaced by a warm glow and a beaming smile accompanied by some loud and atrocious singing, usually a number from Frank Sinatra or Nat King Cole. This particular night was not to disappoint and as they headed down the A45 Philip's dad was already delivering his rendition of 'Unforgettable'. Thankfully the singing would usually cease by the time they exited the M69.

As the darkness slowly began to draw in and the early evening traffic began to dissipate, the majority of vehicles left on the road were of the heavy goods variety. Silence reigned for a while inside the cab as both Philip and his dad paid attention to the road ahead. It was a few miles short of Bromsgrove when Philip carefully poured out two cups of tea from the flasks. He passed one to his dad before clasping his own cup with both hands and sitting back in his seat. He was dying to ask a question and could feel it as it formed and took shape on his lips. He said it over and over again in his head countless times. They had travelled all the way from Driotwich Spa to Whittington before he eventually took his last sip of tea and blurted it out.

"What's wrong with mum, dad?"

They were almost at Brockhill Village before his dad answered. He passed his empty cup back to Philip as he did so.

"I don't know son; I just don't know…"

Despite his wife explaining to him what was wrong, despite their local GP explaining to him what was wrong and despite a bespectacled specialist on the opposite side of a large wooden desk in an office at the hospital explaining to him what was wrong, despite all of this and despite the fact that Francis had understood every word of these explanations, the response he gave was still the most accurate response that he was able to give to his son's question. The simple truth was that he could not comprehend the term 'persistent depressive disorder'. He knew what the words meant and he also knew all about the symptoms that had been meticulously explained to him, such as sleeping too much, fatigue, low self-esteem and a feeling of helplessness. After all he was living with them and trying to deal with them on a daily basis. The stumbling block for him was that depression just wasn't a real illness. He saw it more as an excuse, a way of complaining that your life wasn't the one that you had hoped for, a way of trying to legitimise quitting when life got a bit too tough. For him, it was also something you could snap out of at a moment's notice if that is what you wanted or could be bothered to do. All you needed to do was have a serious word with yourself and a strong cup of tea.

Philip was somewhat frustrated and troubled by the lack of information and the lack of reassurance in his father's response. He waited a few more miles and a few more minutes before asking

"But mum will get better won't she?"

"I don't know son, I don't know, I hope so."

Once again, the response or the lack of response fell a long way short of what Philip was hoping for. However, he decided not to ask any more questions for the time being and wait for what seemed to be a better moment to raise the subject again. In fact it was his dad who went on to ask the next question. They had travelled a few miles further down the road and a little closer to their destination when he turned and looked at his son. He sighed a little before asking.

"Does it bother you...this situation with your mum?"

"Yes, well sometimes it does... I can't explain it really, I miss her even though she hasn't gone anywhere."

Francis Knott turned away from his son and looked up towards the darkening evening sky. He was stunned into a moment's silence by the rather insightful words that had just tumbled from the young boy's mouth. Philip sat motionless, staring long into the distance.

"Out of the mouths of babes," Francis muttered softly to himself before turning and adding a little louder, "maybe the holiday will help, eh."

"Maybe." Philip replied without taking his eyes off the road ahead.

In a desperate attempt to lighten the mood and change the direction that the subject was travelling in, Philip's dad hastily thought of an alternative topic of conversation. However, the choice that he made was about as successful as a hamster on a wheel trying to reach a different location.

"How's the swimming going?" He enquired.

"It's okay but I want to race. My teacher asked again about me trying out for Coventry Godiva's before the holidays. Can't I give it a try?"

Philip's dad immediately became irate, firstly at his son's request, secondly at his son's interfering teacher and thirdly at himself for bringing up the subject in the first place.

"We've been over this son, we don't have the money, you know that. It's okay for your bloody teacher to put ideas in your head. He doesn't have to pay the weekly subs, the contributions for travelling and all the other hidden costs. We only have my wages and they have to take care of all of us as well as pay all the bills. Anyway, swimming clubs are not for the likes of us."

Philip turned his head away and looked out of the passenger window.

Once again, out of desperation to end the conversation on a positive note, Francis scrambled around for the right thing to say.

"Once your mum is better and things are not as bad at home, then maybe we can look at it again." He said.

Philip didn't reply.

"Let's have some music." His dad suggested as he reached for the knob on the radio.

The upbeat rendition of 'I'd Like To Teach The World To Sing' by 'The New Seekers' instantly burst forward and filled the cab. However this particular tune was somewhat unsuccessful in lifting the mood and by the time they drove into the depot in Bristol 'Little Jimmy Osmond's 'Long haired Lover From Liverpool' was also offering very little in the way of a positive outcome.

The return leg of the journey was an equally quiet affair unlike the raucous laughter and the lewd jokes that had emanated from the canteen of the Bristol depot a short while earlier. Philip enjoyed being part of the atmosphere, the backslapping and the story telling, even if he didn't get most of the jokes. He didn't even mind when the noise dropped down to a whisper for the parts that even these guys thought were too sensitive for young teenagers ears. Philip was just happy to sit and eat his sandwiches whilst it all unfolded in front of him.

He had saved his Wagon Wheel for the journey home and just after they exited Bristol on the M32, he tore open the wrapper and clasping it with both hands, took a big bite. The motorway was by now almost deserted. The surface of the road glistened like glass as the cabs headlights shone down upon it. Philip thought about bringing up his mother's illness again but after some careful consideration he decided against it. Instead, he opted to just quietly sit and think about his forthcoming holiday. As his dad had already said, maybe it would help. They were a few miles short of Dursley when the warmth of the cab and the monotonous tone of galvanised rubber rolling along smooth tarmac finally sent Philip off to sleep, leaving his dad to mull over his own thoughts for the rest of the journey.

Chapter 8

Philip and James Knott stood shoulder to shoulder outside their holiday chalet. They gave each other the briefest of glances before continuing to look straight ahead at the row of identical holiday chalets opposite. They stood in complete silence, both trying desperately to comprehend the information that they had received only a few minutes earlier. The silence reigned for a little while longer before James looked again at his big brother and asked.

"Everything?"

"That's what they said." Philip replied.

They both continued to just stand and stare for a few more moments before James inquisitively looked again at his brother. This time however Philip beat him to it.

"Yes James, everything is free."

They were both standing in their respective flared trousers. James was in a pair of dark blue corduroys whilst Philip was sporting a pair of light and dark grey, three buttoned waistband, patched pockets. James was wearing his almost new plastic orange and white training shoes, a white t-shirt and a rather gaudy patterned tank top. Philip had upon his feet his favourite blue and white plastic training shoes. He was also wearing a plain cream coloured t-shirt and a light blue cut off denim waistcoat. They looked like a couple of Bay City Rollers who had not been well.

The issue or rather the barrier that was causing this current lack of activity was quite simply one of choice or in this particular case, too much choice. If you happened to be a child fortunate enough to grow up in a more affluent family, then the Knott brothers' current predicament would have had little impact upon you. If you were fortunate enough to have had more than one holiday every year, skiing trips with the school and summer holidays that had been full of days out then you would probably be quite accustomed to making choices on a far more frequent basis.

For Philip and James however this was the first proper holiday that they have ever had. The closest that they had come to this in the past was four days camping on the bank of the River Severn, almost directly opposite Worcester Cathedral. The highlights of that particular trip had been night fishing and bacon and eggs cooked outside in the morning. Though at the time they were both pleasurable experiences, they now appeared to pale into insignificance at the choices that stretched out before them. Swimming was free, both the indoor and outdoor pools. The cinema was free, the snooker was free, the trampolines were free, the table tennis was free, the chair lift was free, the monorail was free and every single ride at the funfair was free.

They moved…eventually. Once movement had been accomplished however, there was no stopping them and momentum was built up very quickly. The next few days went something like this. Breakfast was followed by a game of mini golf, mainly because this particular activity opened first. After mini golf it was a quick ride on the chairlift which took them over to the funfair. Once in the funfair the most popular rides were the merry mixer, the ghost train, the roller coaster and of course top of the list, the dodgems, where it was every man or small child for himself. James enjoyed the dodgems in particular as in terms of battlefields and combat with his older brother the playing field was much more of the level variety.

After spending the rest of the morning at the funfair, it was back on the chairlift and back to the giant canteen for lunch, second sitting. Once refreshed it was wise not to partake in anything too active, so it was a trip on the monorail and over to the snooker hall for a leisurely frame or two. After the snooker it was time for a more vigorous swim. Although the pool wasn't to the standard of the one back in Coventry, the water still fitted Philip like a Saville row suit. James was equally content just messing around in the pool. They were mindful of the time as it was important to get back to the funfair for the final hour before it closed for the day. Once they had alighted the dodgems for the last time it was a toss-up between the trampolines and another round of mini golf as they both stayed open an hour after the funfair. It was then a case of heading back to the dining hall for dinner, which was consumed as quickly as possible in order to limit the time that was being eaten into the evening's choices. Although these were a bit more limited, there were still decisions to be made. The evening screening at the cinema was certainly a favourite option and by Monday evening they had already watched 'Bed knobs and Broomsticks' and 'The Amazing Mr Blunden'. After the cinema they tended to gravitate towards the Crazy Horse Saloon Bar and play on the replica stagecoaches outside whilst mum and dad enjoyed the evening's entertainment inside. Round about half past nine Francis Knott would appear from inside the bar and send the boys back to their chalet. This instruction would be accompanied by thirty pence between them. This was more than enough to stop off at the seashore café for a hot chocolate and a donut each before heading back to the chalet for a few games of cards whilst they lay in bed and listened out for their mum and dad's return.

Taking into account the odd deviation to the agenda, this was pretty much the way things were heading for the remainder of the holiday. Monday morning had been a particular highlight for Philip. This was due to his dad unwinding a little too enthusiastically the night before in the Crazy Horse Saloon and not feeling well enough to get up for breakfast. Philip and James found themselves being accompanied by just their mum. Despite all of the noise and the hustle and bustle of over four hundred people enjoying and being served breakfast, for Philip as he gazed across the table at his mother, they could have been the only two people there. For a few short hours at least, Philip felt as if he had his mother back. They talked, smiled, and joked as they ate their cereal followed by a cooked breakfast. They even went and played golf together before going their separate ways as the boys headed off to the funfair and their mum went for a walk by the sea. They parted with a ruffle of hair, a gentle kiss on the forehead and a promise to meet up for lunch in the dining hall.

It wasn't until late on Wednesday night that darkness descended in more ways than one and the holiday took a sharp downwards turn. In as many ways as one could suggest, up until this point Wednesday had been another glorious day. It had started off in similar fashion to the previous few days. Despite their mum not being present the boys had still enjoyed a hearty breakfast with their dad. The rest of the day had been filled with an equally hearty measure of funfair rides, golf, trampolines, a trip to the beach, the boating lake and swimming. The early evening sun was still burning brightly when the boys exited the dining hall. They returned to the beach and messed around at the water's edge for a while before taking a short tour of a few of the camp's gift shops, mainly as a reconnaissance mission for later in the week. Once the joints had been cased they headed off to the cinema to enjoy a screening of 'The Horse in the Grey Flannel Suit'. The evening was rounded off with some messing about at the Crazy Horse Saloon until their dad had ushered them back to the chalet at about ten o'clock.

Philip had no idea how long he had been asleep or what the time was. However he eventually became aware of the raised voices that had awoken him and that they were coming from his parent's chalet. A few minutes after Philip woke up, the shouting and commotion from had also woken up James. James sat up in his bed and in the half light of the chalet he looked across at his brother. Immediately concerned and afraid of what was happening, James leapt from his bed and climbed in next to his brother for reassurance and protection. As they sat up in bed huddled together the shouting went backwards and forwards for several minutes before there was a loud crashing sound followed by a short silent respite.

This was almost immediately followed by their mother's distressed voice calling out from the other side of the wall.

"No, don't… no, please don't."

Unsure what was happening James began to sob as his mother's voice continued to seep through the wall.

"Please stop, no…no…"

Philip had a good idea about what was happening and he bizarrely began to feel relieved once his mother had stopped calling out and all he could hear was the sound of her crying accompanied with a repetitive banging sound against the wall. It wasn't long after, that the banging sound ceased and he heard the chalet door slam.

"Stay here." Philip said as he pushed the blankets aside and climbed out of bed.

He tentatively made his way out of his chalet and to the chalet next door. He stood outside in the still of the night for a moment before he slowly opened the door and peered inside. The light above the chalet door illuminated the room just enough for Philip to make out the huddled figure of his mother beneath the bedclothes of the double bed in the middle of the room.

"Mum," he called into the shadowy darkness of the chalet. He waited for a response but all he could hear were gentle sobs that seemed to tumble off the edge of the bed and fall to the floor below. He stepped inside the chalet and called out again.

"Mum, are you alright mum?"

This time around he got a reply.

"I'm fine Philip, now go back to bed."

"Are you sure mum," he looked around the chalet before adding, "where's dad gone?"

Despite the continued sobbing the reply on this occasion was a bit more forceful. "You don't need to concern yourself with where your dad is, now will you please go back to bed."

As he turned to leave and was just about to close the door, he heard his mother call out in a much softer tone. "I'm sorry."

Breakfast the next morning was an equally awkward and troublesome situation for Philip. He was conscious of making as little eye contact as possible with his father. For the majority of the sitting Philip, James and their father sat in silence. It wasn't until the last of the tables were being cleared away before one of them finally spoke.

"What have you boys got planned for today?" Francis asked as he removed his wallet from his back trouser pocket.

Philip just responded with a shrug of his shoulders as he finished drinking his glass of milk.

"Well whatever you are up to I want you to keep away from the chalets today as your mother is not well." He paused as he opened his wallet and extracted two one-pound notes. He placed the money on the table and pushed it towards Philip. "Remember what I said and I'll see you both back here later."

He took his hand away, placed his wallet back in his pocket, got up from his seat and made his way out of the dining hall.

Despite some successful shoplifting, which netted several sticks of rock, thanks to a blind spot in one of the gift shops, and despite netting a further selection of goods which included a box of fudge and an autograph book, the last two days of the holiday were somewhat subdued. Philip had managed to lift a very nice pair of earrings which he was hoping would result in a feel of Lesley Bennet's breasts with his hand under the jumper and who knows maybe even under the bra.

They didn't see their mother again until the morning of the journey home. Philip wanted to talk to her and reassure himself that she was alright but she looked somewhat distant and unapproachable. Both her complexion and her eyes appeared dull and tired. She appeared to be a completely different person to the one that had played golf with him on Monday morning, a morning that now felt like it never really happened. On the journey home his mother just sat with her head to one side and stared out of the passenger window. It was an agonisingly long three hours. The atmosphere in the car was as frosty as a February sunrise. There was a collective and overwhelming sense of relief within the car when they finally arrived home. Once back inside the house Philip headed straight for his bedroom.

He had been lying on his bed for about fifteen minutes when there was a knock at his door. This in itself was a little surprising as people didn't usually knock. He climbed down from his bed and opened the door. His mother was standing on the other side with a letter in her hand.

"This came for you whilst we were away." She said as she handed him the letter. She looked him in the eye and gently smiled before turning away and disappearing into her room.

With the letter tightly gripped in his hand, Philip closed his bedroom door.

Chapter 9

Philip Knott lay on his bed, staring up at the letter that was firmly grasped in both hands. Although he hadn't received that many letters in his short life, he was sure that he had never received one quite like this before. The envelope on its own was screaming quality. This was not the poor standard of envelope that would contain an equally poor standard of Christmas card, like the ones that he would exchange with his school friends at Yuletide. There was a certain amount of thickness to this envelope and it was a cream colour rather than the almost transparent white envelopes that he was more familiar with.

He drew in a deep breath and slowly exhaled as he prepared himself for what he was sure to be bad news inside. Carefully he began to peel the envelope open. It came apart with a sharp clear snap. He peered inside, none the wiser as to its contents. He paused for a moment before taking in another deep breath. His heart rate increased and a few beads of sweat formed on his forehead. He took the crisply folded letter out before carefully placing the empty envelope on the bed. With one more inhale for luck, he began to unfold the letter. All of a sudden his eyes widened and a wave of excitement rushed up from his toes and covered the whole of his body as he saw the Leeds United club badge at the top of the letter with the words Leeds United A.F.C directly beneath it. The tips of his fingers were tingling as he opened up the whole letter. It read

Dear Philip,

I have just received a copy of your entry into the Roy of the Rovers favourite player competition. I would just like to take this opportunity to thank you for your kind words and your praise. It was especially heart-warming to read that you passionately believe in good sportsmanship and fair play, qualities that I hold very dear myself. I hope that I can continue to inspire you and earn your praise in the future. I am sure that you are looking forward to the new season as much as I am. Hopefully it will be a successful one. The whole team are looking forward to having the opportunity to put the F.A Cup disappointment behind them. I hope too that you continue to enjoy reading about Roy and his team every week, it was my favourite comic strip when I was growing up in Scotland. I look forward to your continual support.

All the best, Billy Bremner.

Philip lay on his bed and read the letter several times before carefully folding it and putting it back inside the envelope. He then placed it gently beneath his pillow as if it were a priceless document from the pages of history. He lay back on his bed with his hands clasped at the back of his head and stared up at the ceiling. As he lay and basked in the warm glow that the letter had brought, his bedroom door swung open. His dad entered carrying a suitcase. He dropped it with a heavy sounding thud onto the wooden floor as he closed the door behind him with a swing of his foot.

"You need to empty this." He said as he pointed towards the suitcase. "Put the dirty clothes in the basket in the bathroom and anything that is clean put it back in the drawers. I'm off out, make sure this suitcase is empty by the time I get back and get you and your brother some tea".

He turned to leave, as he reached for the door handle he asked. "Who was your letter off?"

"Billy Bremner". Philip replied.

His dad froze for a moment with his hand still on the door handle before looking over at Philip. "You're joking."

Philip stared straight into his dad's eyes and shook his head.

"Let's see?"

Philip reached under his pillow, retrieved the letter and passed it to his dad. Francis opened the letter a little too vigorously for Philip's liking.

"Careful dad." Philip called out.

Francis rolled his eyes and raised his eyebrows before tentatively removing the letter between finger and thumb. He passed the envelope back to Philip before carefully opening the letter. He read it in complete silence before folding it up again and passing it back to Philip. He waited for Philip to successfully place it back under his pillow before he asked.

"Are you going to write back?"

Francis could see by the expression on his son's face that up until now Philip hadn't considered sending a reply.

"Well whilst you're thinking about it, get this suitcase emptied." Francis said as he made his way out of the room.

Philip jumped down from his bed, unzipped the suitcase and flipped open the lid. Resting on the top of a hastily packed pile of clothes were his swimming trunks. He stood up and retrieved a few coins from the corner of his jeans pocket. "More than enough." He muttered to himself. Chucking his trunks onto the bottom bunk, he scooped up the rest of the clothes and headed for the bathroom. He came out again almost immediately, carrying a clean towel. Once back in his bedroom, he picked up his trunks, rolled them up in his towel, zipped up the suitcase and set off. Within an hour he was poolside, looking down as the sparkling blue water rippled and bobbled in front of him.

Despite the pool being as crowded as one would expect on a Saturday afternoon during the summer and despite the hullabaloo that accompanied it, Philip was more than happy to wait for the optimum moment to dive in. It did not take long before a suitable gap appeared. He pushed forward and leapt into the air. As soon as his feet left the side of the pool and he was completely airborne, everything fell silent around him. The noise that surrounded him instantly dissipated as his out stretched hands made contact with the clear blue water. Once fully submerged, he swam for as long as he could before the overwhelming volume of legs in front of him forced him to come up for air. Once more upon the surface of the water, he did the best he could to continue to swim in a straight line. As he swam he continued to think about his dad's words. For every length that he swam he started the letter at least three or four times. Most of his attempts only got as far as 'Dear Billy'. There was the occasional 'Dear Mr Bremner' and the odd 'Dear Billy Bremner'. On one occasion whilst having to walk the last few feet to the pools edge due to the volume of people in the water he even got as far as drafting a first line. He lost his train of thought though when a rather chubby lad jumped into the water directly in front of him, but the truth of the matter was he had no idea what to write. He continued to do his best to both swim and to get further than 'Dear Billy' for the next hour or so before opting to get his marching orders by doing a 'Scooby' off of the third diving board.

Although Philip was still pondering the possibility of writing back to Billy Bremner when he boarded the bus home, as he got closer and closer to the 'Live and Let Live' terminus, his thoughts turned to Lesley Bennett and the possible rewards his gifts might bring. As soon as he arrived home, he grabbed some clothes pegs from the washing basket in the scullery and hung his towel and trunks on the washing line. Once back in the house, he located the rest of the unpacked luggage, retrieved the items he had stolen from the Butlins gift shops and set off for Lesley Bennett's house.

The journey was short but it was still enough time for his heart to start racing, his mouth to go dry, his tongue to stick to the back of his teeth and his palms to go ice cold and clammy. He duly arrived, not in the best of health and while clutching his gifts in one hand he knocked on the door with the other. Almost immediately the door opened and there stood Lesley Bennett. Her long dark brown hair appeared to shine as brightly as her dark brown eyes.

"Oh it's you". Lesley said with a tone in her voice that not only took the wind from Philip's sails but also took a hold of the sails, threw them to the floor and wiped her feet all over them.

Philip attempted to respond but with his tongue still stuck to the back of his teeth he was unable to say anything. Lesley on the other hand had more she wanted to say and was clearly keen to unburden herself.

"I'm sorry Philip but I don't want to see you anymore."

Philip's jaw dropped, taking his tongue with it. If nothing else, at least it helped to remove his tongue from the back of his teeth which in turn allowed him to reply. "Why not?" he asked.

Lesley shrugged her shoulders as she replied. "I've met someone else."

"When"? Philip asked.

"It's not my fault." Lesley began, "You weren't here."

"I've been on holiday…I've been to Butlins… I've only been away for a week."

"Look Philip, I've met somebody else and that's that."

"Who?"

"It doesn't matter who, you don't know him."

"It matters to me." Philip said as he could feel himself gripping the bag tighter and tighter as he spoke.

"His name's Steve and he plays in my brother's football team."

With this particular piece of information Philip knew that all hope had gone and Lesley was lost. If he played in the same team as Lesley's older brother, he was at least sixteen. With one last futile gesture Philip held up his paper bag. "But I've bought you a present." He muttered.

As he did so a tall, thin lad appeared in the doorway behind Lesley and put his arm around her. He was quite pale with greasy ginger hair that flopped over his shoulders and with a cluster of spots upon his chin.

"Everything okay?" He asked

"Yes." Lesley replied.

"What's that?" the lad asked as he pointed at the bag Philip was still holding up.

"A present." Philip replied.

"Thank you very much," the lad said as he took the bag from Philip's hand and with his arm still draped around Lesley, he pulled her inside and closed the door.

Philip stood on the doorstep for a few moments before turning away and whispering under his breath "Dear Billy."

Chapter 10

"Hot Rice". Craig Swinburn called out as he grasped the tennis ball with both hands. His grip was tighter than the action man he got last Christmas as he spun around and surveyed all possible targets.

It was a glorious August evening. A perfectly round bright orange sun sat alone in a pale blue cloudless sky. The close was full of activity. Babes in arms were toddling around in nappies and vests under the watchful eyes of their mothers. A group of younger children were playing on their second-hand bikes and plastic tractors. The main event however was about to unfold on the green that was partially encased by houses on either side and the three storey flats at the one end.

The rules of Hot Rice were very simple and all over the country the same game would had a variety of different names. As long as you had a tennis ball and at least half a dozen players, the more the merrier, the game was on. Firstly, one player reluctantly agreed or had to be nominated to be 'It'. However, it was not necessarily a bad thing to be 'It' in a game of Hot Rice and it was certainly preferable to being the Germans in a game of 'Escape from Colditz'. To start the game, the tennis ball would be thrown high into the air. The player who was 'It' would attempt to catch the ball whilst the other players would run as far away from the ball as possible. Upon catching the ball 'It' would call out 'Hot Rice'. Everybody would then have to freeze and stand still. This is when the game would begin in earnest. The player 'It' holding the ball, now had to try and hit the other players with the ball. Once you had been hit, you effectively swap sides and the ball could be passed between players whilst trying to hit the remaining players. The last player to be hit was the winner. This game was about survival of the fittest and the best tactic to adopt was to pick off the weaker and slower players first. Once 'It' had the ball in his possession he was not obliged to throw it at another player. He could just opt to throw it into the air a few feet at a time in an attempt to get closer to another player. However he always had to remember that players were free to move when the ball was in flight. They were also free to keep moving if 'It' failed to call out 'Hot Rice' upon catching the ball each time.

Craig Swinburn looked around and immediately identified two possible targets. Martin Matthews was top of the list. As the harsh reality of the game was to pick off the slower runners first and to build up a bigger team for the tougher challenges that lay ahead, Martin was an obvious choice, as nobody on the field of play moved slower than Martin Matthews. Task one for Craig Swinburn was to get a bit closer to Martin. This was quickly achieved by tossing the tennis ball into the air, not too high, in the direction of Martin a few times before catching it again and calling 'Hot Rice'. On the third throw, no sooner had Craig called 'Hot Rice' before he released the ball again, full pelt in the direction of Martin Matthews. Martin turned away and stooped a little. This was unfortunately a mistake as the ball struck him with a marksman's precision on the back of his head. The momentum of the strike sent him toppling forwards and he crashed to the ground with the offending missile coming to rest a few feet away. At this point whilst laughing uncontrollably the rest of the players took the opportunity to run as far away from the sprawled out Martin as possible.

"Grab the ball Martin, you fat twat" Craig called out.

"Piss off". Martin replied as he got slowly to his feet and looked around for the tennis ball.

The next target identified by Craig was a young lad called Anthony King. He was about ten years old but despite his young age seeming an apparent disadvantage, he was not to be dismissed lightly as he was extremely nimble and full of energy. Martin slowly staggered over and retrieved the ball. As he picked it up Craig shouted "Hot Rice" and immediately looked around for young Anthony. Anthony, along with the rest of the players, was some distance away from Craig and Martin. Still giggling at the hit Martin took to the back of the head, Anthony was crouched down with one hand resting on the ground in front of him.

Although Martin was not the quickest, he did possess a half-decent throw and with a bit of teamwork and some short, sharp sprints from Craig, Anthony was soon within range. The youngster still put up a good fight and dodged a few attempts to strike him. He was finally caught by a blow to the knee as he once again attempted to leap out of the path of the ball. Once Craig had somebody with a bit more pace on his side the rest of the players toppled one by one until there were only two remaining, Michael Robinson and Philip. Some quick passing and a good manoeuvre left Philip with nowhere to run and he was easily picked off. This left Michael Robinson to celebrate his victory in a style befitting a cup final goal scorer as he ran around the field with arms aloft doing a very good impersonation of Bob Stokoe after winning the F.A Cup.

After another game of 'Hot Rice' and a game of 'Kick the Can', the number of participants began to decline as one by one they were called in by their parents. By nine thirty only four remained, Philip, James, Craig and Paul. Philip and James knew they were okay for a while as their dad was at work and their mum would have taken her tablets by now and would be fast asleep. After a few games of 'Kerby' the boys went and sat out of sight, round by the garages so that Craig and Paul could smoke a cigarette.

Craig opened the top pocket of his denim waistcoat and took out a ten packet of No6 cigarettes and a box of matches. Opening the packet he took out two cigarettes and passed one to Paul. As he did so Philip reached inside a pocket of his patch pocket flares and pulled out two pieces of 'Bazooka Joe' bubble gum. He passed one to James.

"Have you spoken to Lesley since she dumped ya?" Craig asked before lighting his cigarette.

"No, why would I?" Philip replied.

"Cold that, dumping you whilst you were on holiday and for someone like Steve Watson, he's a right ginger twat. You should have decked him for moving in on your bird whilst you weren't about."

"What's the point? Anyway, I'm better off without her" Philip muttered.

"And he's bigger than you" Paul chipped in whilst smoking his cigarette.

"Yeah, I'm sure you're much better off playing with yourself whilst Steve Watson is getting it done for him" Craig said.

"What makes you think he's getting any further than I did?" Philip asked without really wanting a reply and looking for an opportunity to change the subject.

"Can't do any worse than you did, can he Paul, even for a ginger twat" Craig added.

On this occasion Paul just chose to shrug his shoulders and carry on smoking his cigarette.

"So, you still haven't shagged Claire Chase then?" Philip asked Craig in an attempt to change the direction of the conversation.

"Can't get near her can I at the moment because of her stupid tart of a mother."

"Why what's her mum got to do with it."

"She's been barred from the Livvy ain't she, where you been... Oh yeah that's right it happened whilst you two were at Butlins."

"What happened?" James asked between chews of his Bazooka Joe bubble gum.

Craig took a long drag of his cigarette and shook his head before he responded. "There was some fuckin Irish diddly diddly band playing and as usual she got so pissed up that she lost it. She was dancing on the table when the next thing, her dress was flying across the room. By the time the landlord had got from behind the bar and reached the table, her saggy tits were out and she was pulling her knickers down. You've gone too far this time, he said and then he barred her."

"He won't bar her for long though will he, the amount of money she spends in there." Philip said.

"She's still spending the bloody money, that's the problem. She won't go drinking in the 'Bell' cuz it's too far to stagger home when she's hammered so she's sending Claire to the out sales every night and getting smashed at home. Spark out on the fucking sofa every night, best I can get is my hand in her jeans on the doorstep."

"What you doing on the doorstep with Claire's mum?" Philip asked.

"Funny." Craig muttered with his cigarette hanging from his lips.

"Never mind." Philip said with a large grin across his face.

Rather annoyed by this Craig took the opportunity to hit back. "You know those gifts you nicked from Butlins for Lesley, Steve Watson gave them to his mum for her birthday."

"Bullshit." Philip replied.

"No, straight up, he was going to pinch a hanging basket from some old dear's front garden until your little package fell in his lap. So he got a little box and a piece of wrapping paper. Said he didn't have enough money for a card because he spent it all on the presents. Crafty git but he's still a twat."

Determined not to lose face Philip simply replied. "Oh well at least they didn't cost me anything."

"Nip round to his mum's and tell her that it was you that got them, she might get her tits out for ya." Craig said.

Seeing that Philip was wounded by this piece of news Craig did what all good teenage friends would do and went in for another go. "Did you write to Billy Bremner again? Did you ask him what to do when your girlfriend shits all over you?"

"No, I didn't." Philip said.

"No, you didn't write or no you didn't ask him?"

"No, I didn't ask him."

"So, you wrote to him then?"

"Yes."

"Wow, you nutter, had a reply yet?"

Philip chose not to answer. Craig took one final drag of his cigarette before flicking the smouldering butt away. "Well I'm off to see if the old soak has fallen asleep yet," he said as he stood up. "Look on the bright side", he added as he walked away, "Footie season starts tomorrow."

Chapter 11

Ask any passionate football fan anywhere in the country and they will all tell you the same thing. It does not matter which team you support, you can be an Exeter City fan or an Everton fan, a West Ham fan or a West Brom fan, Doncaster Rovers or Queens Park Rangers. Ask any fan you like which day is the most important or the most anticipated day of the season and they will all say the same thing. The one day that stands above all others in the footballing calendar is the opening day of the season. This is not to say that it is all downhill after that as there are other big days to come during the next nine months. The F.A.Cup third round draw is always a big day, especially if you support a team from the lower divisions or even a non-league club and you have survived the previous rounds. The Boxing Day and New Year's Day games are always special, and even if your team doesn't make it, cup final day is always a big occasion. Especially deciding whether to watch the coverage on ITV or BBC1. In Philip's house BBC1 would usually be victorious mainly because of cup final 'It's a Knockout'. However despite all of these key moments along the way, the opening day of the season was the one that caused the most excitement.

There was a number of reasons for this, reasons which unified fans the length and breadth of the country. From division one to division four on the first day of the season everybody could dream, everybody had hope. Could this be the year you won the title? Could this be the year you won promotion? Could your team survive in a higher league after winning promotion the season before? Could they bounce back after the misery of relegation? There was the possibility of a cup run, the chance to join the list of famous giant killers such as Leatherhead and Hereford. However, the beauty of the opening day was that everybody started the season on the same amount of points. Win the first game and you are, at least for a short while, top of the league. If you lose then Jimmy Hill will remind you at the end of 'Match of the Day' not to be too disheartened as you are still only two points off the top.

Philip needed no further encouragement than the first few rings of his alarm clock to leap out of bed, get dressed and head downstairs for a very quick breakfast before setting off to deliver the morning papers. The excitement and the anticipation had already climbed on board by the time he reached the bottom of the stairs. Francis was sitting at the table, finishing off a mug of tea and smoking a Senior Service cigarette as Philip entered the kitchen.

"Today's the day", he said to Philip. "Some bacon in the pan if you want it." He added.

Philip walked over to the table and took two slices of bread from the breadboard. He went to the pan, took the bacon out with his fingers and placed them on one slice of bread before dipping the other slice into the pan and then placing it on top of the bacon.

"Brentford at home should start with a win." Francis said as Philip sat down at the table and began to eat his sandwich.

"What?" Philip muttered with a mouthful of bacon and bread.

"Brentford at home." Francis repeated.

The penny dropped. "Oh right, Hartlepool." Philip replied as he put his sandwich down and made his way to the fridge.

"And what about your bunch of cheats and divers, who have you got?"

Philip decided not to rise to the bait and simply replied "Everton" as he poured a glass of milk.

"Home or away?" Francis asked.

"Home" Philip replied.

"You need to win your home games, you win now't unless you're strong at home."

"We'll win" Philip said as he sat back down at the table and reacquainted himself with his sandwich. Eager to get to the newsagents, He finished his glass of milk and went to retrieve his paperbag from the scullery. He returned to the kitchen to grab what was left of his sandwich. "Bye dad" he said as he turned to leave.

"Keep the noise down when you get back" his dad replied as Philip disappeared from the kitchen.

As he entered the newsagents Philip was immediately struck by the situation that greeted him. The magazine rack and the section of shelf that usually housed the children's comics and the teenage magazines was no more. The rack had completely vanished and the space on the shelf was now occupied by a selection of knitting magazines and other magazines that were aimed at the more mature lady. The rest of the shelf space was full of the usual products ranging from 'Motorcycle News' on the middle shelf to 'Mayfair' and other adult publications on the top shelf.

Philip looked across at Mr Underwood. "Where have the magazines gone?" He asked

"That's exactly what I'd like to know." Mr Underwood replied.

"You mean somebody has taken them."

"No" Mr Underwood replied, "What I mean is somebody has been taking them."

Mr Underwood motioned towards a handwritten card that was hanging down from one of the shelves. It read 'If you cannot find what you are looking for, please ask behind the counter'.

"He accused me of pinching his stupid magazines."

Philip looked over at the two other boys. They were standing at the far end of the shop waiting for their papers. A boy called Colin Reid was standing with his hands stuffed inside his trouser pockets. He was standing next to the boy who had just spoken. He was a rough and ready young lad from the Manor Farm estate called Paul McBride.

"I did not accuse you of anything Paul, I simply asked if you knew anything about the disappearance of my magazines. Anyway, get a move on and get these papers delivered." Mr Underwood turned to Philip. "What magazines do you want"?

"A 'Tiger' and a 'Shoot'." Philip replied.

Mr Underwood bent down behind the counter for the briefest of moments, however it was long enough for Paul McBride. Mr Underwood reappeared clutching the two magazines Philip had asked for. "That will be twenty-five pence" he said.

"What, no staff discounts?" Paul McBride asked.

"Oh yes and this is some swanky London department store that you three are standing in. Now I suggest that you shift yourselves or you won't be staff, as you call it, much longer."

Philip paid for his magazines, collected his papers and followed the other two boys out of the shop. Once outside Paul Mc Bride nudged Philip. He had a grin on his face that was wider than a poorly timed delivery in a cricket match.

"Miserable old bastard," he said. "He can hide his poxy magazines behind the counter, but he can't hide his chocolate," he added as he pulled out three Fry's Chocolate Creams from inside his jacket. "Here you go lads," he said as he passed one bar to Philip and another to Colin.

Philip smiled as he took the bar of chocolate from Paul.

"Season starts today then" Paul said. "Home to Spurs, can't miss that one."

"You going to the game then?" Philip asked.

"Sure am, if I can sneak in. Come on Sky Blues."

"How do you sneak in?" Philp said with some interest.

"It's easy as long as you're careful. You climb one of the trees that are on the other side of the car park and drop down onto the wall. You gotta be careful though, one slip and it's a bit of a drop. Then you go along the wall and jump across onto the toilet roof. Then you can drop down between the back of the toilets and the wall. It's a bit tight so the chubby pie eaters can't do it. Then along you go and you pop out at the corner of the ground where all the Spaz's sit. Then it's a quick step over the advertising boards before some eagle-eyed steward spots you. Even if they do, they only throw you out and you just head round and try again. Anyway, can't stand here talking to you two boneheads all morning, I've got a game to get to."

The three boys headed off in different directions to deliver their papers and eat their chocolate.

When Philip arrived home all was relatively quiet. The only sign of life was the faint sound of dialogue coming from the television set in the corner of the living room. Still in his pyjamas, James had the volume turned down as far as he could whilst still being able to hear it. He was sitting so close to the set that the screen was almost touching his nose, as he did his best to watch a repeated episode of 'The Double Deckers'. Philip sat down on the sofa directly behind James and took his magazines out of his now empty paperbag.

"Have you had your breakfast James?" He asked.

Without turning around or breaking his concentration James just shook his head. Philip went into the kitchen and returned a short while later, carrying a bowl of cornflakes. He passed the bowl to James and went back to his magazines. On the opening day of the season there was one particular page in 'Tiger' that was of the utmost importance. The page in question was the 'Your Team' page. This was a page that was laid out so the reader could record their own team's performance. There was a team sheet, player ratings, score, referee and a team rating out of ten. Philip set off in search of a pen so that he could fill in as much as he could, which at nine 'o' clock on a Saturday morning wasn't going to be a great deal. He wrote Leeds United in the 'your team' box and Everton in the 'versus' box. He could probably predict the team sheet but he would need to wait until he saw the results in the News of the World on Sunday to confirm the line-up.

James was now engrossed in an episode of 'The Banana Splits' whilst he ate his cereal. Philip meanwhile patiently waited for 'Grandstand' to start. Unfortunately he was in for rather a long wait as it didn't start for another three hours. As he settled in for the long wait, he heard a low voice coming from the kitchen.

"Philip, Philip, where's dad?"

Philip turned around to see his sister's head sticking out from the other side of the kitchen door.

"He's in bed, I think" Philip replied.

Sporting an instantly relieved expression on her face, Philip's sister quietly entered the living room.

"Have you been out all night?" Philip asked with a certain amount of surprise in his voice.

"Ssshhh, keep your voice down."

"Dad I'll kill you if he finds out."

"He's not going to find out and anyway if he so much as lays a finger on me…"

"You'll what?" Philip asked.

"He might get away with treating mum like something he just stepped in but he's not going to do it to me" Grace said as she turned away. "I'm going to get my uniform for work. If dad asks I left at my usual time, okay."

Philip went back to his magazines as his sister quietly headed upstairs to retrieve her uniform. James was still staring at the T.V, now with an empty bowl in his lap. Philip still had two hours and fifty eight minutes to wait until 'Grandstand' started and the time seemed to pass by as quickly as an asthmatic tortoise with a limp. His sister soon reappeared in her Woolworth's uniform.

"I thought you worked at Sketchley's on a Saturday?" Philip asked.

"No" Grace replied, shaking her head. "I haven't been there for weeks." She left as quietly as she had entered.

After a long and agonising wait 'Grandstand' finally started. Once the first bar of the theme tune had struck, then it was official. There was still the best part of three hours until kick-off but once 'Grandstand' had begun then the season had begun and once the season had begun then the Saturday afternoon ritual could begin. It would start with an hour's 'Grandstand' in the safe hands of Frank Bough. This would then be followed by a trip to the bookies in Wood End so that he could place a bet on the 'ITV 7'. The Bookmakers in Bell Green were far more stringent when it came to the law and you needed to be at least sixteen to stand a chance of placing a bet there. However he had no problem in placing his five pence each way at the bookies in Wood End. As long as he just placed his bet and then made a swift exit the bookie there was more than happy to take his money. It was then back home to watch the races on 'World of Sport' before switching back to 'Grandstand' for the half-time score. After the latest update Philip would then find himself caught between a rock and a hard place. It was either rugby league on 'Grandstand' or wrestling on 'World of Sport'. Neither of them appealed and it was just a case of killing time until the vidiprinter began rolling on 'Grandstand'.

The day had followed the designated pattern. His bet stayed alive until the third race. His first two horses 'Visiting Hours' and 'Bring On The Band' had both finished third at prices of seven to one and twelve to one respectively. His third horse however had come in a very disappointing ninth of eleven. By the time the racing was over and the disappointment had subsided, three o'clock had arrived and the games were finally underway. Once they had started Philip would sometimes try and get updates on the radio but living in Coventry this was only really worthwhile when Leeds were playing a Midlands team. This was also the same scenario when he was hoping to see them on T.V. If there was any possibility of seeing them on 'Star Soccer' on a Sunday afternoon, they once again needed to be playing a Midlands team. Hopefully tonight they would be one of the two games featured on Match of the Day.

By the time the half-time scores were in, Philip's dad had got up, gone out, come back in and was now lying on the sofa, slightly drunk and equally slightly conscious. The scores brought good news with Leeds United currently winning 1-0 with a goal from Billy Bremner in as early as the fourth minute. The alcohol fumes from Francis's breath drifted across the room whilst James and Philip stared at St Helens versus Hull Kingston Rovers without actually paying attention to it. Eventually the Rugby League finished and it was time for final score. Francis stirred just in time to see that Hartlepool had opened their account with a 1-0 win over Brentford. He got off the sofa, staggered out of the living room and headed upstairs. Philip had to wait a little longer for the Leeds result but the news when it came was equally pleasing. They had started the season with a 3-1 win with further goals coming from Johnny Giles and Mick Jones.

"Yes." Philip called out as the score came through.

Francis came back into the room. He walked over to Philip and handed him a one-pound note.

"Your mum's not well so after your paper round go to the chippy and get dinner. Get two pieces of fish, you and your brother can share one, two lots of chips and you'd better get something for your sister…get her a fishcake. Don't hang about, I'm getting hungry."

Philip stood up, put the money in his pocket, and picked up his bag which was still lying on the living room floor at the end of the sofa and to the left. He knew he would have to wait a while at the newsagents as it would be some time before the 'Pinks' arrived but under the circumstances and his dad's impatience, it was still preferable to waiting at home.

Chapter 12

 Dear Philip,
 Thank you very much for your letter and thank you for your best wishes with the new season. I also hope that it will be a successful one. I am sorry to hear about the situation with your girlfriend Lesley. I appreciate that this may be of little comfort right now but I assure you that when you look back on this part of your life in a few years from now, you will do so with a smile and with some fond memories. I remember being very fond of a girl back in Scotland before I moved down to Leeds as a sixteen year old. Although she never showed any interest in me, which was rather devastating at the time, I now recall her with great fondness. I sometimes wonder how she is doing now, if she's married, if she has children, and I hope that wherever she is and whatever she is doing, I hope that she is happy. It will be the same for you in time. Your life will take many turns and you will meet many people along the way. Some will be in your life for a short while, others will stay a lot longer. So don't worry too much about Lesley. Just try and stay positive and move on. I guess the new school year is just around the corner. I hope that it goes well and always try to do your best.
 Keep enjoying your football.
 Best Wishes
 Billy.

 Philip had read the letter six times. He was just about to embark on a seventh reading when he heard his mother calling him from the bottom of the stairs.

"Philip can you come down here a minute love." There was a pause but only a brief pause. "Did you hear me Philip?"

"Yes" Philip shouted.

He listened for the sound of his mother heading back into the living room before taking the letter and very carefully putting it back in the envelope. He stood up, bent down and took out the bottom drawer from the chest of drawers. He placed the letter on top of his previous letter that was resting on the floor, before putting the drawer back in its place and making his way downstairs, passing his dad going in the other direction as he did so.

The scene that greeted Philip as he entered the living room can only be described as one of horror for a fourteen year old boy approaching the end of his summer holidays. Philip's mum was standing in front of the sofa, carefully laying out school clothes. James was perched on the arm of the sofa with an equally horrified expression rigidly fixed upon his face.

Philip's mum turned to look at him. "You're as bad as your brother. Don't just stand there like a rabbit on a motorway, come here and help me sort out what's what for school."

Philip could see the rugby shirt that he had put out of his mind for the past six weeks as he slowly edged his way across the room. No sooner had he arrived at the edge of the sofa than his mum started putting items of clothing up to his chest and then laying them back down again.

"What about these, do they still fit?" his mum asked as she passed him two pairs of trousers.

"I'm not sure." Philip replied.

"Well there's only one way to find out Philip." His mum said with a disapproving expression on her face.

Philip walked around to the back of the sofa with a certain amount of trepidation. This was due to one of the pairs of trousers in particular. They were a pair of exceptionally thick, dark blue, corduroy trousers and Philip hated them. He slowly put them on before announcing, whilst still partially hidden behind the sofa, that they were too small.

"Come round here and let me see" his mother said.

Still accompanied by the same trepidation that had escorted him round the back of the sofa, he stepped out and into the open.

"Come here Philip" his mum ordered with a tone in her voice that suggested her patience was beginning to wear thin.

Philip stepped forward the required distance. His mother immediately grabbed the waistband of the dreaded corduroy's and gave them a short sharp tug.

"They fit fine" she said.

"But look!" Philp replied as he pointed towards the floor and attempted to highlight the fact that the bottom of the trouser legs finished about an inch above his ankle.

Not moved by this protest, his mother just looked down briefly before replying "They'll have to do Philip, we're not made of money, now try the other pair on."

Philip's heart sank as he headed back behind the sofa. Trepidation had moved on and had now been replaced by dejection. Trepidation however was soon to make a triumphant return when his mother passed him his blazer. This item was equally short. On this occasion however it was in the arm department. When put together with the corduroy trousers, he could give a very good impression of Max Wall.

For James the issue he faced was quite the opposite, as he knew only too well, if it no longer fitted Philip it was heading in his direction. The problem with this system was that it would take at least another year before the clothes would fit him properly.

"Okay you two, go and get dressed, we need to go into town."

Philip and James both knew that this meant a trip to John Cheatles school outfitters. The prospect of this coupled with Leeds United's trip to Arsenal later that evening meant that a day which had begun so brightly was now rapidly beginning to race downhill. The journey into town was a long and arduous one, starting with the walk to the bus stop and followed by the bus journey itself. There was a time when a journey such as this would have been a very joyous affair. The trip would have comprised of lots of laughter, joking around and chatting. A visit to a few shops and if finance allowed it, a trip to Wimpy for a banana longboat, whilst mum would have a bowl of soup. Days such as this seemed to be little more than a distant fading memory now, almost to the point that, along with other events in his life, Philip was unsure whether they had actually happened at all.

They walked to the bus stop and boarded the bus in complete silence. The mood failed to improve as they travelled into town. Philip and James sat next to each other on a seat in front of their mother. Philip turned and looked at his mother several times as the bus made its way through Bell Green and along the Stoney Stanton Road. On each and every occasion his mother was sat very rigid, looking through the window with her head slightly bowed and ever so slightly tilted to one side. It wasn't until they were all encased within John Cheatles before some sort of communication broke out between them.

If you were to ask any random schoolboy which was their least favourite shop, before answering the question, the school outfitters would surely be given careful consideration. Firstly because there was absolutely nothing in the shop that a schoolboy would actually want to buy and secondly because when you found yourself standing inside one, you knew that your summer holiday, which once stretched out before you, was now on its last legs.

The experience was proving to be equally traumatic for both of the Knott boys, until from nowhere a solitary ray of sunshine fell upon Philip.

"I suppose you had better get yourself a new pair of trousers." His mother said whilst holding a blazer up against his brother's chest.

Philip certainly didn't need a second invitation and even before his mother had reached the 'ers' of trousers, he was on his way. He quickly selected a few pairs of trousers from the racks and disappeared into the changing rooms. Unlike Mr Benn however there wasn't an alternative exit that would lead to a wonderful world of adventure. Once in the changing room, the usual problem occurred. Philip could never quite work out what was the required body shape for a pair of trousers to fit properly. If they were a good fit around the waist, they were too short in the leg and if they were a good fit in the leg department, there seemed to be enough room in the waist to conceal a small number of household pets. Eventually he found a pair that were about as good as it was going to get and far better that the dreaded thick dark blue corduroys. Once his mother had inspected the trousers with a few embarrassing tugs here and there, they were purchased along with some other, much needed, but not exactly wanted, school items, and they left.

Upon exiting the shop the boys were met with an offer that certainly added to the positive direction the day was now taking.

"Who would like a banana longboat?" their mother asked.

"Yes please!" the brothers replied in unison.

They headed up the lower precinct ramp and into the round café that sat majestically on the upper level, overlooking the shops. It wasn't called 'The Round Café', this was simply what everybody called it for the obvious reason that it was round. Once inside and comfortably housed at a table, they waited to order. The young waiter duly arrived and without looking at the menu, their mother ordered.

"A pot of tea for one and two banana longboats please."

The waiter scribbled down the order on his pad. "Anything else?" He asked.

"No thank you."

The waiter turned and left, clutching his pad and pencil as he did so.

The waiter had only departed for a couple of minutes before James was constantly and impatiently turning his head around and waiting for him to return. Philip sat and gazed out of the window at the people passing by. Out of the blue their mother again broke the silence.

"I guess that you two are not looking forward to going back to school?" she asked.

James didn't hear the question but Philip just shrugged his shoulders and replied "Not really."

Philip's mum reached across the table and took a hold of Philip's hands. This immediately caught him off guard and he looked curiously back at his mother. She smiled at him as she gently squeezed his hands.

"Try your best at school son, it's your chance of a better life, you do realise that don't you? Do you want to live your life like your dad and me, always struggling to make ends meet? It only leads to problems, rows and heartache."

Although the psychical connection with his mum was something that Philip had missed and at times he had longed to experience it again, the expression on her face as she spoke left Philip with the feeling that the distance between them had grown. Her smile appeared to drift away as she released his hands and looked across at the waiter approaching the table.

Philip could quite easily put his finger on it, he just didn't want to. But his banana longboat was more bitter in taste than it was sweet. Despite the banana and the three different flavours of ice cream trying their best, the slightly unpleasant taste was still housed at the back of his throat by the time they arrived back home. Carrying his new school clothes, Philip headed straight upstairs to his room. He dumped the bags on his bed and was just about to retrieve his letter when the bedroom door swung open and his dad entered.

"Wanna tag along tonight?" His dad asked.

"No, not tonight thanks dad." Philip replied.

This was not the response his dad was expecting. "Oh right." He said. "Please yourself."

"Can I come with you tomorrow night?"

"I don't know. I'll have to see if there is a space in the cab tomorrow night." His dad said before giving Philip a half smile. Then he added. "You can still make my sandwiches though and put an extra sugar in the flask, sandwiches for your brother too, he's happy to tag along tonight."

With this he turned and left the room.

Once Philip felt sure that his dad had gone downstairs and he felt as confident as he possibly could that he wasn't going to be disturbed, he retrieved his letter from its hiding place and lay down on his bed. After a few more reads, he grabbed his writing pad and a pen and began to craft a reply. He was just about finished thanking Billy for his advice and wishing him luck for the game against Arsenal later that evening when he was summoned downstairs to make the sandwiches. His dad was busy making everybody bacon and eggs for their tea when Philip entered the kitchen.

"Cut some bread and lay the table will you, you can make some sandwiches after tea, how many eggs do you want?"

"Two please dad." Philip replied as he began to gather up the condiments for the table.

"Just the three of us." His dad said. "Your mum is resting and as usual I have no idea where your sister is. We can eat in here."

Philip finished laying the table and cutting the bread just as his dad served up three plates of bacon and eggs. James appeared in the doorway as the plates reached the table. All three sat down and began to eat.

"Back to school next week then," Francis said as he took a slice of bread and walked over to the cooker. He dipped the slice of bread into the bacon fat and pushed it down with his fingers as both boys replied with what can only be described as disgruntled noises.

Francis was shaking his head as he returned to the table. He wafted his grease laden slice of bread in their direction. "Your education is very important lads, unless of course you want to live around here for the rest of your lives. There are some miserable existences around here boys and it is wonderfully easy to join them. If you want your life to amount to something better then you have to make the effort".

"Are you saying that you didn't make the effort dad?" Philip asked.

James instantly froze at hearing Philip's question. He sat motionless for a moment with a piece of bacon hanging precariously off the end of his fork. He looked at his dad. He was expecting a rather angry response but on this occasion however, he was both surprised and relieved in equal measure.

"What they call a comprehensive education today wasn't up to much in Hartlepool at the start of the 1950's son. We certainly weren't encouraged to spread our wings, to see what was possible. The quicker we left school and started to bring a wage into the house the better, especially if there were younger mouths to feed. Look around you Philip and I don't mean at this kitchen, I mean take a good look around the streets as you deliver your papers later. Is this the future you want? Drinking your life away in the Livvy night after night, signing on the dole or in some dead end job. I'm one of the lucky ones, I have a job I enjoy. Most people who work around here hate their jobs almost as much as they hate their lives. Don't rush to join the club son."

Slightly concerned by the second speech about his future in a matter of hours Philip decided not to mention his desire to be a swimmer. Instead he elected to finish his tea, wash up and make his dad and brother's sandwiches before setting off, a little late, to complete his evening round.

Once back home, he spent the rest of the evening patiently waiting for 'Sportsnight' to start. Without really paying much attention to the television, he sat through a quarter-final of 'Ask the Family', an episode of 'Tomorrow's World', a 'Tom and Jerry' cartoon and an episode of 'Are You Being Served'. 'Sportsnight' itself featured some boxing from Cardiff and an ice hockey game between Finland and Czechoslovakia before finally rounding off the programme with that evening's football scores. For Philip it was worth the wait as an up and down day eventually finished on a high. Leeds United had managed an away victory over Arsenal by a score of 2-1, with goals from Peter Lorimer and Paul Madeley. After hearing the result Philip headed off to bed. He attempted to say goodnight to his mum but she appeared to be fast asleep when he looked in on her. As for his sister, he had absolutely no idea where she was.

Chapter 13

It is difficult to put into words, the feelings, the emotions that accompany the final weekend of the summer holidays. If ever there was a vote on the most inaccurate term in the English language, then the term 'endless summer' would certainly be shortlisted, as here they were with just two days left. A summer that once held so much hope and so many possibilities was now about to come to an end and become a page in history. The summer of 1973 was saying its final farewell. As the gang sat scattered about the back of the bus on their way to the swimming baths the usual tomfoolery, the usual fervour was somewhat lacking. A dark cloud seemed to be draped across all of their shoulders. Even Craig Swinburn had lost his usual sparkle and interest in the art of ribbing. He sat looking out of the window, as if he was on his way back from the vets after being neutered. So many hopes had been dashed, so many dreams had faded away under the pressures of reality. Craig did actually feel as if he had been neutered due to his failure to finally crack it with Claire Chase before the end of the holidays. However he was not alone. The same feelings of disappointment also flowed freely through Philip's veins. He had started the holiday dreaming of getting past second base with Lesley Bennett and all he had managed to do was get dumped, and to top it all with a dollop of dread, Leeds were away to Spurs.

They swam, they played, they hung about with their naked backs pressed against the warm glass of the windows that encased the pool. They jumped, they dived, they got thrown out. They went to the café for lunch and stole desert from the pick 'n' mix section of Woolworths, but despite all of this, the day still felt as flat as a layer of skin that had formed on the surface of a cold cup of coffee. It was as if school and all that went with it was reaching back in time and with a cackle and a sneer was squeezing the last few moments of freedom out of their lives.

It was during the bus journey back home when Michael Robinson dropped what was, to Philip, a devastating bombshell. Out of all the kids in the close and those that lived in the flats at the end of the close, Michael was without doubt Philip's closest friend. Since the first year of infant's school they had been in the same class. They had made the school football team together, been caught playing truant together and had experienced the trials and tribulations of adolescent life together.

Without looking at anybody in particular as he spoke, Michael suddenly announced with a soft voice. "We're moving."

Philip instantly turned and looked at Michael. "What?" he said in a voice that was full to the brim with shock.

"We're moving." Michael repeated whilst still managing to avoid eye contact with any of his friends, especially Philip. By now however, everybody was looking at Michael.

"What do you mean, you're moving? When? Why? What? What for?" Philip's words were stacking up, one after the other without spaces in-between as they tumbled from his lips.

"My dad." Michael continued. This time he turned his head and looked directly at Philip. "My dad, he wants to move."

Michael's family had arrived in Britain in 1962 when Michael was a small boy. They were from an equally small town called Linstead in Jamaica. During the early days they moved around a little and had spent some time in London, Luton and Northampton before settling in Coventry in 1966.

As Michael continued to speak the blood started to ebb away from Philips face. His cheap plastic blue and white striped training shoes braced themselves for the large amount of liquid that was likely to imminently arrive at his feet.

"He's gone on about moving for ages, but nothing ever came of it until a few weeks ago."

"So why now? Philip asked.

"All I know is a few weeks ago, I was lying in bed and I could hear them both talking and my mum was crying. Something happened while my mum was shopping in Bell Green. She was walking past Dick Sheppard's when some men started shouting at her and calling her names. It's happened before, but for some reason this time really upset her."

"What kind of names?" Said Craig.

"Oh you know, calling her Nig Nog and Jungle Bunny and telling her to go back home."

"So you're moving back home?"

"No of course not, we're moving to Birmingham."

"Birmingham?" Everybody said at once. Even Martin Matthews, despite him having a mouth full of cheese and onion crisps at the time.

"We've got relatives there and my dad's been able to transfer with his job. We've just been waiting on a flat and we got a letter from the council yesterday."

Michael's dad, Jefferson, worked on the buses for West Midlands Transport as a conductor. He was immensely proud of his job as it took him five years to finally be given the opportunity. Before it came along he had patiently worked in the maintenance shed. Michael can still remember the day his dad came home carrying his conductor's uniform. They had fish 'n' chips from the chip shop in Wood End that night with mushy peas and a bottle of lemonade.

Philip sat trying to take it all in. For him, Michael might as well have be moving back home or to Timbuktu or Outer Mongolia or the moon as it all amounted to the same thing he was losing his best friend.

During a brief silence whilst the bus trundled along the Stoney Stanton Road, Martin Matthews finished what was in his mouth before asking "Why does your dad think it I'll be any different in Birmingham?"

"I don't know." Michael replied. "I don't suppose he does."

"There's more of them over there." Paul Jones muttered.

"More of who?" Michael instantly replied with a stern look on his face. "More nig nogs?"

"Yes, well, no, I didn't mean it like that. It wasn't me that called your mum names. I'm just saying there are more black people in Birmingham."

"There's more people in Birmingham, full stop" Philip said with a sharp tone in his voice.

"Yeah alright, keep your wig on, I must have wagged that particular geography lesson, I probably had better things to do." Anyway, don't take it out on me. It's not my fault his mum got upset and his dad wants to move. I don't want him to move any more than you do but if you want to go and speak to his dad about it, I'll stand behind ya." A couple of streets behind ya but I'll stand behind ya."

After this comment there was almost complete silence for the remainder of the journey. All that could be heard were the soft voices of a conversation taking place towards the front of the bus and the rustling sound of sweet wrappers as Martin Matthews shared out a packet of lemon bon-bons.

The mood was still sombre and predominantly silent as they clambered off the bus and began the short walk home. As they reached the back of the crescent Craig Swinburn turned and headed down an alleyway between two houses and towards a row of garages.

"Where you going?" Philip asked.

"I'm going to the Paki shop to get a Freddo." Craig replied.

Michael turned and followed. "Me too." He announced, as he jogged the short distance to catch up with Craig.

Content with the amount of chocolates they had managed to pinch from the pick 'n' mix counter of Woolworths, Philip and James decided to go straight home. Paul Jones and Martin Matthews paused for a moment before also deciding to go home.

As Philip and James made their way down the side of the house and past the kitchen, they could hear their dad's voice spilling out of the open window. As they walked around the back of the house and into the garden, the voice got louder and louder. As they approached the back door, Philip turned and looked at James.

"Just go straight upstairs when we get in and stay in the bedroom until he's calmed down." Philip said as he reached for the handle on the back door. As Philip swung open the door the boys were instantly greeted with the odour of cigarette smoke and beer. It swept past them with such haste that it suggested there was a train pulling away from a platform and it had a seat reserved.

Their dad was standing in the centre of the room. His face was as red as a communist flag and his forehead was full to bursting with tiny shimmering beads of sweat. Their mother was sitting forward in the middle of the sofa with a cushion resting on her lap and clutching a mug of tea.

"Where is she then?" Francis enquired with a stare that was colder than an igloo's fridge.

"She's at work." His wife replied. "It's Saturday."

"How do you know she's at work? Did you see her leave? Did you see her get ready? When was the last time you actually clapped eyes on our daughter?"

Longing for the conversation to reach its end, the boy's mum paused for a moment and took a drink from her mug before answering. "I don't know" came the reply.

"What don't you know?"

"I don't know when I last saw her."

By now James had managed to make it through the living room and out the other end whilst Philip had retreated to the kitchen. Both managed to reach their allotted destinations unscathed.

Francis continued. "She's seventeen years old and you don't know when you last saw her. Maybe if you could be bothered to pay attention to your family once in a while you would know when you last saw her. Instead she's running around town with every Tom, Dick or Harry and you don't know where she is from one day to the next."

"Well do you know when you last saw her?"

"No I don't but perhaps that's because I work all night and sleep during the day so that the rent gets paid and there is food in the house." Francis wiped his brow with the back of his hand before reaching for his coat that was lying across the chair directly behind him. "And you can tell her from me, the next time you see her that is, if she's not in this soddin' house when I get home tonight, she can bloody well find herself somewhere else to live."

With his coat grasped so tightly in his hand that his knuckles were turning white, he headed out of the back door, shutting it behind him with enough force to cause his wife and Philip, who was still sitting in the kitchen, to jump.

A few moments later Philip's mum entered the kitchen.

"You alright mum?" Philip asked.

She walked over to the sink and rinsed her cup out. She placed it upside down on the draining board before turning around and looking at her son. She sighed a little before speaking. "Yes Philip, I'm fine." She stepped closer to him and stroked his hair. "If you see your sister, tell her to stay home tonight." She said in a soft voice before adding "There's a pound on the sideboard in the living room. Go down the chip shop when you're hungry and get something for you and your brother. If your sister does appear then get something for her as well."

"I'll go after my paper round." Philip replied as his mum left the kitchen and headed back upstairs.

Once all was quiet Philip headed back into the living room and switched on the television. He had to endure the last fifteen minutes of the rugby league fixture between Widnes and St Helens before the football results came on. He emptied his pockets out on to the sofa and passed the time by eating his ill-gotten gains from the Woolworths pick 'n' mix section. No sooner had he eaten his last orange cream than the final whistle blew, the rugby players shook hands and the vidiprinter began rolling. This was always met with a mixture of hope and anticipation. The scores quickly began to come in and a rather trying afternoon concluded with a silver lining as Leeds United made it three out of three with a 3-0 win over Tottenham, thanks to a goal from Alan 'Sniffer' Clarke and two from Billy Bremner. With this result and a chip shop tea on the horizon Philip Knott began to feel just a little bit better.

Chapter 14

"How many fish was that?"

"Two." Replied the stocky, balding, middle aged man standing on the other side of the counter.

"So that's two fish…. Cod or haddock?"

"Cod."

"Two cod, a fishcake, a steak and kidney pie, a saveloy and three medium chips. Is that everything?"

"Yes." The man replied.

Philip Knott was standing patiently in the queue of the Wood End Chip Shop, known locally as the 'Wild West Saloon Bar' due to the amount of fights and brawls that tended to break out on a Friday and Saturday night. Philip wasn't sure if it was true or not but there was one particular story doing the rounds about a man having his arm partially severed by another customer wielding an axe. Why he had had an axe about his person was as vague as the other fine details of the story but apparently the altercation had taken a more violent turn when the man carrying the axe had allegedly taken offence to his victim ordering the last two chicken and mushroom pies.

Although Philip always felt slightly ill at ease whenever he was in the Wood End Chip Shop, this particular time on Saturday night was usually quite safe. Philip looked down the line of customers' there were four people waiting to be served before him. He knew the stumbling block in the queue was the rather large lady directly in front of him. He had needed to step out and look around her in order to count the other people in the queue. Luckily he had headed to the chip shop straight from his paper round and nestled inside his bag was a copy of the 'Pink' sports newspaper, legitimately purchased, and two Fry's Chocolate Creams, illegally acquired. He took out the newspaper and passed the time away by reading the report on the Coventry City game that afternoon, a game in which Coventry drew 2-2 away at Burnley.

He finished reading the report just as the large lady reached the front of the line and was about to be served. The optimism of being next in line and soon being able to leave was quickly dashed as the woman removed and unfolded a piece of paper from her pocket. As each request fell from her lips, Philip's jaw dropped just a little bit further. Philip couldn't help but stare at the woman and look her up and down with a certain amount of annoyance etched upon his face. Her swollen feet were squeezed into a cheap pair of cream coloured plastic shoes. The veins in her neck appeared to be forming an escape committee. A line of sweat rested across her top lip. Her hair was neatly presented and heavily lacquered, whilst her make-up was as bright as the summer's dress that hung over her sizable frame. Eventually her order had been assembled, bagged up and was ready to go. She collected it and made her way out of the shop. Philip stood and watched her as she left.

"Okay young un what can I get for you?"

Philip, momentarily mesmerised by the large lady teetering out of the door, failed to hear the question.

"Come on sunshine, I haven't got all day." The man behind the counter said as he leant forward and gave Philip a tap on the back of his head.

Philip turned around and placed his order. "Two cod, a large chips, a sausage and a bottle of lemonade." He said.

"You'll have to wait for the fish." The man replied as he turned to look at his young assistant. "Put some fish in Glenda." He said before turning his attention back to Philip. "That I'll be eighty five pence young man."

Philip handed over the pound note that his mum had left him as

Glenda dipped two pieces of fish into a tub of batter before dropping them into the fryer. Philip could hear the sizzling, popping sound as they were submerged into the hot oil. Whilst waiting for his fish to cook, he moved away from the counter so that the proprietor of the shop could serve the next customer in the queue. He hovered around just inside the doorway until his order was ready.

"Salt and vinegar on the chips?"

"Yes please," Philip replied.

Once the food was wrapped he placed it along with the bottle of lemonade inside his paper bag. He removed the two stolen bars of chocolate to avoid any unwanted melting scenario, before briskly setting off for home to ensure that the food was still piping hot when he got there.

On getting back home and entering the living room via the scullery and the kitchen, Philip found his brother watching 'Dad's Army' and his sister just finishing off setting the table. Bread and butter, knives and forks, salt, vinegar, tomato sauce, plates and cups for the lemonade were all in place and ready to go.

"Good job I got you something." Philip said to his sister as he removed the two wrapped packages and the bottle of lemonade from his bag, before placing them in the centre of the table.

"What did you get me?" His sister replied.

"Fish." Philip said as he hung the bag over the back of a chair. "Here you go James, come and get your sausage and chips."

The three children sat down around the table and began to eat their tea.

"It's a good thing you came home after work" Philip said to his sister as he reached across and picked up the bottle of tomato sauce.

"Save you breath." His sister replied. "James has already told me all about what dad said."

There was a brief pause in the conversation as James gave a slightly anxious look in his brother's direction.

"He meant what he said." Philip said as he coated the top of his fish in a thin layer of tomato sauce.

"Sorry to disappoint the both of you cause I'm moving out of here anyway. I can't stay here any longer."

"Where are you gonna go?" James asked.

"Karen Fairchild says that I can move in with her. She's got a flat in Clennon Rise. Her twat of a so-called boyfriend left her and moved in with some tart that he met down the town. She's on her own with her little boy and says that she would be glad of the company."

"Dad won't let you do that" Philip said.

"Oh yeah and how is he going to stop me?"

"What will you do for money?" Philp asked.

"Woolies have offered me a full-time job. It doesn't start for a couple of weeks as some old dear is retiring. I was gonna wait until then but if he thinks he is gonna tell me what I can and can't do and when I have to be here, he's got another think coming."

"When are you going?" James asked as he restocked his mouth with a piece of sausage and reached for a slice of bread and butter.

"Tonight." Came the reply. "I'll pack some stuff when I've finished eating this."

Silence took centre stage for the rest of the tea. Once everybody had finished, Philip cleared away the plates whilst his sister went into the kitchen in search of desert. After some rustling around and clattering of pans, she returned some ten minutes later, carrying three bowls of banana and custard on a sunflower design tea tray. As she entered the room James's big round eyes glowed like a full moon on a clear winter's night. This was James's favourite desert and he quickly tucked in to the golden shiny custard and the sweet sliced pieces of banana hidden beneath.

Once tea was over and James had managed to scrape every last remnant of custard from his bowl, Philip and his sister cleared away the rest of the table and went into the kitchen to wash up, leaving James to lie back down on the sofa and get back to watching T.V.

"Listen Philip" His sister said as she ran the hot water and squeezed some washing-up-liquid into the bowl. "You mustn't tell dad where I've gone okay. I shouldn't have said anything in front of James so keep him away from dad."

"What am I supposed to say?"

"Just tell him I've moved out but you don't know where. I'm not telling mum either so you will have to keep an eye on her as well. If anything happens that I should know about, then you'll have to let me know."

"How"?

"Just put a note through the door when you are on your paper round, you deliver in Clennon Rise don't you?"

"Well yes" Philip replied as his sister retrieved a gleaming plate from the bowl and passed it to him to dry. He took it from her as she continued to both talk and wash up.

"I'll be at number twenty nine. If anything happens, you let me know."

"He'll go berserk when he finds out."

"Yeah well let him, he'll calm down once he realises that I am out of his hair."

"You make it sound like he hates you."

Philip's sister paused for a moment with her hands submerged in the hot soapy water, before turning and looking directly at her younger brother. "He hates everybody these days, even himself." She said before looking away again.

It was just coming up to ten 'o' clock when Philip's sister headed down the stairs and into the living room. She was carrying a small sports holdall and two carrier bags. Her hair was still wet and glistening. She placed the bags down at the side of the sofa before rummaging around inside one of the carrier bags and taking out a hairbrush.

"Remember what I said Philip" she muttered as she tilted her head to one side and began brushing her hair. "I've told mum I'm going but I haven't told her where. She isn't really with it so she'll probably forget. Don't tell her okay, he'll find out where I am eventually but by the time he does, he may have got use to me not being here."

After flicking her head back and giving her hair one final brush, she gathered up her possessions and headed towards the back door. "See you later James." She said as she walked past and briefly blocked out his view of the television screen.

James looked up at her as she passed by but didn't reply.

"I'll be back for the rest of my things one night next week when dad is at work."

With this, she opened the back door, stepped into the late evening air, closed the door

behind her and left.

Chapter 15

"I know she's not here. I can see she's not here, that's not the question I asked. I didn't ask you where she wasn't. I asked you where she was. So telling me that she isn't here does not answer the question. It is a response to the question but it does not answer the question. There will be a lot of places where she is not, we could sit here all morning and list the places where she is not. What I want to know is where she, is and if where she is is the same place where she was last night, as she certainly didn't stay here."

Philip stood at the top of the stairs. It was far too early in the day to have such a passive expression on his face but nevertheless, that was what he had. The door to the living room was ajar so he was able to hear every word of the conversation that was taking place. He knew that he couldn't stand at the top of the stairs all morning and he also knew that the scullery door would be locked from the outside, so he would have to go through the living room and the kitchen to retrieve his paperbag. He took a deep breath, double checked that he still had his passive expression on his face and with a large amount of apprehension he slowly began to descend the flight of stairs. As he descended further and further with each step the smell of stale cigarette smoke and beer clambered further and further into his nostrils. When he found himself facing the living room door, he paused for a moment so that he could plan his strategic entrance and swift exit. He pictured the route in his mind. Through the living room door, arc before reaching the dining table, a sharp right just before the sofa and four quick steps into the kitchen and under no circumstances make eye contact with anybody in the room as you travel through.

Unfortunately, just as he had completed the arc and was in the process of taking a sharp right at the sofa, his father asked. "Do you have any idea where your sister is Philip?"

"She's not here" Philip replied whilst still focused upon reaching the relative safety of the kitchen.

"Not you as well" his dad instantly replied. "Your mother's the same. All we need now is your brother to endorse your observations and it will be official."

Philip knew he shouldn't have let it happen, especially when he was only a few short steps away from the kitchen but curiosity got the better of him. "What do you mean, be official?" he turned and asked his dad.

"That I have at some point in the night, unfortunately lost the power of sight. I have officially gone blind. You see, you are the second person I have asked this morning where you sister is and you are the second person this morning to tell me that she is not here. So it's one of two things, either there's an issue with my eyesight or you and your mother have a problem with your ears."

Realising his monumental error and with a hastily thought out attempt to rectify the matter, Philip turned away. "I've got to go dad, I'll be late."

"Get some breakfast inside you" his dad called out.

"I'll have something when I get back" Philip replied as he headed through the kitchen and disappeared into the scullery, out of sight of his father.

As he was putting his shoes on by the side door, his dad appeared in the doorway between the scullery and the kitchen.

"So do you know where your sister is, not where she isn't? I can see where she isn't. Do you know where she is?"

With his eyes firmly fixed upon his laces Philip replied. "No dad, I haven't seen her."

His dad shook his head. "You're not alone there boy, nobody seems to have seen her."

As his dad turned away, Philip grabbed his paperbag, slung it over his shoulder and headed out of the door.

It was the last day of the summer holidays, always a sombre day for any self-respecting council estate teenage boy. However, for a collection of reasons, this particular Sunday morning was much more sombre than expected. Not only was he back at school the following day but his mother appeared to be getting worse and he was seeing less and less of her. His dad was becoming more and more distant, his sister had left home, his girlfriend had dumped him and his best friend was moving to Birmingham. Despite the usual familiarity of the route from house to shop, on this particular morning nothing felt right. Everything was where it should be, everything was the same as the morning before and the morning before that and the morning before that, but as he made his way to the shop, things just didn't feel right. It was as if he was wearing shoes that were a few sizes too small and clothes that were a few sizes too big.

As he entered the newsagents in his ill-fitting attire, his mind was clearly somewhere else. Mr Underwood was still in the back of the shop putting the bundles of newspapers together. Philip was all alone, yet he just stood there with his hands in his pockets. He didn't steal a thing. A few moments later, Mr Underwood appeared from the back of the shop.

"Morning lad" he said as he entered. "I've an extra round going this morning if you want it" he added.

"Yeah sure." Philip replied.

"Here you go" Mr Underwood said as he held out a bar of Fruit and Nut. "A bit of energy for ya. See you when you get back' your papers are ready to go."

Philip made his way along the street. Due to the weight of the now full paperbag, he was leaning to one side as he went, like a ship taking on water. He opened and began to eat his Fruit and Nut. However, as with everything else that morning, it just didn't feel right, it just didn't taste the same. Philip tried to shrug it off and he attempted to put it down to the fact that he had been given the bar of chocolate and it wasn't the result of ill-gotten gains. However, he knew deep down inside that it was much more than that.

Weather wise it was an extremely pleasant morning, sun shining, a gentle breeze. If there had been any trees of note in the vicinity, they would have been stuffed full of colourful birds, all chirping away as if they were in a scene from 'Mary Poppins'. Unfortunately the serene moment and pleasant climate was lost on Philip as he hauled his paperbag along the quiet and deserted street. He was however quite happy to take his time as he was not in any rush to get home. Once he had completed his second cumbersome round of the morning he decided against hanging about at home for too long. Upon arriving back home, he quietly entered through the scullery door, dropped off his bag, placed an ear against the door to the kitchen and listened. All was quiet. As he entered the living room, he could see his dad's feet hanging over the edge of the sofa. He stepped a little closer and peered over the sofa. His dad was thankfully fast asleep. Without pausing or taking a second look Philip quickly made his way upstairs. He grabbed a towel from the airing cupboard and his swimming trunks from his bedroom drawer, and rolled the trunks inside the towel as he descended the stairs and exited through the front door. Once outside again, he headed straight for Michael's flat.

Philip took a deep breath, knocked on the door and braced himself, as he knew only too well what was about to happen. Almost immediately the door to the flat swung open and filling all of the space that had just been created stood a large West Indian lady.

"Oh Lord, Oh Lord" she began. "Somebody needs to call thee doctor, there be a starving, skinny white boy, standing on me doorstep".

Philip looked up and offered a nervous smile in response. He was never quite sure how to react around Michael's mum. "Is Michael in, Mrs Robinson?" he tentatively asked.

Mrs Robinson stood with a rigid posture, her hands resting on her ample hips, looking down at Philip. "You catch me by surprise child, you look too weak to speak. Come bring yourself in and rest a while. Let us see if we can find you something to eat."

This was par for the course. Mrs Robinson believed in a full and varied diet. If she wasn't eating, she was cooking and if she wasn't cooking she was eating. As far as Mrs Robinson was concerned, anyone who was not as plump as Mrs Robinson was suffering from malnutrition and needed feeding immediately. Food was at the centre of her world, it was her passion and she felt it her Christian duty to share this passion with those most in need, and small skinny white boys certainly ticked all the boxes.

Mrs Robinson stepped to one side so that Philip could enter. He in turn, stepped inside and walked the short distance down the hallway before turning left into the living room. As he did so he heard the front door close behind him. In the living room Michael's dad was lying upon a bright brown and orange flower design sofa, a sofa that could be identified in a blizzard with your eyes shut. He was dressed in a white cotton shirt and a pair of faded denim jeans. He had a pair of large black headphones on his head and his bare feet were hanging over the edge of the sofa, tapping away to the music. On seeing Philip enter, he sat up, reached out and unplugged the headphones from the stereo system that sat on top of a wooden cabinet next to the sofa. As he did so the sound of Jimmy Cliff filled the room. Jimmy however, instantly had to move over and make room for Michael's mother as she entered.

"We have an early bird" she said as she stood in the doorway. "One that hasn't caught any worms."

"Leave the boy alone woman, sometimes being skinny can be a good thing you know. The boy is quick and there are times when a boy needs to be quick."

Mrs Robinson just let out a disapproving tut which was accompanied by a disapproving stare in her husband's direction before turning and heading for the kitchen.

"You like 'Jimmy Cliff' Philip?" Michael's dad asked. "This be food boy, food for the soul."

Michael appeared, still in his pyjamas, yawning and rubbing the sleep from his eyes.

"Wanna go swimming?" Philip asked.

"Got no money" Michael replied as his hand disappeared down the back of his pyjama bottoms and began scratching.

"I have," said Philip.

"Yeah sure, I'll go and get me stuff."

Thankfully, despite the flat being relatively small in area and currently full of half-filled cardboard boxes, Michael was able to manoeuvre around his mum and exit quickly without being commandeered and forced to sit and eat some breakfast. He did however grab a cold sausage from the fridge which he immediately started to eat. He also managed to grab two packets of crisps and an apple that he dropped into his carrier bag as the boys left.

"See ya later mum" Michael called out as he closed the front door behind him.

Chapter 16

The two boys must have just missed the previous bus, as the one they eventually boarded seemed to take an eternity to come into view along the Hillmorton Road. This was most frustrating as it took precious time out of what they both knew was to be their last chance to spend the day together. Once they were seated on the back seat of the upper deck, Michael retrieved two packets of cheese and onion crisps from his bag before passing one of them over to his friend. They were through Bell Green and half way down the Stoney Stanton Road, just passing the police station, before one of them spoke' that someone happened to be Michael. He didn't turn to look at his friend as he did so, he just gazed out of the window, looking down upon the street below.

"I don't want to go" he said.

"You what?" Philip replied.

"Birmingham I mean, I don't want to go. I don't want to move to Birmingham."

"Why not?"

"I've been over, I've been to where my uncle lives and it's horrible."

"What's wrong with it?"

"Everything. It's all just tower blocks everywhere, there is nowhere to go and play and that's not the worst of it." Michael turned and looked at Philip. "It's full of Pakis."

"You what?" Philip asked.

"Honest man, I walked down the high street with my dad and my uncle and every shop on both sides, every shop was a Paki shop. Every single one of them were either selling roles of material or all sorts of spices, it was either one or the other."

"Does your mum know?"

"Of course she does, she's been there loads of times."

"No, I mean, does your mum know that you don't want to go?"

The bus slowly began to fill up as it travelled further along the Stoney Stanton Road. Philip slid across the seat to sit closer to his friend.

"Of course she does". Michael replied. "But she hates it here, she hates the abuse, the flat, the neighbours, everything."

"The neighbours?" Philip said with a puzzled expression on his face. "Who's in the flat next to you?"

"You know, that bloody Irish cow Peggy and her miserable bloody husband. They complain about us but they are always shouting and crying and slamming doors, especially when they are both pissed."

Still sporting his puzzled expression Philip replied "What do you mean complain?"

Michael rolled his eyes and let out a heavy sigh as he replied. "They complained to the council once about the smells from me mum's cooking. The pissed up old twat claimed that he couldn't sleep because of the smell. So, they sent a guy from the council round."

"What happened?"

"What do you think happened, he couldn't leave until my mum had fed him. She gave him a plate of curried mutton, rice and dumplings. Even gave him a portion to take home in a plastic tub. Should of seen his face when he left, right big smile, he was well happy. So, they got the hump after that and stuck air fresheners to our front door."

"You what?"

"My dad just took them to the bus depot and hung them up in the toilets. But it was still another reason for my mum to want to move. You wanna smell their flat when they open the front door, stinks of pale ale and bloody cabbage." There was the briefest of pauses before Michael added. "I fuckin' hate cabbage."

Philip just smiled as Michael turned his head away and went back to staring out of the window as the bus continued into town.

No sooner had it pulled into the bus station before the boys were off and heading for the swimming baths. As they entered the building through the double set of glass doors, they were pleasantly surprised by the extremely short queue, especially when you consider it was the last day of the summer holidays. Perhaps the majority of their peers were staying at home to wrap schoolbooks in wallpaper and to draw over newly acquired rucksacks.

As quickly as they could, the boys headed off into the changing rooms, changed, handed their clothes in the metal baskets to the changing room attendants, attached their metal discs to their trunks and made their way up the steps and out into the pool itself.

Although neither boy had seen it with their own eyes, or in the flesh, so to speak and their only experience of it was from the television, nevertheless as they both gazed down at the sparkling blue water, they both independently pictured the vast expanse of the Mediterranean and the sense of freedom it gave them.

They both wanted to dive in but had to wait for a moment as a rather large boy with an extremely red face swam by. Once he was safely out of the way and with toes curling over the edge of the pool, the boys propelled themselves forward and dived in. As if by magic, as both boys burst through the top of the water and disappeared beneath the surface, all of their troubles seemed to wash away and float off upon the Mediterranean tide. For the next few hours at least, nothing mattered. Even the extreme likelihood of this being their last swim together drifted from view as they played, dived, swam and eyed up a couple of girls' at least for the briefest of moments they had hope, until the girl's heads were turned by some older boys in a larger group.

The boys took a time out and sat at the edge of the pool, the sun bursting through the large glass windows onto their backs. In that condensed shortest of moments all was wonderful with the world. But just as they knew the warmth on their backs couldn't last, they also knew that this moment would be fleeting. So make the most of it they did. They got back in the water, they swam, they dived, they splashed, they swam some more, they dived some more, they received their first warning, they received their final warning, they swam, they splashed, they dived, they got thrown out.

The problem with going swimming on a Sunday is that pretty much everywhere else in the town centre was closed. The upper precinct, the lower precinct, Broadgate, virtually the whole town centre was deserted, hardly a soul to be seen. In fact the only places open were the picture houses, the swimming baths, the cathedral and the Wimpy café. Before setting off for home the boys went to the Wimpy and shared a banana longboat. Spoons set on stand-by, they waited impatiently for their order to arrive. Devouring such an item before eating their respective Sunday dinners was seriously frowned upon but somehow or other they both knew that neither one was going to spill the beans. The time that elapsed from the moment the waitress placed the banana longboat on the table until both spoons were tossed rattling into the empty dish was precisely forty three seconds.

As the bus home got closer and closer to 'The Live and Let Live' the metaphorical skies above darkened. By the time it arrived at the terminus the atmosphere had plummeted to such a level that a medieval village, struck by the plague, in a hammer horror film felt decidedly more cheerful. A late summer breeze embraced the boys as they stepped off. It appeared to swirl around them like a dervish as they made the short walk back home. They made their way along the path that snaked its way around the far end of the block of flats and back into the crescent before veering off in slightly different directions towards their respective homes.

"Will you be out later?" Michael asked.

"Depends" Philip replied.

"On what?"

"If my dad goes out. If he goes to the pub, I'll be out, but if he stays in, I'll have to go to bed early cuz it's a school night."

"Might see you later then" Michael said as he reached the entrance to his block of flats and disappeared inside.

As Philip walked along the side of his house and past the kitchen window, he was caught somewhat off guard by the lack of a familiar smell he was expecting to encounter, which would normally be clambering up his nostrils by now. The oh so familiar smell of a Sunday roast being prepared was nowhere to be sniffed. He was instantly apprehensive as to what he would find when entering the house. As he reached the back garden his mouth was drier than an African riverbed in the middle of a drought and the palms of his hands were clammier than a coach load of clams on a clams outing. He opened the back door and stepped into the living room. He was instantly greeted by a different collection of smells that he was rapidly becoming more accustomed to with each passing week. Stale cigarette smoke, sweat and beer rushed to embrace him like a long lost friend or an old flame. He tried not to breathe too deeply as he gently closed the door behind him. Philip's dad was sprawled out on the sofa, fast asleep. The majority of the 'News of the World' had slipped off his chest and was now residing in a V shaped heap on the carpet below. Philip quietly passed by and headed off upstairs in search of more signs of life. He found James lying on his bed, reading a copy of the Beano but to his surprise his mother's bedroom was deserted. Returning to his own room, Philip walked across and peered over the top of James's Beano. He could instantly tell that his younger brother had been crying. James's cheeks were of a fiery red colour, one of his nostrils was running and his eyes had small pools of water resting on the surface.

"Where's mum?" Philip asked.

James didn't reply as such, he just shrugged his shoulders as his bottom lip protruded a fraction.

"What's with dad?"

This time around James responded with actual words. "They were shouting at each other; I could hear mum crying as she came upstairs. Then the front door slammed. I thought it was dad but when I went downstairs, dad just shouted at me to stay in my room."

"When did this happen?"

James returned to just shrugging his shoulders as a way of a response.

"Have you had lunch?"

"No." James replied as he shook his head from side to side.

"Are you hungry?"

"I'm not going downstairs." James said as he edged back on his bed and pressed his back against the wall.

Philip stretched out his hand in his brother's direction. "Come on" he said, "I know somewhere we can go and get something to eat."

Twenty minutes later Philip and James were sitting at the Robinson family dinner table, tucking into sweet potato, yams, spiced pork, dumplings, vegetables and a barbeque sauce. This was followed by baked banana and sweet pineapple, served with a large dollop of vanilla ice-cream.

Chapter 17

As yet, there isn't a word in the English language that can accurately describe this particular feeling. There isn't a word that has the capacity to give it the justice it deserves. True, there are several words to choose from and some of them, especially when they are combined and used in the correct order, manage to come close. However in reality, in the cold light of morning, they still fall short of actually hitting the mark. Yes it is fair to say that the English language has yet to devise a word that encapsulates the feeling of a teenage boy waking up and instantly realising that the summer holidays are over. It is a word that has to define that dreaded first day back at school. It is a sinking feeling that seems to sink further than a German mine in a black and white, Second World War film. A film that would usually star Walter Pidgeon and be set on an American submarine. It is an emotion that goes way beyond the death of a pet or having your dark blue Monza International bike stolen from the garden shed.

With raw emotion and a sinking feeling resonating through every inch of his body, Philip climbed out of bed. As his brother did not need to be up for a little while longer, Philip quietly left the room so that James could have one final hour, before he too would wake and meet the same fate.

After a quick unfulfilling breakfast, he picked up his paperbag and set off for the newsagents. He shuffled along the street with the posture of a condemned outlaw making his last journey to the gallows. Head bowed, shoulders down and one foot dragging along after the other.

"Good morning young Philip" Mr Underwood called out from the back of the shop as Philip entered.

"I think you'll find it's not" Philip replied as his paperbag slipped from his slumped shoulder and onto the floor below.

"Sorry" said Mr Underwood, before he had fully processed Philip's response. "Oh yes, it's back to school today isn't it. That explains the young man wrapped in misery that I see before me."

Philip attempted to offer a gesture of some description in a way of a response but even the gesture would have to admit that is was unprepared for the task that had been set. It just tumbled forward and landed on the floor next to Philip's paperbag and immediately crawled inside in an attempt to hide its shame. The gesture quickly needed to move over so that the required amount of morning papers could also be accommodated inside the bag. Once the papers were inside and without any thoughts of stealing anything at all, Philip slung the bag across his shoulder and headed out of the door.

"Have a good day at school" Mr Underwood shouted as the door closed behind Philip.

Choosing to ignore the comment, a comment that's only intention was to cause annoyance, Philip went on his way and delivered his morning papers before hurrying home to begin the infamous school run challenge.

The school run challenge was so called as it all depended on whether you needed to run or not. There were two buses that Philip, James and their friends could catch for school. Either they caught the 'Twenty Six' from Winston Avenue, which was the closest, or they caught the 'Eight A' from the stop directly opposite Mr Underwood's newsagents. If you were walking out of the crescent, towards Winston Avenue and you were unfortunate enough to see the 'Twenty Six go by, you had to about turn and run as fast as you could in an attempt to catch the 'Eight A' which departed from its terminus in Bell Green at roughly the same time as the 'Twenty Six' departed from Winston Avenue. Failure to catch either of these buses would result in being late for school. If you registered two late mornings in the same week, you were rewarded with an automatic detention.

When he got back home after his paper-round, Philip discovered both his and his brother's school uniforms neatly laid out at each end of the settee, along with their shiny polished shoes on the floor and their bags on the chair. Francis was still in bed and their mother was in the kitchen, patiently stirring a pan of porridge oats.

"Breakfast is nearly ready Philip, can you get some bowls and spoons?" His mother asked as Philip entered the kitchen.

For a moment or two as Philip caught sight of his mother and heard the sound of her voice, the thought of having to return to school briefly faded away. A warm gentle glow seemed to scoop him up in its arms and pull him closer as he stood and gazed at his mother.

"Bowls Philip and don't forget the golden syrup, you know your brother likes it."

"Sorry mum" Philip replied whilst still contently located inside the warm glow.

He quickly found two bowls from the cupboard above the kitchen table before setting them down just in time. Moments later he was carrying two bowls of porridge out of the kitchen and over to the living room table, one for him and one for his brother who was already in position and patiently waiting. Once he placed them down he quickly headed back to the kitchen and gathered up the golden syrup and two spoons. Just as Philip had sat down and was about to bury his spoon deep inside is bowl of porridge, he again caught sight of his school uniform at the other end of the room. His warm glow headed for the nearest exit.

Putting their school uniforms on was a slow and sombre affair. All that was required to make the moment complete was the opening bars of Chopin's Funeral March playing in the background. Like a mummy being wrapped in fresh bandages, the fabric of the uniform appeared to cling to and smother their identities.

The long-suffering drama of getting ready for school inevitably resulted in the boys having to make a mad dash for the bus. Thankfully, due to the volume of children, all looking pristine in their uniforms at the terminus, the boys made it with time to spare. The rest of the group, all bar Michael, were sitting at the front of the bus, upstairs. When Philip and James sat down, Craig and Paul had already removed their ties and were just about to share a No 6 cigarette. The two drags and pass it on rule was very much in evidence as the bus pulled away. As the cigarette rapidly raced towards its demise, Craig was the first person to pass comment upon the day.

"Shit this is." He muttered as he took the second of his two drags. He inhaled deeply as he passed the cigarette to Paul. He then exhaled as he continued. "Shit, shit, shit" he said. The plume of smoke vibrated in front of him as he spoke. "Can't believe, we're back already, can't believe we've got to deal with this shit for another year." He reached out and grabbed the cigarette as it was thrust towards him, the tip getting ever longer and glowing ever redder as the smoke billowed around them.

"At least it is your last year" Philip muttered whilst attempting to waft the smoke in another direction.

"Yeah, that's true." Craig replied. "Unlike that poor bastard" he continued as he waved the cigarette in James's direction before hastily taking his second and final drag. "He's got another four to do yet" he added with a triumphant tone in his voice as the smoke cascaded out and hung around like a groupie at a David Essex concert.

James chose not to respond directly but in a form of a protest, he removed his school tie and shoved it into his blazer pocket, knowing full well that he would have to retrieve it again before he passed through the school gates. Being on school grounds without correctly wearing a tie was another way of finding oneself being placed in detention.

The smoke finally dispersed as the bus trundled along and before they knew it the boys had reached their stop. They all alighted before setting off to complete the rest of the journey on foot. As they got closer and closer to the school entrance, more and more identically dressed children appeared, all walking with a similar gait and at a similar pace towards their reluctant destination and towards the school gates, as if they were being summoned by the Morlocks in a chapter from 'The Time Machine'. James's brain was thankfully still functioning coherently enough to retrieve the tie from his pocket and place it back around his neck as he entered.

Chapter 18

As the rest of the pupils in 'Morgan' house block filtered out of the common room to collect their timetables and make their way to the headmaster's welcome back speech, Philip remained firmly rooted to his chair. He was staring at a piece of paper that Mr Nicholls had thrust into his hand as he had entered the common room approximately twenty minutes earlier. Once those pupils without slips of paper had all departed, he lifted his head and looked around the room. Five or six other boys had also remained in their seats, all of them sporting a slightly bemused expression on their faces and clutching a similar looking, white slip of paper in their hands. After a few further moments of silence, one of the boys finally spoke. That boy was Brian Mason.

"What's this shit all about?" He muttered as he wafted his piece of paper several times in front of his face.

Brian Mason was a bright boy, in fact he was exceptionally bright. However he was also, figuratively speaking, battered and bruised and deeply troubled by the poor quality cards he felt that he had been dealt in life. He lived with his mother and his grandmother above an off-licence on Longfellow Road. As a result of the poor quality hand he was holding, he was openly hostile towards and would challenge anything that he interpreted as authority or as coming from an establishment perspective. As he sat, still waving his piece of paper from side to side, it did not take him long to work out what was going on.

"Oh boy, this one doesn't take a lot of working out, does it?" he said, with a voice loud enough to ensure all of the boys in the room heard.

"How do you mean?" a boy sitting directly behind Brian asked.

"Just look around you, take a good look at exactly who's in here, holding these slips of paper. One thing is for sure, we're not going to any pupil of the year ceremony. I bet each and every one of you ten fags that right now in the other blocks, there are a bunch of kids holding the exact same pieces of paper we are."

"But why, what for?" The boy sitting behind Brian asked.

Brian Mason shook his head and stood up. He pointed at Philip. "Ere Knotty, how many times did you get caned last year?"

"Not sure, a few." Philip replied.

"And how many conduct cards were you on?" Brian Mason didn't give Philip time to answer that particular question before he shifted his questioning to another boy in the room. "What 'bout you Tank?"

A rather large boy with a shaved head looked up from his piece of paper. "All year." Tank replied. "Pretty much the whole year."

Brian Mason looked around the room. "Anyone else care to chip in. I'm telling you now, this is a fit up. The minute we walk in..." He paused for a moment and glanced down at his piece of paper. It quite simply gave the recipient the instruction to report to the school library at 9.30. "The minute we all walk into the library, we are all gonna get clobbered with a conduct card."

"They can't do that, we aint done anything yet!" Tank replied.

"Ah yes Tank, but you will, just by saying that you haven't done anything yet implies that you will at some point do something."

"Of course I will, how else am I going to get the money I need for my fags, cider and the chippy at lunchtime if I don't take it with menace from pathetic little toe-rags desperately trying to avoid being flushed down the toilet."

"Exactly Tank, your money making scheme is what they want to curtail."

"What they want to what?" Tank asked.

"What they want to put a stop to Tank. I have a feeling that we will also get a speech thrown in for good measure."

Round about the time that the boys were heading towards the library, Francis Knott was sitting in his kitchen. He had just lit a Senior Service cigarette and was drinking tea from a chipped and heavily stained mug. As he sat almost motionless, his wife was busily moving around him, clearing away the breakfast things and stacking the plates and bowls in readiness for being washed up.

"So you have no idea what the meeting is about?" She asked with a clearly concerned tone in her voice.

"No, I've already told you, I have no idea but I can guarantee that it won't be good news."

"Is everybody going?"

"I guess so, all I know is that on Friday before I left the yard, Snowy Vest said that we were all to report to the canteen at 10:00am on Monday morning."

Snowy Vest obviously wasn't Snowy Vest's real name. As a matter of fact there were not that many people at the depot who actually knew his real name. He was known as Snowy Vest on account of two things, the first thing being his head of white hair. Secondly, no matter what the time of year or what the weather was like or whether it was a day or night shift, Snowy Vest always wore a vest when he was loading and unloading the lorries in the depot.

Francis finished his mug of tea and stubbed his cigarette out in the small ashtray resting on the table. He stood up and placed his mug next to the rest of the crockery waiting to be washed up. In a rare momentary show of affection, he gently placed a hand on his wife's backside and leant across, kissing her on the cheek as she stood in front of the kitchen sink, filling a plastic bowl with hot water. He turned away, scooped up his cigarettes and matches from the table and departed.

"Come in boys, come in, plenty of room for all, come and take a seat." The Deputy Headmaster Mr Billington was standing at the entrance to the library, holding the door open with one arm and ushering the boys forward with the other one as they approached.

About twenty boys had already arrived when Philip reached the entrance. They were randomly scattered about amongst the four rows of chairs that had been laid out for their convenience. Once everybody was seated Mr Billington closed the library door and walked over to a small rostrum that had been strategically placed in front of the rows of chairs. He turned and mounted the rostrum so that he could look down at his less than enthusiastic audience. As he prepared to address the pupils, two fellow male teachers entered the library and sat down on the back row. They both received a disparaging look from Mr Billington as they did so.

Due to the late arrival of the two teachers and the distraction they caused, Mr Billington cleared his throat in an attempt to focus his audience before he began.

"Good morning boys and let me begin by taking this opportunity to welcome you back. I hope that you all had an enjoyable summer break. I am sure that you are all wondering why you have been invited here this morning. Let me firstly put your minds at rest and assure you that you are not here to receive some form of punishment. Now for the majority of you here today, this is and will be your final year with us. As for us, your teachers and education providers, it is our desire or rather our duty to do all that we can to ensure that you leave here with the best possible chance of success. To leave here with the tools required to have the opportunities to move forward with your lives and become valued members of society."

He paused for a moment to allow himself a glance around the room and check that his audience were focused and paying attention. Despite a collection of blank expressions staring back at him, he decided to continue.

"With your futures at the forefront of our minds, we feel that it is vitally important that you all start the year in the right frame of mind, with the best possible attitude to your studies, focused upon your own futures and upon your own behaviour. This is an opportunity to put the problems and negative situations of last year behind you and to start from day one with a better approach and a better attitude. So to help you begin the year in a positive way we have decided that you will all begin the year on conduct cards."

The news was instantly met with a hostile reaction from the assembled crowd.

"Now boys, settle down. This is not a punishment and should not be viewed this way. You must see this as an opportunity, an opportunity to think about your behaviour, to focus on what is important, to start the school year with a positive attitude. This is the most important year of your lives to date and if you continue with your old ways of recent years, you will leave here as failures and with little chance of success. This is not what we want and if we were to let this happen without trying to intervene, then we also would have failed. So collect your cards from Mr Bell and Mr Bhanot on your way out and remember, the sooner you don't have one the better your chance of success".

Conduct cards and work cards were fairly straightforward in their design and in their desired intentions. You simply handed them to your teacher at the start of each lesson for the whole week. They were signed at the end of the lesson with either a satisfactory or an unsatisfactory. If you received one unsatisfactory during the week, then you were rewarded with another conduct card for the following week. This process would continue until you completed a whole week without receiving an unsatisfactory. If you were on a work or conduct card two weeks running, you also received a detention for each week after the first week that you remained on a card. If you received two unsatisfactory comments in the same week, this was another automatic detention and of course another card. If you managed more than two unsatisfactory signatures in the same week, then you were treated to the full set, a card for the following week, a detention and the cane, one whack on each hand. As far as Philip knew both Brian Mason and a boy from 'Mowbray House' called Kelvin White held the record for the most unsatisfactory signatures in the same week, a total of seven. However Kelvin was currently being educated in a young offender's institute which meant that on a technicality Brian held the record amongst the current crop of pupils. The disgruntled group slowly filtered out of the library and collected their conduct cards as they did so. Round about the time that Philip collected his, Francis Knott was arriving at his works canteen.

Snowy Vest was placing a tray of cups on the canteen counter as Francis swung open the doors and entered. Several of their fellow work colleagues were already present and randomly located at a variety of tables scattered around the canteen. A silvery grey layer of smoke hovered in the air just a few feet above the gathered ensemble.

"Come and get a tea lads" Snowy called out as he placed a large silver teapot next to the tray of cups.

As Francis arrived at the counter and grabbed a cup from the tray, he looked over at Snowy who was busy pouring tea from the rather large pot. "Not good news this, is it Snowy?"

"The boss will be here in a few minutes Francis, he's just on the phone upstairs."

"What do you know that we don't Snowy?"

Snowy placed the pot down on the counter and leant forward towards Francis. "I can tell you one thing Francis, but it won't make your tea taste any better." He picked the pot up again and poured Francis a cup of tea.

"Which is?" Francis asked as he reached over and grabbed a teaspoon from a grey plastic tray.

"It's bad news for all of us Francis…for all of us." Snowy replied.

Francis put two large teaspoons of sugar in his tea, before adding some milk and giving it a petulant, frustrated stir before walking back to his table and sitting down alongside a couple of his work colleagues. No sooner had he returned to his seat than Eddie Wilkinson the boss's son and heir to the business empire entered the canteen. Eddie had run the business alongside his father for the past few years. Edward Snr was now approaching his sixty fifth year and had taken a back seat, so to speak, at the haulage firm, allowing Eddie Jnr to learn the ropes and gradually take control of the company. Eddie navigated his way through the crowd and towards the canteen serving hatch. He quickly made himself a cup of tea before turning to face his staff.

"Thank you all for coming in this morning, my dad and I really appreciate it and all of the hard work that you do on behalf of the firm. I'm not going to weave my way around the houses or beat about the bush, because you all know that we are not here to talk about the staff Christmas do." He paused and took a drink from the cup he was holding before placing it down on the counter.

He continued. "Due to the current economic climate and the strength or weakness of the pound, depending on how you view it, we as a company are currently trying to navigate some rather choppy waters and have been doing so for quite some time. Obviously until now we have not made you all aware of this as we were hoping to ride out the storm and return to calmer waters. However, it is now crystal clear that returning to those calmer waters is no longer possible unless we make some drastic savings, as unfortunately we have been operating at a loss for quite some time now."

Everybody in the room apart from Eddie Wilkinson were sat in complete silence, hanging on to every syllable as it tumbled from Eddie's lips. Eddie himself took the opportunity to replenish and moisten his dry lips with another mouthful of tea before he again continued.

"We have gone over this and over this, looking at every possible option and quite simply we were left with only two. The first option meant having to let some of you go, but to be honest that left a very bitter taste and we did not want to do that, you are all part of the family. So the only other viable option open to us and the one we have decided upon, is to place everybody on a three day week."

A large degree of exhaling and head shaking broke out at each of the occupied tables. The head shaking was still in full flow when a rather portly gentleman, sitting alone at a table directly in front of Eddie spoke out.

"How are we supposed to survive on a forty percent pay cut?"

"I know this isn't easy Tiny" Eddie replied. "But a forty percent pay cut has got to be better than a hundred percent."

"How many people would have to go?" Tiny asked.

"We're not going down that road Tiny, I've already made it clear that we're not."

"How many?" Tiny asked again, however this time around there was more threat embroiled within the tone of his voice.

"Five or six maybe, to begin with and how do we do it, may I ask, names in a hat or last in first out because if we do it that way then you will be out of a job Tiny and I don't want that."

"How do you know so quickly that I'll be one of the ones out?"

"Because we have already considered it, we've looked at all the possibilities."

"Then we'll strike."

"Feel free Tiny, if that is what you feel is best, we have already spoken to the unions but if you want to strike, then strike. At least if you do then we will break even this week for the first time in seven months and in three week's time we can shut up shop and we'll all be out of a job."

"Is it really that bad?" Francis asked.

"Yes Francis, I am afraid it is. Nobody is importing and if they are then nobody is spending, end result is we have very little to move about the country and distribute. You must have noticed you wagons getting emptier and emptier. I'm hoping that it will be temporary, it could last only a few months, weeks maybe. We need to just hang on in there and weather the storm."

"Easy for you to say" Tiny exclaimed as he stood up abruptly, knocking his chair over in the process. "Maybe you'll have to sell your flash motor?"

Eddie shook his head as he replied. "I'm sorry everybody but I don't have a bottomless pit of money and I have already sold the flash motor, it paid your wages last week. If we can get through this then hopefully we can save all our jobs, if we don't it will mean all our jobs. So from today we are on a three day week, I'll be able to let you all know which three days, later today and for most of you it will be Monday, Tuesday and Wednesday. I can't say anymore that that at the moment lads. Now if you'll excuse me, I have a business to try and save." With this Eddie walked past Tiny and threaded his way once again between the tables and left the canteen.

After drowning his sorrows in the 'Jolly Collier' public house and losing more than he could afford to in the bookies on Hamilton Road, Francis arrived back home a little after four o'clock. As he climbed out of his car he noticed Philip standing at the edge of the green with his hands stuffed inside his trouser pockets, staring up at the block of flats. Francis walked over to his son.

"What you doing son?"

Philip turned to look at his dad and then back at the flats. "He's gone dad. I thought he had a few more weeks before they moved. He said he had a few more weeks."

Francis turned and looked at the flats. He could see Michael's flat with 'Windowlene' smears over all of the windows. "Perhaps he didn't know he was going today, perhaps his mum thought it was for the best, perhaps she just wanted to leave without a fuss."

"But I'll miss him dad, he was my best friend. He wasn't at school today but I just thought he wasn't well or he was packing his stuff, I didn't even say goodbye. We went swimming yesterday but he didn't say anything about leaving today, not a word."

Maybe, he didn't want to upset you, or maybe he didn't know."

"How could he not know?" Philip asked.

"I don't know son. Maybe his parents didn't want anybody knowing, so they didn't tell him." Francis placed his hand gently around his son's shoulder. He could see the tears beginning to well up in his eyes.

"Looks like we have both lost plenty today son, come on let's go and get something to eat. Life can be hard at times Philip for people like us. You just have to try and be strong and get on with it. How was your first day back at school?"

"Not now dad, not now" Philip replied.

Chapter 19

As Philip Knott stepped off the 8a bus at the end of the school day on Wednesday afternoon, he had two things on his mind. The first thing was whether Billy would reply to the letter he had written on Monday evening and posted the day after on his way to school. The second thing on his mind was whether Leeds United could continue their perfect start to the season later that evening when they had a home fixture against Wolverhampton Wanderers. Wolves had made a good start to the season as well, winning two of their first three games. They were a half decent team with a strong goalkeeper in Phil Parkes. They also boasted a couple of quality strikers in Alan Sunderland and their talisman Derek Dougan. Dougan was a no nonsense, roll your sleeves up, feisty player in a similar mould to Billy Bremner. When he was on song Dougan had the ability to turn defenders inside out and round and round until they felt as if they had spent the whole afternoon on the waltzers. However Philip was confident that Billy had the capacity to keep Dougan quiet and as they had home advantage, he also felt that this would be enough to ensure a positive result.

Philip had already chosen to ignore the 'Unsatisfactory' he had received on his conduct card earlier in the day and was determined to not let it spoil his evening, because alongside his two thoughts about the evening ahead there were also two reasons why he was not going to let his 'Unsatisfactory' take centre stage. The first of these was the inevitability factor: receiving a further Unsatisfactory was bound to happen before the week was out. In fact it was more of a certainty than the reception on Radio Luxemburg later that evening being weaker than an asthmatic boy with a fever. The second reason for giving his Unsatisfactory no more thought than he felt it deserved was due to the ridiculous manner in which it occurred.

It happened in his geography lesson whilst the majority of the class were working on their European rainfall bar charts. Philip was sitting next to his friend and fellow classmate Chris Burns. Whilst playing catch up and completing his average European sunshine bar chart, Chris Burns burst into song, giving the class his rendition of Bill Withers 'Ain't No Sunshine'. As it was a song that Philip knew well, on account of hearing it several times in Michael's flat, he couldn't help but join in. It was the ignoring of the third request from their teacher to stop singing that ultimately resulted in his Unsatisfactory but...

'I know, I know, I know, I know, I know, I know, I know, I know, ain't no sunshine when she's gone.'

When Philip arrived home and walked past the kitchen window he caught sight of the tall figure of his dad moving about inside. He continued around the house to the back door and entered the living room. On doing so he heard his dad call out.

"Is that you Philip?" Francis swung open the kitchen door and peered into the living room. "Where you been, your brother was home over an hour ago, come and open this tin of ham, James lay the table and be quick, these chips are nearly ready."

Philip closed the door, dropped his school bag onto the floor and headed into the kitchen. Sitting on the table was a tin of ham, fenced in by three plates and the kitchen wall. "I was running late so I did my paper round straight from school." He said.

"Where's your paperbag"? Francis asked.

I used a spare, Mr Underwood has a few in the back of the shop."

"Well get that ham open. Plenty of jelly on mine" Francis said, rubbing Philip's head as he went past. "How was school?" He asked as he turned his attention back to the chip pan.

"Unsatisfactory." Philip replied.

Francis gave his son a puzzled look, in the belief that he would get more information. However Philip just focused on the task he had been set. Francis decided to leave it for now on account of the chips needing to be removed from the pan. James entered the kitchen in search of knives, forks, bread, butter, salt, vinegar and tomato sauce. This particular quest was accomplished in two visits and within five minutes of Philip arriving home the three of them were sitting down to tea. Other than James asking what was for afters, not a great deal was said whilst they ate. The boys both got a wagon wheel each for desert, then Philip washed up whilst James dried and their dad prepared his flask and sandwiches for work.

'Nationwide' had not long departed the screen and the two boys were enjoining a 'Tom & Jerry' double bill on BBC1 when their dad entered the living room dressed for work in his Wilkinson's overalls. Tom was once again prematurely and quite foolishly lighting a victory cigar as Francis sat down on the settee next to Philip.

"So what did you mean by unsatisfactory." He asked as the shouts of "Thomas! Thomas!" could be heard coming from the T.V.

Philip looked at his dad with an expression etched across his face that simply translated to 'What?'

"School today, you said earlier in the kitchen that your day had been unsatisfactory."

"Oh that." Philip replied. "It doesn't matter."

"Yes it does, I'd like to know what you meant."

Philip turned away from the sight of Thomas running through the house, trying not to be struck by the large broom that was raining blows down upon him. "I got an Unsatisfactory on my conduct card in geography."

"You what, you're on a conduct card already, you've only been back three days, what on earth did you do?"

"Nothing."

"You must have done something?"

"I didn't." A slightly agitated Philip replied. "A whole group of us got put on them on Monday. We hadn't even had a lesson, I hadn't had the chance to do anything."

"So what did you get an unsatisfactory for?"

Philip hesitated before answering, giving James enough time get off his seat and relocate himself on the living room floor, closer to the T.V.

"Singing" Philip eventually replied; a response that was even captivating enough for James to spin round and turn his attention away from Thomas's woes and Jerry's inevitable victory.

"Singing?" Francis said. "In a geography class? And what do you do in your music lessons, go bloody orienteering?"

Philip chose not to reply. Instead he just waited for his dad to continue. He didn't have to wait long.

"And what exactly were you singing may I ask?"

"Ain't no Sunshine". Philip replied.

"What?"

"Ain't no Sunshine, by Bill Withers."

"Who?"

"Bill Withers."

"Well that explains it. No wonder you got an unsatisfactory singing that rubbish."

"It's not rubbish."

"Clearly your teacher thought it was, you need to sing something like Nat King Cole, nobody can give you an Unsatisfactory for singing a song by Nat King Cole."

Francis started to sing as he got up from the settee and headed towards the kitchen to collect his flask and sandwiches. "Gee it's great after being out late, walking my baby back home." He returned a few bars later. "I've got a stop to do before I go to work, so you two keep the noise down, your mother's got another headache or something along those lines… and make sure you are both in bed by 9.30." He returned to his song on the way out. "She says if I try to kiss her, she'll cry, I dry her tears all through the night."

Chapter 20

Grace Knott was sitting at the better end of a rather distressed looking, worn out settee. She was wearing a pair of pink fluffy slippers and a pair of baggy fitting pink cotton pyjamas. Her hair was wrapped in a white towel and her hands were firmly clasped around a smoked glass cup of coffee. She was just settling down to watch 'Coronation Street' on the twenty two inch colour television set, rented from Redifusion for a pound a week, when there was a knock at the front door.

"Can you get that Grace?" Came a shout from the kitchen. "It's probably my mum and I'm in the middle of doing baby's bottle."

Grace put her smoked glass cup down on a small smoked glass coffee table that sat directly in front of the distressed settee and with a sigh as heavy as a coal merchant's lorry, she stood up and made her way to the front door. Upon opening the door, her slightly tired, glum expression instantly changed to one of surprise, mixed in with a splash of horror.

"Dad!" She said with an obviously startled tone to her voice.

"You still recognise me then" Francis replied.

Grace's expression immediately changed to one that resembled a scrunched up piece of paper. "Not anymore." She replied.

A reply that put Francis even further onto the back foot.

"What do you want Dad?"

"I want to talk to you."

"What about?"

"Can I come in?"

Grace moved to one side and made a space for her dad to enter. He stepped inside. Grace closed the front door before squeezing past her dad and returning to the living room. Francis followed. As he entered the sparsely furnished living room, he looked around, stopping his gaze at the settee.

"I think an elephant has been sitting on your sofa whilst you weren't looking" he said.

"If you've come to criticise dad…"

Before Grace could complete her sentence, her dad interrupted.

"No, no, it was just a little joke" Francis said as he weighed up where best to sit.

Next to the sofa was an equally distressed looking armchair, sporting a rather worn out orange and brown stripped pattern. It did however look slightly sturdier than the settee. Francis walked over and cautiously sat down.

"How did you know where I was?" Grace asked as Francis got comfortable and reached inside his overalls pocket for his cigarettes.

"Don't be silly" Francis replied. "I knew where you were moving to the day before you moved."

"Did Philip tell you?"

"No". Francis replied with a rather surprised look on his face. "Did he know?"

"I don't know" Grace quickly answered. "Somebody might have told him, somebody told you."

There was a moment's silence, just long enough for both of them to briefly look away from each other before once again making eye contact across the room. As they did so Grace asked. "Who did tell you?"

"It's not important." Francis replied.

"Would you like a drink dad?" Grace asked whilst hoping her offer would be declined.

"No thanks sweetheart, I haven't got long, I'm already running late for work."

Francis was just about to continue when he was distracted by the 'Coronation Street' theme tune which was quickly followed by an advert for Sunlight Soap, featuring a glamourous young lady in an equally glamourous bathroom.

"Could you switch that off?" Francis asked as he motioned towards the T.V set.

Grace stood up and reached over for the off switch. With one short click, the glamourous lady and her glamourous bathroom were gone.

"So." Grace said as she reached for her cup of coffee and sat back down.

Francis hesitated for a moment.

"What is it dad?"

"This isn't easy." Francis replied.

"Is it mum, has something happened, is she okay?"

"Your mum is fine…well when I say fine, I mean that she's the same as usual but it's not about your mum as such."

"Then what is it dad, what do you want?"

This time around Francis managed to say what he had come to say. "I need you to come back home." He said, looking past his daughter and at the wall directly behind her as he did so.

The shock of what she had just been asked caused the coffee in her mouth to scramble for every available and viable exit. Some managed to head south and work its way down her throat, some shot forth out of her mouth and some exited via her nose. As she gasped and spluttered, she managed to wipe away coffee with one hand whilst placing the cup on the coffee table with the other. Once all of her airways were once again clear, she was able to offer a response.

"Are you serious, you actually want me to move back home?"

"No". Francis replied. "I need you to move back home."

"Oh that's nice. So you're not going to try and force me to move back home, you're not going to start throwing your weight around as usual."

Francis took a moment to light a cigarette before responding. As he did so, Grace reached over and passed him a small glass ashtray that had been resting on the coffee table.

"Look." Francis began as he exhaled a plume of silver smoke into the room. "Believe it or not, I'm actually very proud of you. Becoming independent, getting a full-time job, standing on your own two feet, paying your own way in the world and taking care of yourself and if it wasn't for the current situation that I find myself in, I wouldn't be sitting here now."

Grace was just about to enquire as to the circumstances that her dad was referring to and the words were all neatly lined up on the tip of her tongue when there was another knock at the door. In quick fashion the words moved over to one side to allow another group of to form in response to the knock at the door.

"That I'll be Karen's mum bringing her little boy back."

Grace stood up, turned and opened the living room door. As she entered the hall, Karen appeared from the kitchen.

"It's okay Grace, it I'll be me mum" Karen said before adding "Who's in there?"

"Me dad" Grace replied.

"Oh." There was a pause. "What does he want, he's not going to start any trouble is he?"

"No, don't worry, anyway he will be going any minute now, he's on his way to work."

Karen opened the front door. "Hello mum and how is my beautiful little boy?"

"He's asleep" said a rather large lady who was standing on the doorstep with both of her hands firmly placed on the handle of a dark blue pram. She had a blue seashell patterned silk scarf on her head that was doing its best to conceal the curlers in her hair. A cigarette hung from her bright red lipstick covered mouth. A long gentlemen's overcoat a pair of dark brown slacks and a pair of dark brown slippers completed the ensemble. She turned a little, manoeuvred the pram and entered the flat.

"I'll have to wake him, he needs his feed" Karen muttered as they entered. "Do you want a tea mum?"

Grace was just about to return to the living room when the door opened and Francis stepped into the now rather cramped and busy hallway.

"Hello Francis" Karen's mum said as she moved to one side, allowing Karen the room required to take her son out of his pram. "On your way to work?"

"No, no I'm not, I'm off down the community centre to audition for the role of Mary in this year's nativity. Anyway should you be using four letter words in front of your grandchild?"

"Four letter words?" Karen's mum asked with a puzzled expression on her face.

"Work." Francis replied. "Seeing as nobody in your house has done a day of it for the past decade.

Karen's mum's facial expression instantly changed to one of hostility and she removed the cigarette from her lips before replying "Alfie can't help it if his health has let him down and he can't work; he is sick you know."

"Well he does look worse for wear when I see him in the boozer every weekend" Francis quickly added as he squeezed past and made his way through the still open front door.

"Dad!" Grace said with a clearly uncomfortable tone to her voice.

Karen's mum stomped into the kitchen with Karen and child quickly following behind as Grace stepped into the stairwell after her dad.

"What did you say that for dad?"

"Oh do me a favour Grace, she's a nosey cow and her old man is nothing more than a work shy scrounger. They need to have a bit of respect and start providing for their family instead of sitting on their lazy arses and expecting other people to do it. Look, have you started full-time at Woolies yet?"

"No, I start Monday but I am in Friday and Saturday as usual, why?"

"I meant what I said, I need you to move back home."

"I can't dad."

"We can't discuss this now, not with the busy body in there listening and wanting to know our business. I bet you a daytrip to Margate that her ear is pressed to the other side of that door as I speak and don't you go saying anything in front of her. When you finish work Saturday come home and we'll talk then."

With this Francis turned away and headed down the stairwell. Grace stood and watched as his footsteps faded away and he disappeared out of sight.

Chapter 21

Philip had had to wait until Thursday morning before finally being able to find out the score against Wolves from the previous evening. As far as he was aware, Harry Carpenter had neglected to give out the results on 'Sportsnight' but he couldn't be sure on account of drifting off to sleep for a brief moment whilst attempting to remain interested in the boxing. He had also drawn a blank on the Ten O'clock News and as for the Radio Luxemburg reception fading in and out on his Benkson transistor radio, there was obviously no joy there either.

The minute he entered the newsagents on Thursday morning, he scooped up a morning paper in his eager hands and headed straight for the back pages. On the inside back page of the 'Daily Mirror' he found the score along with a match report. An impressive 4-1 victory had maintained their one hundred percent start to the season with goals from Mick Jones, Billy Bremner and two from Peter Lorimer, one from the penalty spot.

Unfortunately, a certain amount of shine was taken off the result later that day when he picked up another Unsatisfactory for his behaviour in his English lesson. Another one duly arrived in science on Friday, when he had attempted to ignite Dave Berry's school tie with a Bunsen burner, bringing the weekly total to four. Any connoisseur of the work / conduct card system would tell you that four unsatisfactory signatures in one week meant one thing and one thing only, there was only one course of action that could now be taken. The card had to be destroyed and the best way to destroy it legitimately was for it to find its way into the wash. So on Saturday morning when his mother had asked him to bring down anything that needed washing and check the pockets, he was more than happy to do so. He made doubly sure that his conduct card was firmly and safely located in a pocket his school trousers before handing them over. He hovered around the kitchen until he witnessed the trousers going into the washing machine, without being checked. Once the door had been shut, he returned to his room and picked up where he left off with his recently purchased copy of that week's 'Tiger' comic. Settling back into his still warm bed, he was halfway through 'Roy of the Rovers' and Melchester Rovers latest fixture when the post arrived. Moments later his bedroom door swung open and his mother entered with a letter clasped in her hand. As Philip saw her approach and despite Melchester Rovers being on the verge of losing at home to Carford City, his comic was cast aside.

"You have a letter" his mother said as she handed it to him. "Is it from your footballer Bobby"?

"It's Billy mum" Philip replied as he took the letter from her hand.

"Oh sorry, Billy" his mum replied with a smile on her face. A smile that Philip hadn't seen for a while.

"Thanks mum". Philip said as she turned away and left the room.

Philip waited for a few minutes until he was sure that he was alone and unlikely to be disturbed before slowly peeling back the seal and looking inside. He carefully removed the letter, placed the envelope on his pillow and then unfolded the letter.

Dear Philip,

How nice to hear from you again, wee man, although it does appear that you are once more having a tough time of things. It never rains but it pours, or so they say. First you break up with your girlfriend and now your sister has moved out of home and your best friend has moved away. I am unsure as to what I may be able to say that could offer you some crumbs of comfort during this difficult time. Life can have a habit of unravelling at the drop of a hat. One minute you are sailing along and everything appears to be going smoothly and then in the blink of an eye, sweeping changes come rushing into view and turn everything upside down. It was very much like that when I first moved to Leeds as a teenager. There I was in Stirling as a young lad, not much older than yourself, playing football with my friends and for my local team. Then the next thing I know, I am living in lodgings in Leeds, with complete strangers.

Don't get me wrong, it was an exciting time and I had a fantastic landlady who looked after me but the change was still a shock to the system and there were days when I felt incredibly homesick. As I mentioned when I wrote to you before, friends like girlfriends, will come and go, in and out of your life. but I know from my own experience that it is tough to lose a close and best friend. Some gaps are difficult to fill. Just try and hang on in there. I am sure that things will get better in time.

Yes indeed as you mentioned, it has been a very good start to the season. The atmosphere in the dressing room is very good at the moment and it is a positive place to be. Big Jack is always telling a few jokes, trying to get Norman to laugh, but of course he doesn't crack. You know Norman, he cannot be seen to have a sense of humour or a soft side. Hotshot is taking bets on how many goals he will score this season. By the time you receive this letter we will have played Wolves and possibly Birmingham City. No disrespect to these teams but we see them both as winnable games, so hopefully our good start will continue for little while longer. Fingers crossed that when I next write to you we are still unbeaten. Hang on in there Philip, keep working hard at the things you are good at and even harder at the things you are not.

All the best,
Your friend Billy.

Philip lay in his bed and read the letter twice more before carefully folding it up and just as carefully placed it back in its envelope. He climbed out of bed and removed the bottom drawer from his chest of drawers. He then safely placed the letter alongside his previous two letters before putting the drawer back. He climbed back into bed with a newly acquired warm glow and reunited himself with his comic. He had just finished reading how Roy's injury time strike from just inside the eighteen yard box had salvaged a 2-2 draw against Carford City when his mother came back into the room.

"Do you have any plans for today?" She asked.

Philip shrugged his shoulders and shook his head. "Nothing planned" he replied.

"Would you mind nipping up to Bell Green for me and doing a bit of shopping?"

Philip thought that was as good a reason as any to get out of the house before his dad got up. He had been woken up by his dad crashing about and stumbling around downstairs the night before, so he knew the mood his dad would be in when he eventually got up would be somewhere between a bear with a sore head and a bear with a sore head whose chair had been sat in and whose porridge had been eaten.

"Yes sure mum" he said.

Ten minutes later Philip had brushed his hair, cleaned his teeth and was standing in the kitchen. He looked at the shopping list that his mum had just handed to him, then shoved the list into one pocket of his jeans and the money that his mother had placed on the kitchen table into the opposite pocket before grabbing his school rucksack from the scullery floor and setting off for Bell Green.

"Be straight back and don't lose the change." His mother called out as he closed the scullery door behind him. He headed out of the crescent, past the 'Live and Let Live', down Skinner's Hill, across the small bridge that took him over an equally small stream, through the children's park and into Riley Square at the far end of the Bell Green shopping centre.

The first shop Philip walked past, or rather attempted to walk past was 'Dick Sheperds' bicycle shop. He couldn't help but stop and admire the gleaming, shimmering, pristine bicycles in the large windows. Despite there being several bikes on display, there was one bike in particular that continued to catch his eye. It was a predominantly bright red 'Team Europa' road racing Raleigh bike. He stood and gazed affectionately at the bike, admiring the red and gold paintwork, the silver handlebars, the gleaming chain, the slim sleek tyres and the perfect gear levers. As he stared he drifted away into a make believe rendition of a television commercial. He was somewhere in the highlands, mountains in the background, the sun shining down onto a glistening stream as he cycled over an old stone bridge, towards a small quaint Scottish village, coming to an effortless gentle stop outside an equally small and quaint Scottish café. As he dismounted, he stepped back into the present and found himself back outside the bicycle shop. With one final lingering look at the bike, he turned and went on his way to do his mum's shopping.

Reality was firmly asserted and he was completely back in the moment as soon as he took his first step inside Sainsbury's. The aisles stretched out before him. However he could see very little of them due to the overwhelming volume of little old ladies, bobbing and swaying like a flotilla of tiny boats anchored in a small seaside harbour. They were all almost identical in their appearance. All were wearing thick, long, fur collared coats with a few inches of leg sticking out at the bottom, before a slightly varied selection of fur lined boots covered the feet, ankles and lower leg. A plethora of headscarves, all double knotted beneath the chin, shifted from side to side. Each and every little old lady was clutching a small shopping trolley in one hand and a Sainsbury's shopping trolley in the other. Philip collected his trolley from just inside the entrance, took out his list, took a deep breath and took off down the aisle. The metallic clanking sound of shopping trolley crashing into shopping trolley could be heard up and down every one of the four aisles. It took the best part of forty minutes for Philip to manoeuvre his way through the melee. All he needed to get was two tins of baked beans, two tins of spaghetti, one tin of mushroom soup, one tin of tomato soup, one white sliced loaf, one crusty white loaf and a bottle of washing-up liquid.

When he finally exited the supermarket and walked past Woolworth's next door, he caught sight of his sister dismantling a back to school display just inside the entrance. Philip pulled open the glass door and stepped inside.

"Hello Sis" he said.

Grace stood up and turned around. "What are you doing here?" she asked.

"Mum wanted me to do some shopping."

"Is she okay?" Grace asked with an immediately concerned expression on her face.

"Yeah, she's fine." Philip replied, a reply that in turn received an instant disapproving scowl from his sister.

"Well you know what I mean, nothing's happened." Philip quickly added.

"Have you still got your paper round?" Grace asked.

"Yes, Why?"

"I've been looking out for you the last couple of mornings, that's why."

"Oh right, I think I only come into your block at night, I don't think anybody in your block has a morning paper. What do you want me for anyway?"

"Dad" Grace replied.

"What about dad?" Philip asked.

"Is there anything I should know about?"

"How do you mean?"

"Has anything happened, it's just that he came to see me Wednesday night..."

Philip quickly interrupted with a horrified expression on his face. "He knows where you live."

"He's always known apparently."

"I didn't tell him."

"I know you didn't, look that's not important right now, he said that he needed me to move back home."

"Oh right" Philip said.

"Do you know why?"

"I might do, it's his job, he's been put on three nights a week."

"So that's what it's about" Grace said, nodding her head in the process. "It's not about me or mum or you two, it's about needing my wages."

Just then a middle-aged lady with rouge covered cheeks, bright red lipstick and hair sprayed stiffer than a broken zip approached.

"Come on now Grace" She said. "You should have done that by now dear."

"Yes Miss Jones" Grace replied. "I'm just about done."

"Good, once you have finished, you can give Miss Dodd a hand checking the stock." With this Miss Jones turned away and walked over to another of the junior shop assistants.

"Hang on there a minute" Grace said as she picked up a box in front of her and hurried off.

No sooner had Grace disappeared before she reappeared and quickly scurried towards Philip. Upon reaching him, she thrust some coins into his hand. "Go to Gladding's and get a cake" she said, squeezing his hand tight as she spoke.

"What kind of cake?" Philip asked.

"Just get a jam sponge and don't squash it on the way home. I've got to go, I'll see you when I finish work."

Grace disappeared again; if anything, her disappearance was even quicker this time around. Philip shoved the money into his pocket and headed out of the shop to continue his shopping. Next stop was the post office to purchase two second class stamps before heading to the fruit and veg shop. Though much smaller in scale, the fruit and veg shop was equally as chaotic as Sainsbury's and sporting a very similiar cliental. However despite being penned in with nowhere to go on more than one occasion, he finally emerged with carrots, onions, a cauliflower and potatoes safely purchased. The chemist was next to drop off a prescription. He was told by the lady behind the counter, 'It will be ready to collect on Tuesday'.

Now he could head for Gladding's. After the bike shop, Gladding's was his next favourite shop in Bell Green. If the wonderful window display of golden sponges, soft white creams and bright red fruits in mouth-watering pastry cases didn't hook you, then the wonderful aroma as you entered the shop certainly would. The gentle heat and sweet smell rushed to greet him as he stepped inside. He closed the door behind him and was more than happy to stand and wait for his turn to be served. A few minutes later a lady behind the counter asked "And what can I get for you?"

"A Victoria sponge please." Philip replied as he stepped a little closer.

The lady turned around and grabbed a flat piece of white cardboard. With a few well practised twists and turns of her hands, it became a cardboard box. She put it on the counter before carefully gathering up a Victoria sponge from one of the racks below and placing it inside the box. As she looked at Philip, she closed the lid.

"A treat?" She asked.

"A peace offering, I think." Philip replied.

"Will there be anything else?" The lady asked.

"No thank you." Philip said as he handed over the correct amount of money and picked up the box. He gently brought it to rest on top of the shopping in one of the carrier bags he was now carrying, and after one final deep inhale, he left the shop and set off for home.

Chapter 22

Reminiscent of a cartoon sketch of a deserted tropical island in the middle of a deep blue ocean, complete with solitary palm tree, the Victoria sponge sat alone and proud in the middle of the dining room table at the far end of the living room. At the other end of the room, James was sitting on the sofa with his head in his 'Beano' comic. He was halfway through this week's adventure of 'Billy Whizz', engrossed in Billy's trials and tribulations as he desperately tried to get to his school sports day on time.

Philip was positioned at the other end of the sofa, resting on the arm rest and staring at the television as the football scores began to come in. A big smile appeared upon his face as the rolling vidiprinter revealed that Leeds United had continued their fine start to the season with a comfortable 3-0 victory over Birmingham City, thanks to a hat trick from Peter Lorimer. As he saw the result come across the screen, he sat back on the sofa, enjoying the moment. Whilst continuing to watch as the rest of the day's scores came in, he caught sight of his sister in her Woolworth's uniform in the back garden as she approached and opened the back door.

"Did you get a cake?" she asked as she swung open the door and stepped inside.

"Yes, it's on the table," Philip replied as he gestured towards the table at the other end of the room.

James managed to tear himself away from Billy Whizz long enough to give his sister a smile as she closed the door behind her. As he returned his attention to his comic, his dad entered the room at the far end at exactly the same time as his mother appeared from the kitchen.

"Can you set the table Philip?" she said before she had noticed Grace standing next to the television set. "Oh hello Grace, are you hungry? It's just egg and chips I'm afraid but there is enough to go round."

"Thanks mum that will be great," Grace replied.

As Philip stood up to make his way to the kitchen, his dad asked him how Hartlepool had got on.

"They lost 2-1 at home to Reading dad," Philip said as he passed through the gap between the chair and the sofa and disappeared out of view.

"At home," Francis mumbled to himself as he shook his head and sat down at the table. He pulled his chair in a fraction and stared at the Victoria sponge in the centre of the table.

Philip quickly returned, carrying an assortment of items in his arms. A bottle of tomato sauce, a half used loaf of sliced white bread, salt, vinegar, knives and forks. He plonked them down on the table with all the finesse of a northern darts champion, before instantly heading back into the kitchen. He bounced around the kitchen and his mother whilst gathering up side plates, margarine, three plastic cups and a bottle of Corona Cherryade. Once back at the table he proceeded to lay everything out in its rightful place. As he did so, he glanced over at his dad, who was still sitting at the table and still staring at the Victoria sponge. Francis's concentration was finally broken a few minutes later when a plate of egg and chips was placed in front of him. As everybody came to the table, Philip sat down with an expression on his face that clearly demonstrated a certain amount of pleasure. He tried his hardest but he couldn't remember the last time that all five members of his family had been sat around the same table at the same time, eating dinner. He poured himself some cherryade and buttered a slice of bread.

"Do me a slice," his dad asked.

"And me," James piped up before adding, "can you pass the cherryade?"

Once he had buttered two more slices of bread and poured his younger brother a drink, he covered his chips with the required amount of salt, vinegar and tomato sauce, picked up his fork and tucked in. For Philip, for a few minutes at least whilst everybody focused on their dinner, everything felt like it used to be. Unfortunately it didn't feel that way for long.

"What's with the bloody cake?" Francis asked as he reached for another slice of bread.

"How do you mean?" his wife replied.

As quickly as it took his dad to wave his fork in the direction of the Victoria sponge, Philip felt the tension enter through the soles of his feet and race upwards through his whole body.

"So you think we can afford to go out buying fancy cakes?"

"No Francis, no I don't think we can afford to buy fancy cakes."

Francis was just about to respond to his wife's comment when Grace interrupted.

"I bought it dad," she said.

"Oh right, nice to see that you've got money to waste."

"It's just a cake dad, I know you've got problems at work and money is tight, so I thought I'd treat us all to a cake, we all need a treat now and then."

"What we need Grace is food on the table, and how exactly do you think you know about my problems at work?" Francis asked with a stern expression etched across his face.

"The same way that you knew about where I live, I guess." Grace replied.

"Yes, well you won't be living there much longer."

"Says who dad?" Grace said with a tone in her voice that suggested she was beginning to wish she had gone straight home after work.

"Says me young lady." Francis replied as he slapped his fork down on to the table with such force that it caused bubbles in the bottle of cherryade to rush to the surface.

Grace pushed her chair back and was about to stand up when her mother reached across and grabbed her by the hand. "Finish your tea," she said in a soft voice before turning her head and looking over at her husband. "Your father didn't mean it, he… well he just wants what's best for you that's all. Now let's all stop arguing and finish our tea."

The tension that was now swirling without a care in the world through Philip's body moved over to allow the icy chill that followed a bit of elbow room. Silence descended like a February fog on a crisp cold morning and just like a morning fog it seemed to take root and stubbornly refused to move. There were moments when words formed on the edge of tongues, only to receive a last minute message from the brain department, just as they were about to depart, that perhaps remaining silent was a better option.

Once everybody had about finished and James was just mopping up the last remnants of egg yolk and tomato sauce with a piece of bread, his mother stood up and began to gather up the empty plates.

"Who's for cake?" she asked.

Philip nodded in the affirmative as he finished off his cherryade and placed his cup on the table.

"I'll have a small slice mum," Grace said.

"Not for me", Francis said. "I fancy some banana and custard, what about you James, would you like some?"

As soon as Francis had finished speaking, a dilemma pricked up its ears like a Meerkat and scampered in great haste towards James, instantly embracing him upon arrival. The dilemma looked him squarely in the eyes. He was thinking faster than a Mexican bandit with an angry posse on his tail. A quick glance at the Victoria sponge was followed by an equally quick look at his dad. And equally as quickly he reached a decision and plumped for banana and custard. The rationale behind his decision as he saw it, went as follows; there was a better chance of getting a slice of cake later in the evening than there was of getting banana and custard. Once he had reached his decision, he sighed with relief, said bon voyage to the both the dilemma and the Mexican bandit and sat back in his chair.

James was the only person still sitting at the table by the time his dad appeared from the kitchen carrying two bowls of banana and custard. Philip was sitting on the sofa waiting for an episode of The Pink Panther Show to start. His sister and mother had made their way upstairs and had gone to their mother's bedroom. Francis sat down opposite James and passed one of the bowls of banana and custard over. He then held out a spoon that James eagerly clasped in his hand. They exchanged smiles before tucking into their deserts. Francis paused for a moment to just sit and look at his youngest son as he gobbled up the shiny golden custard and sweet sticky banana underneath. He leant across and gently ruffled his son's hair before turning back to his own bowl of loveliness. As he was clearing away the empty bowls, Grace came down the stairs and back into the living room.

"Philip, you can wash up and James can dry." Francis said as he took the bowls into the kitchen. On his return he added "Do it now as I want to speak with your sister."

"What do you want now dad, I've got to go home, I'm babysitting tonight for Karen, she's going out."

"This is your home," Francis replied with a tone in his voice that caused Philip and James to quickly scurry to the relatively safe distance of the kitchen.

"Not this again dad, I thought we were done with this, I thought you were pleased that I'd moved out."

"You're too young to move out, you are only seventeen."

"You didn't say that the other night."

"Well I'm saying it now and if I say you are moving back in here where you belong, then you are moving back in here and that is the end of the matter."

"You can't make me dad."

"Yes I can, you are only seventeen".

"For a few more weeks dad, only a few more weeks and then I'll be eighteen."

Francis paused, Grace didn't. "If that is what you want, you can force me to move back in but I won't stay here and all you will manage to achieve is make things worse and why would you want to do that. If it's about money and needing some help then I can give you some out of my wages each week to help out but I've moved out dad and you need to accept that and that's that."

Grace stood with her back to the living room door and stared hard at her dad who was sitting at the dining table. Waiting for a response she clenched her fists tight and tried her best to remain calm. She could feel her heart as it pounded rapidly beneath her Woolworth's uniform. For her, she knew the enormity of this moment. It was as if they were standing at opposite ends of a dusty strip of land in a small wild west outpost. Grace found the waiting unbearable. The silence hung heavily as she felt her nails begin to dig into the palms of her hands. Any moment now she expected a ball of tumbleweed to roll its way along the living room. Eventually Francis looked into her eyes and spoke.

"Is there nowhere else you can move into?"

"What's wrong with where I am?" Grace replied as her fists relaxed a little.

"They're bad news Grace, the whole family are, they're nothing more than a bunch of scroungers and parasites. According to that fat cow of a wife, her husband has only got enough strength to walk to the bloody post office once a fortnight to cash his giro yet he's propping up the bar of the 'Livvy' night after night and as for his miserable bloody wife, she's no better, in fact she's far worse. I just don't want you living there Grace, they'll just sponge off you, always looking to borrow money and never pay it back."

"Karen's not like that dad, she hasn't even asked for any rent until I get my first full weeks wages."

"Of course she hasn't, she isn't paying the bloody rent, the social are paying it. As soon as you start giving her your half, it will go straight into her pocket along with the other money she earns."

"What other money?"

"What?"

"Karen doesn't work, so what other money does she earn?"

"Of course she doesn't work, can't go against the family motto, 'In benefits we trust'. They'll disown her if she goes out and gets a job and stop being so naïve Grace, you don't have to have a job to earn money."

Silence entered the room again, only this time around it was accompanied by Philip and James. Grace turned away from her dad and looked over at her brothers. "I've got to go now," she said as she gave her brothers a half smile. She looked back at her dad. "Thank you for showing that you care dad, I'd forgotten that you used to do that but don't worry, I'll be fine."

Grace turned and left the room, moments later the front door could be heard opening and closing. Philip switched the television on just as the opening titles of 'Bruce Forsyth's Generation Game' were rolling across the screen. A couple of minutes later they heard the front door open and close again. They both turned around to see a vacant chair, an empty space and the living room door ajar.

"Where's dad gone?" James asked.

"Where do you think?" Philip replied.

Chapter 23

"No, no, I give up, you're going to have to tell me Knott. I have no idea, I couldn't even hazard a guess, you'll just have to tell me what it is that I am holding in my hand." Mr Spencer stared across his desk at Philip Knott. His elbow was resting on the surface of the table and in between his thumb and middle finger he was holding a small bedraggled looking piece of white card.

Philip looked somewhat nervously back across the table as he replied. "It's my conduct card sir, from last week."

Every Monday morning, directly after assembly, all the boys that had been on either a work card or a conduct card the previous week lined up outside Mr Spencer's office to hand them in. The content of their cards would determine their fate in that instance and for the next week. On this particular Monday morning Philip had been summoned in first.

"Oh I see, this is your conduct card." Mr Spencer replied. "It looks rather worse for wear does it not Knott. What happened to it, I suppose the dog washed it."

Philip was caught slightly off guard and responded with a puzzled expression on his face. "We haven't got a dog."

"We haven't got a dog, Sir," said Mr Spencer, before continuing. "So, when did this act of sabotage take place, did you throw it into the washing machine whilst your mother's back was turned or was it stuffed into your trouser pocket deeper than a Scottish lumberjack's voice?"

"It wasn't deliberate Sir, it was an accident."

"And exactly how many unsatisfactory's has this unfortunate conduct card managed to conceal from us?" Mr Spencer asked.

"Two Sir."

"Two."

"Yes Sir."

Mr Spencer stood up from behind his desk and picked up the long, thin, wispy cane that was displayed proudly on top. "Step outside Knott," he said as he stepped forward.

Philip turned and walked the short distance out of the office. Outside the office was a small square shaped space with another office positioned on the other side. Along the exterior wall of each office ran a small wooden bench and a couple of chairs. On each bench sat a collective of boys, all of them tightly holding their work or conduct cards, awaiting their turn to be summoned into Mr Spencer's office. Philip stepped into the space, rubbing his hands on the outside of his trousers as he did so.

"Okay Knott, you know the drill. Hold out your hand."

Philip raised his arm and put his hand out in front of him. Mr Spencer rested the cane gently on the palm of Philip's hand.

"How many unsatisfactory's was it?"

"Two Sir."

"Then two it shall be...on each hand."

Mr Spencer raised his arm and with it the cane until it was pointing over his shoulder, before bringing it crashing down onto the palm of Philip's hand. Philip winced as the thin smooth strip of rattan collided with the soft pink flesh of his hand. As soon as it had made contact, Mr Spencer lined it up again for the next swipe. As the second swipe came hurtling down, Philip's eyes narrowed and he sucked in a deep breath.

As he lowered his stinging, scorched palm, he could feel the eyes of the other boys burning just as intensely as they stared hard at his face. They were looking for any sign of weakness, anything that would go against the rules of being caned. The rules were quite simple. You weren't allowed to let your eyes water, cry or wet yourself. Many a boy had failed.

Many a boy had leaked fluid from more than one area of their anatomy and many a boy had had to spend the rest of the day attempting to come to terms with the ridicule and shame whilst wearing damp clothing. You were however allowed to blow on your palms or shake your hands but only after the final stroke had been dealt. One stroke on each hand was comfortably manageable for somebody of Philip's experience. Two strokes was much tougher and the maximum of three strokes on each hand was a bridge he had thankfully yet to cross.

Philip held out his other hand before he was asked to do so. Such an act earnt respect amongst those gathered to receive the same punishment. He stared straight ahead and stood as rigid as an old oak on a stormy night as Mr Spencer lined up the first swipe. Mr Spencer prided himself on being able to strike to soft fleshy centre of the palm with more accuracy than any of the other teachers and as the cane crashed into the flesh he would always have a satisfied expression upon his face. If the child moved and the fingers were struck or the wrist area bore the brunt of the swing, then it simply didn't count as a stroke and the whole process had to begin again. Children quickly learnt to keep their hands still.

The second stroke soon set off on its journey and duly arrived with the same amount of force and accuracy as the first. Once it had struck, Philip quickly lowered his hand and began the good fight to not allow his bottom lip to buckle or his eyes to water. He was quite relieved when Mr Spencer pointed with his cane for Philip to return to the office, where he would be out of sight of his peers.

Mr Spencer followed him inside and proceeded to shut the door. He gently placed the cane back on his desk before returning to his seat. Philip stood in front of the desk with his hands clasped tightly together. Mr Spencer opened the top drawer of his desk and took out a new, undamaged, pristine conduct card. He wrote Philip's name in the space provided and then handed it to him.

"And don't forget detention tomorrow Knott." He said as Philip reached out and collected the card.

"Detention for what?" Philip asked.

"You get another card for getting two unsatisfactory's on your previous card. You get the cane for getting two unsatisfactory's on your previous card. You get a detention for lying to me and claiming that there were only two unsatisfactory's on your previous card." He paused for a moment before adding, "And don't let the dog wash this one."

Philip folded the card and carefully slipped it into the outside breast pocket of his blazer. He was just about to leave when Mr Spencer asked. "Any movement on the swimming front?"

"How do you mean Sir?" Philip replied.

"Your dad, has he managed to give any more thought to you trying out for Coventry Godiva?"

Philip's demeanour instantly changed, his shoulders dropped and his head bowed. To the naked eye he appeared to lose a couple of inches in height but at least the change of topic had taken his mind off the burning sensation that was emitting from the palms of his hands.

"Not much chance of that at the moment Sir."

"Why's that?"

"We can't even afford a cake at the moment. My dad has lost half his job, so I don't think he would be able to find the money needed for me to join a swimming club."

"Half his job, how do you mean, he's lost half his job?"

"He's only working three day a week at the moment, not really sure why or for how long, he hasn't really said anything."

"Oh I see. It's happening a lot at present I'm afraid. The economy is on its knees and so is the country for that matter. He's better off than some though, at least he has still got a job."

"Yeah well, membership fee, weekly subs, travel costs, training costs, not going to happen is it Sir."

"Are you managing to do any swimming at all?"

Philip shrugged his slouched shoulders as he answered. "Not really Sir. I mean I go swimming with my friends at the weekend but it's a bit too busy to actually swim. We just mess about and have a laugh."

Mr Spencer sat back in his chair and looked directly at Philip. "You could use the pool here," he said. "After school I mean. I could arrange it. I know it's not exactly Olympic size or anything like that but at least it would be empty. It would be a bit like that film, the one with Burt Lancaster in." He paused. "What's it called?"

"The Swimmer," Philip softly said whilst looking past Mr Spencer and into the distance.

"That's it, you know it then?"

"Yes Sir, I know it."

"Well it would be like The Swimmer but on a much smaller scale."

Conscious of the queue that was still waiting outside his office, although he was more than happy to make them sweat a little longer, Mr Spencer stood up and walked the short distance to his office door. "I tell you what Philip," he said as he opened the door. "You go the whole week without an unsatisfactory on your conduct card and I'll arrange for you to have access to the pool after school. Now get yourself off as you don't want to be late for your first lesson."

Philip walked away, his hands still tightly clasped together as he heard Mr Spencer summon the next victim into his office.

Chapter 24

Philip took his conduct card out of his blazer pocket and skimmed it onto the top of the chest of drawers next to his bed. With an equal amount of frustration and vigour the aforementioned blazer quickly followed. What chance had he got of going the whole week without getting an unsatisfactory on his card, especially when the second lesson on Tuesday of week two of the fortnightly rolling timetable had been French in the languages lab?

A French lesson in the language lab was always seen by certain boys as an opportunity to play what was generally known as the booth scoring game. This was the number one priority of the lesson: actually bothering to learn any French came about quatrieme or cinquieme on the list, well below eating any sweets you may have in your possession, writing your name on the desk or trying to irritate the boy in the booth next to you until they could take no more and handed over any sweets that they had.

The game itself tended to be played mostly by boys who were on conduct cards. The correlation between these two seemingly separate pieces of information was fairly obvious. Even for those boys who actually wanted to learn French in the misguided belief that some day on their respected council estates they would be fortunate enough to stumble across a lost tourist from Toulouse and be able to offer them some kind of assistance. Even for those boys the correlation between conduct cards and playing the game was apparent.

On this particular Tuesday morning there were three conduct

card-carrying boys in the class, Philip and two boys who were also in his maths and general science classes. One was a large boy, with an impressive collection of spots on his face, called Robert Mara, otherwise known as spotty Bobby, (although nobody had as yet been brave enough to call him this to his face). The other boy was equally unpleasant in appearance due to his yellow teeth and greasy hair which seemed to be ever stuck to his forehead; his name was Derek Windass and there were no prizes on offer for guessing what his nickname was.

"You playin' Phil?" Bobby asked as the boys gathered outside the language lab and waited for the teacher to arrive and let them in.

Philip dropped his bag on the floor and leant against the wall. He looked across at Bobby and Derek. He smiled, "Does the Pope shit in the woods," he replied.

The actual lesson and in turn the game itself received an unexpected bonus when an unrecognisable and unknown teacher entered the block via the double doors at the far end of the corridor and began to walk in their direction. Carrying a brown leather satchel and wearing a brown jacket with brown leather elbow patches, he had supply teacher stamped all over him. By now the lesson was approximately three minutes behind schedule and their usual French teacher Mr Franks was nowhere to be seen. The teacher got closer and closer before beginning to squeeze his way past the gathering of boys waiting to enter the lab, the final squeeze being the most difficult one to orchestrate as Bobby Mara was stood directly in front of the door.

"Mr Franks is not here today boys, so I will be taking the lesson. My name is Mr James," he said as he managed to edge Booby over to the right a little with the aid of his leather satchel in order to insert the key and open the door.

No sooner had it opened than Bobby, Philip and Derek rushed past Mr James and into the room. The supply teacher foolishly mistook this act as a keen desire to learn French when in fact it was vital to acquire booths fourteen, fifteen and sixteen if the game was to be played properly.

The rules of the booth game were fairly straightforward. In the languages lab there were sixteen booths in four rows of four with a narrow corridor down one side for access to the booths. Each booth was clearly numbered. To be able to score the most points possible and to make the game more interesting, the players needed to acquire the aforementioned booths, depending on the number of players. According to the size of the class, there would be one or two boys in each booth. (Each booth came equipped with a built in tape recorder and two sets of headphones. However this particular piece of information was surplus to requirements in respect of playing the game.)

As soon as Philip, Bobby and Derek had made it to the required booths, Bobby delved deep inside his school rucksack and rummaged around in search of some paper and a pen.

"Get the scorecards ready Bobby," Derek said with a certain degree of excitement in his voice.

"I'm on it, I'm on it," Bobby replied.

The scorecard was simply a piece of paper, lined or plain, it didn't really matter. The paper had three columns etched onto it. Column one was for the booth number, column two was for the signature of one of the boys in the corresponding booth. This was for verification purposes at the end of the game; no signature meant no points scored. The final column was for the points scored.

Rather than a normal desk, the Languages lab had a small raised platform at the front of the classroom with a desk perched on top. The desk itself had a built in switchboard so that the teacher could start the tape recorders collectively and when needed, stop them collectively as well.

Bobby passed a sheet of paper to Philip and another one to Derek. "Pens at the ready," he said.

"Who's first?" Derek asked.

"You can go first," Philip said, looking at Derek as he spoke.

"Who's timing it?" Derek said.

"We'll take it in turns," Bobby replied.

Mister James climbed the raised platform and looked down at the class. "Before we start, I believe that there are a few of you who need to hand in your work cards or your conduct cards," he said as he began fumbling around inside his jacket pockets for a piece of paper.

"Ere Phil, take them up to him before he spots where we are sitting," Bobby said as he passed his card over and nudged Derek at the same time, prompting him to do likewise.

Philip did as he was asked. As he reached the raised desk clutching the cards, Mr James had found the piece of paper he was looking for and was just about to call out the names inscribed upon it. Philip handed over the cards and as he returned to his booth, Mr James cross referenced the names on the cards with the names that were written on the piece of paper.

The rules of the game were quite simple. Once the lesson had commenced, whoever's turn it was had three minutes to leave the booth and move stealth-like, reminiscent of a big cat in the wild, stalking its lunch. The objective was to get to another booth, get a person in the chosen booth to verify the successful attempt by signing the scorecard and then return to your own booth without being spotted. You could only visit a booth once and the person who visited the most booths by the end of the lesson was the winner. The first few booths were relatively easy, especially to the seasoned professional. The game really came into its own once the only booths left were located on the first two rows, booths one to eight. These booths were vitally important because in the event of a tied game, the person who had reached the lowest number booth was declared the winner.

Philip's downfall came the very next run after Derek had been caught on all fours, in the walkway along the side of the booths, in an area known as 'no man's land', as he was trying to reach booth five. It was always risky to go straight after a failed run but if you don't set off within the first minute of your allotted time then you forfeit your turn, and with the game so evenly poised, it was a risk worth taking.

Philip knew his game was up when he popped his head up in booth number three and glanced over at the raised desk, only to find the supply teacher Mr James staring straight back at him.

With a somewhat dejected and deflated tone in his voice Mr James asked. "And you are?"

"Knott, Sir", Philip replied.

"You certainly are not", the teacher replied, before adding "Have you actually managed to learn any French today"?

"Oui Monsieur". Philip replied.

"Tres bien, tres bien. Autre chose".

Not entirely sure what the teacher had just asked, Philip thought for a moment, knowing that he needed to offer some sort of response. Clutching desperately at a straw, he muttered "Bon appetit."

"Oh I see." Said Mr James. "So whilst you are checking in at the airport, handing in your luggage, going through passport control and customs, finding your departure gate and boarding your flight, at some point in all of this, you will tell one of the members of staff that you encounter along the way to enjoy their meal."

"It could be an early morning flight Sir and one of the check in staff might be enjoying a croissant," Philip said.

Mr James stood up and stepped down from the platform. "If you think that my appearance in some way suggests that I am likely to engage in futile conversations, then you are very much mistaken. So I suggest that you return to your own booth immediately and when you get there, perhaps you could humour me and make some token gesture towards actually learning something."

"Could I just get Burgess to sign my scorecard please Sir? Now that I'm here."

"Sign your what?"

"My scorecard Sir, for the game."

"I know what card I will be signing Knott, now get back to your seat."

Philip picked up his scorecard and pen and turned away to head back to his booth. "Oui Monsieur, excellente." He said as he set off on his journey. He was met with broad smiles on the faces of his friends and fellow competitors when he reached his destination.

The lesson ended with a comfortable win for Bobby by three clear booths. It also ended with an unsatisfactory for both Philip and Derek Windass. Philip's first Unsatisfactory of the week was quickly followed by his second in the following maths lesson for hurling a clear plastic protractor across the room. Or rather for hurling a clear plastic protractor at Cliff Cain for his relentless ribbing after hearing of Philip's previous Unsatisfactory and three booths defeat.

Thursday morning's Geography lesson saw his third and final Unsatisfactory of the week. This was for getting embroiled in a pointless debate about the Arctic Circle not actually being a circle which inexplicably progressed into a debate about England's chances of qualifying for the 1974 World Cup finals. This in turn developed into a discussion about England's strikers and whether they were better than the Italian strike force. Due to Allan 'Sniffer' Clarke being one of the England strikers, Philip came down on the side of England. By the time Mr Billington, the geography teacher, clicked the top of his pen and entered an Unsatisfactory on Philip's conduct card, the conversation had moved on to why India and Pakistan were both equally rubbish at football. Although the group discussion failed to reach a definitive answer, Martin Potts had suggested that it was something to do with the weight of their turbans as this caused problems in lifting their heads and thus being unable to both play the long ball and cut out the long ball.

Upon returning home from school on Friday afternoon, Philip stood in his bedroom, frantically processing his thoughts in a desperate attempt to locate a silver lining like an old lady at the checkout of the local Spar, rummaging in her purse for the money off coupon on a tin of Crosse and Blackwell baked beans. Normally she would only buy the Spar own brand baked beans, but as she had a coupon, she thought that she would have a little treat.

After a short while Philip managed to take a firm hold of a couple of silver linings. The first one simply being it was Friday which hopefully meant his dad would be spending the evening in the pub as he didn't have to go to work. This in turn meant that Philip would be able to play out until late. The second silver lining was the fact that Leeds United were away to Wolves on Saturday and there was a good chance that the game would be one of the two featured games on 'Star Soccer' on Sunday. There was also an excellent chance of a positive result seeing as Leeds had managed to comfortably beat Wolves only recently.

Philip headed out of his room and for the newsagents to complete his evening paper round. He took enough money with him so that he could buy this week's copy of 'Shoot', if he had to. He'd managed to lift a copy of this week's 'Tiger' when he had gone to do his paper round that morning. He was saving the reading of that particular publication until after his paper round on Saturday morning.

Chapter 25

"Dad, dad."

Grace stopped walking and stared intently at the figure in the distance that had now changed direction and was briskly walking away from her. Quite sure in her assumption that it was her father that she had called out to, she called out again. Only this time around she called out a little louder to accommodate for the fact that he was now a good distance further away than the last time she called.

"Dad, dad."

The figure in the distance didn't turn around but instead continued to walk briskly towards Broad Park Road. Carrying a bemused expression on her face, Grace continued along Roselands Avenue, before turning right along Clennon Rise. A few short steps later, Grace arrived at the entrance to her block. Just as she entered the block she took a final glance towards the figure she had called out to. By now he had reached Broad Park Road and was almost completely out of sight.

As Grace entered the flat, her friend was walking into the kitchen, carrying two cups in her hand. Grace followed and stood in the doorway.

"My dad hasn't just been here looking for me as he?"

Karen turned away and began to rinse the cups out under the tap. "Your dad?" She asked. "No he hasn't called by here, why?"

"Oh, no reason," Grace replied before walking over to the kettle. "Tea?" she asked.

"No thanks Grace, I've not long had one.... How come you're

home so early?"

"They've given me a half day as they want me to go in and help stocktake again tomorrow." Grace filled the kettle, flicked the switch and crossed the hallway into the living room. This time it was Karen's turn to follow.

Picking up the ashtray from the coffee table Karen asked "After your cup of tea, you couldn't make yourself scarce for a while could you Grace?"

Grace reacquainted herself with her bemused expression as if they had never been separated. "Oh… sure, if you like, any reason why?"

"I've just got somebody coming round that's all and I want to make a good impression." Karen immediately considered how that must have sounded to Grace and quickly tried to make amends. "No, sorry Grace, I didn't mean it like that, I just…oh, you know."

"Yes, I know. Where's…"

"He's with me mum" Karen interrupted.

"So, who is he, anybody we know?"

Grace could sense that Karen was becoming more and more agitated and was busily passing the ashtray between her hands as she replied.

"No, you don't know him, he's not from around here."

"Oh, where did you meet him?"

"I'll tell you all about it later Grace, he's gonna be here soon, I'm just going to get ready." Eager to get out of the room, Karen took the ashtray with her and made a swift exit. Grace went into the kitchen to make herself a cup of tea.

Fifteen minutes later a rather more glamourous Karen re-emerged, only to instantly become annoyed on discovering that Grace was still in the flat. "Please Grace, he's going to be here any minute," Karen said as she placed the now empty ashtray back down on the coffee table.

"Grace!" she snapped again as the sound of the ashtray colliding with the glass top of the coffee table echoed around the room.

"Okay, okay. I'm going," Grace replied, and she stood up to take her cup into the kitchen.

Karen quickly grabbed it and took it from Grace's grasp. "I'll do that," she said, "just give us a couple of hours, okay."

Karen turned and still clutching the empty cup, opened the front door to let Grace out. Grace departed, walked down the two flights of stairs and out of the block, back onto the street. She made her way back towards Roselands Avenue. As she was about to turn off Clennon Rise, a mustard coloured, two door, Vauxhall Viva caught her eye as it went past. The car pulled up directly outside the entrance to Grace's block. As Grace turned back into Roselands Avenue, she glanced over to her left and towards the car, just as the driver's door opened. She watched as a tall, heavily set, middle-aged man clambered out and closed the door behind him.

'That's Martin Matthews's dad.' Grace said to herself. She slowed down a little and observed as the man walked towards and entered the block of flats. As he disappeared from view, Grace came to a complete stop, still looking over at the block of flats. She stood motionless for a moment and then shook her head in an attempt to remove the current unpleasant thought that was lodged within. Unable to do so and with two hours to kill Grace headed back to her family home.

When she arrived, Grace elected to walk around to the back of the house rather than let herself in through the front door with the key she still had in her purse. She made her way along the side of the house and into the back garden, listening out for any raised voices as she went. As she reached and opened the back door, the only noise she could detect was being emitted by the television set. Grandstand was on and a neglected Frank Bough was trying his best to be both informative and entertaining whilst discussing the table tennis that was about to start but nobody in the room was paying him any attention. Grace closed the door and stood next to the television set just as a match between world champion Xi Enting of China and Dragutin Surbek from the Socialist Federal Republic of Yugoslavia was about to commence. The only other person present was James. He was lying belly down on the settee, resting his head in the palms of his hands, reading the 'Beano'. He had just finished reading about Lord Snooty before turning the page and settling into this week's story of The Three Bears. He paid his sister no attention.

"Where is everyone James?" Grace asked.

"I'm here, mum's asleep upstairs, Philip is upstairs and dad's out," James replied without interrupting his flow of The Three Bears. Pa Bear had entered the Bear Territory Open Golf Championship on the grounds of there being a banquet for the winner; Teddy Bear was his caddy.

Grace walked the short distance towards James, leant over and snatched his comic away.

"Hey!" James called out.

"The Beano," Grace said. "You're still reading the Beano. What a baby! You're too old to still be reading this."

"And you're too ugly to be allowed out during the day," James replied.

"Ha, ha," Grace said as she tossed the magazine back at James.

James quickly retrieved his comic, found his page and returned to the adventures of the Three Bears just as Philip entered the room. He was carrying two rolled up towels under his arm.

"What are you doing here, you been sacked?" Philip asked upon noticing his sister standing by the settee.

"No I haven't, no," Grace replied. "And why is he still reading the Beano?" she added as she pointed at James.

"Probably because he hasn't finished it yet, he only started reading it about half an hour ago."

"Oh very funny. I didn't mean that particular copy, I mean the Beano full stop, he's twelve years old. If other kids find out he still reads it, they'll take the piss out of him."

"Leave him alone Grace," Philip said with a sharp tone in his voice that was accompanied with an equally sharp stare. "There's no law against it, he's not hurting anybody, he can read what he wants to read and if anybody has an issue with it then I'll deal with it. James, I can't find your goggles, you'll have to go without them."

"Are you two going swimming?" Grace asked.

"What gave it away, was it the snorkel and flippers I'm wearing or was it something else?" Philip replied.

Grace took a small step backwards so that she was no longer in James's eye line and motioned towards the kitchen at Philip. "Oh so much wit and humour. I can't believe that you haven't been invited to be on the 'Comedians.' Every Saturday night I tune in expecting to see you on the screen."

Grace headed into the kitchen Philip followed. As for James, he had just finished the Three Bears and was now onto this week's adventures of Little Plum. As Philip entered the kitchen Grace closed the door behind him.

"How's mum?" Grace asked.

"Okay I guess." Philip said.

"What do you mean, 'okay I guess'? You're supposed to be keeping an eye on her and keeping me informed."

"What do you want me to tell you? She's in bed, occasionally she gets out of bed and then she goes back to bed." Philip said with a clearly impatient and annoyed tone to his voice.

"Where's dad?" Grace asked.

"Bloody hell Grace, where do you think he is, he's gone out, he's either in the bookies or the Bell."

"When did he go?"

Philip raised his eyebrows and exhaled. "I don't know exactly Grace, he doesn't exactly say goodbye you know. I guess about an hour or so ago, what's the big deal?"

"I saw him a little while ago when I was walking home from work," Grace said. "He came around the corner and was walking towards me in Roselands Avenue but when he saw me, he turned and started walking the other way."

"I wonder why?" Philip interrupted.

"I'm being serious Philip. I shouted after him twice but he just kept walking."

"Are you sure it was dad?"

"Of course I'm sure. When I got home I asked Karen if he had called at the flat and she said no. So where had he been, where was he going?"

"I don't know Grace, maybe he had called at the flat but Karen didn't hear him, maybe she was in the bath or drying her hair."

"Yeah but if he had been looking for me why did he walk the other way and anyway he knows I'm at work so why go to the flat?"

"Do I have to get a certain amount of these questions right Grace, because to be honest with you, I haven't got a clue what you're on about?"

"Oh it doesn't matter." Grace said. "You just run off to the swimming baths with your little friends; maybe you'll get lucky and some fat girl's top may come undone."

"Don't take it out on me Grace, if you're that bothered then go up the Bell and speak to him about it," Philip said as he opened the kitchen door and shouted over at James. "Time to go James, get your shoes on and grab your coat."

"He won't be there." Grace replied. "He was walking towards Broad Park, he'll probably be in the White Horse."

"No chance," Philip said as he disappeared into the scullery in search of a carrier bag. As he returned, he added. "You know what he thinks of the people who drink in there. They're even lower than the cliental of the Livvy and you know what he thinks of them."

Philip exited the kitchen and placed the rolled up towels inside the carrier bag. With the bag then safely tucked under his arm, both he and James headed towards the back door. As they did so Grace sloped out of the kitchen and flopped onto the settee, exhaling deeply as she landed. She immediately lifted up her bum a fraction and removed the comic she had just sat on.

"Come with us if you want." Philip said as he went to close the back door.

"No thanks." Grace replied. "The last thing I need right now is your sad friends staring at my tits for the next two hours."

"Don't flatter yourself." Philip replied. "They'll be plenty of other tits to stare at, not just yours."

As Philip closed the door Grace called out. "Don't mention any of this to dad, okay. Don't tell him that I've been here either."

Philip raised his eyebrows again and shook his head before he disappeared out of view. Grace found herself sitting alone and staring at the table tennis on 'Grandstand'. After watching for a little while longer Grace made her way upstairs to look in on her mum. On discovering that she was fast asleep she left quickly and quietly, heading instead to Bell Green to kill some time window shopping. On returning home a little while later Grace found her flatmate sitting on the settee in a white fluffy dressing gown and a towel wrapped tightly around her head, smoking a cigarette.

"How did it go?" Grace asked

"How did what go?" Karen replied.

Somewhat surprised by Karen's response. "Your date?" Grace asked.

"My what?" Karen paused for a moment. "Oh that, he didn't turn up," she added as she stubbed her cigarette out in the ashtray, placed her hand on the towel to hold it in place, stood up and left the room.

"Was it something I said?" Grace muttered to herself as she switched on the television set and sat down.

Chapter 26

Two goals from Alan 'Sniffer' Clarke had helped to secure a 2-1 win at Southampton and had also helped to stretch Leeds's one hundred percent start to the season to seven games. One crucial deciding factor that may well have contributed to the continuation of this winning streak was the absence of Mick Channon from the Southampton line up.

It didn't really matter who you supported, when it came to acknowledging the quality of opposition players and drawing up a wish list of those that you would like to see in your particular team colours, a player of Mick Channon's quality would undoubtedly make the list. Being a Leeds United supporter, Philip definitely felt that his list would be a lot shorter than most other fans' lists but he would still have a list and, Mick Channon would be on it. Ray Kennedy would also have a better than average chance of making the cut, along with Ron 'Chopper' Harris at a push. After that, trying to add any further names would be as problematic as trying to keep hold of a recently caught rainbow trout after dipping your hands into a vat of lard.

No sooner had the warm glow of viewing the league table in the paper on Monday morning wrapped itself around him, than Philip's attention had turned itself to the next league game. Even the minor distraction of the midweek European fixture against the Norwegian minnows Stromgodset couldn't turn his attention away from such an important match.

One key component of the game of football that the young fan learns very quickly is that no matter who you support, some fixtures are far more important than others. In fact stating that there are certain games that are more important is rather an understatement. There are certain fixtures in every team's season where the thought of losing does not bear thinking about. Defeat would send a chill down the spine so cold that it could live next door to an Eskimo. Ask any Notts County fan, and although they wouldn't enjoy it, they could cope with losing to Doncaster Rovers, Oldham Athletic or Grimsby Town. But losing to Nottingham Forest is a whole different level of hurt. It is the same story up and down the land. Aston Villa fans shudder at the thought of losing to Birmingham City. Sunderland fans are reduced to tears if Newcastle United turn up and win, and so it goes on. Victory however in such a fixture is a completely different story. Victory in such a fixture is the sweetest tasting ambrosia known to every man, woman and child who has ever stood on the terraces. For this particular fourteen year old Leeds United fan a fixture of this magnitude was fast approaching: a home game against Manchester United.

To a Leeds United supporter, Manchester United were the footballing equivalent of something you have just stepped in on the high street and were now busily trying to scrape it off your shoe whilst sporting a disgusted expression. So it came as no surprise that whilst Philip stood in Mr Spencer's office on Monday morning, he was having a great deal of difficulty holding on to the conversation.

"So all this time that I thought you were serious, it now appears that I had got it wrong," Mr Spencer said whilst he twirled a pen between his fingers and stared across his desk at Philip.

Philip didn't reply.

"Are you listening to me Knott?"

"Yes Sir." Philip said.

"Then what did I just say to you boy?"

"You asked me if I was listening Sir?"

Mr Spencer's expression quickly changed. "Don't get smart with me Knott. Boys who foolishly believe they can get smart with me very quickly live to regret such reckless endeavours."

Philip just wanted the conversation to be over as quickly as possible. He wanted his inevitable punishment over with as quickly as possible so that he could focus on more pressing matters such as writing a very important letter to Billy, wishing him and the rest of the team luck for the forthcoming fixture against Manchester United.

Mr Spencer continued. "I thought you were serious about your swimming but obviously not."

"I am serious about it Sir." Philip replied.

"Not according to this conduct card you're not. I offer you the chance of your own pool to train in and you throw it back in my face. All I can assume from this is that the admission price is too high for you."

"It's not Sir."

"One week Knott, that's all you had to do, just one week without earning yourself an unsatisfactory and here you are with two. One more and no doubt the dog would have been doing the washing again this weekend."

Mr Spencer allowed himself a little chuckle. Philip just rolled his eyes as he shifted his weight for one foot to the other.

Mr Spencer opened the middle drawer of his desk and removed a pristine, unblemished stack of conduct cards, held together by a thick elastic band. He removed a singular card from the top of the stack and placed the rest back in the drawer. As he went to close the drawer, he paused for a moment. With the drawer half open, or half closed, depending on your point of view, he looked up at Philip and then back inside the drawer. He removed a large brown envelope, placed it on the top of his desk and closed the drawer. He picked up his pen, clicked the little silver button at the top of the pen and proceeded to write Philip's name in the designated place on the conduct card.

"One last chance." He said as he passed the card to Philip. If you come back next week with one single, solitary Unsatisfactory on this card then the offer is off the table. However if you manage to achieve an Unsatisfactory free week, you can bring your swimming trunks and towel with you."

Philip took hold of the card and braced himself for what he thought was about to come next. However this time around it didn't happen. Instead Mr Spencer opened the large brown envelope and took out a couple of A4 pieces of paper, stapled together in the top left hand corner.

"I take it that you are aware of our annual trip to Dol-y-Moch in Wales which we run every year for the fourth year boys?" Mr Spencer asked.

"Yes Sir." Philip replied.

"You haven't put your name down."

"No Sir, it's not really for me, it's all that outward bounds stuff, all walking boots and map reading."

"I think you might actually enjoy it and you'll gain a lot from the experience. It might actually do you some good and there's a lot more to it than walking boots and map reading."

Philip shrugged his shoulders. I don't think we can afford it anyway Sir."

"Look, take this home and have a chat with your mum and dad about it. There are a few places left, we don't go until January and you can pay weekly. The cost is £8.00 and you need to have paid it all by Christmas." Mr Spencer handed the paperwork over to Philip. "It tells you more about it in here. You can let me know next week when you return with your rolled up towel under your arm. Now get yourself off, you don't want to be late for your first lesson."

By the end of his first lesson of the day, geography, Philip had completed his first draft. By the end of his second lesson, history, he had made the necessary adjustments to the first draft. Due to the nature of his next the lesson, his final lesson before lunch, general science, working on his letter was always going to prove difficult. However by the midway point of lunchtime, he had managed to obtain an envelope from the headmaster's secretary and was on his way to the school library to complete the final version.

Although the library was a rather unfamiliar setting, it was also a location where he could almost guarantee that he would not be disturbed by any of his friends and could therefore work on his letter until the start of the afternoon lesson. The school operated on a two week timetable and the afternoon of the second Monday meant a double lesson of religious education, R.E for short. For a fourteen year old boy growing up on a rundown, sprawling enclave on the outskirts of the city, R.E had the be the most irrelevant subject imaginable. It would be closely followed by history but R.E would undoubtedly cross the pointless subject finish line first. Philip failed to ascertain how the Sermon on the Mount, the Sea of Galilee or the last supper had any relevance whatsoever to his life. He felt equally perplexed by the need to know anything about the kings and queens of the fourteenth and fifteenth century, Sir Walter Raleigh, Sir Francis Drake, the Black Death and the gunpowder plot.

The double whammy of a double block of R.E was the fact that the R.E teacher was the most boring teacher in the whole school. The moment that you crossed the line and entered Mr Swan's classroom it was as if you had entered into a different dimension in time. A minute spent on the outside of this particular vortex appeared to last at least ten minutes on the inside. The lesson itself seemed to acquire the pace of an asthma sufferer attempting to climb a steep hill whilst carrying their cumbersome and overweight grandmother on their back.

Mr Swan was quite obviously a well-meaning teacher who cared passionately about the subject he taught and its importance. He also cared equally passionately about the lives of the boys he taught. The problem was that in all of his forty seven years, he seemed to have managed to avoid concepts such as fun and humour within the art of storytelling. When you mixed together the subject matter and his dry flat monotone voice, you unwittingly created the perfect storm.

Philip spent most of the lesson staring out of the window and away into the distance, gazing out upon rolling empty playing fields and trees swaying in the light afternoon breeze. The rest of the time was spent creating an animated drawing of a stickman footballer scoring a match winning goal in the corners of the pagers in his R.E book. As minute collapsed on top of minute his thoughts slipped further and further into the unknown. Eventually the final minute of the lesson stretched out its exhausted hand and grasped hold of the piece of chalk in Mr Swan's hand, thankfully bringing the proceedings to a close. Almost immediately a collection of relieved young faces filed out of the classroom and began to acclimatise themselves with a more familiar time zone, immediately forgetting the homework task they had just been asked to complete.

Philip stood by the school gates and waited for James. As he stood amongst the mass of children leaving school, he spotted Martin Matthews making his way up the hill and towards the gates. However Martin was focused more on the bar of chocolate he was eating than the world around him and as he passed through the gates he failed to notice Philip. As the swarm of children continued to pass him by, Philip, by choice, managed to avoid the attention of his other friends. He continued to stand and wait for James. The thronging mass had slowly transformed into a steady trickle when James finally appeared at the bottom of the drive.

"Where have you been?" Philip asked as James finally reached the summit of the hill.

"Miserable old Compy kept me back at the end of the lesson because I forgot to bring in my homework".

"Did he give you a detention?"

"No." James replied. "But if I don't bring it in on Wednesday the miserable old sod said that he will."

"Better get it done then, when you get home."

"I have done, I just forgot to bring it in, I think it's on the table in the living room."

"Yeah well, can we get a move on? I want to call in to the post office on the way home," Philip said as he turned around and headed away from the school gates.

The early evening skies had begun to darken and light wispy droplets of rain had started to fall by the time the two boys stepped off the number twenty six bus. They got off two stops early on Broad Park Road so that Philip could call into the post office.

"Why did we get off here?" James asked as he raised the hood of his Parka coat over his head.

"I told you, I wanted to go to the post office."

"What for?"

"I need a stamp, I've got to post a letter, anyway if you stop moaning, I'll get you a freddo."

"But I'm getting wet." James muttered as they approached the post office. "Can I have a comic as well?" He added.

As they entered the Post Office, Philip reached inside his blazer pocket and pulled out a handful of coins. He pushed them around his palm with his finger whilst calculating the cost of a stamp, comic and two Freddo's.

"Yes you can have a comic." He said once he had worked out if he had enough money to complete the transaction.

Philip made his way to the counter to purchase his stamp whilst James walked over and began looking at the comics. There were a few people in front of Philip, so he joined the back of the line and waited patiently to be served. By the time he had reached the counter, James had joined him, carrying a copy of 'Whizzer and Chips' in his hand.

"Can I have a first class stamp Please?" Philip asked the lady on the other side of the counter, before turning to James. "Quick James go and get two Freddo's," he said as he took the comic out of James's hand.

The lady flipped open a large black book, found the correct page and carefully removed one first class stamp.

"That will be three pence." She said, passing the stamp to Philip just as James returned.

"And these." Philip said as he placed the two Freddo's and the comic on the counter.

The lady looked down at the items. "That's ten pence in total please, young man."

Philp handed over the exact money. He picked up the stamp and one of the Freddo's in one hand before passing the other Freddo and the comic to James. They both turned away from the counter and left the post office.

The rain was still falling as they exited. James quickly took his bag off his shoulder and safely placed the comic inside, whilst Philip took the letter out of his bag, licked and attached the stamp and walked over to the post box directly opposite. He inserted his letter in the slot, listened as it dropped inside and then put his bag back over his shoulder.

As they walked home past Clennon Rise and through Roselands Avenue, the rain began to fall heavier and heavier. They turned into Monkswood Crescent with the rain drops bouncing off them as they went. It took a few more strides along the crescent before they both realised that the ambulance they could see in the distance was parked outside their house. Once realised, they both sprinted quickly up the street, crashing through the newly formed puddles as they went. As they reached the ambulance, they could see the back doors open and Francis was climbing inside. With rain running down their foreheads, they peered inside. They could make out the figure of their mother, lying on a stretcher. Her eyes were closed and a transparent oxygen mask was covering the majority of her face.

"Dad." Philip called out.

"Get yourselves in the house boys and get dried off." Francis said as he sat down opposite his wife and next to an ambulance man. "There's nothing to worry about. Philip sort yourselves out some tea and I'll be back as soon as I can."

With this the ambulance driver appeared and closed the doors. Without saying anything, he disappeared just as quickly as he had appeared and climbed into the cab. The engine started and the ambulance pulled away, leaving the two soggy boys standing outside the house as the incessant rain continued to tumble down.

Chapter 27

Philip. Grace and James were all sitting in the visitor's waiting room of the Walsgrave Hospital. They were sitting in a row with James in the middle. He was clutching a small bunch of flowers that Grace had bought from the florist in Bell Green before they had caught the bus. Philip looked around the room at the other visitors patiently waiting for the clock on the wall to reach 6pm. Two seats down to the left sat an Asian lady in her late fifties. She was sitting with her hands placed neatly in her lap and her head bowed, looking at her feet. Along the left hand wall sat what looked like a young married couple. He was wearing a pair of dark blue, rather grubby looking work overalls whilst his wife sat with a small brown paper bag and a couple of magazines resting on her lap.

'Perhaps we should have bought some magazines' Philip thought to himself before turning his attention to the next person in the waiting room, a frail looking elderly gentleman who was sitting directly opposite him. Philip couldn't help but think how alone and scared the old man looked. He found himself staring intently at the old gentleman. His skin was almost falling from his face, his eyes were sunken and glazed, with his left eye in particular looking rather bloodshot. His attire, like his skin, appeared to be gradually slipping towards the floor; it was a battle that gravity was well on the way to winning. His wrists rested on his thighs with his hands curled up and clenched tight. His protruding knuckles shone a bright red colour under the waiting room lights, whilst the skin on his hands, just like the skin on his face, was drained of colour as if he had been admitted to the hospital with the worst case of seasickness ever recorded. Philip looked directly at the old man and smiled. The man didn't smile back. Feeling slightly uncomfortable by the lack of response, Philip was just about to turn his attention away from the old man, when the waiting room door opened and two nurses stood in the doorway. The first nurse quickly glanced around the room before stopping at the old man.

"Mr Williamson," she said.

The old man turned his head and looked up at the two nurses.

"Would you mind coming this way Mr Williamson? The doctor would like to speak with you."

"There's nothing wrong?" he asked. "My Mary's okay isn't she?"

Neither of the nurses replied, instead they just repositioned themselves in the doorway to make enough room for the old man to get through. Slowly he stood up and picked up his hat and coat which had been resting on the chair next to him. As he went to leave, he looked across at Philip. Philip smiled at him again and again the old man did not smile back. Philip watched as the old man put his coat over his arm and whilst holding his hat, he left the room followed by the nurses.

"That doesn't look good does it?" Philip said as the waiting room door closed and he turned to look at his sister.

"What doesn't?" Grace replied

"That old man," Philip said.

"What old man?" Grace said with a small splash of annoyance in her voice.

"Doesn't matter." Philip said, shaking his head as he spoke.

Still making sure that Philip could detect the annoyance in her voice, without the need for a map and compass, Grace turned and looked at him as she spoke. "Can I remind you why we are here?"

"I know why we are here, we are here to visit mum."

"And to find out what happened." Grace said as she stared hard at her brother.

"You're not still going on about that are you, do you really think that dad pushed mum down the stairs."

"I don't know Philip, I wasn't there was I?"

"No, nobody was there." Philip replied.

"Except dad," Grace said before adding, "A bit of a coincidence, don't you think?"

"Oh yes, of course it was, he works nights, so he's at home during the day, you don't live there anymore and anyway you were probably busy helping yourself to the pick'n'mix in Wollies and James and me were at school, so it's a real coincidence that it was just mum and dad that were at home at the time."

Grace's eyes widened as she looked at Philip before she turned to look at the clock, exhaling loudly as she did so.

It seemed to take a whole lot longer but three minutes later the clock finally reached six 'o' clock and the visiting bell rang out. Grace, Philip and James stood up and made their way out of the visitors' waiting room, along the corridor and onto the ward. There was a row of evenly spaced beds along either side of the ward. As they looked down the ward, they saw that their mother was in a bed four beds down on the left hand side.

"There she is," Philip said as he stretched out his arm and pointed in the right direction.

As soon as he spotted her, James rushed over and attempted to hug his mum whilst still clutching the bunch of flowers.

"Mum!" he called out as he opened up his arms to their maximum wing span.

They embraced whilst Grace and Philip completed the journey to their mother's bedside. There were two chairs at the side of her bed. Once he had been released from his mother's grip, James sat down, still holding the bunch of flowers. Grace took the other seat, next to her younger brother, whilst Philip stood near the end of the bed.

"What are you all doing here?" their mother asked with a broad smile across her face.

"We wanted to see you," James said.

"That's sweet," their mother replied as she leant across and gently rubbed James's head. "Are they for me?" she added, pointing at the flowers in his hand.

James smiled and nodded as he passed the flowers over to his mum.

"Keep your eye out for a nurse," she said as she rested them gently on her bed. "I'll get her to put them in some water."

"How are you mum?" Grace asked.

"I'm fine darling."

Rather annoyed by the sheer lack of information in her mother's response, Grace quickly said. "How can you be fine, have you not noticed where you are, you're in hospital."

"Oh stop fussing Grace, you'll upset the boys. I'm fine, a bit bruised and a bit sore, if you really want to know but thankfully, nothing broken."

Still unhappy and still eager for much more information, Grace continued. "So what actually happened?"

"Didn't your dad tell you?"

"Not exactly." Grace said. He didn't say a lot, he just said that you had fallen down the stairs."

"Well to be fair Grace, that's about all there is to tell you. I fell down the stairs."

"But how?" Grace asked.

"I'm not sure that I understand the question Grace." Her mum replied. "How many ways are there for a person to fall down the stairs? You either fall down the stairs or you make it safely to the bottom."

James chuckled at his mother's response; Grace certainly did not. Her blood pressure was rising quicker than the current price of oil. She was just about to fire off another inquisitive question in her mother's direction when a nurse appeared behind Philip, holding a chair.

"Would you like a chair son?" she said. "Would you like me to put those in some water?" The nurse added as she placed the chair in position so that Philip could sit down.

The nurse made her way along the chair-free side of the bed, reached over and took the bunch of flowers off the bed. "Mmm, they smell lovely." she said as she held them to her nose and inhaled deeply. No sooner had she turned and walked away than Grace asked her question.

"But what actually happened?"

"Oh Grace, to be honest I can't remember a lot of it."

"Please mum, can you at least tell me what you can remember."

"I remember your dad coming into the bedroom, saying that he wanted to get a couple of hours sleep. He had to go to work later. So, I got up and went downstairs."

"And you fell down the stairs; where was dad?" Grace interrupted.

"No Grace, that's not when I fell down the stairs. Now if you want me to tell you what happened, then listen. You know what your dad can be like, sometimes it is just easier to stay out of his way. Anyway, I lay downstairs for a while on the settee and watched some television. Crown Court had just finished when your dad came back down. I made us both a cup of tea and then I went back upstairs. I lay down for a while. I wasn't planning on falling asleep as I knew that the boys would be home from school soon. Well I obviously drifted back to sleep as I woke up a little later. I jumped out of bed and looked around the room for my dressing gown and slippers. I couldn't find them so I thought that I must have left them downstairs. I do remember feeling a little light headed when I got out of bed but I just went to go downstairs. The next thing I remember was when I was in the back of the ambulance with an ambulance man and your dad staring at me, on the way to hospital. Thankfully it looks like I slipped and slid down the stairs on my back rather than tumbled forward."

"So there is more than one way to fall down a flight of stairs!" Philip said.

His mother smiled. "Yes I suppose there is." She replied.

Philip and James were still laughing when a very serious Grace asked

"Where was dad?"

"What?" came the rather terse reply.

"When you fell down the stairs, where was dad?"

"I've no idea where your father was Grace, now stop going on about it. The way you are carrying on, anybody would think that your dad had pushed me down the ruddy stairs".

Grace stared at Philip and in turn Philip stared at Grace. The staring competition had reached its fourth second when the nurse returned carrying a large glass vase of flowers.

"There we are," the nurse said as she gently placed the vase on a small wooden cabinet next to the bed. Philip turned to admire the vase of flowers as the nurse walked away, allowing Grace to claim a moral victory of sorts.

"Is your dad getting you both up for school?"

"No, I am." Grace said. "Dad asked me to stay at home until you got home."

"Well I should be home in a couple of days, they just want some swelling at the base of my spine to go down before they can discharge me. What about your paper round Philip, did you do it tonight?"

"No mum, not tonight. I told Mr Underwood this morning that I was visiting you tonight and that I couldn't do it. He said that one of the other boys could do it."

"Well you don't have to come and visit me again, I'll be back home in a couple of days. Don't want you losing your job over this."

"I won't mum."

After some more discussion around getting to bed on time, eating a good breakfast, cleaning their teeth, having a bath and keeping the house tidy, it was almost time to go. Both Philip and James were keen to get back home. The first international episode of 'It's a Knockout' was on at eight o' clock, with a team from Bristol representing the UK. They all got up to leave and gave their mother a kiss. As the two boys walked away, their mother kept hold of Grace's hand until they were both out of earshot.

"Grace, just try and keep out of your dad's way until I get home okay. Things will be different soon, I promise."

Grace nodded, smiled and gave her mother another kiss before catching up with her brothers.

As they passed the visitors waiting room, Philip noticed the door to the room directly opposite was half open. He glanced inside and saw the old man from the waiting room crouched forward with his head in his hands and a nurse sitting next to him with her arm around his shoulders.

Chapter 28

No matter how you viewed it. No matter the angle that you approached it from. You could sneak up behind it, on tiptoes, in the dead of night. You could dress it up any way you liked. You could even put a nice satin bow around it, pink in colour. The fact however remained the same. A goalless draw at home to Manchester United was about as satisfying as last night's leftovers, as comforting as standing in the queue for the nit nurse and as aesthetically pleasing as Albert Steptoe's front room. The only crumbs of comfort to be gleamed from such an awful result were the facts that they were still top of the table and still unbeaten. These crumbs of comfort however were very small indeed, crumbs that a pigeon on a paved patio carrying a magnifying glass would have great difficulty in locating. The simple truth was that Manchester United, the current Manchester United, were a poor side. They were not the conquering European winners of a few seasons ago, they were not even the same side as two years ago. They had already tasted defeat this season at the hands of Leicester City, twice, Arsenal and Ipswich Town. The genius that once was George Best was now well past his best and a faint, just visible shadow of the player he once was. The legendary Bobby Charlton was no longer in the squad; nor was the great Dennis Law. And no matter how hard they tried or how well they performed on an individual basis, even the likes of Brian Kidd, Sammy McIlroy and Willie Morgan, all good footballers in their own right, could not transform or inspire what was quite frankly little more than an average team.

Philip was standing in the newsagents with a paper bag full of 'Coventry Evening Telegraphs' resting against his legs. He and another paperboy were waiting for the 'Pinks' to be delivered to the shop when the door swung open and Paul McBride walked in.

"Alright Paul," Philip said.

"Not really Phil," Paul replied, shaking his head as he did so.

"What's up?"

"Oh, you wouldn't believe it, you just wouldn't believe it, I still can't believe it and I was there. We threw away a two goal lead. We were strolling it Phil, they were shit. Then out of nothing, halfway through the second half we gift them a goal, their first shot on target the whole game. All of a sudden it's a different game, they now believe that they can get something out of the game. We stopped playing, lost our way totally. All of a sudden it was Newcastle United against Ken sodding Dodd's diddy men. Then they go and grab a point in the last minute, the last bloody minute. If it wasn't for the fact that I sneaked in, I would have demanded my money back. John Fuckin Tudor in the ninetieth minute. Geordie twat."

"Language!" Mr Underwood shouted from behind the counter. "If you are going to use profanities like that young man, then take it outside."

"Pro what?" Paul asked, scratching his head as he spoke, before adding "What about your bunch of queers, how did they get on, I haven't seen any results yet."

"Bout the same as you, drew nil – nil against Manchester United."

"What, you're joking, you couldn't even beat them? Were you at home or away?"

With his head bowed, Philip replied. "We were at home."

Paul's head was still set on disbelief auto shake when the door opened and two further paperboys entered the shop. Their heads in turn nodded in acknowledgement of their fellow paperboys as they went to collect their papers.

"The Pinks are late." Philip said as they squeezed past.

"I'm not surprised they're late. The City match reporter is probably still crying into his notebook," Paul said.

As he spoke, the newsagents' door swung open again and a rather red faced, disgruntled looking delivery driver tossed a bundle of 'Pinks' into the shop. The door immediately slammed shut and no sooner had the bundle landed on the floor and slid to a stop, than the driver was back in his van and racing towards his next drop off.

Mr Underwood came out from behind his counter. He was carrying a small Stanley knife in his hand. He bent down and sliced apart the metal strip that had been holding the bundle of Pinks together. "Okay boys, come and collect your Pinks and then get your skates on, we are all running a bit late tonight."

Philip took the opportunity to take one more Pink than he needed before picking up his bag and quickly stepping outside the shop. Once outside he folded the 'Pinks' and put them inside his bag. Paul was next to exit the shop, only a matter of seconds behind Philip. As he stood next to him and took in the evening air, Philip foraged inside his paperbag.

"Here you go, something to help get over your disappointment," Philip said as he passed Paul a Fry's Chocolate Cream.

"Cheers Phil, when did you inch that, I didn't even see you move, did you palm it before I got there?"

Philip didn't reply, he just looked straight ahead as the rest of the paperboys filed out of the shop and set off on their respective rounds.

"Seriously Phil dude, that is a real gift that you have there. You don't want to be wasting it on chocolate bars and comics, you need to be thinking bigger." Paul was just about to set off on his round when he added, with a mouthful of Fry's Chocolate Cream. "How's your mum?"

"Oh she's okay." Philip replied.

"Is she out of hospital yet?"

"Yes, she came home on Thursday, it wasn't anything serious. How did you know that she was in hospital?"

"I was in the offie at the Livvy last night getting some sweets when that woman, don't know her name, the alcy, you know the one, she lives near you, always stripping off, she was in there with her daughter, buying some fags and vodka and she was going on about it."

"What do you mean, going on about it, going on about what?"

"Bout your dad pushing her down the stairs."

Philip's face instantly shifted its expression to one of horror. It was as if an old tramp had just inserted a dirty, wet finger into his ear. With a segment of Fry's Chocolate Cream wedged halfway down his throat, he quickly responded.

"What, he didn't push 'er down the stairs, she slipped, who told you that he pushed her?"

"I just told you, the pisshead in the offie last night."

"But who told her, why is she going around saying things like that?"

"I don't know Phil, I didn't ask her. It's just what she was saying to the woman behind the counter when I walked in. Anyway, I had better go. Thanks for the chocolate, see you later."

"He didn't push her down the stairs," Philip called out as Paul set off to deliver his papers.

With the inside of his mouth sufficiently coated in Fry's Chocolate Cream, Philip shoved the empty wrapper into his coat pocket and marched off to deliver his papers. He marched as quickly as the weight of the paperbag would allow him so that he could get to Clennon Rise and his sister's flat as soon as possible. Once there and still struggling to contain his anger, he banged hard on the door several times. At least this sudden turn of events had taken his mind off of the football scores.

His patience ran out quicker than the good luck of a cat who had just stumbled into a dogs pound. His clenched fist was only moments away from once again connecting with the front door, when it swung open and Grace was standing in front of him.

"Hello Philip, what are you doing here?"

"What are you playing at Grace?" Philip began. "Why are you going around telling people that dad pushed mum down the stairs?"

"You what," was the rather startled response. "What are you talking about?"

"You know exactly what I am talking about Grace, exactly how many people have you told?"

Grace's eyes continued to widen as Philip spoke and she glared at her brother. She leant forward and took a firm hold of the fake fur lined hood of his Parka coat. With her hand clenched tightly Grace dragged Philip inside before frogmarching him down the hall, past the living room on the right and the kitchen on the left, the first bedroom on the right and the bathroom on the left before pushing him into the last room on the right.

"Ssshh," Grace said. "I'll be back in a minute." Moments later after going and closing the front door, Grace returned. "Keep your voice down." Grace began. "The baby's sleeping and I do not want everybody knowing our business. Now start at the start Philip because I don't know what you are going on about."

"You know what I am going on about, how many people have you told that dad pushed mum down the stairs?"

"I have already told you, I haven't told anybody."

"Then why was Claire Chase's mum telling anybody that would listen in the Live and Let Live last night?"

"I've no idea Philip and keep your voice down because if Karen hears you, then you might as well put it on the front page of the Telegraph."

"It's a bit late to worry about that now Grace, if everybody in the 'Live and Let Live' knew last night, then just how many people bloody well know by now, I can't believe you!"

"Philip, on mum's life, on my life, I haven't said anything to anybody. The stupid cow has obviously gone and decided this for herself so that she can gossip about somebody and be the bloody centre of attention, with her clothes on for a change."

Suddenly there was a knock at Grace's bedroom door. Grace looked directly at Philip and placed her finger over her lips before turning and opening the door.

"Grace," Karen said whilst trying to peer over Grace's shoulder and see who was in her room. As soon as Karen determined that it wasn't anybody of interest, she turned her attention back to Grace. "I'm just popping down Broad Park, Grace, to get some fags and a bottle of Cinzano, oh and a couple of Babychams for my mum, she's popping round in a bit. Can you listen out in case he wakes up, he shouldn't do, he's just had a big feed, I won't be long."

"Okay." Grace replied as she closed the door again and waited a few seconds with her head tilted towards the door. Once Grace was happy that Karen was out of range, she straightened up and turned her attention back to her brother.

"Listen Philip, I think that maybe, just maybe, dad did push mum down the stairs. Let's face it, they don't exactly get on anymore and that is putting it nicely. But I haven't said anything to another living soul, except you."

"Well where would she get it from?"

"I don't know Philip, probably nowhere. Dad might have even mentioned to one of the neighbours that mum had fallen down the stairs. They mention it to somebody who mentions it to somebody and it eventually reaches her. She then chooses to fabricate what she has heard so that she can get some attention."

"But what if dad hears about it?"

"Then she'll get what she deserves, the nasty cow. That's if he does find out, you know what he thinks about the type of people that drink in the Livvy. According to dad, they're either Irish, alcoholics or benefit cheats and in most cases all three. And anyway you are forgetting one very important thing, even the cliental of the Livvy don't believe what she says; they all know what she's like. I suggest you go and finish your paper round before you find yourself delivering more of yesterday's news and then get yourself off home. If you do hear anything else though, make sure that you let me know."

Philip gathered up his bag of newspapers and as he was leaving the flat Grace asked "Do you know when mum's next hospital appointment is?"

"No," Philip replied.

"Try and find out if you can. Ask mum. That's if it's worth her going. They'll probably just keep on giving her more pills instead of actually trying to help her."

Philip didn't reply, he just made his way down the stairs and back outside beneath the darkening skies.

Chapter 29

Philip found himself in familiar surroundings, familiar in relation to both time and space. It was Monday morning and he was once more standing in Mr Spencer's office, in front of Mr Spencer's desk. He had just handed over his conduct card from the previous week and was patiently awaiting a response. Mr Spencer was taking far too much time for Philip's liking and he had already turned the card over at least three times, inspecting the signatures on both the front and the back of the card. Eventually Mr Spencer placed the card carefully on the desk in front of him, puffed up and blew out his cheeks, sat back in his chair and looked up at Philip.

"Well then, the fact that I have this particular conduct card in front of me can only mean one of three things. Firstly you and I Knott have entered some kind of parallel universe, a different dimension in the galaxy, set adrift to spend the rest of our days floating aimlessly away from the universe that we are more familiar with. However, seeing as that particular scenario is highly unlikely, after considering all the facts, I think that we can safely dismiss it and turn our attention to the second option, wouldn't you agree Philip?"

Philip though it would be best to refrain from saying exactly what it was he was thinking and just nod his head in agreement.

Mr Spencer continued "The second option being that the card that I have had presented to me on this fine September morning is actually a forgery." Mr Spencer paused and stared hard at Philip for a few seconds, looking for some kind of reaction. Philip stood firm on this occasion, Like Alec Guinness in 'The Bridge On The River Kwai'.

"Yes Philip, you heard me right, a forgery. Some of you boys think that we dumb teachers haven't got a clue what goes on in our own school. Well I am sorry to disappoint you but not only do I know what goes on but I can also tell you who the best forgers of teachers' signatures, and I also know how much they charge for their services.

Shaking his head from side to side Philip muttered. "I don't know anything about that Sir, I've never been offered one," whilst attempting to look as innocent as possible, although as he did so, he convinced himself that he wasn't doing a very good job. It was a little like the policeman in the street scenario. Whenever you see a policeman on the beat walking towards you down the high street, no matter how hard you try, you can't help feeling that the expression on your face suggests that you have just committed the most heinous of crimes.

Mr Spencer picked the conduct card up from his desk and looked over the top of it, directly at Philip. "Based upon your rather botched attempt to sabotage one of your previous conduct cards, I'm inclined to believe you on this occasion." Mr Spencer paused, and continued after a deep breath. "So that just leaves us with option number three and this one is by far the most unbelievable and unimaginable of the three options. This option would suggest that you actually listened for once. That you actually took on board what I said and I am actually holding a genuine conduct card in my hand, a conduct card without a single, solitary, Unsatisfactory emblazed upon it."

Mr Spencer folded the card carefully and placed it back on his desk. "However, I don't want you thinking that you are out of the woods just yet. Because I can assure you, every direction that you care to look in, all you can see is trees. The precarious ice upon which you currently stand is thinner than a flea's eyebrow. Are we clear?"

Philip nodded. "Yes Sir." He said.

"Because if I see you in my office again or hear of you receiving a detention chit between now and half-term, you'll be back on a conduct card quicker than it takes Yul Brenner to get a haircut."

Philip replied with a slightly sarcastic laugh before picking up his bag and turning to leave Mr Spencer's office.

"What's your hurry Knott?" Mr Spencer asked. "I believe we made a deal. Instead of wasting your life in detention tomorrow, I suggest that you bring your swimming kit to school. Be at the pool at home time and don't be late."

"Yes Sir," Philip said as he picked up his bag again and made his second attempt to leave Mr Spencer's office. However just like Angus Lennie's dash for freedom in 'The Great Escape', it was to no avail.

"Have you thought any more about this outward bound trip to Wales in the New Year?" Mr Spencer asked.

"Yes Sir, I'd like to go, I think I might be able to save the money and my sister said she would help."

"I tell you what." Mr Spencer said as he opened a drawer of his desk and took out a plain white card. "Why don't you bring what you can each week and I'll keep a record of it on this card. Where are you going to get the money from, did you say?"

"I have the money from my paper round and my sister works at Woolworths."

"Okay Philip, come and see me at the start of each week and give me as much as you can. Fifty pence a week should just about cover it, think you can manage that?"

"I think so." Philip replied.

Mr Spencer stood up, walked around his desk and opened his office door. "And don't forget your swimming kit tomorrow," he added as Philip collected his bag for a third time and finally left the office.

Tomorrow couldn't arrive quickly enough for Philip, except that is for the lump-in-the- throat, break-into-a sweat-moment which occurred after lunch on Tuesday, when he was asked for his conduct card at the start of his geography lesson.

"I'm not on one this week sir."

"Why not?"

"I didn't get an Unsatisfactory signature last week sir."

Philip's geography teacher stood up from behind his desk and walked towards Philip. He was wearing a plain brown shirt, beige slacks and a beige corduroy jacket with dark brown leather elbow patches. Also from the autumn collection, he was sporting a rather puzzled expression. "Are you sure, I'm sure I gave you an unsatisfactory last Thursday and as I recall there was already an Unsatisfactory on your card from the day before."

Philip quickly reacted. "No sir, I think you are thinking of the week before, I got a couple of Unsatisfactory's that week. Perhaps you are mixing me up with somebody else."

With the puzzled expression still evident and standing over Philip at the front of his desk, his teacher said "No, no Knott, I 'm not mixing you up with anybody else. Well so be it, if you are not on a card then you are not on a card. We need to get on with the lesson, so I suggest that you attempt to avoid earning yourself a fresh card today."

Thankfully the rest of the lesson and the following lesson passed by without further incident and as soon as the bell went for the end of the school day, Philip quickly headed for the swimming pool. As he approached the entrance to the pool, he noticed Mr Spencer and another man standing in the doorway.

"This is Mr Kennedy, Philip. I've asked him along to watch you swim. He's the head coach and Coventry Godiva."

"I haven't got long sir," Philip replied. "I need to get back home for my paper round."

"Then you'd better get a move on hadn't you lad. Believe it or not, but we haven't got all day either. We'll see you in the pool in two minutes."

Philip quickly vanished inside the changing room and equally as quickly, he disrobed and put on his trunks. He left his clothes in a pile on the bench, as tidy as the inside of hippy's rucksack and made his way poolside. On exiting the changing room, the comforting smell of the pool clambered inside his nostrils. On catching sight of the water, he breathed in deeply and exhaled slowly, before stepping towards the edge of the pool. Mr Spencer and Mr Kennedy were standing at the side of the pool.

Mr Kennedy asked. "What's your favourite stroke… Philip is it?"

"Yes," Philip replied. I like freestyle but I also like the butterfly."

"Who taught you?" Mr Kennedy asked.

"Nobody," Philip replied.

Rather taken aback by Philip's response, Mr Kennedy asked. "Nobody, then how did you learn to do the butterfly?"

"I just watched it on TV."

"You learnt how to do the butterfly by watching it on TV and do you think you are good at it?"

"I don't know." Philip said as he shrugged his shoulders. "You didn't ask me what I was good at, you asked me what my favourite strokes were."

"Don't be rude Knott," Mr Spencer interjected.

"I tell you what Philip, give me a few lengths of freestyle to start with and we will have a look at your butterfly in a while. Did you learn how to turn by watching TV as well?"

"No, I'm not very good at turning, especially in the shallow end."

"Well don't worry about your turns and don't try and break any of Mark Spitz's records. Just swim at a gentle pace for me so that I can get a good look at your action okay?"

Philip nodded and prepared to dive in.

"Okay, go on my whistle. Are you ready?"

Philip nodded again and waited for the whistle. The sound of rang out and he sprang forward from the pool's edge and dived into the cool water. As soon as the tips of his fingers broke through the surface, a warm contented glow swept through his body and towards his feet. Once fully submerged, the pool once again seemed to fit itself around him like a made to measure, high-end suit. By the time he resurfaced he was already halfway down the pool. Three effortless strokes later and he had reached the far end. One slightly awkward turn and he was on his way back towards the shallow end. He caught sight of Mr Kennedy watching his every action as he swam past. Another slightly more awkward turn in the shallow end and he was once more gliding serenely through the water.

After swimming a few more lengths, Mr Kennedy ushered Philip over to the side of the pool. He took his time to speak, gliding his index finger back and forth across his chin as Philip patiently waited in the water for his assessment.

"We can work on the head and your arms are a fraction too high, would cost you valuable time, especially in a short race but it wouldn't take a lot to address that. What is your best time for fifty metres?"

"I don't know," Philip replied. "I've never been timed officially."

"Well that doesn't matter now, we can soon sort that out. Right then, let us have a quick look at this self-taught butterfly of yours."

Philip made his way back to the shallow end of the pool and climbed out of the water.

"Ready?" Mr Kennedy asked.

"Ready." Philip replied.

"On my whistle."

Mr Kennedy blew and Philip once more dived into the pool. As soon as he resurfaced his arms began to rotate in perfect unison, coming over his shoulders, crashing into the surface of the water, disappearing beneath the surface and then almost instantly reappearing as one. After just a couple of lengths this time around, Mr Kennedy's whistle found itself once more perched between his lips. A short shrill sound immediately followed and echoed around the pool. Philip came to a stop before swimming over to the side of the pool. As he reached the edge, Mr Kennedy stepped a little closer and looked down at Philip.

"You've got a good T.V," he said.

"We rent it," Philip replied.

"We need to have a better look at you in a bigger pool. We train every Wednesday night at 6pm."

"I can't come then," Philip replied. "My dad doesn't leave for work until then and anyway he wouldn't let me come as I have to look after my younger brother."

"When we're not competing we also train on a Sunday morning at 9am. Can you make it then?"

Philip quickly thought it through. 'Get up, do paper round, go home, have breakfast, get kit, catch bus'. "Yes, I can come on Sunday," he said.

"You're a bit raw around the edges and a bit shy when it comes to finesse but swimming isn't all about finesse and you have potential. You need to become a member of the club before you are eligible for selection and able to compete but that is another thing we can get to."

Philip decided against highlighting that particular obstacle at that particular moment and just nodded his head.

"When you arrive just tell the lady at the desk that you are here to try out for the swim team, so that she doesn't try and charge you. And don't be late, we don't do late, and don't be late for your paper round either. I'll see you on Sunday."

Chapter 30

As soon as Philip opened the back door and stepped into the living room, he immediately spotted the gleaming white envelope being propped up by the salt and pepper pots on the dining table at the far end of the room. As James allowed his school bag to fall to the floor before he himself flopped onto the sofa, Philip pushed past him and rushed over to pick up the letter. Even though it was not at an ideal angle, before he had even reached the table, Philip could tell that it was from Billy. With the envelope firmly clasped in his hand, he rushed out of the room and headed upstairs to get changed out of his uniform. Minutes later he reappeared, still clutching the letter. He raced through the living room, through the kitchen, into the scullery and out again, with his paper bag in one hand and the letter in the other. Once out into the crescent, he threw the bag over his shoulder, to free up both hands and with giddy, heart-racing excitement, he carefully began to open the letter.

Dear Philip,

How nice it was to hear from you again. Your kind and positive words were as always an inspiration. Unfortunately, on this particular occasion we were unable to live up to both your hopes and the high standards that we set ourselves. As I am sure you can imagine, we were all very disappointed in the dressing room after the Manchester United game. It was a very frustrating ninety minutes for us all. They clearly came with a game plan and to be fair to them, they executed it very well. I am sure that their manager was very happy with the final score. Teams will often adopt a defensive approach against us and are happy to play with nine or ten players behind the ball. I have the utmost respect for these tactics, although it has to be said, it is not especially enjoyable to watch. However it is up to us to find a way through and try to break them down.

To say that both Peter and Norman were rather cross in the dressing room after the game is putting it very politely! However they both felt that we had two good shouts for penalties. Norman felt, as he put it, that the referee had "lost his bottle", especially with the second shout as it was so close to the end of the game. I have to admit, I couldn't really see the first incident when Peter was brought down as I was too far away but there were certainly strong claims for the second one as Norman was clearly clattered from behind. At the end of the day though, you cannot go relying on referees to help you win football matches. We didn't create enough chances and we weren't good enough on the day, it's as simple as that. What we have to do now as a team is to take the positives out of the game and turn our attention to the next, away at Norwich. We need to focus on the facts that we are still top of the league and we are still unbeaten.

As I have said, on Saturday we didn't take our opportunities when they came along and I am rather concerned that when it comes to you and your swimming, you are in danger of doing the same. If your teacher is presenting you with an opportunity to swim, then you must grab it with both hands. The current situation may well change with your dad's job and you may yet get the chance to join the swimming club; if that chance does come along then you need to be ready. I know this only to well as I speak from experience. When I was growing up, I had a very close friend back home in Stirling. We played for the same teams together as we grew up. Everybody called him Tavi. To be honest, for a long while he was a much better player than me. Tavi was small like me but skinny. The kind of kid that if he turned sideways, you had to reach out and feel for him. But boy was he quick, a natural winger if ever there was one. Still to this day, with the exception of Johnny Giles, I've never seen anybody who could cross a ball the way Tavi could. Whether he was standing still or was in full flight, he could just wrap his foot perfectly around that ball and send over the most delightful of crosses. However, there came a time when he seemed to lose interest, he started to miss training and matches; he became unreliable. 'Other fish to fry Billy' he used to say to me. When the day came and the scouts came calling, I was prepared and I was picked to sign for Leeds; Tavi wasn't. Things turned sour after That. I moved away and down to Yorkshire and Tavi continued to play local league football. He had a couple of trials for some Scottish clubs, so I heard, but nobody signed him up. With local league football you don't get the protection or a proper physio. A few too many bad tackles and playing on poor quality pitches ruined him and ruined his knees. He had to stop playing at the age of 22. That is no age for a career to be over, especially when you were once as good as he was. He would have played for Scotland, no doubt about it. So please just keep this in mind as sometimes in life a chance may only come along the once and you may never know when you have missed it.

Sorry to hear that you mother is still finding life a struggle. In such difficult times all you can do is be strong and be there for her. At least you have a big family occasion just around the corner with your sister's 18th birthday. It is moments like these when families can find joy and strength in each other, which in turn can help us to get through challenging moments in life. I hope that you all enjoy the day, especially Grace, and I hope that we have a positive result at Norwich on Saturday.

Write again soon Philip.

Your friend,

Billy.

Philip's already meandering pace came to a complete stop at the bottom of Monkswood Crescent. He stood and stared at the letter in his hand until his eyes began to water and the words began to dissolve on the page. Before they had disappeared completely and fearing that they would be lost forever, Philip wiped his eyes with the sleeve of his coat and carefully folded the letter. Once it was safely back in the envelope, Philip placed it safely inside his paperbag before crossing the Henley Road and continuing on his way to the newsagents.

As he entered the shop, Paul McBride turned and looked him straight in the eye.

"Where you been dude, I've been havin to make up some right shit excuses to hang about. I've tied my shoelaces three times and I've even tucked my shirt in. Hurry up, I'll see you outside."

Paul picked up his bag, marched past Philip and out through the newsagent's door, leaving it to swing shut by itself. As it closed Mr Underwood appeared from the back of the shop.

"Where have you been? I'd almost given up on you! Your papers are over there, all ready to go. I suggest you get a move on, we don't have all night."

Philip walked over to the counter and the large stack of newspapers waiting for him. Thursday night was the worst night of the week. It wasn't quite as bad as Sunday morning in relation to bulk and thickness of the papers needing to be delivered, but it wasn't far short. Thursday night was classified night and forty two extra thick 'Coventry Evening Telegraphs' waited to be stuffed inside Philip's paperbag.

Being extra careful not to damage his letter, Philip loaded up his bag until the stitching began to stretch. With a deep breath, he heaved the bag onto his shoulder and made his way out of the shop. Once outside he walked over to the impatiently waiting Paul. He let his bag slip off his shoulder and onto the floor below and reached into his coat pocket. He retrieved two Bar Six and passed one over to Paul. Paul smiled and without any words being exchanged, he reached inside his jacket pocket, took out a folded piece of paper and passed it to Philip.

"What's this?" Philip asked

"It's whatever you want it to be Philly boy," Paul replied as he waited for Philip to take the piece of paper from his hand. "It's just a list of words, or a shopping list, a wish list, an opportunity, an earner, it's up to you Phil."

"I don't follow," Philip replied as his curiosity won out and he relieved Paul of the piece of paper that was still hanging between his fingers.

"I've told you before Phil, you have a talent but as I have also said, it is wasted, get my drift," Paul said as he waved the recently stolen bar of chocolate in Philip's direction.

Philip looked at the piece of paper, then at Paul and then back at the piece of paper. It read.

'Box of Black Magic chocolates 'large'
Travel alarm clock
Old Spice gift set
Dressing gown 'pink'
Cliff Richard LP 'Cliff Live in Japan'
Space Hopper
Pocket transistor radio
View master Projector
Evil Knievel stunt cycle
Fishing reel
Foot pump
Guinness book of records
Panasonic cassette recorder'.

"Don't hang about for too long though Phil, things don't stay on the list for long."

"But I don't understand," Philip replied. "Who wants these things?"

"Get real Phil, all sorts of people. Lads like you and me that need to get presents for people but can't afford the full price. Lads desperate to get further than squeezing tits over the bra. People who need things for their holidays or just need a new one of whatever it is. Others just want them because they want them but like I say, times are hard for a lot of people at the moment and they can't afford the shop price. This is where people like us come in but things won't stay on the list for ever. I mean who would want two Cliff Richard LP's?"

Philip took another look at Paul and attempted to pass the piece of paper back. Paul however picked up his bag and began to unwrap his Bar Six. He raised it up a little in Philip's direction as he did so.

"Look Phil, it's up to you, every item you manage to get and I can sell on, we split the proceeds fifty fifty. Anyway, I've got to go, these papers are not going to deliver themselves."

It wasn't until later that evening when Philip and James were in bed, that Philip could get a better, more considered look at the items on the list. After returning home from his paper round, he had gone straight upstairs and placed the piece of paper along with his letter from Billy, under his pillow. Now with his dad in the pub and his mother having been in to say goodnight, he was able to retrieve the piece of paper from under his pillow and take a longer look.

As the light in the room began to fade, Philip found himself looking from the list to the letter and back again as if he was watching Vitas Gerulaitis and Jimmy Connors trading shots on centre court. However, he found himself being continually drawn to one particular line of the letter before turning his attention back to the list. The line that he could not draw his attention away from read 'sometimes in life a chance may only come along once'.

"What are you up to?" James called out form the bunk below.

"Nothing," Philip replied. "Go to sleep," he said before adding. "Where would you get a foot pump from?"

"You what?"

"A foot pump, where would you go if you wanted to buy a foot pump?"

Philip waited for a reply but all remained silent in the bunk below. Philip leaned over the edge of his bunk and looked at James. "Do you know where a fishing tackle shop is?" he muttered.

"No." James replied. "But I don't think they would sell foot pumps."

Philip flopped back onto his pillow. "Just go to sleep James", he said.

Philip closed his eyes. As the ever-increasing darkness galloped towards them, he slowly drifted towards sleep.

"So you think you can swim?"

Philip turned and looked at the man standing next to him at the edge of the pool. He had short shimmering thick black hair and a thick black moustache. He was wearing a dark blue pair of swimming trunks with dark blue goggles to match. A rolled up white towel was draped around his neck and was being gripped tight at both ends. Philip turned away and looked down at the water.

'Mark Spitz'. he thought to himself. 'It's Mark Spitz'.

"Want to race then lad?"

Philip looked back in the direction of Mark Spitz. He attempted to reply but the words he tried to get out lodged themselves fast in the back of his throat, allowing only enough room for air to still pass through. So he just nodded instead.

"You'd better put that letter down then, you'll get it wet," Mark said as he removed the towel from around his neck and tossed it behind him.

Philip looked down and discovered that he was holding the letter from Billy in his hand. He glanced around the edge of the pool a couple of times before he noticed the envelope resting upon a starting block a few feet behind him. He turned and walked over to the starting block. He carefully returned the letter to the envelope before making his way back to the edge of the pool.

"Ready now?" Mark enquired.

Now able to speak, Philip replied. "Yes."

"Then choose your stroke?"

"Butterfly," Philip said.

"One length of the pool. I'll give you a ten stroke head start."

Philip nodded, edged forward slightly, curled his toes over the side of the pool and got himself set.

"On the count of four, okay." Mark said.

"Okay." Philip replied.

There was a moment's silence within which Philip could hear his heart beating.

"One, two, three, four, go."

Philip sprang forward and crashed through the surface of the water. As soon as he resurfaced, he began to count his strokes whilst listening out for the sound of Mark Spitz diving into the pool. He swam as hard as he could but the other end of the pool seemed to remain just as far away as when he had set off. He could hear the swimmer behind him getting ever closer, until he could see their arms out of the corner of his eye. However as the swimmer glided effortlessly past, it was no longer Mark Spitz and was now Mr Spencer.

By the time that Philip finally reached the other end of the pool, Mr Spencer was already out of the water and sitting poolside with a rolled up towel draped across his shoulders. He looked down at a red faced, out of breath Philip.

"Both hands lad. When chances come along in life, you need to grab them with both hands," Mr Spencer said before getting up and slowly walking away, leaving Philip all alone in the pool.

Chapter 31

"But you've got to have a party!" Karen exclaimed passionately. She was standing in the kitchen with her arms folded, leaning with her back resting against the sink. On the cooker was a pan of water and in the pan was a baby's bottle three quarters full of milk.

Grace was standing in front of the small kitchen table with her back to the cooker, buttering two slices of toast.

"What are you going to do if you don't have a party?" Karen asked.

"I was just gonna go down the Livvy," Grace replied.

Karen found herself somewhat horrified by the reply. "You what? The Livvy? On your eighteenth! With all those old soaks! You were planning on spending your eighteenth in the bloody Livvy. You're not even gonna go down the town?"

Grace continued to busily butter her toast. Once completed, she placed the knife on the table, picked up one of the now buttered slices, took a big bite and whilst still holding the toast in her hand, turned and exited the kitchen.

"I'm gonna be late for work," she called out as she headed down the hallway and into the bathroom. She reappeared some fifteen minutes later, wrapped in a bath towel and minus her slice of toast. Karen was waiting in the hallway.

"I'll arrange it," Karen said. "We can still go the Livvy for a few if you like, then we can come back here. I can grab my dad's record player. Can you get hold of a couple of LPs from work and take them back on Monday?"

"It's not a library Karen, it's Woolworths."

"That's a good idea," Karen said. "They have LPs at the library in Bell Green."

"Oh yeah they do," Grace said as she shook her head. "Several classic albums by Beethoven and Mozart, a country and western compilation LP featuring the likes of Jim Reeves and Slim Whitman, two Cliff Richard LPs and a scratched Mungo Jerry LP if the Jamaican guy who usually borrows it has remembered to take it back."

Grace crossed the hallway and this time disappeared into her bedroom, closing the door behind her as she did so. When she reappeared another fifteen minutes or so later, in her Woolworths uniform and with a damp towel draped over her arm, the hallway was deserted. Grace headed towards the kitchen in search of her second piece of toast, dropping the damp towel off in the bathroom en route. She picked up the now cold piece of toast before quickly popping into the living room of the flat. Karen was now sitting in the armchair next to the television, giving her little boy his morning bottle. A smouldering cigarette rested in the ashtray which in turn rested upon one of the arms of the armchair.

"I'm off, I'll see you later," Grace said.

"So, are we having this party or not?" Karen replied.

"I don't know," Grace replied as she turned and disappeared out of sight.

"But I need to know," Karen called out. "I need to go and get the record player." Grace didn't reply; instead all that Karen heard was the sound of the front door slamming shut.

Philip was sitting at the dining table in the living room. He was casually flicking through the pages of his recently illegally acquired copy of 'Shoot' magazine whilst patiently waiting for his sausage sandwich to arrive. James was sitting on the settee at the other end of the room, watching an episode of 'The Banana Splits'. Francis Knott was in the kitchen, cooking the aforementioned sausages. Back in the living room, three plates sat upon the table. On each plate were two slices of buttered bread, to which tomato sauce had been liberally applied.

Philip was about a third of the way through an interview with Chelsea player Peter Bonetti and his hopes for the England team in qualifying for next summer's World Cup, when Francis entered from the kitchen, carrying a frying pan crammed full with sizzling sausages. 'The Banana Splits' appeared to deflate in acknowledgement of defeat as James's attention instantly shifted towards the sounds coming from the pan in Francis's hand. He leapt from the sofa and followed his dad towards the dining table. Francis dished out the plump, shiny sausages before placing the empty pan on top of a placemat in the middle of the table. Just as Philip was carefully lining his sausages up to a satisfactory standard on one of his slices of bread, his mother shouted down from her bedroom.

Francis Frowned. "Go and see what your mum wants Philip but be quick cos if your sandwich starts to go cold, then your brother and me are eating it," he said before sinking his teeth into the soft warm sandwich he had in his hands.

Philip covered his symmetrically positioned sausages with the other slice of his bread, got up from the table and made his way upstairs. As he entered the bedroom his senses were mugged by a stale odour that was screaming out for a day off. It made his nose twitch and his eyes water at the same time. He managed to keep his mouth closed tight so that it was unable to crawl down the back of his throat. His mother was sitting up in the bed.

"Open the curtains for me Philip," his mother asked.

To the odour's dismay and disbelief, Philip shut the bedroom door and with it blocked out the shaft of light that was coming from the landing. He walked across the room and opened the curtains before turning to look at his mother. He was slightly taken aback when he gazed at her. Her skin looked pale and almost translucent with the sun now shining upon it. Her eyes were dull and devoid of any remnants of shimmer or sparkle and her hair lay flat and lifeless down the side of her face.

His mother looked back at him and attempted a smile as she gently patted the bed for him to sit down.

"So, how's school?" she said in a soft voice as Philip walked towards her and sat down. As he did so his mother tentatively rubbed the back of his head.

"It's fine," Philip replied.

"Keeping out of trouble?"

"Yes mum, I'm fine."

"Are you going swimming today?"

"No, not today. I was thinking about going tomorrow after my paper round."

"Oh, but you normally go on a Saturday."

"Yeah I know, but Sunday's are so boring, especially now grandad doesn't get to visit as much as he used to. So I thought that I would go tomorrow instead."

Philip's grandad on his mother's side was a kind and gentle, softly spoken man who, during the later years of his life, had taken immense pleasure in visiting his grandchildren as often as he could. He lived in Ledbury on the edge of the Malvern Hills and he would travel over every fortnight on the Midland Red. He would set off very early in the morning and would arrive back home very late in the evening. He would come armed with a bag of sweets for each of his grandchildren, a comic each for the two boys, a girl's magazine for Grace and a shiny ten pence piece for each of them. However in recent times and especially since the turn of the year, his health had begun to suffer somewhat and the journey itself involved a lot of travelling on several buses. Firstly from Ledbury to Worcester, then Worcester to Bromsgrove, Bromsgrove to Birmingham, Birmingham to Coventry and a final bus from Coventry bus station to Henley Green. He would be able to stop for a few hours before setting off to make the long journey back again. When he did visit, Francis tended to stay in the pub for the majority of the lunchtime session before returning home and sleeping off what he had just spent the previous three hours consuming. This was on account of being reminded several times over the years that he hadn't been good enough for the woman he married.

"We could go and visit grandad if you want."

"I'd like that." Philip replied.

"Maybe we can go tomorrow." his mother said before pausing and then adding, "No, we can't go tomorrow, it's your sister's birthday."

The odour in the room clung to Philip like a limpet on its favourite rock. He stood up and walked over to the window, opening it upon arrival and embracing the morning air as it pushed past and began to fill the space behind him. He stood for a moment to feel the cool morning breeze rest upon his skin before turning and walking back over to his mother. He sat down again. Whilst he was opening the window his mother had reached under her pillow and taken out a small brown purse that she was now holding in her hands. Pulling the metal clasp apart, she opened the purse and peered inside. The tips of her fingers disappeared inside the purse, before re-emerging, clasping hold of three, one pound notes.

"Can you take this?" she said, passing the money over to Philip. "Can you go into town and get your sister a bottle of Charlie perfume. Make sure that it's Charlie mind and can you also get a birthday card from her dad and me. I guess you haven't got her a card yet?"

Philip shook his head as he took hold of the money.

"Well there should be enough left to get her a card from you and your brother. And get a sheet of wrapping paper as well, nice wrapping paper, not some with racing cars or footballs on it. You may still have enough left over to get yourself some lunch from the Wimpy or Fishy Moors. Now put that money in your pocket and don't lose it."

Philip stood up and pushed the money deep into one of the pockets of his flared jeans before sitting down again.

"Have you had breakfast?"

"Not yet, it's downstairs, dad made us sausage sandwiches."

"I don't suppose he made one for me, did he?" His mother asked.

"I don't think so mum but I can make you one," Philip replied.

"Yes please sweetheart that would be lovely."

Philip stood up and made his way out of the room. With the stale odour still pressed up against him, he headed back down the stairs and into the living room. He entered the living room just as Francis was leaning over the dining table to take possession of Philip's sausage sandwich.

Managing to snatch his plate away just in time Philip asked. "Do we have any more sausages dad?"

"No." Francis replied.

Philip stood and held the plate which housed his sandwich and thought for a second or two before turning and heading back upstairs. As he re-entered his mother's room, the atmosphere within seemed to have lifted somewhat. The room felt brighter as the curtains ruffled in the breeze coming from the open window. Philip looked at his mother.

"There's no more sausages." He said. "But you can have mine, it's still warm."

"Why don't we share it?" His mother replied.

Philip sat back down on the bed. He took one of the sandwiches off the plate and then passed the plate to his mother. Halfway through his half of the sandwich, he turned and looked at his mother.

"Mum," He said, "can I ask you something?"

A moments silence was able to squeeze in between the subsiding odour and the morning breeze before his mother replied. "What's on your mind?"

"Are you getting better?" Philip asked.

His mum placed her half eaten sandwich down on the plate and looked directly at her son. She reached out and stroked the side of his face with the back of her fingers, letting out a little sigh as she did so. "I don't know," she said.

She could instantly detect by his expression that her response troubled Philip. "It's not really something that you can measure in such terms Philip. It's not like a cold or an ingrowing toenail. I don't have something that you can see getting better or feel getting better. It's just not that simple, I am sorry to say."

"Dad says that you are just unhappy."

"I'm afraid that your dad doesn't understand, or he just refuses to understand. But I suppose that in a way he may be right. I'm very unhappy but not in the way he thinks or means, and it is not because of you or your brother either."

Silence once again took centre stage for a minute or two whilst they both finished their respective sandwiches. As soon as they had both finished, Philip asked, "Do you want a cup of tea mum?"

"Oh yes please, that would be lovely," his mother replied.

Philip picked up the empty plate and went back downstairs. As he entered the living room Francis was in the process of clearing away the table.

"What are your plans for today?" Francis asked as they both headed towards the kitchen.

"Mum wants me to go to town and get something for Grace's birthday."

"Oh right," Francis replied. He placed the frying pan and the empty plates he was holding on the draining board and took his wallet out of his trouser pocket. He opened it and took out a one-pound note.

"Take this and get her something from you and James," he said as he passed the note to Philip. "Talking of your sister, do you know what time she starts work?"

"I'm not sure dad, I think she starts about half eight."

"Can you tidy up the kitchen and do the washing up before you go to town. I'm off out, got a few things to take care of, I'll see you later."

Philip hung about in the kitchen and waited to hear the sound of the front door opening and closing. He stacked the washing up in a neat pile before making his mum a cup of tea. He took the tea upstairs and opened the bedroom door, only to find that his mother had fallen asleep. He placed the cup of tea down on the small bedside table and as quietly as possible, he closed the bedroom window, pulled the curtains together and left the room, closing the door behind him as he did so. On returning to the living room, he found that James had himself returned to the sofa and was once again engrossed in the television.

"James," Philip said, however he didn't get a response.

"James!" He repeated, a little louder this time, but still nothing.

He called out again, only on this occasion the call was accompanied with a firm shove of the back of James's head.

"What?" James replied with a certain amount of annoyance in his voice.

"I'm going into town after I've done the washing up but I want you to stay here and look after mum."

"But I want to go to town," James replied.

"I'll pay you to stay at home."

"How much?"

"Twenty pence."

"Fifty pence."

"Thirty pence."

"Okay," said James. "But I want the money before you go."

"If anybody asks you though, you have to say that you wanted to stay at home, okay…OKAY!"

"Yeah okay," James said, still annoyed that he was being distracted from the programme he was trying to watch.

Philip shook his head before heading back into the kitchen to take care of the washing up. James turned his attention back to the television and the episode of 'Lizzie Dripping' that had just started on BBC 1.

Chapter 32

Francis Knott lay back in bed, one hand pressed between the back of his head and the plywood headboard, the other laid over the side of the bed with a Senior Service cigarette between his fingers. A thin wispy line of silver coloured smoke drifted upwards towards the ceiling. One leg was outstretched with his foot exposed towards the bottom of the bed; the other was bent at the knee. Semi naked, wearing just a white vest, he casually continued to smoke his cigarette. As he took one final long drag and stubbed it out in the ashtray that was resting on his stomach, the bedroom door swung open.

Carrying a mug of tea in each hand, Karen walked in. She passed one of the mugs to Francis before sitting down near the end of the bed. "You'll have to go when you've finished that," Karen said.

"Another customer?" Francis replied.

"No, I wasn't expecting any 'customers' this morning as you call it, not until you turned up unannounced. I have things to do."

"Like what?"

"None of your business, just finish your tea and piss off. Don't forget to leave the money before you go. You can have the tea for free, the other service you have to pay for."

Francis placed his mug down next to a small lamp with an orange flowered lampshade sitting on top of the small bedside chest of drawers. He reached across for his cigarettes and matches and lit up another Senior Service whilst the previously discarded one was still smouldering in the ashtray.

"No rush is there?" He said as he let the cigarette momentarily hang from his mouth unaided.

"Yes there is actually. I don't want you in my flat any longer than needs be and what if your daughter should walk in and find you here?"

"Yeah well you were the one that let her move in here. What on earth did you do that for?"

"You mean you haven't worked it out yet?" Karen asked as she turned her head to look at Francis. "She didn't want to move in here, she just wanted to move away from you."

Francis instantly felt the anger begin to swirl around inside him and race towards the surface, like a cork in a barrel of wine. "If Grace ever finds out about this…"

"You'll what?" Karen interrupted as she continued to stare at Francis.

"You'll find out soon enough and if you ever get her involved in anything like this."

"Oh right, that's just typical of somebody like you. It's okay for you and those other sad drunken soaks to come and shag someone like me because you don't want to sleep with your tired, miserable old wives anymore, but not your precious daughter."

Francis sat upright, tossed the blankets aside and began to get dressed, cigarette still hanging from his lips. "My Grace has got a future, a good job, can work her way up at Woolworths. What have you got? You're nothing! You come from nothing. Just look at your sorry excuse of a father. Never done an honest day's work in his life but he still managed to find the money to become an alcoholic! I wonder whose tax contributions paid for that?"

"Oh fuck off. Like you're any better than any of us. You've got a daughter that can't stand the sight of you and was so desperate to get away from you that she moved in here and a wife that hates you. Maybe you should be out buying your daughter a birthday present instead of coming here to spend your hard-earned money."

"And what are you going to do if I don't pay you?"

"And what will you do if I go and do some shopping in Woolworths?"

"You wouldn't dare."

"Wouldn't I?"

Francis rammed his half smoked cigarette down into the centre of the ashtray, sending a mixture of embers, ash and smoke into the air. He leapt towards Karen, grabbing her dressing gown firmly by the collar and pushed her against the bedroom wall. With his hand clasped tightly, he held her there and stared straight at her. Karen in turn attempted to look in every direction other than at Francis. Moments later both their attentions were distracted by the sound of Karen's baby boy crying in his cot in the corner of the room. Francis released his grip and Karen broke free before scampering over to the cot. She leant in and scooped her baby up in her arms and turned back around to look at Francis.

"You still here?" She said.

Francis removed his wallet from the back pocket of his trousers and opened it up. He removed the last two remaining pound notes and tossed them towards the bed, watching as they tumbled through the air before coming to rest on the blankets below. He then turned and left, slamming the bedroom door behind him as he did so. Karen, clutching her baby in her arms, stood and waited, listening out for the sound of the front door opening and closing. A solitary tear slid down the side of her nose and came to rest upon her top lip as she heard the front door slam shut.

Francis arrived back home about ten minutes after leaving Karen's flat. He was somewhat surprised and annoyed when he walked into the living room and found James lying on the sofa, watching the television.

"What are you doing here?" Francis asked.

"Nothing." James replied.

"Where's Philip? Is he still here?"

"No, he's gone to town dad."

"Why didn't you go?"

"Eager to get away from the conversation as quickly as possible,

James replied whilst turning his attention back to the television. "I didn't want to go dad."

Francis spent the next couple of minutes wearing out the living room carpet. He paced up and down the room, constantly rubbing his chin, his cheek, the back of his neck and the back of his head as he did so. Eventually he stopped walking and stood in the middle of the living room, listening out for any sound of movement coming from upstairs. After satisfying himself that all was still and quiet, he slowly and silently made his way upstairs. He stood outside his wife's bedroom door and listened once more. He reached for the door handle and slowly pushed it downwards. He held it steady for a few more seconds before opening the door just enough to move forward a little and peer inside, releasing his tight grip on the handle as he did so. Once he had reassured himself that his wife was asleep, he pushed the door open a little further and tiptoed into the room. He moved towards the dressing table that sat beneath the window, as silently as an early morning breeze. On the right hand side of the dressing table were three drawers. Francis leant over and slowly pulled open the bottom drawer, looking over at his wife as he did so. He inserted his hand into the drawer and began fumbling around inside. His facial expression changed as his fumbling became a little more frantic. He repeated the same process with the next two drawers, the search becoming slightly more uncontrolled with each drawer.

Once he had accepted that the item he was searching for was not to be found in any of the drawers and after one final search in the bottom drawer, he stood upright and glanced around the room. He walked over to the side of the bed and looked down at his wife as she lay sleeping. He leant across, slid his hand under her pillow and began to feel about as gently as he could. After a few seconds of feeling about, using a gentle pat and move motion, the tips of his fingers landed upon the item he was looking for. He stretched out his fingers and gripped it tight. He carefully removed his hand from beneath the pillow. He stood upright once more, opened his clenched hand and gazed down upon his wife's purse.

Francis stood motionless, not even daring to breath. He could feel the sweat forming between his thumb, finger and the small smooth silver ball of the claps on the purse. He applied just about the right amount of pressure so that one silver ball rolled across the surface of the other silver ball and the purse popped open. Once opened, he quickly peered inside before carefully removing a one-pound note. He stuffed the pound note into his trouser pocket with one hand whilst he reunited the silver balls of the purse's clasp with the other, the slight clicking sound causing his heart to skip a beat. Once his heart had dusted itself down and regained its composure, he leant forward and slipped the purse back under the pillow. He stepped back and waited for a brief moment before turning and softly walking towards the bedroom door. As quietly and as carefully as he had entered the room, he opened the door and left. As he slowly pulled the door closed behind him, his wife opened her eyes, waited for the door handle to be released and then sat up in her bed.

Once Francis felt that he was clear of the bedroom door, his pace increased as he headed back down the stairs and into the living room. James was still lying on the sofa, his head resting on a cushion and one arm dangling towards the floor whilst he watched an episode of Mr Benn, 'The Balloonist'.

"Keep the volume down on that T.V." Francis said. "Your mum's asleep and I don't want her being disturbed."

James didn't reply.

"Did you hear what I said?"

"Yes dad." James replied.

"Then answer me next time. I'm off out, remember what I said and don't lie there all day watching the television." Francis turned away and left the room. Approximately twelve minutes and forty seven seconds later he pushed open the double doors and entered the bar of the Bell Inn.

"The usual?" The barman asked as Francis approached the bar.

Francis nodded as he removed the pound note from inside his trouser pocket. He rested his elbows on the bar and waited for his drink to arrive.

"There you go Francis, that's thirteen new pence please," the barman said as he placed a pint of bitter down in front of Francis.

Francis handed over the pound note and took a large mouthful of his pint whilst he waited for his change. After it had arrived, he picked up his pint and walked over to a table already occupied by four other men.

"Hello Frankie boy, want in?" one of the men said as he tossed a two pence coin into an ashtray in the centre of the table.

Francis looked down at the small collection of coins in his hand. "Not today," he replied.

Chapter 33

Philip sat alone at a window booth of Wimpy's restaurant on Fairfax Street. He gazed out through the large pane of glass at the world as it passed by and went about its business. The street was awash with teenage boys in flared denim jeans and denim cut off waistcoats, middle aged men with middle aged waistlines wearing brown slacks, Asian ladies covered from head to toe in brightly coloured, flowing swathes of material and old ladies hesitantly trying to navigate a clear path through the crowds as they attempted to reach Sainsbury's on the corner of the street.

His attention was finally redirected when he realised that a waitress was standing at his table, holding a pad and pencil in her hand. He had no idea how long the waitress had been standing there but he guessed that it had been a while by the way that she was tapping the pad with her pencil. Thankfully he was able to save her some time by not needing to look at the menu before he ordered.

"Can I have a cheeseburger, fries and a glass of lemonade please?" Philip said.

The waitress scribbled the order down on her pad, dropped the pad and pencil into the pouch at the front of her apron, turned and walked away. As she approached the serving hatch at the far end of the restaurant, Philip took a folded sheet of paper from the back pocket of his jeans, unfolded it and placed it neatly upon the table. He wasn't exactly sure why he needed to look at the list of items on the paper at that particular moment in time as he could recite every last item that was scrawled upon it.

Moments later the waitress duly returned with his glass of lemonade. Without paying attention she plonked it down directly on top of his piece of paper with such force that some of the contents leapt from the glass and onto the paper. Still unaware of her actions, she turned and walked away. Philip quickly removed the offending item from on top of his piece of paper. He picked the sheet of paper up and attempted to shake the pools of lemonade off with a few rapid flicks of the wrist before folding it back up and returning it to the safety of his pocket. He then turned his attention to drinking what was left of his lemonade whilst once more gazing at the passers-by. However, this time around he would turn his head one hundred and eighty degrees every so often so as to have prior warning of the waitress approaching with his food. It was round about head turn number seventeen when he noticed the waitress heading in his direction carrying his cheeseburger and chips. As with his glass of lemonade, his plate was placed on the table with all the finesse of an elephant sitting on a suitcase.

After adding the required amount of tomato sauce, salt and vinegar, Philip tucked in. Within minutes his plate was empty and his food was all washed down with the final two mouthfuls of lemonade. When attempting to get his bill, it took him just as long to attract the attention of the waitress as it had taken for him to eat his meal.

"Do you want a desert?" the waitress asked as she sloped towards the table.

"No thank you," Philip replied. He was just about to ask for the bill when the waitress tore a slip of paper from her pad and placed it on the table. She turned and walked away as Philip picked up the piece of paper. It read cheeseburger and fries 36p, glass of lemonade 7p, total 43p.

Philip picked up his bag which had been lying on the bench next to him, made his way towards the young lady sitting at the till, handed over the slip of paper along with a fifty pence piece, collected his change and left. Once outside, he walked along Fairfax Street, past Sainsbury's on the corner and headed towards Broadgate. His first stop was Owen Owen.

He knew the risks of Owen Owen, he was well aware of the degree of difficulty associated with Owen Owen, especially the formidable ladies on the perfume counter, but a busy Saturday afternoon could work in his favour he thought to himself as he entered the department store.

Once inside, Philip headed straight for the perfume and cosmetics counter. The sickly sweet aroma in the air informed him that he was getting closer. As he approached, he had already attracted the attention of one of the female sales assistants.

A short, plump, middle aged lady with make-up plastered on her face thicker than a village idiot's thick friend, bright red shimmering lipstick spread lavishly across her lips and eyelashes that were crying out to be released back into their natural habitat, stared at Philip as he reached the counter. Her rigid and lacquered hair sat motionless upon her head as she turned and walked towards him.

"Are you lost?" she enquired whilst successfully attempting to look down her nose at Philip.

With an equally scornful expression on his face, Philip replied, "No, I'm not lost, I would like to buy some perfume."

"Oh I see," the sales assistant replied. "And who is this lavish purchase for, your fictitious girlfriend perhaps."

"No, it's for my sister. It's her eighteenth birthday tomorrow and my mother has sent me to buy her some gifts as she is unwell and one of the gifts I have been asked to buy is a bottle of perfume." Philip paused for a moment before looking over the shoulder of the sales assistant and further along the counter. "Could I possibly be served by somebody else?" he added.

"No, all the other sales assistants are busy." the sales assistant replied without even bothering to turn around.

Philip glanced at the sales assistant's name badge. "Well Gwendoline, can I please see what perfumes you have for sale that are priced at three pounds or less."

There was another moment of silence as sales assistant and potential customer stared intently at each other. Philip knew how vital it was not to flinch, not to back down, not to be defeated; this was a stand-off that he could not afford to lose. Thankfully as he was just seconds away from cracking, Gwendoline crumbled first and with a demeanour full to the brim with contempt, she reached under the counter and began to retrieve boxed up bottles of perfume. Allage by Estee Lauder, Diorella by Dior, Charlie by Revlon, Clara by Revlon and finally Charlie Blue by Revlon. Upon placing the final perfume onto the counter Gwendoline looked at Philip.

"These are all priced between two pounds fifty and three pounds, which one would you like?"

"What do they smell like?" Philip asked.

"Perfume, they smell like perfume," Gwendoline replied.

"They can't all smell the same?" Philip said whilst picking up one of the shimmering glossy boxes.

"Does it matter, will your sister mind which one you get?"

"Could I try a sample?" Philip asked as he pointed towards some bottles of perfume on the shelf directly behind Gwendoline.

"No, I haven't got time." Gwendoline replied.

"Then perhaps I can be served by somebody that has got time or perhaps somebody in a managerial capacity," Philip said.

Becoming somewhat irritated by the scruffy teenage boy at her cosmetics counter, Gwendoline turned to grab the sample bottles from the shelf. After grabbing the first bottle, she glanced over her shoulder at the perfume on the counter.

"Here you are," she said as she placed the bottles on the counter. "Allage, Diorella, Clara and Charlie Blue. Which one would you like to try first?"

"This one," Philip replied as he passed one of the bottles to Gwendoline.

Taking the bottle, Gwendoline sprayed a small amount of perfume onto her wrist and rubbed her wrists together before thrusting her arm in Philip's direction. Philip leant forward and sniffed. His eyes instantly and simultaneously widened and watered. He felt a burning sensation immediately grab at the back of his throat. He leant backwards a lot quicker than he had leant forwards, coughing as he did so.

Gwendoline smiled. "Not for you?" she asked. Seeing the discomfort displayed across Philip's face, Gwendoline immediately went in for the kill, picking up the next bottle on the counter and giving it two healthy sprays upon her wrist. After rubbing her wrists together, she leant across the counter and thrust her arms towards the still recovering teenage boy. It was like watching a boxer on the ropes. Another assault upon the nostrils was like another right hook making contact with an unguarded head, blow upon blow raining down, referee poised to step in and stop the fight. Along with the smell of perfume in her own nostrils, Gwendoline could also smell victory. She could see Philip swaying in front of her, desperately trying to make sense of his surroundings. He reached out and placed a hand upon the counter, just as a large helping of perfume number three was thrust under his nose.

"How about this one?" Gwendoline asked with obvious delight in her voice.

Philip shook his head in an attempt to clear his nostrils. He looked at Gwendoline with tears running down his cheeks. With a sparkle in the corner of her eye, Gwendoline reached for another sample of perfume. Philip raised his hands and took a step backwards, making sure that he was more than an arm's length away. Realising that victory was hers, Gwendoline placed the bottle back onto the counter.

"So which one will it be?" She asked. "Or would you like to go away," Gwendoline paused for a moment, "and think about it?"

With his eyes still streaming, Philip nodded and walked away.

It wasn't until Gwendoline had put the sample bottles back on the shelf and was returning the boxed products to their usual place, that she slowly came to realise she was a perfume short. The victorious, triumphant expression on her face quickly readjusted to one of shock, followed by one of rage.

"Where's my Charlie?" She said in a voice several octaves louder than she intended. She quickly turned to look in the direction of her two colleagues, checking to see if her outburst had been heard. Thankfully her two colleagues were engaged in their own conversation at the far end of the counter. After some frantic fumbling and checking, Gwendoline, under her breath on this occasion, muttered "That little bastard stole my Charlie."

She immediately stood on her tiptoes and attempted to survey the area. Her head twisting from side to side as she desperately tried to spot Philip. However it was far too late, Philip had already doubled back and walked along the opposite side of the cosmetics counter and was now leaving the department store by the side entrance, his bottle of Charlie safely concealed inside his bag. His eyes were still watering but he was sporting an enormous grin across his face as he pushed open the doors and exited the store. He knew that he could acquire other items on his list from Owen Owen but thought that it was far too risky with Gwendoline on the lookout. He was able to obtain, without too much fuss, a travel alarm clock and an Old Spice gift set from Woolworths. The transistor radio proved to be a bridge too far as the electrical shop in the lower precinct had a higher than average proportion of young eager staff working their Saturday jobs. He knew of a smaller electrical shop, next door to a travel agent on the Albany Road in Earlsdon, but it was problematic due to the proximity of the staff in relation to the only exit. He had better luck in the market. He was able to obtain an orange space hopper, some cheap make up products for his sister and although they were not on the list, two Leeds United bracelets. After visiting a couple more shops and legitimately exchanging cash for the items he wanted, he celebrated with a banana longboat in the round café, where he put on one of the bracelets before heading home in time for final score.

Philip returned home to find his dad asleep on the sofa, the all too familiar aroma of beer and tobacco hanging in the air. He headed straight upstairs and into his mother's room.

"Hello love," his mother said as he entered the room. She was sitting up in her bed, flicking through the pages of an old magazine.

Philip sat along the side of the bed and placed his bag on the floor, directly in front of him. He opened it up and took out the perfume, make-up, wrapping paper and two birthday cards.

"How much was all that?" his mother asked.

"Four pounds give or take." Philip replied.

"But I only gave you three."

"Dad gave me some and I added a bit myself."

His mother smiled as she reached for the bottle of perfume. "I'll wrap these up later, you and your brother will need to write your card. You can drop them off in the morning on your paper round. Be sure to tell your sister to come for Sunday lunch tomorrow. James has fetched her a cake from Gladding's."

Philip closed his bag, nodded at his mum and picked up one of the cards.

"Your dad brought a bag of chips home, they're wrapped up in the oven. Can you heat them up for you and James? I think there's some eggs in the fridge but make sure you save a couple for Yorkshires tomorrow."

Philip nodded again and then made his way back downstairs. There was no sign of James but his dad was still fast asleep on the sofa. Philip tiptoed past the sofa and switched the T.V on, making sure the volume was turned down before the picture burst into life. The wrestling from Bedworth Civic Hall was just finishing, so he quickly turned over to BBC1 just in time for the vidiprinter to start rolling. After a few silent minutes of waiting, the all-important score came through. Norwich 0, he held his breath and clenched his fist tight, Leeds United 1. As soon as the result had disappeared off the rolling screen, Philip got up off the floor and made his way into the kitchen. He opened the oven and took out the bag of chips and collected the eggs from the fridge. He proceeded to cook the eggs and reheat the chips for him and James. When he came out of the kitchen to set the table, he discovered that his dad had gone and James was now sitting on the sofa, watching The Pink Panther Show.

"Where's dad?" Philip asked.

James just shrugged his shoulders. "Dunno," he muttered.

It was when he returned to the kitchen to collect more items for the table that he heard the raised voices coming from upstairs. By the time he had finished setting the table and had returned to the living room, carrying two plates of egg and chips, the voices had become much louder and more uncontrolled to the point where his mother and father were just attempting to shout louder than each other. James's eyes began to fill and he had an all too familiar fearful expression upon his face.

"Don't worry." Philip said as the voices coming from upstairs continued to get louder. Suddenly their mother's voice became much more audible on account of the bedroom door being swung open. Despite the thumping sound of footsteps bounding down the stairs, they could hear every word.

"Yeah that's right, you have it, take it, take all of it and then you can tell your kids why they have nothing to eat because you've drank it all away in the soddin pub, you bastard."

The footsteps got louder, before the boys heard the front door open and slam shut. Except for the sound coming from the television set at the other end of the room, all fell silent. 'Voyage to the Bottom of the Sea' had just started. James began to ever so softly sob and sniff as he ate his egg and chips. In an attempt to reassure his younger brother, Philip gave him a big smile and poured him a glass of lemonade.

"I'll bring us some chocolate back after my paper round," he said. "Then maybe we can go to the off sales for some more lemonade."

James wiped his eyes and smiled.

"I'm just gonna go and see if mum is alright," Philip said as he stood up and left the room. Moments later he was standing outside his mother's door. He stood and listened but he couldn't detect any sounds coming from inside. He opened the door very slowly and rather nervously he entered. The early evening sunlight shone across the room and onto the bed where his mother was laying. She was lying on her side with her eyes wide open, looking towards the window and the shaft of sunlight. She didn't seem to notice that Philip had entered the room. Her eyes were full of tears on the verge of being set free and Philip could clearly see the bright red imprint of a hand across her cheek.

"Mum," he said softly. But he didn't get a response.

"Are you okay?" he added, but again his mother didn't respond, she just continued to stare towards the window.

Philip was just about to leave when he noticed the purse lying on the bedroom floor with a small number of coins scattered in close proximity. He bent down and gathered up the coins before putting them back in and closing the purse. He went to place the purse on the small bedside table when his mother reached out and clasped his hand. Without saying anything or even looking in his direction, she squeezed his hand tight for five or six seconds before letting go again and turning to face the bedroom wall. Philip let go of the purse and quietly left the room, closing the door gently behind him as he did so.

As he entered the living room again, he suddenly became conscious of the time. He quickly ran back upstairs and grabbed the items he needed from his bag, raced back down and dashed through the living room, kitchen and scullery. He called out to his brother not to disturb mum and that he would be back soon. Once in the scullery, he scooped up his paperbag, dropped the items he was carrying inside and left. Less than five minutes later and quite out of breath, he arrived at the newsagents. As he approached the door, Paul McBride and another boy exited.

"Alright Phil?" Paul said.

Philip motioned with his head for Paul to join him, away from the other paper boy.

"What gives?" Paul asked as he walked towards Philip, leaving the other boy to set off on his round.

Philip opened his bag and Paul peered inside.

"Oh nice one Phil, what you got?"

Paul reached inside and took out a travel alarm clock, a space hopper and an Old Spice gift set.

"Any luck with the Cliff Richard L.P?" Paul asked.

Philip shook his head.

"Yeah, proving a bit tricky that one and I'm running out of time. The lad that wants it, wants it for his nan's birthday and I think it's in a few days' time. Might have to settle for a cake of some variety, they are easy to get your hands on. Never mind. I should be able to shift these tonight. I'll weigh in when I see you tomorrow. I should have a new list by then as well, doubt Cliff bloody Richard will be on it though."

Philip just nodded as Paul put the items inside his bag. They then headed in different directions; Paul set off on his paper round and Philip entered the shop.

Chapter 34

Philip stood in the kitchen, reading the note that had been left for him on the table by the fridge. Next to the note were the presents his mother had wrapped and two birthday cards. One was from his mum and dad, the other one was from his granddad. He could tell who it was from by the handwriting on the envelope. The note itself simply read 'Please drop these off for your sister on your paper round and remind her to come for dinner at 2pm, Mum'.

Philip's dad was nowhere to be seen and as Philip hadn't been greeted by the usual smell of stale tobacco, sweat and beer when he entered the living room, he assumed that his dad hadn't returned home the previous evening. After breakfast and before setting off on his paper round, Philip went back upstairs and collected the birthday card from him and James.

Once inside the newsagents, he filled his bag with unnecessarily swollen newspapers. He dragged the strap up his body before taking a deep breath and planting it onto his unfortunate shoulder. Leaning over to one side like an old drunk man staggering along the street and with the cards and gifts contained within a carrier bag, hanging from the opposite arm, Philip stumbled out of the shop. Thankfully by the time he reached the entrance to his sister's block of flats, he had delivered enough papers to be able to stand upright. As he climbed the stairs and approached the door to his sister's flat, he noticed that it was ajar. He could see splintered fragments hanging from the door frame and the faint sound of voices, laughter and music coming from inside.

Rather carefully and with extreme caution, he pushed the door open a little further and stepped into the hallway. Reminiscent of a Michael Caine spy thriller, he silently stepped towards the sounds he had heard as he had entered the flat. He stood facing the door to the living room. As with the front door, this door was also slightly ajar. He took a deep breath, puffed out his cheeks and pushed the door open. He stood in the doorway and looked around the room. There were about six or seven people in the room. All of them except one were teenage boys about two or three years older than Philip. The exception was a man in his early fifties, known locally as Bob Dylan. His real name was Brian Webster but ever since the summer of love and Woodstock, he had been converted by the whole free love ideological dream. He had not long returned from India and was happily impressing his young audience with tall tales, whilst sharing some of the illegal hashish that he had managed to smuggle back into the country. Sitting in the dip of the rundown sofa and looking a few shades whiter than a ghost's skiing holiday snaps was Lesley Bennett's new boyfriend Steven Watson.

The room itself was littered with an assortment of beer bottles and beer cans. An empty vodka bottle lay on its side on top of the coffee table and judging by the state of the floor, at least two full ashtrays had been sent tumbling at some stage of the previous evening.

"Alright Phil," Steven said. "What's in the bag?"

"Newspapers." Philip replied.

"Ha, ha, very funny. What's in the other bag?" Steven asked as he pointed towards the carrier bag in Philip's hand before adding. "More gifts?"

"Yes actually." Philip replied. "Only this time they are not for you or your mum."

Philip turned away and continued to walk down the hallway. As he passed Karen's room, he noticed the door was half open and he could see Karen asleep on her bed. He could also see that Karen was half naked, except for a pair of blue cotton knickers. She was asleep and lying on her back with her breasts exposed. Putting aside the naked flesh that he had seen on television, 'Twins of Evil' being a particular favourite, this was the most he had ever seen of a real life naked girl. He was transfixed for a moment as he stood and gazed at every inch of Karen's body, paying particular attention to her breasts. Suddenly he heard a sound coming from behind him. A rather pale and groggy looking teenage boy staggered out of the bathroom, wiping his mouth with the back of his hand as he did so. Philip quickly leant forward, closed Karen's bedroom door and continued down the hallway towards his sister's bedroom.

With the image of Karen's breasts still clearly visible in his mind, he knocked on his sister's bedroom door, an action that was rewarded immediately with a response of 'piss off' from the inside the room.

"It's me," Philip replied.

"Who?"

"Me, Philip, your brother," Philip said.

A few moments later Grace opened the door. "Sorry Phil, I thought it was those twats in there again," Grace said, before turning away and walking back to her bed. Dressed in pyjamas, dressing gown and slippers, it was clear that Grace had been awake for some time.

"Are you okay?" Philip asked as he stepped into the room and closed the door behind him.

"No, not really Phil, seeing as you asked," Grace replied before adding, "What do you want Phil?"

"Happy Birthday." Philip said as he held up the carrier bag in Grace's general direction.

Grace sat up, reached out and took hold of the carrier bag. "Thanks," She said with a half-smile on her face as she peered inside the bag.

"Mum said to tell you to come for lunch today," Philip said as Grace took the birthday cards from inside the bag.

Grace instantly froze with birthday cards in one hand and the carrier bag hanging open in the other. She turned and looked at her brother. "I don't think so Phil," Grace said.

"Why not, mum will be expecting you, she's got a cake from Gladding's."

"Will dad be there?" Grace asked.

"Probably." Philip replied. "Why?"

"Did you notice the front door on your way in?" Grace asked.

Still struggling to make sense of the conversation, Philip opted to just nod his head.

"Yeah, well, do you know who did it?"

Though he was beginning to suspect the direction the conversation was now heading, Philip wasn't given the time to formulate an answer.

"Dad, that's who. What state was he in this morning? No doubt he was sprawled across the settee, sleeping it off when you got up. When he turned up here last night, he was absolutely smashed. I'd never seen him that drunk before."

"He wasn't there," Philip said. "and judging by the lack of evidence or lack of odours, I don't think he has been home all night."

"Yeah well he certainly came here last night, that's for sure."

Philip stood in silence, desperately searching for something to say before he finally muttered, "Who are those idiots in your living room?"

"Oh, nobody important, just a stupid bunch of twats but they're the least of my worries right now. When Karen wakes up, I doubt that I'll still have a living room."

"How do you mean?" Philip asked.

"Because when she gets up, she'll probably tell me that I have to move out."

"Why? It's not your fault that dad lost it."

"Lost it!" Grace interrupted. "I wish that's all that it was. The front door wasn't the only thing he broke last night."

Philip took a deep breath and braced himself for what he was about to hear.

Grace began. "As well as breaking the front door, he managed to break a tea pot, several plates, a window in the kitchen and to top it all off, Karen's dad's nose."

"You're joking." Philip replied.

"I wish I was Phil. He was breaking so many things, I was about to give Roy Castle a call. And that's not the half of it. You should have heard what he was shouting about. He's really losing it Phil, you need to try and stay out of his way and make sure that James does as well."

"Why, what was he saying," Philip asked.

"Oh I suppose most of it was the usual when you think about it. It was just more the way he was saying it, there was just more venom and more anger in his voice. He was out of control. Calling Karen's dad a scrounger and a benefit cheat. Kept going on about how somebody on benefits could have enough money to become an alcoholic. Then when Karen stepped in and asked him to leave, he turned on her. Started calling her a slag and a prostitute. Then Karen's dad tried to land one on him but dad just whacked him one, right in the face. Sent him stumbling backwards into the kitchen table, breaking the teapot."

"What about the other stuff... the kitchen window?"

"Oh, that all got broke in the melee that followed when about four or five of them were trying to get dad out of the flat."

Grace lay back on her bed. "I hate Sundays." She said as her head collided with the pillow. "There's never anything to do."

"I'd better go," Philip said. "Will you be okay?"

No sooner had Grace's head made contact with the pillow, than it set off again in an upward trajectory as Grace sprung up in her bed. "I know, let's go and visit Grandad."

"I can't today," Philip replied.

"Why not?" Grace asked.

"I'm going swimming." Philip answered.

"You can miss swimming for one day, we can take James as well, we can all go."

"I can't," Philip repeated. "I'm not just going swimming."

"What do you mean, why, what else are you doing?"

"If I tell you Grace, you've got to promise not to tell anybody, you can't say anything."

Grace nodded, but for Philip this wasn't enough. In fact it fell a long way short. If he could, he would get something in writing, preferably countersigned by a witness.

"I mean it Grace, you can't say anything, you can't tell anybody."

"Yes." Grace said with a large amount of annoyance evident in her short response.

With obvious excitement in his voice, Philip said, "I'm trying out for Coventry Godiva's."

Grace's reaction to this piece of information, or rather her lack of reaction, was the exact opposite of Philip's excitement. "Oh right," Grace said. "Is that it?"

"Yes." Philip said with his own personal supply of annoyance in his voice.

"Can't you do that next week?" Grace asked.

"No," Philip quickly replied with annoyance now being shovelled in faster than a stoker on a steam ship. "I'm going," he added. "I've got to finish my paper round, I have to be at the baths by nine."

"How long will it take you to finish your stupid paper round?" Grace asked.

"If I ever get round to finishing it, it should take me about half an hour or so."

Grace jumped off her bed and with gazelle like movement, leapt past Philip. "Okay," she called out as she exited the bedroom and disappeared into the bathroom.

With far less vigour on display, Philip turned and made his way back down the hallway towards the front door. He stopped at Karen's bedroom door and listened. He could still hear voices coming from the living room. He waited a moment before gently pushing Karen's bedroom door open a little, in an attempt to get one last look at her exposed breasts. However to his disappointment, Karen had turned over onto her side and all he could see was her bare shoulders. He continued down the hallway and set off to finally finish his paper round.

By the time he got back home, Grace was already there, sitting on the settee. James was sitting next to her, looking as excited as a puppy with a new squeaky toy.

"We're going to see Grandad," James said as Philip opened the back door and stepped inside.

"Are you?" Philip replied.

"We all are," James said. "Mum too."

Rather surprised by this piece of news, Philip asked, "Where is mum?"

"She's in the kitchen making sandwiches," James replied.

With a rather unpleasant look aimed in Grace's direction, Philip headed for the kitchen.

"Cheese, egg or crisps," his mother asked as he entered.

"Sorry?" Philip replied.

"In your sandwiches, what do you want, egg, cheese or crisps?"

"I can't go mum."

"Don't be silly Philip, of course you can go."

"Honest mum, I can't."

"But it's your sister's birthday and how is your grandad going to feel if you don't turn up? You know how much he thinks of you. What is so important that you can't go?"

"What?" Philip said with equal measures of surprise and sarcasm. "You mean Grace hasn't told you?"

"No she hasn't, but you can tell me," his mother replied as she continued to butter several slices of bread.

"I'm going swimming mum."

Philip's mum slammed the knife she was holding down onto the table. "You think you are missing visiting your grandad, just so that you can go swimming..."

"I'm not just going swimming," Philip interrupted. "I'm trying out for Coventry Godiva's. If I don't show up Mr Spencer will go mad and I won't get another chance."

"I thought we had discussed this Philip. We told you that we couldn't afford for you to join a swimming club, especially at the moment with the situation with your dad's job and everything. And exactly what has Mr Spencer got to do with it?"

"He arranged it for me. One of the coaches at the club came to watch me swim in the pool at school."

"Did he now? and when did he come to the school and watch you swim?"

"He came last week," Philip replied before adding "I've been saving up, I can pay for it myself. I've got to be there by nine."

"Oh I see," his mother said. "You know what will happen if your dad finds out and I don't know how you are going to keep it from him."

Choosing to ignore this minor detail for now and looking directly at his mum as he spoke, Philip said. "Can I go? If I don't hurry, I'll miss the bus."

"I suppose you had better go and get yourself ready then. Now do you want egg, cheese or crisps? You still need to take something to eat with you."

"Crisps," Philip replied as he turned and went upstairs to collect his swimming trunks, goggles and a towel from the airing cupboard. Once he had gathered up all he needed, he made his way back down the stairs and into the kitchen. His mum was waiting with a wrapped up crisp sandwich in her hand.

"We won't be back until late," his mother said as she handed over the sandwich. "So you'll have to sort yourself out some dinner when you get home. "I'll leave your dad a note, telling him where we have gone. I'll tell him you had already left to go swimming with your friends before we decided to go and visit grandad."

"Thanks mum," Philip replied as he stuffed his towel, trunks, goggles and sandwich into a carrier bag. He turned to leave and just as he did so, his mother called out.

"Good luck."

Chapter 35

Around about the time that Philip was stepping off the number twenty-one bus in Pool Meadow and sprinting towards the swimming baths, Grace, James and their mum were boarding a different number twenty-one bus outside the Live and Let Live public house. At the same time in a house in Aldermans Green, Snowy Vest was standing and facing the bedroom door of his spare bedroom. He still had the instructions, just received from his wife, ringing in his ears. He knocked apprehensively on the bedroom door a couple of times, waited a respectable amount of time for a response, took a deep breath, opened the door and stepped inside. He instantly took two large strides towards the window, threw the curtains open, opened the window with the same amount of force, shoved his head into the open space and took a deep breath.

He then turned and looked at the figure still lying asleep in his spare bed, walked over to the side of the bed, reached out, grabbed a shoulder and shook it.

"Francis! Francis!" Snowy said. "Francis, you need to wake up."

Francis didn't stir. Snowy took a firmer grip of Francis's shoulder and with several degrees more intensity, he shook again.

"Francis!" Snowy shouted as he continued to rock his unwanted guest from side to side.

This time around, Snowy's goal was reached and Francis began to respond. It took him a few moments to acclimatise to his unfamiliar surroundings and to realise exactly where he was. The inside of his head felt like it had been set on fire and all that remained were a few charred embers and a small plume of grey smoke, drifting off into the distance. With his eyes flickering faster than a discotheque's lighting system on a Saturday night, he attempted to focus on the figure standing over him. After a few moments of blurred vision, Snowy was still very much of the soft focus variety but it was as good as it was going to get.

"Alright Snowy," Francis muttered.

Unfortunately Snowy wasn't alright, he was under pressure to get the job done and he knew it. "There's a cup of tea for you in the kitchen Francis, then I need you to get on your way. We're visiting the wife's sister in Kettering today and we need to be getting on our way."

The part about the cup of tea in the kitchen was true; however the other part about visiting the sister-in-law was not. For Snowy, this was a necessary fabrication to get Francis out of the house as quickly as possible.

"Everything alright Snowy?" Francis asked as he tossed the blankets aside and sat up.

"Not really, no, the wife ain't best pleased."

"Why Snowy, what have you done?"

With a puzzled expression on his face and raised eyebrows offering their full support, Snowy replied. "I haven't done anything Francis. You on the other hand."

With a puzzled expression of his very own, Francis reached for his trousers that were lying on the bedroom floor. "Me, what have I done?"

"Oh nothing Francis. Just waking half the street up by banging on our front door and shouting at the top of your voice at two o' clock in the morning."

"Sorry about that Snowy, I had nowhere else to go."

"Why couldn't you go home?" Snowy asked.

Francis finished dressing before sitting back on the bed to tie his shoelaces. He chose not to reply to Snowy's question.

"Everything alright Francis?"

"No Snowy, not really," Francis replied as he stood up and walked towards the door. "Don't worry about the tea. I'll see you at work." He added as he left the room.

Philip Knott pushed open the glass doors and entered the swimming baths at precisely six minutes past nine. He attempted to bypass the payment counter in the centre of the ground floor and head straight for the changing rooms. However he was stopped in his tracks by a rather rotund middle aged lady with heavily lacquered hair and a facial expression equally stiff.

"And where are you off to in such a hurry?" the lady asked.

"I'm here for the training," Philip replied. Seeing as his response made no impression he quickly added, "Coventry Godiva."

"Do you have your membership card?"

"No." Philip replied.

"Then I can't let you in."

"I'm not a member yet," Philip said with a certain amount of panic in his voice as he saw the clock behind the lady's left shoulder tick ever closer to ten past nine. "I was told to come this morning and try out for the team."

"By who?" The lady asked.

"I can't remember his name, he came to watch me swim at my school and told me to turn up this morning."

"Wait there," the lady said, before walking away and disappearing through a door.

Philip stood and watched the clock. Each second seemed to go quicker than the previous one. After a hundred and forty six seconds, the door opened again and the woman returned. She walked back across the tiled floor, towards Philip.

"Go on then," She said, "and tell the changing room attendant that you are here at the invitation of Mr Kennedy."

Philip raced into the changing room, grabbed a basket as he ran past them and was changed into his trunks in a time that would have impressed Billy Whizz. He handed his basket to a less than enthusiastic attendant, told him who he was there to see, collected his metal disc, pinned it to his trunks, ran up the stairs, past the showers and out into the pool. He arrived poolside at nine seventeen and twenty three seconds. He looked around the pool as he entered. There were several swimmers in the water. Approximately three to four swimmers in each lane were being put through their paces. Standing a few feet away from Philip and with his back to him, stood a tall wiry man in a white tracksuit and a pair of flip flops. He was randomly shouting instructions to different swimmers as they made their way up and down the pool. Catching sight of Philip's reflection in the water as he approached, the coach turned his head.

"Can I help you sonny?" he asked.

"I'm looking for Mr Kennedy," Philip replied. "He asked me to come along today."

The coach turned his attention back to the swimmers in the pool. "And what time did Mr Kennedy ask you to be here for?" the coach said before blowing his whistle and shouting some instructions to a boy in the third lane.

"Nine 'o' clock," Philip replied.

Without responding to Philip's answer, the coach blew two short blasts on his whistle and signalled to another coach who was standing on the other side of the pool. Both Philip and the coach stood in a silence that was perfectly designed to make Philip feel uncomfortable, as the other coach slowly made his way around the edge of the pool. As he got closer, Philip could see that it was Mr Kennedy approaching.

"This young man is looking for you," Mr Kennedy's colleague said once he was in earshot.

Mr Kennedy looked straight past his colleague and directly at Philip. "You're late," he said with a no-nonsense tone to his voice. "If you want to be in the team, this is the first and last time that you are late."

"My bus was late," Philip muttered.

"Take a look in that pool son, there are thirty kids in that pool and each and every one of them was here on time. If your bus is going to get you here late, then I suggest that you get an earlier bus."

"But I have to do my paper round first," Philip said.

"Look son, I'm not going to waste my time standing here and arguing with you. It is up to you to sort it out, you either turn up on time or you don't turn up at all."

Mr Kennedy turned to his colleague. "Can you take him through to the other pool and run your eye over him, see what he's made of. He needs to work on his turns, watching the T.V. hasn't taught him how to do that yet."

"Oh", Mr Kennedy's colleague said, "so, this is the boy with the T.V."

"It's rented." Mr Kennedy replied. And while you're there, get a time for his freestyle over twenty-five metres, and his butterfly."

"Follow me," the coach said.

Philip followed as they both made their way along the main pool, through a glass partition, past the baby and toddler pool before duly arriving at the edge of the twenty five metre pool.

"Get yourself some starting blocks from over there," the coach said as he pointed to a stack of blocks resting against the wall along the side of the pool. "Then in you get and warm up with a couple of steady lengths."

Philip grabbed a starting block and carried it over to the middle lane. Once he had placed it in position, he eagerly stepped onto it and dived into the pool. No sooner had the cool water encased him than he once again felt at ease and confident. On returning to the surface of the pool, he swam to the far end, turned and swam back again. As he arrived back at his point of departure, the coach was standing next to his starting block.

"Right then, let's have a closer look at that start," the coach said. "The start is crucial, especially in the shorter distance races," he continued as Philip climbed out of the water. "Races cannot be won at the start, but they can be lost. Now onto the blocks and get yourself ready."

Philip climbed onto the starting block.

"Now lean forward so that your head is over the water and your shoulders are in line with the edge of the pool. Good. Now bend and curve your back. Bending the knees a little, now you need to grip the starting block with the tips of your fingers, just gently coil them around the block."

Philip continued to follow his instructions.

"It is very important that your knees remain bent as you use this to propel yourself forward. If you have to bend your knees first, you are giving your opponents a head start, an advantage. And when you enter the water, you do not dive as deeply as you just did, you are not diving for pearls, this is not a Roy Orbison song."

Philip sprang forward, leapt off the block and dived into the water. He quickly came to the surface and looked around for the coach.

"Your line was good and a good body shape but you are still too deep. Come back and try again. You must remember, you swim faster on the surface than you do below it, so the quicker you return to the surface the better. As soon as your toes disappear below the surface, you need to start kicking your legs. This time, when you come to the surface, keep swimming, I'll tell you when to stop."

Philip swam back to the edge and once more climbed out of the pool. His heart was beating faster than a cannibal's drum at dinnertime. The thought of actually being coached sent waves of excitement rushing through his body and his enthusiasm didn't wane for a moment, even when he was climbing out of the pool and diving back in again for the ninth time. As he resurfaced following his ninth dive, he heard the coach blow his whistle. He stopped swimming and turned around.

"Getting better," the coach said. "Take a five-minute break and then we'll have a look at your turns."

The coach walked away and out of view, leaving Philip to his thoughts. He sat at the edge of the pool with his feet submerged in the water below. A few minutes later the coach returned with a vending machine coffee in one hand, a stopwatch around his neck, a pencil behind his left ear and a wooden board with a piece of paper attached in the other hand.

"The turn is all in the timing and knowing exactly when to turn." The coach said as he approached Philip. "Turn too early and you're reaching for the wall, turn too late and your body position is all wrong when you need to gain maximum distance from the push off the wall."

Philip listened to every word, nodding frantically as he did so.

"Right, back on your block and let's give it a go. Dive in and swim to the other end. Listen for the whistle; on my whistle you need to turn. Head and arms tucked under the body, you need to then twist your body. Feel for the wall with your feet and push off the wall. Don't worry, it takes a while to get it. Most people struggle with it at first."

Philip dived back into the water and began to swim to the other end of the pool. He heard the coach shouting and telling him to slow down a little but the adrenalin and his nerves propelled him forward. As he swam, he pictured a majestic and graceful turn in his head. Unfortunately the reality was a very different picture altogether. As he heard the whistle ring out around the pool, he ducked his head and his arms and attempted to roll beneath the surface of the water. He instantly lost his bearings. His arms flapped around like a little old lady in battle with a persistent wasp on a hot summer's day. By the time he remembered to stretch out his legs, his toes barely made contact with the pool wall and as a result he lacked the momentum needed to push himself away. As he resurfaced, the coach signalled for him to keep swimming.

"Try again at the other end," he called out as he walked along the side of the pool, drinking his cup of coffee.

However, this attempt to turn was equally inept as the first. At one point Philip found himself almost motionless on the bottom of the pool but at least he was facing the right way, though he needed to use his hands to push himself forward.

As he once again resurfaced, he heard the coach's whistle ring out and fill all of the empty space that surrounded him.

"Okay, okay we can work on that," the coach said as he scribbled a few notes onto his sheet of paper. There's not long left of the session, so let's record some times. We'll start with the freestyle; twenty-five metres, that's one length of the pool okay, and remember what you have learnt about your starts."

Beginning to feel a little tired, Philip extracted himself from the water once more. He felt as if he had been in and out of the water more times than a fisherman's float in an angling competition.

"Okay sunshine, on to your starting blocks. On my whistle, one length of the pool as fast as you can."

Philip climbed onto the block as the coach raised the whistle to his lips. "Ready," the coach called out just as the whistle arrived at its destination. Philip assumed his starting position and nodded his head.

"Don't forget, not too deep, back to the surface as quickly as possible. Three, two, one." The whistle reverberated off the walls of the pool and Philip immediately sprang forward into the water. Once submerged, he frantically began kicking his legs. When he surfaced, he glided down the pool, reached the other end and stopped. As his hand connected with the end of the pool the coach stopped his watch. He stared at his watch for a couple of seconds before writing the time down on his piece of paper.

"Okay, a gentle slow swim back and then we'll go again," the coach shouted.

Philip certainly did go again. He swam another twenty-five-metre freestyle, two fifty metre freestyles, two twenty-five metre butterflies and two further fifty metre butterflies.

"Okay son, session's over." The coach said just after he had pressed the stop button of his stopwatch for the last time. "Go and get changed." he added.

Philip climbed out of the pool and walked back past the toddler pool, through the glass doors and along the side of the main pool towards the changing rooms. The main pool was by now deserted except for Mr Kennedy who was walking towards him.

"Get yourself showered and changed lad." he said. "I'll come and have a chat with you in a few minutes." Mr Kennedy continued past Philip and approached the other coach as Philip disappeared into the changing area.

"Well Craig, what's your assessment?"

"Well…" Craig replied. "His dive is okay, just needs a bit of work. His turns are hideous, it's like watching an articulated lorry trying to fight its way out of a cul-de-sac. He certainly hasn't learnt how to turn by watching T.V."

"Oh right," Mr Kennedy replied with a rather disappointed tone to his voice.

"No, wait; there is a silver lining."

"Which is?"

"Which is, oh…my…god, the boy can swim," Craig said as he handed over his clipboard.

Mr Kennedy took hold of the clipboard and quickly scanned the notes that were scrawled upon the piece of paper, before reaching the times that had been recorded at the bottom of the page.

Craig waited patiently for the reaction. He knew it was coming but it took a lot longer to arrive than he anticipated. It took so long to arrive that Craig felt as if he had ordered it out of the Gratton catalogue. Finally it arrived. An instant drying sensation raced along the sides of Mr Kennedy's throat. His eyes bulged and his lips attempted to weld themselves together; thankfully they were unsuccessful.

"These times that you have written down here," Mr Kennedy said.

"Yes, what about them?" Craig replied.

"Are you sure they are right?"

"Of course they are right."

"Sorry Craig, I wasn't suggesting…"

"That's okay," Craig interrupted.

"These times for the fifty metres, does that include his bad turns?"

"Yes."

"So with a bit of training we could take another couple of seconds off these times?"

Craig just nodded.

"Do you know what this means Craig."

"It means that we have found ourselves an exceptional swimmer," Craig said.

"Indeed it does but it also means that we have got a massive headache coming our way."

"How do you mean?" Craig asked.

"Think about it Craig, he can't just walk straight into the team, or rather, swim straight into the team."

"But if he's good enough, then he's good enough." Craig said.

"Oh my word, he is definitely good enough! Even with his bad turns, he is the best swimmer we have in his age group, but it's not as simple as that," Mr Kennedy said as he removed the piece of paper from the clipboard, folded it and put it in his pocket. "He can't just turn up and push somebody else out of the team."

"What does that matter?" Craig asked with a puzzled expression on his face. "As long as the team is winning."

"Mr Kennedy shook his head. "These parents don't care about the team winning, they only care about their little stars being in the team. Need to tell all their friends at the tennis club how well their little angel is doing. Just to add to the mix as well, this lad is from the wrong side of the tracks. As soon as they find that out they'll be rushing off to the chemist to buy a bottle of head lice solution. Little Timothy who plays the oboe and can speak Chinese is not going to lose his place on the team to some ruffian who has just walked out of the pages of a Dickens novel."

"What are you going to do?"

"Well first of all we need to sign him up. He can't swim for anybody until he has done that, and then we will tread need to very carefully indeed. He may be a great swimmer but we can't afford to lose half our team because of it. Can you finish tidying up? I'm gonna go and have a word with him."

Chapter 36

Although it was obviously no louder than on any other morning, Philip's alarm clock seemed to ring out with a force that grabbed him by the scruff of the neck and pinned him against the wall in some dark and unsavoury alleyway, before rifling through his pockets. It was only as he reached out to switch it off that the pain instantly flashed up his arm and across his shoulders. He let out a small incoherent murmur as his finger connected with the switch and the room once again fell silent. He lay still for a moment but when he finally attempted to climb out of bed, things actually managed to take a further turn for the worse. The pain in his arms and shoulders were forced to doff their cap to the pain in his legs. His inner thighs were stiffer than the collar of a starch salesman's shirt. His calf muscles began to sob at the thought of having to take part in any sort of physical activity. He sat on his bed, breathing rather heavily and with eyes beginning to water. 'If this is what it feels like after a training session,' he thought to himself, 'how on earth are you supposed to swim in an actual competition?' He stood up and slowly dressed. He left the bedroom and clambered down the stairs with a posture similar to that of a grey-haired pensioner with two heavy bags of shopping attempting to alight from a double decker bus on a windy day. As he slowly made his way through the living room and approached the kitchen door, he was taken by surprise by the sound of movement coming from inside. Upon entering he found his dad sitting at the kitchen table and in the process of lighting a Senior Service cigarette.

"Morning Son." his dad said as Philip opened the scullery door. "You want some breakfast?"

"No thanks Dad," Philip called out from inside the scullery. "I'll get it after my paper round."

"I've done you a fried egg sandwich," his dad said.

"I haven't got time," Philip replied.

"Haven't got time, haven't got time for a fried egg sandwich? How long does it take to eat a fried egg sandwich for Christ's sake?"

Philip peered around the scullery door and looked at his dad before looking at the fried egg sandwich that was resting upon a plate on the kitchen table. He walked over to the table, removed his paperbag from his shoulder, hung it over the back of the wooden chair, sat down and picked up the sandwich. He took a big bite and as the warm yolk of the egg burst inside his mouth, his dad leant back in his chair, opened the fridge door took out a bottle of milk and plonked it down on the kitchen table.

"Have you seen your sister recently?" he asked as he poured Philip a glass of milk.

Philip shook his head as he wiped yolk from his chin with the back of his hand.

"Not even yesterday, on her birthday?"

Philip took a swig of cold milk before answering. "I saw her but I didn't see her," he said before taking another bite of his sandwich.

"How do you mean? You either saw her or you didn't."

Philip again waited a moment to clear his mouth before responding. "I just dropped some cards and a present off, whilst I was on my paper round but I didn't stop."

"Oh, I see, did she say anything?"

"What about?" Philip replied before going in for another bite.

"Oh anything really, nothing in particular. Is she getting on okay? Are there any problems at the flat?"

"I don't think so," Philip said. "She didn't say anything if there are."

Francis finished his cigarette as Philip ate the rest of his sandwich.

"I'm off," Francis said as he stubbed the cigarette out. "I'm off to the depot; Snowy Vest has got some jobs for me, a bit of maintenance work, cash in hand, help out a little whilst things are a bit tight. Don't be late for your paper round or school. I'll see you tonight, think you mum has something planned as there's a cake in the fridge."

Francis departed the kitchen, leaving Philip to take the last mouthful of his sandwich and milk before he in turn collected his paperbag and made his way through the scullery. Each step on the journey to the newsagent's, each raising of the leg and crashing of the soles of his shoes onto the pavement beneath sent a searing pain through his aching calves and thighs. As he tentatively and carefully made his way along Henley Road, Paul McBride came cycling towards him on a blue and red Raleigh racing bike, coming to a stop just as Philip was about to cross the road.

"Where you bin?" Paul said as he delved inside his paperbag and took out a folded piece of paper.

"Where'd ya get the bike?" Philip asked.

"Now that would be telling, Philly boy, good deal though, only cost me four quid, almost brand spanking too." He passed the piece of paper to Philip. "Some new ones on the list, still need that fishing reel, if you can get a good one, I can get a good price for it. You'll be pleased to hear that I don't need the Cliff Richard L.P any longer. Fat Bobby Cowley managed to get it on cassette from some petrol station. Do you know him?"

"No." Philip replied. "I don't think so."

"He's alright, bit of a twat, he lives in Potters Green, goes to Woodway Park, bit thick but a good lifter though. He needs to be cus the fat fucker ain't running far if he gets caught. Here's your money for the stuff you got the other day." Paul reached out and handed over Philip's share before turning away. "Gotta go," he said. "Running late but not as late as you."

As Paul cycled off into the distance, Philip shoved the piece of paper and the money into his pocket. He hurried along as fast as his aching legs would allow him, towards the newsagent's. On arrival, he was greeted by a rather disgruntled looking Mr Underwood and a lonely, isolated bundle of morning papers resting on the counter.

"I'd nearly given you up," Mr Underwood said.

"Sorry." Philip replied. "I was having breakfast with my dad and I lost track of time," he added as he put the pile of newspapers into his bag.

"Well off you go. I'll see you this evening, on time hopefully, unless you're having dinner with a great aunt."

Philip didn't reply. Instead he carefully placed the bag onto his aching shoulder and left the shop. He was about halfway through his paper round and was just coming out of Watcombe Avenue before the strap of his bag stopped cutting into his severely sore shoulder blade. The weight and thickness of the morning papers, as a rule, were not cause for concern, but on this particular morning, it felt as if the bag was made of concrete and each of the papers inside were made of thick shiny strips of steal. It wasn't until he was working his way along Ellacombe Road and was down to his last few papers that he was able to walk with a more upright posture. As the final paper disappeared through the letterbox and landed upon the mat on the other side of the door, he breathed a heavy sigh and gave his shoulder a gentle rub. Then as fast as his body could muster, he made his way home.

Needless to say, he was late getting home, late eating his breakfast, late getting dressed for school, late leaving for school and inevitably late for school. James had had the foresight to leave without his brother as he had realised, with room to spare, that Philip wasn't going to be ready on time. Philip, on the other hand, wasn't even out of Monkswood Crescent when the number twenty six bus he was meant to be on pulled away from the terminus on Winston Avenue. As he knew that his chances of reaching the Henley Road in time to catch the '8A' were slimmer than a catwalk model's shadow, he accepted his fate and opted to catch the next twenty six. He eventually arrived at school a full twenty two minutes late. As he arrived, his name was taken by the prefects on the gate. Gone were the days when he was able to run past them, shouting out a false name as he did so. Now he would even receive a hello or a good morning from the prefect as he walked past.

Philip entered 'Morgan House' common room just in time to hear his name being called out. He knew exactly what that meant and as soon as the assembly had finished, he headed for a very familiar location on a Monday morning, outside Mr Spencer's office.

As he sat and watched a procession of boys receive their punishment from Mr Spencer, checking of course for any signs of weakness, any trembling lips, any teary eyes, any leakages, it suddenly dawned on him that he had no idea why he was there. He hadn't been on a work card or a conduct card the previous week and as yet, Mr Spencer would not have known that he was late that morning as the prefects would still be on patrol. So why oh why was he there? Why had his name been called out during the roll of honour in assembly?

About third from last to feel the thin wispy strip of cane come crashing down upon his soft fleshy palm was a small boy in a blazer that had clearly belonged to his older, bigger brother at some point in the past. He was a year two boy, year three at most. Philip would have waged his dinner money on the boy buckling, if anybody had been laying bets that morning. Thankfully for Philip, they weren't as the young boy held firm and hardly flinched as Mr Spencer dished out his just deserts.

Moments later Philip was the only boy left, sitting outside Mr Spencer's office. As for Mr Spencer himself, he had just dispensed with the final culprit from the previous week. The boy, with his hands frantically being rubbed together, had been sent on his way and Mr Spencer had stepped back inside his office.

"In you come Knott." Mr Spencer called out.

Philip stood up slowly and walked into the office.

"Shut the door boy," Mr Spencer said as he sat down.

Philip turned and closed the door, before positioning himself on the other side of Mr Spencer's desk.

Mr Spencer was just about to speak when there was a knock upon the office door. Rather irritated by the interruption, Mr Spencer raised his eyes towards the ceiling, before asking Philip to open the door and establish what the person knocking on the other side wanted.

Philip opened the door and proceeded to do exactly what he had been instructed to do. He asked the prefect, standing in front of him, what it was he wanted. The prefect ignored Philip, took a step forward and peered around the door.

"The late book sir," he said as he made eye contact with Mr Spencer and held the book in the air.

"Well give it here then lad. Don't just stand there waving it around like a poorly designed kite."

Philip stepped aside as the prefect entered the office, handed the book to Mr Spencer and quickly retreated, leaving the door ajar as he did so.

Still holding the book in his hand, Mr Spencer shook his head. "Close the door Philip, we haven't got all day," he said as he placed the book on his desk.

For the second time in as many minutes, Philip closed the door and repositioned himself in front of the desk.

"Now then lad, first things first. Do you have any money for me towards the outward bound trip in January? Fifty pence a week, I think we agreed upon."

Philip had forgotten all about the school trip and the agreement to pay off a certain amount each week. "Yes I have sir but I forgot to bring it with me, I can bring it tomorrow," he quickly replied.

Mr Spencer leant back in his chair and stared directly at Philip. "See that you do," he said. "There are only so many places on the trip and I'm sure that I can find another boy that would be happy to take your place, if needs be."

In an attempt to relieve the stiffness in his legs, Philip swayed from side to side for a moment or two as if he had just been gathered up by a stiff breeze.

"Anyhow," Mr Spencer continued. "That's not the main reason I wanted to see you," he added as he leant forward again, placed his elbows on the table and rested his chin upon his overlapping hands. "What's this I hear about you not being able to attend training on Wednesday."

Not quite sure if he was relieved or not to discover the reason that he had been summoned to Mr Spencer's office, Philip took a few seconds to think before he replied.

"It's difficult Sir," He eventually muttered.

"In what way?" Mr Spencer asked.

"It starts at six and my dad doesn't leave for work until about that time."

"Can't your dad leave a bit earlier and drop you off or can't you leave before him so that you can get there on time?"

"Not really Sir."

"Why on earth not Knott?"

There was a moment's silence that lasted far too long for Mr Spencer's liking and nowhere near long enough for Philip's liking.

Eventually Philip spoke. "My dad doesn't know I'm going sir and if he found out, he'd do his nut and there's also my brother sir, I need to be at home to look after him."

"Oh, I see, tricky. What about your mother, is she still unwell?"

"Good days and bad days sir...mostly bad."

Mr Spencer sat back in his chair again. "Well lad, you're going to have to get this sorted out and quickly. I cashed in a favour to get you a shot at this. I believed you had the ability. I don't want you letting me down. You can't be expected to be selected for the team if you are not prepared to attend training. You'd better get off, don't want you being late for your class."

With his shoulders still feeling like they were on fire and with stiffness still dominating the feeling in his legs, Philip turned and left the office.

Chapter 37

No sooner had the teacher completed his sentence and informed the class that the lesson was at an end than Philip had shoved his text books into his rucksack, fastened the straps whilst walking and headed out of the door.

He had given James similar instructions to be as quick as he could but he still found himself waiting impatiently at the school gates for two full minutes before spotting his brother casually making his way up the hill. As soon as he felt that James was in earshot, Philip called out for his brother to hurry up. To his frustration, he watched James continue to plod along up the hill. Philip marched down the hill, took hold of his brother's arm and pulled him along like a small boy dragging a parent towards the entrance of a fun fair.

"What's the rush?" James called out as he was dragged through the school gates and towards Belgrave Road.

"You know what!" Philip replied. "I told you this morning."

"Oh yeah." James said as he broke into a small trot, in order to keep up with his brother.

The pair hurried along at a strong pace with Philip always a few yards ahead and continually turning his head to make sure that his brother was not falling too far behind. The bus arrived within a couple of minutes of the boys reaching the bus stop along the Ansty Road.

Once they had alighted at the end of their journey, Philip marched on ahead. Only on this occasion, he wasn't bothering to turn around and check on the progress of his brother quite as often. He quickly glanced back as he entered Monkswood Crescent but James was still ambling along Henley Road.

As soon as he entered the house, Philip dropped his school bag on the floor of the scullery and raced upstairs, grabbing a towel from the airing cupboard before dashing into his bedroom. He quickly removed his blazer, jumper, tie and shirt, leaving them to fall at his feet. He took hold of the towel and wrapped it around his naked torso as tightly and as flat as possible before putting a t-shirt and his school jumper over the top. He tucked the t-shirt tightly into his trousers, to hold the towel in place. Just as he had finished tucking the t-shirt in and had begun to search for his swimming trunks, his dad walked into the room.

"Where's your brother?" he asked.

"He'll be here in a minute dad, he's just taking his time as usual."

"And what's your rush?"

"Mr Underwood wants me to do an extra round tonight, one of the other lads is sick."

"Well I've got to leave a little earlier myself. Snowy Vest wants to see me about something or other. I'll get some tea for James and me; you'll have to sort yourself out when you get back."

"Okay dad," Philip replied.

"And see if your mum wants anything when you get back, she's asleep at the minute."

"Okay dad," Philip said again, hoping that his response would be sufficient enough for his dad to leave the room.

Thankfully, without any further discussion, his dad did indeed turn and leave the room. Upon his dad's departure, Philip quickly gathered up everything else he needed and concealed the items about his person. His swimming trunks were neatly folded and placed down the back of his trousers. His goggles were concealed in his left sock and some money, along with the swimming club membership form he was given after the session on Sunday, were placed in his trouser pocket. Then as quickly as he had arrived, he left.

He passed through the kitchen, where James was now sitting at the small kitchen table and his dad was placing the chip pan on the cooker. Philip headed out of the house via the scullery, collecting his paperbag as he did so.

It would come as no surprise to discover that he was the first paperboy to arrive at the newsagents. In fact to his immediate annoyance, he had arrived before the evening papers and spent the next twelve minutes pacing up and down outside the shop looking along the road in search of the black, 'Evening Telegraph', delivery van.

Whilst he was waiting and watching impatiently, a steady stream of paperboys filtered past and disappeared inside the shop. The next paperboy to arrive was Paul McBride on his new Raleigh bicycle.

"Alright Phil?" he said as he dismounted and leant his bike up against the shop window. "Papers here yet?"

"No, not yet," Philip replied before adding, "Any chance I can borrow your bike?"

"You what, no chance mate. I'm hardly gonna lend it to you then do my flamin' paper round on foot."

"No, I mean after. After you have finished your round, can I borrow it then, just for tonight, I'll bring it back first thing tomorrow morning?"

"Sorry mate, no can do. However, I am prepared to discuss the possibility of you loaning it, for a small fee of course".

"How much?" Philip asked.

"That all depends."

"On what?"

"On what you want it for, how long you want it for, where you're taking it, if you will be leaving it unattended for any length of time and if you have adequate security provisions such as an acceptable, strong padlock."

"Adequate security provisions?" Philip asked with a puzzled tone in his voice.

"Yes Philip. I don't want it getting nicked, that's what happened to the last bloke which owned it." Paul paused for a moment before adding, "You'll need some lights as well."

"Could you get me a bike?" Philip asked.

"Well I could certainly put the word out for you and I can add it to the list. Will you be wanting lights and a good padlock as well?"

"I guess so," Philip replied. "How much will it cost?"

"A bike like this with a good padlock and lights, you're looking at about six or seven pounds."

"How much?" Philip said with a large dollop of shock sploshed on top of his words. "I can get a second-hand one out of the paper for that."

"Ah, yes you can Phil, but as you have just stated, it will be second-hand and not a brand spanker like this one."

"But it won't be nicked either."

The two boys were so engrossed in their conversation that neither of them noticed the 'Evening Telegraph' delivery van pull up and the driver drop off three bundles of newspapers inside the newsagent's door, before climbing back into his van and speeding off towards the next delivery.

"Another valid point Phil, it won't be nicked. A bike like this one is about twenty pounds in Dick Sheppards. I can get you one for about seven. Or I can get you a less impressive looking, cheaper one for about three or four quid, lights and lock included, hopefully. At the end of the day Phil, it's up to you."

The newsagent door swung open and Mr Underwood popped his head outside. "Are you two delivering any papers tonight?" he asked as a steady stream of paperboys began to exit the shop.

"Just let me know Phil," Paul said as he headed into the shop.

"What about me using your bike tonight?" Philip replied as he followed Paul into the shop.

"Get some lights and a good padlock and we can then enter into negotiations about you loaning my bike."

"Can't I just use yours?" Philip asked.

"You can when I get some, they're on the list," Paul replied as he began to fill his bag with that evening's edition of the 'Evening Telegraph'. He then turned away from the counter and headed for the door. "Catch you later." he said as he opened the door and stepped back out into the early evening chill.

Philip suddenly noticed that he was the last paperboy in the shop and Mr Underwood was now standing in front of him, clutching an armful of newspapers. Realising his literal schoolboy error and how much time the distraction had cost him, he quickly filled his bag with copies of the evening paper and dashed out of the shop.

Chapter 38

"Look son, you're a good swimmer, in fact, you are a very good swimmer. In fact, you are one of the best young swimmers I've ever seen and I've been coaching young swimmers for nearly twenty years. You do the maths, if your maths is half as good as your swimming, you should be able to work out that comes to a lot of swimmers."

Philip was sitting on a small black imitation leather chair, in an equally small office which was on the first floor of the swimming baths. It was located just before you reached the café and the stairs that led up to the public seating gallery.

In between Philip and the seat currently being occupied by Mr Kennedy was a large wooden desk. To the left of the desk stood a metal filing cabinet with a white electric fan perched on top. To the right of the desk and in line with Mr Kennedy's chair was a small white fridge. A faint smell of chlorine and disinfectant hung in the air, suggesting that the office had had a past life as a store cupboard. There were no windows in the office and the bright glow from the neon light in the ceiling filled the room with a soft golden haze.

"Would you like a drink lad?" Mr Kennedy asked as he reached over and opened the fridge.

"Yes please," Philip replied.

"Lemonade okay?"

"Yes please," Philip said again.

Mr Kennedy took two small glass bottles of lemonade out of the fridge and placed them on the desk. With one swift action, he closed the fridge and opened the top drawer of his desk. He took out a bottle opener, opened both bottles, reached across and passed one of the bottles to Philip, then returned the opener before closing the drawer again.

"Do you know the worst thing about coaching?" Mr Kennedy said as he raised his bottle of lemonade to his lips.

Philip very quickly realised that he had just been asked a rhetorical question.

"I mean besides the early starts and the late nights, always having wrinkled toes, verruca's and having to constantly wear flip-flops. Above all that and above all else, it's the parents."

Mr Kennedy paused and took another mouthful of lemonade, shaking his head as he did so.

"You see the parents all believe that their little darlings are going to be the next big thing, the next David Wilkie." He paused again before asking. "You know who David Wilkie is, don't you?"

"Yes." Philip replied. "He got a silver medal at the last Olympics."

"Yes, well, these parents all expect their kids to do the same and that makes them the worst type of parent. Do you know why?"

Pleased that he spotted this particular rhetorical question quicker than last time around, Philip shook his head.

"Because they are middle class parents and there's nothing worse than middle class parents. All in their semi-detached homes with their own driveway. Living along the Allesley Road, or Binley Woods or Stychale. Beige carpets on the landing, magazine racks in the lounge, spice racks in the kitchen and prawn cocktail in the fridge. You understand what I'm trying to say, no right-minded person would entertain the thought of eating prawn cocktail, would they?"

Philip knew that this question required an answer but as he didn't have one, he just shook his head and carried on drinking his lemonade.

"So we can't very well have a Bash Street Kid turning up and taking young Cuthbert's place on the team. Especially a Bash Street Kid that turns up late for training, if he bothers to turn up at all. Do you know who the Bash Street Kids are?"

"Yes," Philip replied. "They are characters in the Beano."

"Good," Mr Kennedy said. "Then you understand what I am trying to say."

Philip didn't reply, he simply carried on drinking from his bottle of lemonade. Mr Kennedy placed his empty bottle on to the desk before continuing.

"So do you see why it is more important for you that you turn up for training and you turn up on time? You give them the slightest reason to want you off the team and I'll have a queue of parents lined up outside my door, banging on it like a bunch of extremely irate chimpanzees, understand?"

This time Philip was able to reply. "Yes," he said.

"Good, now have you bought your membership form and your money with you?"

Holding his lemonade bottle in one hand, Philip leant to one side and with his other hand, he reached inside the back pocket of his flared denim jeans and retrieved a neatly folded piece of paper and an equally neatly folded one-pound note.

"Have your parents signed it?" Mr Kennedy asked as he reached across and took the form and the money from Philip.

"Yes." Philip replied.

On top of the pound it cost to join the Coventry Godiva's Swimming Club, the forged signatures had cost him another thirty pence. Although Mr Kennedy would have no idea if the signatures were fake or not, Philip didn't want to take the chance and felt that it was money well spent.

Philip took the last mouthful of lemonade from his bottle and placed it on the desk. He sat back in his seat as Mr Kennedy looked over his membership form.

"It usually takes a week or two to get you registered and you cannot compete until you have your registration number. We have a home meet on Sunday but you won't be registered in time for that. However, I still want you to be here so that other people get used to seeing your face about the place. The next training session is next Wednesday. Don't forget it is twenty five pence for every session you attend. We have another meet the following Sunday in Birmingham, hopefully you should be registered by then. You need to be here by twenty past eight at the latest. Bus leaves at eight thirty sharp. It's fifty pence for the bus and fifty pence for the meet. We'll need to work on those turns but I want you to swim the fifty metres butterfly, fifty metres freestyle and swim the butterfly leg of the medley relay, okay?"

Philip was lost for words. With his mouth opened wide and his face aglow, he simply nodded.

"Right lad, get yourself off home," Mr Kennedy said as he gathered up the two empty lemonade bottles from his desk. "Be here by nine on Sunday," he added. The sound of the glass bottles colliding with each other filled the room as Mr Kennedy leant over and placed them in a waste bin by the side of his desk.

As Philip exited the swimming baths and made his way along Fairfax Street, the cold autumn air rested upon the surface of his skin and nestled into his still damp hair. Darkness had descended and soft hazy drops of rain that were only visible when you looked up towards the street lights had begun to tumble towards the ground. Beyond the glow from the lights and further up the outline of silvery grey clouds were just about recognisable as they hovered in front of the thick blanket of darkening sky. Philip continued along Fairfax Street, crossed the road by Sainsbury's and walked towards the bus shelter outside of the Coventry Theatre and directly opposite the fire station. He leant against the outside of the bus shelter and waited patiently for the number twenty one bus to arrive. By the time he reached home, his hair was once again quite wet but the rest of him was only ever so slightly damp, like a flannel that had just been used to wipe away some vanilla flavoured ice-cream from a small child's face.

Philip opened the back door and stepped inside. Sitting on the sofa, cuddled up under a blanket were James and his mother. An episode of 'Softly Softly' had just drawn to a close and the titles were beginning to roll across the television screen.

"And where exactly have you been?" his mother asked before looking a little more closely and noticing Philip's still damp hair. "Have you been swimming? Did you go straight after your paper round?"

The paper bag draped over his left shoulder was a big clue to the answer to the third question. The first two questions were also answered when Philip removed his rolled up towel and trunks from inside his paper bag.

"Who said you could go swimming on a school night?"

"It wasn't swimming, it was training," Philip replied.

"Training, swimming, it's the same thing and anyway I thought you went training on Sunday?"

"I did but they train twice a week."

"I don't care how many times a week they train Philip, you cannot simply take off without telling anybody where you have gone."

"But if I don't turn up to train, I can't compete," Philip said, still holding his rolled up towel in his hand and with his paper bag still draped over his shoulder.

"Go and put those things in the wash basket and hang that paper bag up." his mother said as she stepped out from beneath the blanket. "I'll make us all a hot drink before bed. James, would you like a Horlicks?"

James nodded as he scooped the blanket up and wrapped it around him. Philip did as he was asked, before returning to the living room and sitting on the sofa next to James. Sportsnight was on after the news with European highlights fingers crossed it would be highlights of the Leeds United game.

A few short minutes later Philip, James and their mother were all sitting on the sofa with the blanket draped across their legs, all holding a mug of hot, milky Horlicks and not paying attention to the nine o'clock news. As Philip gently blew the skin on the top of his drink to one side of the mug, his mother asked,

"So what is this competition?"

"They're not called competitions in swimming mum, they're called meets," Philip replied.

"Oh so sorry, do forgive me. So they want you to compete in a meet, how sweet," his mother said whilst sending a smile in James's direction.

James smiled back. Philip wanted to feel annoyed but it was the first time in a long time that his mother had made a joke and smiled in such a short space of time that he elected to savour the moment instead.

"There's a meet in Birmingham in a couple of weeks' time. The head coach wants me to compete for the club. But I have to attend training if I want to be selected."

"I thought you had to be a member of the club to be able to compete. Your teacher said…"

"You do mum," Philip interrupted. "I joined tonight."

Philip held his breath and stared at his reflection wobbling upon the glossy surface of his drink as he awaited a response. It took a little longer than expected but eventually his mother asked,

"I thought it cost money to join this club. How did you pay for it?"

"Money I'd saved from my paper round."

"And what do you think will happen when your dad finds out? You know how he feels about this."

"You won't tell him, will you?" Philip asked with a certain amount of dread in his voice.

"No, I won't tell him, he already thinks I have no idea what my children are up to but he will find out eventually and when he does…" His mother replied with an expression upon her face that was accompanied by a shrug of the shoulders.

"But I can pay for it myself out of my paper round money and Grace said that she would help out."

"That's not the point Philip as you well know."

His mother was about to add something else, just for good measure, when she was distracted by the 'Sportsnight' theme tune as it sprang from the television set and filled the room. She once again moved the blanket to one side and got to her feet. "I want you both in bed as soon as this finishes." She finished off her drink and took her empty mug into the kitchen, before heading back through the living room and up the stairs. "Wash the mugs up before you go to bed Philip," she called out as she exited the room.

The door closed behind her, leaving Philip and James to watch 'Sportsnight'. Unfortunately for Philip, Harry Carpenter introduced highlights of Liverpool's finely balanced European encounter against Luxembourg minnows Jeunesse Esch, though he did see the results of all the other games. Leeds United had a convincing 6-1 win against their Norwegian opponents, to go safely through to the second round of the European Cup, 7-2 on aggregate.

Chapter 39

Philip arrived home, after completing his paper round on Saturday morning, feeling decidedly chilly. A sudden cold snap overnight had left him ill prepared as he had set off an hour or so earlier and by the time he arrived back home, his nose, ears, finger tips and toes were beginning to sting. Inside his paperbag however was a stolen copy of 'Shoot' magazine which he had been able to slide in when he had legitimately purchased this week's copy of 'Tiger'.

To his surprise, as he hung up his paperbag in the scullery, collected his magazines and entered the kitchen, he found his mother already up, dressed and sitting at the kitchen table. She was eating a bowl of porridge oats and, resting upon a small plate, next to her bowl of porridge, sat half a grapefruit with a sprinkling of demerara sugar on top.

"You look cold," his mother said as he closed the scullery door. "Sit yourself down and I'll get you a bowl of porridge."

Philip stepped over to the table, placed his magazines on top and then sat down. He watched his mother as she collected a bowl from the cupboard above the table, journeyed to the stove, took hold of the wooden spoon resting in the pan and filled the bowl with porridge. She took out a spoon from the cutlery drawer en route back to the table before placing both items down in front of Philip.

"There you go," she said. "That will help keep the cold out."

Philip stood up and from the other side of the cupboard that housed the crockery, he retrieved a tin of Lyons Golden Syrup. This time it was his mother's turn to watch him. Philip prized the lid off the tin with the handle of his spoon before diving in and scooping up half a spoonful of sticky, shiny golden syrup. He then held the spoon about six to eight inches above his bowl of porridge and allowed the syrup to slowly lose the inevitable battle with gravity. The syrup drizzled off the spoon and all over the bumpy surface of his breakfast. Once that particular task had been completed, he pressed the lid back on to the tin of syrup before taking a bottle of milk from the fridge and pouring some on to the surface of the porridge, watching carefully as it began to mix with the syrup. As he sat down again and picked up his spoon, his mother looked across at him and smiled.

Philip was scraping the last remnants of porridge from his bowl when his mother asked. "What do you have planned for the rest of the day?"

Not wanting anything to get in the way or cause unnecessary distractions for what he had planned and not being in the position to be able to discuss what he had planned, Philip shrugged his shoulders as he replied. "Not sure."

"Well would you mind taking your brother to Saturday morning cinema at the Odeon?" His mother asked as she stood up and began to clear the table.

Philip had a shoplifting list, recently acquired, sizzling away and burning a hole in his back pocket, so much so that he felt that he could smell the material smouldering as the smoke drifted up towards the ceiling. The last thing he needed right now was to get lumbered with having to chaperone his brother.

"Do I have to?" he replied with desperation clinging to every word, like dust on a strip of Sellotape, as they fell from his lips.

His mother didn't answer straight away. Instead she just gave him a look. Though very subtle in its design, the information contained within it was plain to see. After a few further moments of silence, she asked, "What's up, I thought you enjoyed Saturday morning cinema? You used to go nearly every week."

Saturday morning cinema was very much aimed at the younger audience. A little something for everyone, the advertisement outside the cinema claimed. The advertisement even went as far as claiming two and a half hours of pure fun. The fun would start at 10am with a couple of 'Bugs Bunny' cartoons. This would then be followed by an episode of 'Disney Time', where a random selection of scenes from a library of 'Disney' films and documentaries would be packaged together into a thirty-minute medley. This would then be followed by the dusting off of a thirty-minute episode of the 'Lone Ranger' or 'Casey Jones' or 'Champion the Wonder Horse'. If you were really fortunate it might be an episode of something a bit more relevant and closer to home such as Here come the 'Double Deckers'. A brief intermission would then follow, giving the audience an opportunity to purchase a choc-ice from one of the usherettes that had appeared, as if by magic, at the front of the screen. Once all transactions had been completed, the lights would be dimmed once more, in time for the main feature. If you were lucky you would be treated to a Disney film of clout or a Ray Harryhausen classic such as 'Jason and the Argonauts' or 'The Golden Voyage of Sinbad'. If you were extremely lucky, luckier than an Irishman standing at the end of a rainbow with a four-leaf clover in his sweaty palm, you may well be rewarded by a screening of 'Godzilla vs Gigan' or 'Godzilla vs The Smog Monster'. However, the last time Philip went, a few weeks before the summer holidays, he had to sit through something called 'The Million Dollar Duck'.

As the awful memory of 'The Million Dollar Duck' pushed and shoved its way to the forefront of his thoughts, Philip turned to his mother. "I just don't enjoy it much anymore," he began. "it's for younger kids and I guess I've just grown out of it."

"Well you'll just have to loosen that waistband a little and squeeze back into it one more time, because I don't want James being left on his own or around the house today."

"But why?" Philip asked

"Because I've got an appointment at the hospital this morning and you know what your father thinks about that, so I don't want him waking up in a foul mood, with a sore head and James finding himself in the firing line." She paused for a moment. "Or you for that matter."

"Can't we go swimming instead?"

"No, you cannot. James said that he wanted to go to the cinema and I promised him you'd take him. You can go swimming next week."

"But mum," Philip muttered. However, his protest was cut short by a far sterner interruption.

"Please Philip, just do as I ask. I'll give you the money to get in and enough left over for you both to go to the Wimpy for some lunch and an ice-cream. Now can you go and get your brother up, quietly, don't wake your dad, and tell him to come and get some breakfast, whilst I clear away and wash up these things. I need to be getting ready as well, we can catch the bus together."

"Why isn't dad going with you?"

"Because he doesn't want to and I don't want him to." With this, she turned away and began running the hot water into the plastic bowl waiting in the sink.

Philip got up from the table. Realising that there was no avoiding the inevitable, he collected his comics and left the kitchen. He tossed the comics onto the sofa on the way past and went upstairs, quietly, to wake up his brother.

Philip, James and Mrs Knott arrived at the number twenty-one bus stop, opposite the Live and Let Live public house, at exactly eleven minutes past nine. According to the timetable in Mrs Knott's handbag, the next bus was due to depart at nine seventeen. Running a few minutes behind schedule, the bus eventually arrived and departed again, upon the return journey to the town centre, at nine twenty.

To both Philip's surprise and enjoyment the journey into town was quite a pleasurable one. So pleasurable in fact that it completely took his mind off the money he needed to raise for the stolen bike he wanted to order, the money he needed to raise for his school trip and the money he needed to raise to cover his swimming club costs. For the majority of the journey, Mrs Knott was very chatty and jovial. Philip couldn't put his finger on why his mother was in such good spirits and he was more than happy not to go in search of an answer. Instead he just sat back and chose to enjoy the moment. The reason itself was quite simple. Just being out of the house and away from her husband for a few hours was more than sufficient to allow some sunlight in to her usually dark world.

As the bus reached the end of Stoney Stanton Road, near the Swanswell Park, Mrs Knott rang the bell to alight and make the short walk to the Coventry and Warwickshire Hospital. As the bus came to a stop, she leant forward and gave James a kiss on the cheek. Feeling that her eldest boy believed he was now too old for a kiss, she simply placed her hand on the back of his head for a few seconds as she stood up.

"Be good you two and I'll see you both later. I'll get some boiled bacon for tea." She said as she walked towards the back of the bus and stepped off the platform.

Ever since his mother had mentioned taking James to the cinema and reminiscent of a bout between Kendo Nagasaki and Giant Haystacks, Philip had been wrestling with his conscience. Several headlocks, throws against the corner posts, half nelsons and body slams later, he still hadn't been able to reach a decision. As the bus pulled away and his mother disappeared from view, he found himself being thrown to the canvas once more. As he lay there, he could feel the full weight of both Kendo and Giant Haystacks pressing down upon him. Turning to look at his brother as if he was a member of the audience only made matters worse and he knew the next headlock was only moments away.

The dilemma that he was wrestling with was quite simply this, should he go to the cinema with his brother and pass up the opportunity of earning some much needed revenue, or should he leave his brother in the cinema and head off into town in an attempt to acquire some of the items from the current updated shoplifting list? As the boys stepped off the bus and walked up to the Odeon cinema, the turmoil began to subside as Philip finally came to a decision. On this particular occasion the risks were just too great. The 'what if's' in the negative corner had out fought the 'what if's' in the positive corner.

Although there were only two 'what if's' in the negative corner, they were both menacing in their appearance and of the heavyweight variety. 'What if' something happens in the cinema and I'm not there, stood shoulder to shoulder with the even more threatening, 'what if' I get caught shoplifting and I'm not there to meet James when the show finishes. This particular 'what if' was a double whammy 'what if' and could not be ignored. Not only would he be in trouble for shoplifting but he would be in even deeper hot water for abandoning his brother.

Philip was able to console himself with the reassurance that he had enough money in reserve to cover this week's outgoings and although the funds needed for the bicycle were still some way off, if he went without sweets at the cinema and a desert in the Wimpy, he could syphon off a little of what his mother had given him.

"Two please". Philip said as he looked at the lady inside the ticket office in the centre of the foyer and pushed the money beneath the gap at the bottom of the glass panel.

"Can we get some sweets?" James asked.

"I'll get you something during the intermission," Philip replied as he collected the two tickets. "Let's hurry before all of the good seats are gone."

They continued on through the foyer, down a small flight of steps and across the plush carpeted floor towards the screen itself. Philip handed the tickets to the usherette standing by the doors, before pushing them open and both walking into the darkened room.

The boys located a couple of satisfactory seats in the middle of a row, about a dozen or so rows back from the front. No sooner had they sat down than the final pre-show advertisement finished, the lights came up and the curtain swung across the stage, covering the screen. Every child in the auditorium knew exactly what this meant. Inside a minute, the lights would set off in the opposite direction and travel all the way down to complete darkness. The electric curtain would exit stage left, the projector would begin to whirl and a customary cheer would ring out. The screen would then flicker into life and the show would commence.

Fully expecting the 'Lone Ranger' to burst upon the screen, Philip slumped into his chair a little. To his surprise, though not exactly a vast improvement, this time around the show started with an episode of 'Champion the Wonder Horse', entitled 'Canyon of Wanted Men'. This was followed by two 'Mr Magoo' cartoons, an episode of 'Disney Time' and then an episode of the 'Lone Ranger' brought the first half of the show to an end and steered the audience safely into the intermission. As the credits rolled and the lights came up, two usherettes had magically appeared in front of the stage.

James, still enthralled by the episode of the 'Lone Ranger' and perched on the edge of his seat, turned to his brother and asked, "Can we get some sweets now?"

"What do you want?" Philip replied.

"Can I have a box of chocolate raisins?"

"Do you want a drink as well?"

"No thanks, I'm alright."

Philip stood up, squeezed past his brother and half a dozen or so other boys of a similar age, before stepping into the aisle and joining the queue for the usherette. Upon reaching the front of the queue, he purchased two boxes of chocolate covered raisins and then set off on the journey back to his seat. Both boys sat in silence for the rest of the intermission and ate their respective boxes of chocolate covered raisins.

After a few more minutes of serving eager young children a selection of sweets and drinks, the usherettes made their way back up the aisles and out of view. The lights dimmed once more and the curtains departed in anticipation of the main feature. Luck held out for Philip, the projector whirled once more and filling the screen in glorious technicolour was the opening credits to 'Godzilla vs Hedorah'.

For whatever reason, Philip absolutely loved these films. The poor quality, rock bottom budget special effects didn't impact upon his enjoyment one iota. The equally poor quality scale models of Japanese cities, villages, countryside and oceans didn't matter either. Nor did the poor quality scale model of the nuclear power plant that was destroyed in every film, matter. For Philip it was the fact that these films were so far removed from anything else he came into contact with, which gave them a mystical quality. They were just so different, so unique that he simply sat back in his seat and absorbed every last frame.

As Godzilla let out one final flame throwing roar of defiance before disappearing beneath the ocean surface, leaving the emotionally scarred but ultimately thankful Japanese townsfolk to rebuild their lives, Philip exhaled a breath that had clearly been building up for quite some time.

The credits began to role, the lights came up and the cinema rapidly emptied. Young boys and girls, mainly boys, spilled out onto the street, adjusting their eyes to the early afternoon autumn sunshine as they did so, some being met by parents or other age responsible relatives, the rest scattering in a range of directions.

Philip and James set off towards Fairfax Street and the Wimpy café. Once seated inside, they both ordered a bowl of tomato soup. James had a glass of lemonade whilst Philip chose a glass of milk. For desert they shared a banana longboat, though Philip only had a couple of spoonful's before letting his brother eat the rest.

The boys arrived home a little before three o' clock. At first, upon entering the house via the back door, they thought that nobody was home, until they heard movements coming from a room upstairs. Spotting the comic he had discarded earlier that day, James picked it up, sat down on the sofa, opened it and began reading this week's adventures of Little Plum. Philip on the other hand, headed upstairs. Following the movement he could hear as he climbed the stairs, he soon found himself standing outside his mother's bedroom door. The door was slightly ajar. With a certain amount of trepidation, he pushed the door open sufficiently to allow him to step inside.

As he entered, he found his mother standing in the epicentre of chaos and devastation. It was as if a hurricane had just passed through the room and the tailwind has only just receded. Items of clothing were scattered everywhere, drawers were open wide, previous contents now strewn over a wide area, perfume bottles and hairspray cans lay upon the floor. His mother was picking items of clothing up, carefully folding them and placing them neatly on the bed. She looked across at her son as she continued to fold the jumper in her hands.

"What happened?" Philip asked.

"Your father happened," his mother replied.

They both stood in silence for a moment before his mother added as she placed the jumper on the bed. "Looking for a way to take the bitter taste out of his mouth."

Realising what his mother meant by her choice of words, Philip quickly turned and left. Moments later he entered his bedroom and looked across at the window sill. Standing on the sill was a bright red plastic, pig-design money box, about twelve inches high. He had had the money box since he was about nine years old. Both ears were chewed to the point that the plastic was now an off-white colour. Philip rushed over to the window, picked up the pig, turned it upside down, removed the stopper and shook the pig, whilst holding his other hand underneath. A fifty pence piece and two ten pence pieces fell into his hand. He turned the pig upside down again and peered inside. To his horror it was empty. The two, one-pound notes that should have been inside were gone. Pig in one hand, stopper and seventy pence in the other hand, he stood in disbelief. Lost for words, emptiness as vivid as the inside of his piggy bank gripped him tightly. He returned the coins and the stopper, placed the piggy bank back on the window sill and headed back down stairs. He switched the television set on and sat down in the chair. Although he sat and stared at the wrestling from Bedworth Civic Hall, he was located in a place much further away. So far away in fact that he didn't even move to turn the television over in time for the vidiprinter to start rolling. He watched the scores on 'ATV'. A 1-1 draw at home to Stoke City failed to raise his spirits from their current location beneath his feet. Not only was he unable to say anything about the money that had disappeared, for fear of the trouble it may cause but he no longer had enough money to pay for his swimming subs and his school trip, even if he added the money that was left over from the cinema trip.

Chapter 40

The swim meet was entering its latter stages with Coventry Godiva several points clear of its nearest pursuer, the City of Birmingham Swimming Club. Philip was sitting in the stands, busily transferring information of Leeds United's 1-1 draw with Stoke City from the 'News of the World' to the appropriate page in his 'Tiger' comic. Exactly as he was beginning to write down the names of the Stoke City line-up, his father, Francis Knott, was pushing open the saloon bar door of the Green Man public house in Alderman's Green. Although it was only a few minutes walk from the Bell Inn, the Green Man was an establishment that he had not frequented until now.

As the door swung shut behind him, Francis scanned the crowded room from left to right. Turning his head back towards its starting point on the second sweep, he caught sight of Snowy Vest. Snowy was standing up, waving an arm above his head and looking in Francis's direction. Both men weaved between and around crowded tables as they set off towards each other. As soon as the two men were close enough to make themselves heard above the hustle and bustle of the Sunday lunchtime chatter, Snowy pointed towards the bar.

"Bar," he called out as he pointed in the necessary direction.

With one final table between them, both men turned and headed for the bar.

"What you havin' Francis?" Snowy asked as they reached the bar.

"Bitter," Francis replied.

"Two bitters Jack and a Guinness." Snowy called out, in the direction of the man behind the bar.

"Hold your horses Snowy, I've only got the one pair of hands."

"No problem Jacko, when you're ready, when you're ready," Snowy replied as he placed his hand inside his dark blue blazer in search of his wallet.

With his lips pursed and his cheeks puffed out, as if he was about to whistle, Snowy exhaled. "What a week Francis, what a long week it has been!" he said as the men waited for the barman to pour the drinks.

"For some…" Francis replied.

Snowy raised his eyebrows. " Mmmm," he muttered. "Still not looking great at the moment is it."

"Have you invited me here to tell me things I already know Snowy or are you going to let me look through your soddin' understatements of the year yearbook 1973?"

"Relax Francis, relax," Snowy replied. "I didn't mean to cause offence."

Snowy was rescued from his awkward moment by the placing of two pints of bitter upon the bar in front of him. "Your Guinness will be here in a minute," the barman said before adding, "that will be forty eight pence Snowy."

Snowy picked up one of the pints of bitter and placed it down in front of Francis before opening his wallet and removing a one-pound note, which he proceeded to hand to the barman. "Have one yourself Jack," he said as he released the note.

"Thank you Snowy, I'll just have a half, I'll leave it in the tap for later. That's fifty seven pence altogether."

Snowy collected his change, placed it into his trouser pocket, picked up the pint of bitter in one hand, the pint of Guinness (which had by now arrived), in the other, turned away from the bar and headed back to his table. He weaved in, out and around the tables that lay in his path with Francis following closely behind. On arriving, he placed the pint of

Guinness down in front of a large balding gentleman with a round face and swollen neck before turning to Francis and motioning towards an empty chair with his now free hand.

"You know Lousy, don't you Francis?" Snowy asked as they both sat down.

"Guess so," Francis replied.

Lousy's real name was Albert Burns. He was one of the managers who worked upstairs in the office at the depot and was responsible for despatches. It was his job to check that the correct shipment found its way on to the correct lorry, left the depot at the correct time and reached the correct destination. If you were ever to find yourself in a conversation with Albert Burns, and it did not matter one iota how many times you found yourself in a conversation with Albert Burns, the nature of the conversation would always arrive at discussing, or rather listening to his tale about his ex-wife. You could be talking about your summer holiday or a fishing trip you recently went on, your verruca, your dog's bad breath or the difficulties of growing cucumbers without a greenhouse, yet sooner or later the conversation would arrive at his ex-wife. Or more precisely, as Albert would put it, 'how she cleaned me out, took the lot she did, left me with two saucepans, and one of them had a loose handle, a Whipsnade Zoo souvenir mug, a purple rug and a deck chair'.

Lousy was known as lousy due to his shocking inability to make a decent mug of tea. It had reached a point in the office where Lousy was no longer allowed to make tea, and to compensate for this shortfall was now duty bound to supply more biscuits than the other members of staff who worked in the office. The name itself was established when a colleague cried out one autumn afternoon, 'who the hell made this tea? it's lousy'!

Once the three men had introduced themselves to their respective drinks and Francis had lit a cigarette, Snowy muttered, "How's things Francis, financially I mean, I guess these short weeks are beginning to bite?"

"You could say that the dog's teeth are firmly sunk into soft pink flesh," Francis replied before taking a large gulp of bitter from his glass.

"You're not wrong there Francis," Lousy muttered. "Not wrong at all, not looking good for any of us."

Snowy took a sip of bitter from his glass, placed it gently on the table, then leant a little closer to Francis. In a soft voice, he said, "What if Lousy and me were able to put a bit of extra funding your way, would you be interested?"

"What do you mean?" Francis asked. "What is it, is it legal, on the level, above board?"

"Of course it is," Lousy replied. "That's why we are sitting in the corner of a pub, whispering to each other."

"Alright Lousy, settle down, the man's just asking." Snowy turned to Francis. "In answer to your question Francis, no it's not legit, legal, on the level or above board. Are you interested? Are you interested in making a few extra pounds to help you through these rather turbulent financial times?"

"I could be, but why me?" Francis asked.

"Because you are a man who can be trusted and like the rest of us Francis, you are also a man who needs the money."

"But why now?" Francis asked before taking a large drag from his cigarette.

"Because a window has been opened Francis, a vacancy, you might say, that need filling."

Lousy Piped up. "Yeah, George bloody Meadows has gone and moved on."

"Lousy," Snowy snapped, rather too loudly for his own liking, before glancing around the room to see if he had attracted any unwanted attention. "Francis doesn't need to know the reason for the vacancy, he just needs to know that there is a vacancy," he added in a much quieter voice once he was happy that nobody was listening.

Snowy continued. "Keep it under your hat Francis but George is leaving at the end of the week, well Wednesday in fact as we are still on these short weeks. His brother-in-law has offered him full-time, driving for his removals firm."

"I thought he didn't like his brother-in-law."

"He doesn't Francis, fuckin' hates him but it's full time and like I say we all need the money. Don't think he actually wanted to take the job but the wife, you know what it's like."

"Can't believe you need the money Lousy, on a management wage and all that?" Francis said.

Snowy raised his eyebrows, closed his eyes, sighed, opened his eyes again and looked down at his pint. He knew exactly what was coming. As sure as Wednesday followed Tuesday, flared trouser had patch pockets and every boy between the ages of ten and fourteen had a Parka coat, he knew what was coming. Sure enough, it arrived almost immediately.

"You're joking ain't you Francis?" Lousy Began. "I need the money more than any of you. My bloody ex-wife cleaned me out. Took the lot she did. Left me with two saucepans, and one of them had a loose handle, a Whipsnade Zoo souvenir mug, a purple rug and a deck chair. Even had to sell me house. Over twenty years paying for that house, just so she could click her solicitor's fingers and walk off with it. Nice detached house in Atherstone it was. Now all I've got to show for it is a shitty little semi in Barwell. So don't go thinking that just because I drive a cream coloured Rover and wear a suit to work that I am sitting at the top of the hill with a fat fuckin cigar in my mouth Francis, cuz I'm not."

Snowy slipped a hand inside his blazer pocket and retrieved his brown leather wallet. He opened it and carefully extracted a crisp, flat one pound note. "Why don't you go and get the drinks in Lousy," he said as he gently placed the pound note on the table before closing his wallet and putting it back in his blazer pocket, "whilst I have a chat with Francis."

Lousy placed his hands on the edges of his chair before levering his large, bulky, overweight frame into the air. Once he was upright and stabilised, he collected the money from the table and set off in the direction of the bar. Snowy watched and waited until Lousy was well on the way towards his destination before he once again leaned a little closer to Francis.

"Listen here Francis, it's rather straightforward really. Every now and then a few boxes or packages, as we all know the way gravity works, from time to time fall off the back of lorries. It just so happens that we are in a position to choose the lorry and what it is that falls off it."

"But surely somebody knows if items have gone missing?" Francis replied.

"Only if it looks like they have gone missing, if the paperwork is in order. You'll only go looking for something if you know it isn't there."

Snowy paused for a moment and filled the time by having a quick look around the pub to check that Francis was the only person paying attention to what he had to say. "Look Francis, Lousy over there, he picks the load. Not much value in having it away with a dozen boxes of washing up gloves. However, a few boxes of nice Italian leather shoes, now there is money to be made there. As I was saying, Lousy gives us the nod, I mark the boxes and load them accordingly onto the lorry. You drive the lorry, you meet our contact just outside Rochdale, he takes them off your hands and the rest of the load reaches the depot. Our man in the office at the other end fills in the paperwork."

"But at some point, somewhere, somebody is going to discover that they haven't got as many pairs of nice Italian leather shoes as they should have," Francis said before finishing off his drink and stubbing out his cigarette.

Snowy glanced over Francis's right shoulder and spotted Lousy setting off on his return journey with two pints of bitter and a pint of Guinness delicately grasped between both sets of his fat, stubby fingers. "Listen Francis, why don't you have a think about it? You'll have to come off the Bristol run of course. We can talk again in the week. But listen Francis, if you're not interested, that's fine, but if you're not, then this conversation never took place."

Snowy stared hard at Francis for a few seconds before sitting back in his seat. Francis reached for his cigarettes as Lousy reached the table and placed the drinks down.

"Anybody for a game of three card brag?" Snowy asked as he reached for his drink.

Chapter 41

Philip arrived home, looking and feeling slightly windswept, on a blustery Wednesday afternoon. He had been delayed somewhat by a rather drawn out conversation with his religious studies teacher about his lack of interest in the subject, and as a result, he had just missed the 8A bus. The bus itself had pulled away from the stop as he reached the top of Arch Road. Rather than wait for the next bus or walk in the wrong direction along the Ansty Road to catch the twenty-six, he opted to carry on walking down Wyken Croft with the strong wind swirling around him.

As he came through into the living room, Philip immediately noticed the letter, propped up against a tomato sauce bottle on the dining table. Francis was sitting at the table, directly behind the letter, eating a bacon sandwich.

"Here you go, I believe this is for you," Francis said as he held the letter up.

"Dad!" Philip replied with clear annoyance in his voice, as he rushed over to grab hold of the letter.

"What?" Francis asked.

"You'll get grease stains all over it," Philip said as he took hold of the letter and began inspecting it before attempting to brush away the thumb print that was clearly visible in the top right-hand corner.

"It's only a letter son, it's not the bloody crown jewels."

Philip turned away from his father, still rubbing the envelope, so that Francis could not see the less than impressed expression on his face. After accepting that the grease stain was now a permanent feature, he headed off into the scullery to collect his paper bag. He very carefully placed the letter inside the bag, before equally carefully removing the bag from one of the coat hooks by the side door. As he headed back through the living room on his way to collect his swimming gear from upstairs his dad asked.

"So this footballer is still writing to you then?"

"I guess so," Philip replied.

"What do you talk about?"

"Nothing much".

"Oh I see, he just sends you blank pieces of paper does he?"

Philip shrugged his shoulders whilst edging a little nearer to the door. "He just tells me about the games and I tell him about school and stuff."

Francis raised his head considerably higher and looked over the top of the sandwich in his hand at Philip. "As long as that's all you talk about. I don't want this family's business being discussed in the bloody Leeds United dressing room. Don't you tell him anything about your mother either?"

"I won't," Philip replied as he reached for the door handle.

"Good. Before you dash off, I'm away early again tonight. Snowy is changing my route."

"Why?" Philip asked.

"Never mind why. I'm on the Rochdale route from next week, so he wants me to go along for the ride with George Meadows tonight as it is his last run. Sort yourself and your brother something to eat when you get back from your paper round, unless your mother can manage it."

Philip finally managed to exit the room. He quickly bounded up the stairs, two or three at a time. On entering the bedroom, he found James, lying on his bed reading his comic. Once again Billy Whizz was making rather hard work of arriving at his desired destination on time.

"Dad's leaving for work soon," Philip said. "Once he's gone, go and get yourself some cereal for your tea okay?"

James didn't offer a verbal reply, he just nodded and carried on reading his comic.

Once a towel, a pair of trunks and a pair of swimming goggles had been concealed beneath his school uniform, Philip turned and left. Being sure not to make eye contact as he passed through the living room, he called out "See you later dad."

"Night son." Francis replied.

Philip left the house and set off for the newsagents. As soon as he reached the end of the close and before it became too dark, he retrieved the letter from the paper bag. With the care and precision of a bomb disposal officer, sweat upon his brow and tightly holding a small set of pliers, Philip prized open the seal of the envelope. He slowly removed the letter and before unfolding it, He placed the envelope back inside his bag.

Hello Philip

I am sure that you will agree, it was another slightly disappointing result again yesterday against Stoke City. Once again, we were unable to take advantage of the few chances that we created. Sniffer was feeling quite low after the game as he felt that he missed a couple of very good opportunities. As with the pattern of most games this season, teams will defend deep and in numbers, especially when we are at home. It is up to us to show that we can adapt and find a way to break them down. In the main and looking at the bigger picture, we are still controlling games and are, I suppose, struggling to win rather than struggling to draw. We just need to be more clinical, more ruthless and more creative when we are in possession. If we can do this, then I am sure that this recent run of draws will soon transform themselves into wins. However, sport is all about building upon the positives as well as working on the negatives, and positively speaking, we are still unbeaten in the league this season.

So it is back to work on the training field in readiness for the next match against Leicester and then a very big game that we will need to be prepared for against Liverpool. Remember Philip, preparation is everything in sport. If you ignore this and fail to prepare properly, you will never reach your full potential.

So glad to hear that you have been selected for your swimming club and your first competitive meet is just around the corner. I'm looking forward to hearing all about it and of course, to hearing how well you did. When there are troubles and issues in other areas of your life, moments like these can offer you so much. They can provide great rewards and a great sense of achievement. They can, even if it is just for a short while, offer an opportunity to escape, to step away from those other concerns. They allow you to be free, nothing pinning you down or holding you back. Like I say, even if it is only for a short while, you need to make the most of it. Take in the atmosphere, soak it up, take the time to look around you and take a breath but above all be ready, be prepared. When you find life difficult and there are times when it all feels too much, sport can be that oasis, that shaft of light in an otherwise dark space.

Remember to let me know all about your swim meet; I look forward to hearing all about it. Hopefully by time I write again we will have had a few more encouraging results. Be in touch again soon,
Billy.

Philip was just about to start reading the letter again when he was distracted by the sound of somebody calling out from the other side of the Henley Road.

"Phil! Phil!"

Philip looked up from the letter to catch sight of Paul McBride. Paul's arms were frantically flailing above his head, like a cotton sheet on a washing line, in a strong wind. As soon as he was confident that he had attracted Philip's attention, Paul called out again.

"Quick Phil, I've got something for ya."

Philip placed the letter carefully inside his bag before gently jogging across the road in the direction of both Paul and the newsagents.

"I've got one." Paul said as Philip approached.

"One what?" Philip asked whilst checking his letter was lying flat at the bottom of his bag.

"What do you mean, one what?" Paul replied with a certain amount of surprise in his voice. "A bike, I've got you a bike."

Philip instantly gathered up and cradled a certain amount of surprise of his own. Paul continued.

"You'll need to come and collect it tonight, after your round."

"I can't tonight." Philip said. "I've got swimming."

"Not tonight you aint, you'll have to miss it. I've got to shift it Phil. If you don't want it, just say the word. I've got other customers that do want it and they can pay c.o.d."

"Pay what?" Philip asked.

"Cash on delivery or collection in this case." Paul replied.

"Can I collect it tomorrow?"

"It's got to be tonight Phil, it's in my dad's shed. I am offering it to you first because I know why you need it. But if you want it, you have to get it tonight."

"Can't he hang on until tomorrow."

"You are missing the point Phil. My dad doesn't know that it is in his shed and he is not going to find out it's in his shed, cause you're gonna come and get it as soon as you have finished your round. I can't risk my dad finding it and if he doesn't find it, there is a strong chance that it will be nicked by tomorrow night, you know where my dad lives."

Paul McBride's dad lived on the Manor Farm estate. If you or an immediate member of your family wasn't a burglar or a thief of some description, if you weren't in receipt of benefits or faking some sort of hard to disprove disability, such as a bad back, if you didn't have a drink problem or a drug habit, then you had no place or no business living on the Manor Farm estate. Paul McBride's dad was able to fulfil at least two of the above criteria, and on the odd occasion he could possibly attempt three.

Paul turned away and headed towards the shop. As he approached the door, he paused and waited for Philip to catch him up. As Philip approached Paul asked, "Whereabouts do you finish your round?"

"Top of Ellacombe Road," Philip replied.

"Head back towards Broad Park when you finish and I'll be waiting outside the White Horse."

Paul pushed the door open and stepped inside the shop. Philip followed.

"Evening boys," Mr Underwood said as he looked up from a pile of 'Evening Telegraphs' that lay upon the counter. "I've an extra round going tonight if anybody is interested." He added.

"Can't tonight." Paul replied. "I've got to help my dad clear out his shed."

"What about you Philip?" Mr Underwood asked as he walked around the counter, clutching a stack of papers.

Avoiding eye contact as if he were a small child that had just been disturbed with his hand deep inside the biscuit barrel, Philip shook his head. "No can do, dad's at work early and I need to get home," he said.

"Oh well, I'm sure one of the other lads can do it," Mr Underwood replied as he motioned for Paul to hold his paperbag open. Once he had inserted the papers inside Paul's bag he returned to the counter and scooped up another bundle.

Upon noticing Mr Underwood approaching, Philip quickly removed his letter from the bottom of his bag before holding the bag open. Once the papers were safely placed inside, he carefully returned the letter.

"Away you go then boys," Mr Underwood said as he held open the shop door. As he did so, two more boys and an elderly gentleman attempted to enter the shop. After some initial confusion and a brief moment of manoeuvring by all involved, Philip and Paul found themselves outside the shop. As the door closed behind them, they could hear Mr Underwood enquiring about the spare round that was up for grabs.

"Outside the White Horse as soon as you finish," Paul said as he removed two Fry's Turkish Delight's from his coat pocket and passed one to Philip, a broad smile appearing across his face as he did so.

Philip took the bar of chocolate from Paul and nodded before they both departed and set out on their rounds.

Chapter 42

Francis Knott drove his dark green Ford Corsair through the entrance of the Wilkinson's transport depot at a speed of about twelve miles an hour but still in fourth gear. He drove towards the staff parking area and swung the car around whilst still maintaining his current speed, before briefly coming to a standstill, causing the vehicle to rock a little, then reversing into an available space. He switched off the engine and the car appeared to sigh with relief before falling silent. Francis reached across to the passenger seat and attempted to grab hold of his flask and sandwich box. As he picked up the sandwich box, the packet of cigarettes that had been resting on the top slipped off and landed on the floor below. With a disapproving shake of his head, he stretched out an arm in an attempt to retrieve his packet of Senior Service cigarettes. With a hand open wide and a flat palm he patted the floor a few times before striking lucky and landing upon the offending article. He grabbed hold of the cigarettes and as he sat back upright in his seat with the cigarettes firmly clasped in his hand, he noticed a tall thin figure walking towards the car. In the fading light he could still make out that the person approaching the car was George Meadows.

Francis opened the door and clambered out of the car just as George reached the bonnet. George paused for a moment and removed a comb from his back pocket. "Snowy's been looking for you," he said as he began to comb his jet black, thick, greasy hair.

"Where?" Francis replied as he closed the car door.

"What?" George said.

"Where has he been looking for me?"

"In the depot," George replied.

"I take it he hasn't found me yet."

Both puzzled and troubled by the conversation he now found himself in, George was keen to find the exit. He made one final sweep through his hair before giving the back of his head a gentle pat and returning the comb to his back pocket. With an uncomfortable glance in Francis's direction, he turned around and walked back towards the main depot building.

Francis stood by the car and waited for George to complete the short journey across the yard and disappear into the building. Once George was out of sight, he locked his car and made the same journey towards the same depot entrance. Without clarifying exactly through the use of a tape measure, he was approximately halfway between car and depot when Snowy Vest appeared and stood in the entrance.

"I've been looking for you," Snowy said as soon as he was content that Francis was within earshot.

"Yes, somebody said," Francis replied as he reached the entrance.

"Have you forgotten that I need you ride shotgun with George tonight?" Snowy said.

"You what?" Francis replied as he came to a sudden stop directly in front of Snowy. Francis hadn't forgotten but there was no harm in having a little fun at Snowy's expense, he thought to himself.

"Tonight, I need you to go with George, to Rochdale. He's gonna show you the route." Snowy paused and looked from side to side before leaning a little closer to Francis. "He'll introduce you to our man up there."

"What about my run to Bristol?"

"You don't need to concern yourself with that Francis but to put your mind at rest, I'm taking it."

Francis smiled. "So it looks like I'm riding shotgun. Who am I, Yul Brenner or Steve McQueen?"

"You can be whoever you want to be Francis. You can be 'Abbot and Costello' or 'McMillan and wife' for all I care, so go and put a nice frilly dress and some lipstick on if you want, just as long as you are in that cab and ready to go in ten minutes."

Snowy turned away and headed towards the small office situated in the far left corner of the building. Francis headed in the opposite direction and made for the works canteen. Once inside he sat down at the nearest table, poured out a cup of coffee from his flask and lit a cigarette.

Philip Knott stood uncomfortably outside the White Horse public house on Broad Park Road. Although the pub had yet to open for the evening session, there were still several other places that he would rather be. The White Horse's reputation for drunken fights, rowdy disputes, random acts of vandalism and general disorder could only be surpassed by that of the Shire Horse public house, an establishment located on the Manor Farm estate.

Whether either pub was open or not, on the occasions when Philip found himself walking past them, he always tended to walk a lot quicker than normal, reminiscent of the way people would walk in old black and white newsreels of the twenties and thirties. So for Philip, having to actually stand still outside the White Horse was an extremely unpleasant experience.

The relief that rapidly ran through the whole length of Philip's body the moment he spotted Paul McBride on the horizon could only have been measured by somebody working for the local council and in possession of a pedometer. Any other measuring device simply would not have been adequate enough to do the job.

As Paul approached he removed the last remaining 'Evening Telegraph' from his bag, folded it in half and in half again before pushing it through the letterbox in the left side door of the White Horse. As he did so, the sound of dogs barking could be heard on the other side of the door. Philip had already moved a few feet away from the pub entrance but upon hearing the dogs, he elected to move even further away.

"Stupid fuckin dogs," Paul said as he turned away from the door and looked at Philip. "Bloody vicious though. I'm sure he electrocutes their bollocks just to get them nice and angry." Paul added.

The dogs themselves were a recent addition to the pub; they had only been in residence for a few months. The landlord decided to get them after one particular evening pushed him over the edge. The evening in question saw three separate incidents occur in swift succession. The first was a fight between two men over an alleged unpaid wager that had been placed on a world cup qualifier involving the Scottish national team. The qualifier in question had seen Scotland secure a place at the 1974 World Cup with a 2-1 victory over Czechoslovakia. The bet in question revolved around a belief that Scotland would fail to qualify for the 1974 World Cup. The second incident took place a short time later when a lady, for want of a better term, in her late fifties, took exception to the way her third husband was looking at the barmaid and proceeded to smash a pale ale bottle over his head. The third and by far the most troublesome incident, as far as the landlord was concerned, occurred shortly after the ambulance had left. This was the theft, whilst the pub was still open, of the cigarette machine that had been attached to the wall in the bar. The free-standing cigarette machine that used to be in the bar had suffered the same fate only a few weeks before. The landlord's misguided belief that having it replaced by a machine attached to the wall would stop it being stolen only added to his misery. Three large men, all wearing masks and carrying crowbars, walked into the bar, forcefully removed the machine from the wall, carried it out of the pub, threw it into the back of a waiting van, climbed into the van and drove away. From start to finish the incident was over in a matter of two minutes.

"We need to get a move on," Paul said. "Wanna be gone before my dad wakes up."

"Wakes up?" Philip asked as he hurried along to catch up with the fast moving Paul.

"Yeah, wakes up," Paul replied as Philip arrived by his side. "If I know my dad, he'll have spent the lunchtime session propping up the bar in the Shire Horse before taking a carry out home. He'll fall asleep on the sofa, wake up, eat a fried egg sandwich and then stagger back to the pub in time for the evening session."

As darkness fell, the two boys quickly walked along Broad Park Road, across Henley Road, down the track that ran along the side of the local primary school playing field, past the community centre and into the Manor Farm Estate. They headed towards the sixteen storey tower block that sat in the middle of the estate. With several weaves left and several weaves right, they worked their way past the tower block and further into the estate. A final few twists and turns brought them to a row of small back gardens on the left and even smaller front gardens of equally small houses on the right. Three gardens down, Paul stopped, opened the gate and the two boys stepped inside.

The 1963 Atkinson lorry had just bounded down the slip road of junction two and on to the M6 motorway when George pointed towards the glove box in front of Francis.

"Have a look in there Francis?" He asked. "I think there may be a bar of chocolate."

Francis leant forward, opened the glove, peered inside, looked around, fumbled about under a couple of folded maps and a few other sundry items before spotting a bar of Turkish Delight at the back. He reached in, removed it and held it out, in George's direction.

With a rather disappointed expression on his face, George looked at the glistening purple wrapper of the bar of chocolate and then at Francis as if he was in some way responsible for the bar of chocolate he was holding. "Is that it?" George asked.

"I think so," Francis replied before taking one quicker look inside the glove, just to make sure. "Yeah that's it," he said as he closed the glove for a second time.

"Oh well, it will have to do," George said as he took the bar of chocolate from Francis. "Want some?"

"No thanks." Francis replied.

With a scrunched up expression on his face and with eyes squinting as if he had just exited the cinema on a gloriously sunny afternoon, George took a bite of his Turkish Delight.

"So, you're moving on then?" Francis said before lighting a cigarette and winding the window down a few inches.

"That appears to be the case," George replied before taking what appeared to be another unpleasant bite of his Turkish Delight. "I'll tell you what," he added. "If Turkish people find this a delight, I wouldn't fancy a bar of Turkish shite."

Francis smiled. "Bit of a surprise though."

"What is?"

"You, packin' this in and going to work for your brother-in-law."

George waited for a moment until the latest bite of Turkish Delight had departed his mouth, then he replied. "Out of my hands Francis, out of my hands." Again he paused for another brief moment before adding, "and I'm not going to work for my brother-in-law, just by way of clarification."

"Oh I see," Francis replied. "I guess then I've been unreliably informed."

"Only fractionally Francis, I suspect only fractionally. I'm going to work with my brother-in-law, alongside my brother-in-law, not for my brother-in-law."

Silence reigned for the next few miles of motorway, whilst remainder of cigarette was smoked and remainder of chocolate bar was consumed. As they rolled past the Dunlop factory, George could see the curiosity etched upon Francis's face. He could almost reach across and scoop the questions from Francis's mouth as if he was filling a sand castle bucket with water from the ocean on a summer's day. He decided that he couldn't watch Francis suffer a moment longer.

"He wants to expand the business," George began. "He believes that with all this economic uncertainty and collapse of industry, people are gonna be on the move, relocating where the work is."

"Yeah well, I hear there are a load of jobs in a place called jeopardy, according to the news last night, Problem is, I can't find it on the map."

George chose to ignore Francis's attempt at humour and continued. "He wants to expand, set up another base further south, Bedford way I think. Problem is he needs investment, banks are reluctant to loan due the current uncertain climate, unless you can bring more than a Victoria sponge to the table, so he came to the wife."

"How come?" Francis asked. "She got a Battenberg and a tray of eclairs stashed away or something."

"Or something," George muttered. "When their dad passed away, it was his business, the brother-in-law just ran it after the old boy retired. He left it to the pair of them, equal split. Well what did the Mrs want with half a removal business? So the brother-in-law bought her out. On the proceeds we bought the house. Now he wants her to invest, buy back in, so to speak. So we've re-mortgaged the house. But she would only do it if it was a partnership and I got a full time position with the firm."

"You happy about it then?"

"Yes and no Francis, yes and no. I don't exactly want to work with the arsehole but I shouldn't have to deal with him too often. I 'm going to be here and he is going to be spending most of his time in Bedford. The way it is with this job, I can see this firm going under sooner rather than later. I need security Francis. I've got three daughters, one gets married in the spring. How do I pay for that if I am out of work? Country's down the toilet Francis, the economy with it. Strikes all over the place, shorter weeks. What next? Don't look great does it?"

"I know it doesn't look great," Paul McBride said as he and Philip stood in the open doorway of his dad's garden shed.

"I don't know what it looks like," Philip replied. "I can't see it."

"Hang on a minute, there's a torch in here somewhere," Paul replied as he started to carefully move around in the darkness.

"Maybe you could do with a torch to help you find the torch," Philip said.

After a little more fruitless fumbling, Paul eventually found a small plastic-cased torch. With a click of a switch, a shaft of light shone across the inside of the shed.

"Quick Phil, shut the door." Paul said.

As Philip turned and closed the door behind him, Paul aimed the beam of light onto a rather sorry looking, rather worse for wear racing bike. In its prime, this was a brick orange 1972 Eddy Merckx twelve gear racing bike with drop handle bars covered in gleaming white tape. However, this particular bike was now a long way short of the pristine bike it once was. Unlike the great Eddy Merckx, this bike's better days were certainly behind it. A tour of the garden looked like a challenge too far, never mind a Tour de France.

"I know it's not spanking," Paul said as he shone the beam of light away from the bike as not to reveal any further horrors. "But if you were to respray it. You can easily lift some from Dick Shepperd's. They're in a blind spot. I can put some on the list for you if you want."

The circle of light from the torch in Paul's hand gently swayed around on the floor of the shed before he pointed it back towards the bike. "You'll have to walk it home though." Paul continued. "The back tyre's flat. It comes with a pump though." He added as he shone the torch onto the black pump that was attached to the frame of the bike. "You'll need to get a repair kit and some oil for the chain and some new tape for the handle bars."

Sensing he was beginning to lose his audience somewhat, Paul completed his sales pitch on a positive note by shining the torch onto the black leather covered seat. The seat's okay though," He said.

"Where did it come from?" Philip asked.

"Not exactly sure," Paul replied. "Someone's garden down the Windmill Road, I think. Fat Bobby lifted it."

"How much do you want for it?"

"I was looking for three quid, I told Fat Bobby that I would give him one fifty. But seeing as it's you and I know you need it for this swimming thingy, he will settle for a quid and you can have it for two."

"Two pounds?" Philip replied.

They're about fifteen quid brand new and if it was in better condition, then you'd be looking at five or six quid at least. A little bit of work and you've got a good bike."

"But I haven't got two pounds," Philip said.

"You can owe it me." Paul said as he grabbed hold of the bike and began to wheel it towards the door of the shed.

Quickly taking stock of the current situation, Philip decided that having a bike was preferable to no bike at all. He took hold of the handle bars and carefully wheeled the bike out of the garden shed.

"I'll see you tomorrow morning." Paul said as Philip and the bike made their way out of the garden. "I've got an up to date list, if you are interested."

Philip just raised a hand in the air before setting off for home. He heard the garden gate close behind him.

Nobody can be sure what the dispute was over but by the time Philip arrived home, the back tyre of the bike had parted company with the back wheel. This made things rather tricky as the bike became difficult to manoeuvre but eventually it was safely secured in his garden shed.

He went into the house and spent the rest of the evening watching television with his brother. He caught the end of 'Oh Father' before sitting through an episode of 'Search Control' and an episode of 'Softly, Softly'. He them made them both a hot Horlicks drink whilst the news was on. However, he drew the line at watching 'The Horse of the Year Show' and instead elected to lie on his bed reading his most recent copy of 'Shoot'.

Located just off junction twenty one of the M62, along the A640, situated between Milrow and Figmore and approximately three miles from Rochdale sits a rather basic lorry park. The park does however boast a wonderful range of potholes and no matter the weather or the time of year, the holes always seem to be full of brown murky water. To say that the lorry park lacked amenities would certainly be an understatement. The gents toilet was located behind a thick, overgrown bramble bush. There had never been a need for a female toilet but if a lady were ever to find herself in need of the toilet whilst in this particular lorry park, then the same flat piece of earth behind the same thick, overgrown bramble bush was her only option.

George and Francis arrived a little after 10pm. The lorry lurched from pothole to pothole as it made its way to the relatively deserted far end of the lorry park. George pulled up in a spot he was happy with, parked and switched the engine off. The only other lorries nearby were a Preston's of Potto lorry some fifty or so yards away and a blue and white Welch's Transport lorry parked on the other side of the Preston's lorry.

George glanced at his watch. "Won't be long." He said, even though he could not quite make out the time.

No sooner had Francis wound his window down a little and lit a cigarette than a dark coloured Austin Morris 1300 appeared in the entrance of the lorry park. The car stopped and Francis could just make out an outline of the driver looking around the lorry park.

"Here we go." George said as he flashed his lights and began to step out of the cab. The car drove towards them and came to a stop, facing the cab about ten feet away. The driver's door of the car swung open and an extremely heavy set man with a thin greying moustache and a centre parting wider than the grin of a Cheshire cat shuffled about and moaned and groaned until he eventually popped out of the driver's seat. Once fully erect and after arching his back with a grimace on his face, he closed the car door. He walked towards George and Francis, who by now had also climbed down from the cab.

"This is Francis," George said before adding "Snowy said…"

"I know what Snowy said," the man interrupted as he looked directly at Francis.

Francis held out his hand.

Still looking directly at Francis, the man removed a brown envelope from the inside pocket of his jacket and passed it to George. "You're not a poof?" He said

"Sorry," Francis replied.

"Sorry? Sorry? You sure you're not a poof? You sound like one."

"No," Francis replied.

"Good, you better not be a poof. I don't do business with poofs. Can't be trusted see. When the chips are down and the backs are against the wall, they crack, they're weak, no backbone, no fibre, can't be trusted."

"Oh right," Francis said as he looked across at George.

"Francis." The man said as he glanced around the lorry park. "That's an Irish name isn't it. You're not Irish are you? Cause I don't do business with them either, just as bad as the poofs. Another lot that can't be trusted. Sell their own grandmother for a food hamper and a crate of beer that lot."

"No, I'm not Irish," Francis said.

"Good job. Tell Snowy I'll be in touch." The man said as he turned back towards his car. As he reached the car he turned again and looked at Francis. "Don't let me down Francis, you wouldn't want to do that." He muttered as he began to clamber back into the driver's seat. By the time he had completed the task, George and Francis had already climbed back into the cab. They watched in silence as the Austin Morris completed a rapid three point turn, before driving out of the lorry park.

"Short and sweet," Francis said as the car disappeared from view.

"Onwards and upwards Francis, onwards and upwards," George replied.

"I'm just glad he left his headlights on whilst he spoke to us," Francis said as he turned to look at George. "Saved him the trouble of asking me if I was black."

Chapter 43

"He's not gonna make it, I'm telling you man, he's not gonna make it," Craig Swinburn said as he stood on the platform at the back of the number twenty-one bus.

"He will, he'll make it," Paul Jones replied.

Paul, Craig, Philip and James were all standing on the platform at the back of the bus. They were all looking out, across the roundabout and down the Deedmore Road.

"You wanna bet? I'll bet ya," Craig said. "I bet you a crash, the fat twat doesn't make it."

Paul instantly understood the terms of the bet; it was simply to determine which one of them got the cigarettes out once they were seated upstairs at the back of the bus. "You're on," Paul replied before leaning out and shouting, "Come on Martin, hurry up." However, the words of encouragement were only because he now stood to profit from Martin's success.

Martin Matthews however, was far too far away to hear the words of encouragement and support that were now being offered from the back of the bus. To say that he was sprinting would be unfair both to those who could sprint and to Martin who clearly couldn't. Certainly his feet crashed into the pavement beneath him with a greater degree of force than they would have if he was merely walking, but to conclude that he was actually travelling any quicker was more difficult.

Martin slowly got closer and closer to the roundabout and in turn the bus. For the majority of the onlookers, his lack of progress was excruciating to watch. He appeared to be moving with all the speed of a cross-channel ferry. His lumbering from side to side was also reminiscent of a cross-channel ferry, only this time it was attempting to cross the channel during a rather violent storm. Craig was the only onlooker enjoying the spectacle and the sight of Martin's heavy frame clambering towards the roundabout. Craig was busily looking down the road at Martin, then turning to look down the bus at the back of the driver sitting in his cab, before turning back to look and see how much ground Martin had covered.

Martin was by now just crossing the dome shaped roundabout and the momentum gained on the downward slope propelled him closer to the bus as the engine burst into life. Both Craig and Paul turned to look at the driver; they stared intently at the back of his head. They watched as he flicked his cigarette butt out of the window, closed it, placed his foot on the clutch pedal, put the bus into first gear and indicated to pull away from the bus stop.

"Run Martin run!" James shouted.

Martin was just metres away as the bus lurched forward and attempted to pull away. Martin was by now so close that the other boys could see the redness in his face, the veins in his neck, the sweat pouring down his cheeks and his thick brown hair stuck to his forehead.

The sudden sound of a car horn caused the bus driver to brake sharply. A moment later a Vauxhall Viva that had appeared out of nowhere came off the roundabout and shot past the now stationary bus, the driver of the car frantically shaking his fist as the car sped along the Hillmorton Road.

As the bus went to pull away for the second time, Martin threw himself into the air and onto the platform. He came crashing down with such force that the carrier bag in his hand slammed onto the floor and its contents spilled out. Two packets of salt and vinegar crisps, a smaller plastic bag of lemon bon-bons and a packet of Rolo's broke free as if they had just been liberated from a chain gang and were running towards the woods.

"Bollocks," Craig muttered as the other boys helped Martin to his feet. Martin looked as if he was being helped from the canvas after being counted out by the referee. A victorious Larry Holmes with arms raised in triumph bounced around the ring whilst the crowd roared with pleasure and Martin was helped back to his corner.

Wheezing, breathing deeply and attempting to speak with little success, Martin pointed at his selection of sweets with a shaking arm and an outstretched finger. "My………my……….my sweets," he eventually exclaimed.

Martin was desperate to retrieve the items in question before the bus reached the first stop, outside the chemist's, further along Hillmorton Road. Everybody helped out, even Craig, who was still upset about losing his bet. An elderly lady further up the bus retrieved his packet of Rolo's from beneath her feet and handed them back to Martin.

Once all of the items were safely back inside the carrier bag and Martin felt that he could manage the climb, the boys finally made their way upstairs and sat down. The bus was just turning into Almond Tree Avenue when Paul rubbed his hands together and looked at Craig. Craig made a half-hearted attempt to declare the bet null and void on account of the Vauxhall Viva but he knew he was clutching at straws and as his protest faded away, he took out a ten packet of Embassy Regal from the pocket of his Parka coat, removed two cigarettes and reluctantly passed one to Paul. He placed the other cigarette between his lips before putting the packet back in his pocket.

As soon as he had lit his cigarette and was contently savouring its victorious flavour, Paul looked over at Craig and asked, "so you didn't get anything last night then."

"No, I told you, nothing, we just watched T.V, the bloody 'Horse of the Year' show." He paused. "She likes horses," he added.

"Is her mum still barred from the pub then?" Philip asked.

"Bloody hell Phil, where you bin? She's been allowed back in for ages. I think the landlord was losing too much money by her being barred. Probably costing him a holiday every year, if she weren't allowed back in. She has had to agree to keep her clothes on though."

"So how come you spent the evening just sitting and watching T.V?" Paul asked.

"I managed to feel her up." Craig said in a clear attempt to salvage some shred of credibility. "We didn't just watch T.V."

"Under or over?" Paul asked.

"Over," Craig replied with a tone in his voice that had been gift wrapped and tied with a bow by a member of the sales team at the defeatist counter.

"Over," Philip said. "Over, you got that far months ago. You reckoned you would have gone all the way by the end of the summer holidays, at this rate…"

Annoyance instantly pushed defeatism to one side and interrupted the last statement on behalf of the both of them.

"So? So what? It's a bit difficult to get under her top, or inside her jeans when her stupid little brother is sitting there. He's worse than a fat kid hanging around the buffet at a wedding. Anyway, exactly how far did any of you lot get last night? I'll tell you how far you got, absolutely nowhere. You were sitting at home all alone on a Friday night, feeling a right tit. Whereas I was at least feeling a pair of tits."

Craig took a large drag of satisfaction from his cigarette. Eager to direct the conversation away from his lack of progress with Claire Chase, he looked over at Phil as the smoke drifted from his mouth.

"Anyway Phil, you want to get yourself round to Lesley Bennet's house, you might be able to get back in there."

"No thanks," Philip replied. "She's seeing that what's his face, that Steve, whatever his name is."

"Not anymore she's not, he dumped her last week." Craig replied.

"How do you know that?" Philip asked.

"He told me. I see him at football practice don't I? He said she was a waste of time. All they did was necking and it took him two months to get to that. He reckons he's seeing some sister of a kid from another football team, Small Heath F.C, I think he said. By all accounts, if you buy her a four pack of Babychams, she'll let you do anything you want."

Silence descended quicker than an evening's mist in a horror film as the four boys all sat and pondered the similar picture they had in their mind. The bubble was burst by the appearance of the bus conductor at the top of the stairs.

"Fares please," he said.

Each boy in turn specified the ticket they required and handed over their money in order to purchase their ticket. Martin had some difficulty making himself understood on account of still being in the recovery phase of his run for the bus. The fact that he had three bon-bons in his mouth didn't help either. The bus conductor took an educated gamble on him wanting the same ticket as everybody else and acted accordingly. Martin nodded in appreciation as the conductor handed him his ticket and his change. As soon as the conductor had continued on his way, Martin was forced to share out the remainder of his bon-bons.

A thin wispy layer of silver smoke hovered just above the heads of the passengers of the upper deck as the bus approached the city centre. The boys all alighted outside Sainsbury's and into the fresh air, before making the short walk along Fairfax Street towards the swimming baths.

The news of Lesley Bennet's break up was still whirling around at the forefront of Philip's mind as they arrived at the swimming baths. He thought about procuring a gift of some sort. However, he was struggling to think of something he could steal from Dick Sheppard's bike shop that Lesley would like or want or in turn would loosen any possible items of her clothing.

"Last one in the pool's a knob." Paul called out as he pushed through the doors of the changing rooms, grabbed a basket and sprinted ahead of the rest of the group. Within four minutes, four of the boys were already encased within the cool blue water of the pool. There were no prizes on offer for guessing who trailed in in last place and spent the next ten minutes being called a knob.

As usual, the pool was busy and as usual it was proving extremely difficult for Philip to find some space to actually swim in. The situation didn't improve much over the next few hours, culminating in Philip being the first one to be ejected from the pool. A poorly executed bombing attempt off the second diving board had resulted in the pool attendant blowing his whistle and pointing in the direction of the changing rooms the instant that Philip's head resurfaced.

However, good fortune had opted to climb aboard the good ship Philip when it had mattered most, inside Dick Sheppard's bike shop. The shop was thankfully quite busy when Philip and James had entered. Both Mr Sheppard and his young sales assistant were helping their respective customers as Philip and James stood inside the doorway and looked around the shop. Mr Sheppard was helping a married couple and their four year old daughter choose her first bike, whilst an elderly gentleman with a small purse in his hand was being served by the young assistant. The elderly gentleman required bicycle clips, chain oil and a rear light.

Philip sent James to the counter so that he could legitimately purchase a puncture repair kit whilst he casually manoeuvred around the tight confines of the shop. As James patiently waited to be served, two more customers entered the now rather crowded shop. Despite the occasional glance in his direction from Mr Sheppard, Philip was able to acquire three cans of spray paint without any difficulty at all. As a way of a bonus he was also able to conceal about his person two rolls of sky blue handle bar tape.

"Can I help you?" The young sales assistant asked James as the elderly gentleman attempted to leave the shop.

"A puncture repair kit please," James replied.

In no time at all the sales assistant had reached beneath the counter and placed one puncture repair kit on top of the counter. "Anything else?" he asked.

"No Thank you," James replied.

"That will be eight pence."

James handed over a ten pence piece and waited for his change. By the time it arrived, Philip was standing by his side. James collected the change and the puncture repair kit before both boys quickly left the shop.

The newly found good fortune was kind enough to stick around a little while longer as firstly the boys returned home to discover that the house was quiet and their dad was nowhere to be seen or heard and secondly as the scores came in Philip discovered that Leeds Untied had remained unbeaten and had secured a 2-2 draw away at Leicester City. Unfortunately however, during the small hours and in the still of night, good fortune upped sticks and slipped silently away.

Chapter 44

"I'm sorry son but you can't swim."

Philip was sitting in front of the wooden desk in the small office on the first floor of the swimming baths. Resting on his lap in a carrier bag was his swimming kit and a pair of swimming goggles, and hanging from the back of the chair was his paperbag. On the other side of the desk stood Mr Kennedy. His hands were placed flat upon the surface of the desk as he stared intently at Philip.

It was incredibly safe to assume that Mr Kennedy was not best pleased. The wide eyed expression, the flared nostrils, the protruding veins in his neck and the tone in his voice all pointed towards his obvious annoyance better than a billboard sign on Broadway.

"If I could, I would, but I can't," he continued. "My hands are tied," he added as he thrust his hands forward and held them together, leaving Philip to picture the imaginary rope that was binding them together.

"But why not?" Philip asked.

"It's the rules son, the club rules. Have you actually read them? No, of course not. If you had read them then you would have turned up for training on Wednesday night. I thought about phoning Mr Spencer when you didn't show and your parents but something told me that wouldn't be a good idea, so I thought I'd wait and see what you had to say when or if you turned up today."

Philip could feel his hands gripping his carrier bag so tightly that his knuckles were beginning to turn white. The expression on his face clearly demonstrated to even the most casual of observers that he still had no idea why he couldn't swim. Mr Kennedy provided the additional information that he needed for the penny to drop.

"Look son," Mr Kennedy said. "The rule is, if you don't attend the training session prior to a meet then you forfeit your opportunity to compete. It's the same rule for everybody. I can't have people just turning up for competitions and expecting to swim but not showing up for training."

"But, but…" Philip attempted to form a fuller sentence; however he was not given the opportunity.

"There's no buts about it son, I can't allow you to swim. There would be uproar, complaints from parents stretching as far as the eye could see. You've only just joined and I'm already letting you break the rules. Can't happen, it's as simple as that. If you want to swim for the club then you've got to demonstrate that you are part of the club."

Philip looked down at his lap. The weight of disappointment was resting on the back of his neck. He managed to lift his head and look at Mr Kennedy. "I'm sorry," he muttered.

"Sorry wouldn't cut much ice with these parents son. You were late arriving today and you didn't show at all on Wednesday. Why not?"

"It was because of training that I missed training," Philip replied.

"How do you mean son, I don't follow."

"Well you see a friend of mine was selling a bike. He said that I had to collect it Wednesday night or he would sell it to somebody else that wanted it. It's not exactly road worthy at present so I had to walk it home. But I'll have it fixed in a day or two and then I can cycle here straight from my paper round."

Mr Kennedy looked at Philip, shaking his head and gently sighing as he did so. "Listen son, this is your last chance. You are getting another chance because I know it isn't as easy for you as it is for others on the team. Get the bike fixed and turn up to training, on time. Now go and get yourself on the minibus. We need to get going or we'll all be late.

Even though you can't swim today, I still want you to be part of the team."

A sixteen seater red Barton Bedford minibus was parked in the layby outside the entrance to the baths. It was already quite full when Philip climbed aboard. There was an unoccupied seat at the back of the bus. Philip walked past his fellow teammates and sat down. As he did so, a boy sitting in the seat directly in front of Philip turned to look at him.

"Why are you here? You can't swim, Why did you even bother to turn up?" he said.

"Mr Kennedy wants me to come along so I can be part of the team," Philip replied.

"You'll never be part of this team," the boy said as he turned away and smiled at the boy he was sitting next to.

Philip decided not to reply. Instead he elected to wait for a more opportune moment. He sat back in his seat and removed his copy of 'Tiger' from his paperbag.

Approximately thirty five minutes later and a few minutes late the minibus arrived at the City of Birmingham Sports and Leisure Centre. As the team members on board the bus climbed down and made their way across the car park, Philip saw his opportunity. Once he felt that there was a safe distance between himself, the boy and Mr Kennedy, Philip grabbed the collar of the boys coat from behind and lifted him up so that he was walking on his tiptoes.

"Oi! Oi! What you doing?" The boy said.

"Listen here you," Philip replied as he leant a little closer to the boy's ear. "You speak to me like that again and I'll take that silver spoon out of your mouth and I'll shove it up your arse. You understand me you double barrelled twat. And if you mention this conversation to the coach, I'll fuckin drown ya. If you mention it to mummy and daddy, I'll fuckin drown ya. If you mention it to any of our teammates, I'll fuckin drown ya. In fact you're gonna have to try really hard not to get wet."

Philip released his grip of the boy's collar and the boy's feet duly returned to a more natural walking position. As soon as they did so, he quickly sped off, so that he could put some distance between him and Philip. Philip turned to the boy's friend and smiled.

Once inside the building, Mr Kennedy sent Philip to watch the meet from the public viewing gallery. As soon as he had selected a seat, Philip retrieved a stolen Sunday newspaper from inside his paperbag and attempted to use it so that he could fill in his match report inside his comic.

However, the information gleaned from the match report and the team sheets failed to do justice to what was a fantastic game of football. Leicester had established a two goal lead. The second of their goals was an absolute screamer. It was scored by Alan Birchenall from about twenty five yards out, a bullet of a shot that flew into the top right hand corner of the goal. The outstretched hand of David Harvey in the Leeds goal got nowhere near it. Leeds United, to their credit, rallied and manged to get a goal back, a close range tap in from Mick Jones after a glorious long pass from Johnny Giles and a cross to the near post from Peter Lorimer. The equalizer was rather fortunate as the decision to award Leeds a free kick for hand ball, just outside the box, was a rather dubious call. However Peter Lorimer's quick thinking and taking the free kick before the Leicester players were ready, allowed him to thread a through ball to the unmarked Billy Bremner who slotted the ball home from twelve yards. Leeds United almost stole the win late on with a shot that crashed against the cross bar but in the end both teams had to settle for a point.

It was about halfway through the meet and a rather bored Philip was aimlessly flicking through the pages of his stolen newspaper. He paused briefly on each occasion when he came across a seductive image of a young lady in a state of undress. As he was looking at a picture of a very shapely Diana Dors in a bikini, he felt a tap on his shoulder. He closed the newspaper and turned around to see Michael Robinson standing behind him.

"I've been looking for you everywhere," Michael said. "I thought you were swimming. I was just about to leave," he added as he climbed over the row of seats in front of him and sat down next to Philip.

"He wouldn't let me."

"Who wouldn't?"

"The Coach."

"Why not?"

"Because I missed training on Wednesday and apparently it's a club rule that if you miss training before a meet, you can't swim."

"Why didn't you go training?" Michael asked as he pulled two packets of salt and vinegar crisps from his coat pocket and passed one of them to Philip.

"Paul Mc Bride had got me a bike and I had to go and collect it. He insisted, he said that he couldn't wait until Thursday. It had to be there and now, after my paper round. He had it stashed in his dad's shed but his dad didn't know."

"Oh right, I guess it was a stolen bike then."

"A good guess. Fat Bobby Cowley had nicked it from somewhere. That's probably why it had a puncture."

"What do you want a bike for?" Michael asked.

"So I can get to training."

"So you missed training so that you could go to training."

"I've already had this conversation today Michael, can we talk about something else?"

The two boys sat and ate their crisps as the sound of whistles being blown and spectators cheering washed over them with every passing race.

"So how is living in Birmingham?" Philip asked as he licked crisp residue from the tips of his fingers.

Michael shrugged his shoulders. "Okay I suppose."

"Want some chocolate?" Philip asked. He didn't bother waiting for a reply as the two boys exited their seats and went in search of a vending machine. It didn't take long to find one.

"What do you want?" Philip asked as they both stared through the glass frontage of the vending machine at the products on the other side.

"I'll have an Ice Breaker," Michael replied.

Philip put in the required amount of money to purchase two bars of chocolate, ten pence in total, before setting free from the confines of the machine one Ice Breaker and a Bar Six.

"How's your mum?" Philip asked as they headed back to their seats.

"Oh, she's okay, seems a lot happier here. There's a West Indian centre at the end of the road. She spends a lot of time down there. I tell you what Phil, you thought my mum was big, you should see the size of the women down there. You know those people who try and get as many people as they can in a phone box, some of these women, you wouldn't even get their lunch in it. They all turn up with tins full of cakes under their arms or tubs full of rice and dumplings. They all just sit around and talk and eat and knit. Virtually every night my mum is in the kitchen baking something to take with her the next day."

"What about your dad?"

"Oh, he's alright. Keeps out of it doesn't he. As long as my mum's not upset, he's happy. Happy with his job too, he loves being a bus conductor."

"What's your school like?" Philip asked as they sat back down in their seats.

"Alright, I guess. I'm in the school football team, no great achievement that though, if you're not Pakistani you're in the team. You know how shit they are at football and virtually every kid in the school is Pakistani, it's like a school on the Foleshill Road. We played a team from a school in Small Heath last week. Our team had eight black kids and three ginger Irish twats. They were all Paki's with hankies on their heads, we beat them eleven-nil. What about you, how are things at home?"

Philip sighed a little and stared at his feet for a moment before he answered. "About as bad as they can be," he began. "My mum is getting worse, I hardly see her these days. My dad is hardly sober, my sister has moved out. It feels like I've been run over and whilst I'm lying in the road, somebody comes along and robs me. My sister had a party a few weeks ago for her eighteenth. In this flat she's sharing. My dad turned up, drunk as a skunk and started fighting. Broke some bloke's nose and smashed up the kitchen. He had to be thrown out. My sister thought she would be as well as it's the other girl's flat. He's even taken money from my savings box in my room so he can go and get drunk."

"That's bad, what you gonna do?" Michael asked.

"What can I do? Keep out of his way as much as possible. Can't wait to see what happens when he finds out I've joined the swimming club. I can't decide whether it would be better if he was drunk or sober when he finds out."

"You mean he doesn't know."

"Of course he doesn't."

Michael pulled a face that said all it needed to with a little extra thrown in for good measure as he put the last piece of his ice breaker between his lips.

"Where's your sister moved to?" he asked.

"She's sharing a flat in Clennon Rise with Karen Fairchild."

Michael froze except for his eyes which instantly widened in disbelief. If he hadn't just swallowed the last bit of his ice breaker, as sure as a detention follows a day at school, it would have become lodged in the back of his throat. "You're joking?" Michael finally muttered before adding, "You know what she does then?"

"She's working in Woolworths." Philip replied.

"You what, Karen Fairchild is working in Woolworths?"

"No, my sister is working in Woolworths. Karen doesn't work."

"Oh yes she does!" Michael said with a look on his face that was now causing Philip concern.

Philip licked the last remnants of bar six from his lips. "What are you on about?" he asked.

"She's a prossy man, on the game." Michael answered.

"You what?" Philip replied. "Of course she's not."

"Oh my god Phil, take a vacation will you and when you get back, go and ask her. I thought that everybody knew that."

Philip was stunned into an almost petrified silence. He could feel the inside of his head start to dissolve and run down the back of his neck.

"Listen Phil. If your sister doesn't know, you need to tell her and if she does know, you need to tell her to move out. She must have been desperate to move out of your house."

"She was," Philip managed to say.

Michael glanced out towards the pool and caught sight of the clock on the timekeeping scoreboard. "I need to go Phil," he said. "My mum wants me back home for lunch. Do you want to come, I'm sure she will have cooked plenty?"

Philip shook his head. "Can't," he replied. "I have to get the minibus back after the meet and anyway, I need to get that bike fixed. "Can you get over to Cov at the weekend? I can meet you at the baths on Saturday."

"Dunno, maybe. My mum ain't that keen on me going over. If you're here again and you will be swimming next time, let me know."

Michael, got out of his seat, said goodbye, climbed the steps towards the exit and disappeared out of view, leaving Philip to watch the last few individual races of the meet and the relays, surrounded by a crowd of cheering spectators.

Chapter 45

On Wednesday the 17th of October 1973 as the boys made their way to school there was only one topic of conversation and this particular topic of conversation remained the only topic of conversation for the whole of the day. In classrooms throughout the school, lessons were conveniently side tracked so that the topic of conversation could take centre stage. In staff rooms and offices, at breaktime and lunch time, even in the canteen and the caretaker's office there was only one topic being discussed. The topic on everybody's mind was the World Cup qualifier between England and Poland. The game kicked off later that evening at 7.45pm. It was being screened live on ITV. It was so important that even Philip's swimming training session had been cancelled. The coach made the announcement on the minibus whilst travelling back from the meet in Birmingham on Sunday afternoon. The news was a double thumbs up for Philip as he now had longer to get the bike fixed and he could also watch the match.

The game itself was a game that England could not afford to lose, or even draw. Only a victory would see the team and the nation qualify for the 1974 World Cup which was to be held in West Germany. Failure to qualify was unthinkable, unimaginable, for two reasons. Firstly, since their first World Cup in 1950, England had never before failed to qualify for the finals and secondly, Scotland, who were also playing later that day in Czechoslovakia, had already qualified, thanks to two victories against Denmark and a home win in the first fixture against Czechoslovakia.

England had started their World Cup campaign in November the previous year. A successful, if not convincing 1-0 win away to Wales in Cardiff, thanks to a goal from Colin Bell. However, this was as good as it got and the home fixture against the same opposition in January ended in a disappointing one-one draw, despite an absolute screamer of a goal from Norman Hunter.

The team and the nation had to wait the best part of six months before playing their next qualifier, away to Poland in Chorzow. A Polish goal early in each half had resulted in a shattering 2-0 loss. Unbeknown at the time, this particular game was to mark the end of an era. This fixture turned out to be Bobby Moore's last competitive game in an England shirt. The hero of 1966, that now world-famous tackle in the 1970 World Cup quarter final against Brazil. The infamous jewellery scandal and the arrest over the alleged stolen bracelet at the same tournament in Mexico. All of this was about to become another finished chapter of England's football history. The defeat against Poland was to be the last of Bobby Moore's one hundred and eight England caps.

Poland's victory against Wales in September had left them top of the group with four points. England had three points and Wales, who had played all of their fixtures, also had three points. It all came down to this final game, a game that England simply had to win.

Philip and James had rushed home from school as fast as they could along with most other boys as one by one they sprinted through the school gates and headed for their respective places of habitation. With the bike still not road worthy and still in need of lights, Philip had to complete his paper round on foot. However, he did so in record time. Once he was back home, he waited for his dad to leave for work before he made himself and James something to eat. Francis was not best pleased about having to miss the match on T.V and had to settle instead for listening to the radio commentary in his cab as he headed towards Rochdale.

Once the coast was clear, Philip cooked beans on toast for him and James. For desert they shared a tin of rice pudding with some sugar sprinkled on the top. Philip washed up, made a cup of tea for himself and took one up to his mum. His mum was asleep when he entered the room, so he placed it by the side of the bed and quietly left. Once back downstairs the two boys settled down and by 6.30pm they were both sitting in front of the television. They still had over an hour to wait until kick-off, so to pass the time James read his comic and Philip aimlessly watched the end of 'Nationwide' before paying even less attention to the programmes that followed.

The game was finally about to start. England fielded a strong team as one would expect for such an important game. There were players from all the big clubs, Derby County, Arsenal, Tottenham Hotspurs, Leeds United, Liverpool, Manchester City, Sheffield United.

The nerves were already jangling as James and Philip were poised on the settee, waiting for the referee to signal to his linesmen and blow the whistle.

England produced a lovely sweeping move early in the game, eleven passes and nine players involved. The move resulted in a shot from Tony Currie which whistled over the Polish crossbar. There were clear signs of confidence flowing through the team. Philip and James watched intently as they listened to the enthusiastic commentary of Hugh Johns.

'Well read by Madeley, Colin Bell through to Chivers, Peters, on again for Bell and he's still got it. Emelyn Hughes, support from Hunter, good ball, Bell, Peters, Clarke, Channon, back for Currie to hit. Well this is the sort of start England wanted'.

A forty-yard pass from Madeley, one touch football, Channon on a driving run as he fires just wide. A free kick sent high across the goal mouth to the far post, knocked back into the six-yard box by McFarland but it is cleared away. Chance after chance comes England's way. Channon heads over from six yards out. A strike from Colin Bell brings out a fine quality save from the Polish goalkeeper. The next attack sees the goalkeeper off his line and flapping about near the edge of the box but somehow the Polish defence smuggle the ball to safety. Another cross, another shot, another block, another save, another header from Channon, late into the half, is again well saved by the Polish goalkeeper.

The commentator's voice fills the room. *'This is the most incredible first half of football I've seen for a very very long time'.*

The whistle blows, half-time the score is 0-0.

Philip and James feel exhausted, as if they had just played the first forty-five minutes themselves and in need of some half-time refreshments. Philip heads into the kitchen and returns a minute or two later with two plastic cups of Corona Limeade and some malted milk sports biscuits on a small plate.

The second half is soon under way and an early chance goes begging as Currie slices a shot wide from just inside the box with only the goalkeeper to beat. Then twelve minutes into the second half, the unthinkable happens. The normally reliable Norman 'Bite Yer Legs' Hunter comes off second best after a weak tackle on the halfway line. Time suddenly becomes distorted and the next ten seconds seem to be over in a flash and last forever at the same time, as over a hundred thousand fans in the stadium and the millions watching the TV screens, stare in horror and disbelief. One forward run, one pass, one shot. Hughes fails in his desperate lunge to block the shot. Shilton drops to the ground but the ball goes beneath his body and nestles into the corner of the net. The unthinkable is now very much at the forefront of the nation's minds.

Things now go from bad to worse when a Mick Channon equalizer is ruled out by the Belgian referee. A foul by Clarke in the build up or was it Chivers, nobody knows as the commentator explains. *'There didn't seem to be anything wrong with that at all'.* Whilst the millions of fans at home watch the replay.

Then a piece of good fortune, perhaps a moment of guilt from the referee, perhaps an opportunity to redress an earlier error, he awards England a penalty so soft that you could curl up and fall asleep on it.

GOAL!!! Clarke scores. He sends the keeper the wrong way and fires the ball high into the roof of the net. Now the search for a winner begins. Another shot by Currie, another save. A corner from Currie, a header from Clarke, cleared off the line with the keeper beaten. McFarland stabs the loose ball wide. The crowd groan as one, heads are firmly placed inside hands up and down the nation. The last chance, the last throw of dice and another goal line clearance in injury time as a shot from Colin Bell is cleared away. Then it rings out louder than a clap of thunder, the final whistle blows.

'it's over, it's all over. And for England one of the blackest days they have ever had.'

The two boys sat motionless in disbelief. In total silence they sat and stared at the TV screen. Images of dejected, isolated England players standing on the Wembley turf with hands on hips, socks rolled down and looking towards the night sky with shattered expressions on their faces. Hugh Jones commentary now seeped out of the television set and spilled onto the floor below, failing to reach its audiences ears.

In a layby on the A580, approximately thirty five miles from Rochdale, Francis sat and stared through his windscreen and in to the darkness with a bewildered expression upon his face. He leant across and switched the radio off, sitting in the empty space with his forearms resting on the steering wheel. He puffed out his cheeks and exhaled before reaching for and lighting a cigarette. Glancing at his watch as he returned the packet of cigarettes to the top pocket of his overalls, he started the engine. He put the vehicle into first gear, released the handbrake, switched on the headlights and with cigarette hanging from his lips and his head still shaking from side to side, he pulled out of the layby. He knew that he was going to be late arriving at the depot in Rochdale but at that precise moment in time it didn't seem to matter all that much.

Philip puffed out his cheeks and slowly exhaled before reaching for his cup of limeade and the last sports biscuit that was resting on the plate between him and James on the sofa. He bit into the biscuit as he watched the England players laboriously trudge off the Wembley turf and down the tunnel. The Polish players' jubilation, in blunt stark contrast, was there for all to see as they hugged each other, cheered, danced and waved at their travelling supporters.

Philip had seen enough. He got up from his seat and turned the television set off. He grabbed hold of the now empty plate and the two plastic cups and took them into the kitchen. Before returning to the living room, he went through the scullery and checked that the side door was locked, rinsed the plate and the cups and switched off the kitchen light.

"I think it's time for bed," Philip said.

James didn't hear him at first as he had already moved on from the England defeat and was busily reading of the adventures of Minnie the Minx and her failed attempts to destroy her school report card.

"James, it's time for bed," Philip repeated.

"Can I read my comic in bed?" James asked without taking his eyes off the page.

"As long as you're quiet and don't wake mum," Philip answered.

James climbed off the sofa and with comic in hand, made his way out of the room and up the stairs. Philip checked that the back door was locked, unplugged the television set and followed shortly after, checking that the front door was also locked on his way past.

Chapter 46

Philip woke up earlier than usual for a Saturday morning. However, although there was a hugely important game upon the horizon, it wasn't Leeds United's home fixture against Liverpool later that day, that was playing on his mind. It was the conversation with Michael at the swimming meet the previous Sunday and more specifically the revelation about Karen's job description. He just couldn't get it out of his mind. Even as the game got closer and closer, the mighty Liverpool, current league champions with their collection of big hitters, such as Hughes, Keagan, Heighway and Toshack could not dislodge his concerns about the possible occupation of his sister's flatmate from the centre of his thoughts. It was stuck faster than a handkerchief on the head of a northerner spending a day at the beach, and no amount of huffing and puffing was going to shift it.

Philip got dressed quietly and quickly before heading downstairs. He ate his breakfast whilst adopting the same noise and speed he had used to get dressed, and the policy remained in place until he had exited the house. Once outside he paused for a moment on the side step. He was deciding whether to turn right and head straight for the newsagents or to turn left and collect the now roadworthy bike from the garden shed. After a quick attempt to weigh up the pros and cons, he turned left and went to collect his bike. However, this did delay him somewhat due to the random pieces of rope he had tied around the bike by way of a deterrent to any possible theft attempts. The garden shed had a padlock on the door but as yet the bike did not. After unravelling all of the knots and removing the pieces of rope, he wheeled the bike out of the shed and set off for the newsagents, making up for lost time as he peddled down Monkswood Crescent and along the Henley Road. He climbed off the bike upon arrival and leant it against the newsagent's window before entering the shop to collect his bundle of morning papers.

"You've two additions today," Mr Underwood said as he pointed to Philips pile of newspapers resting on the counter. "A 'Sun' in Watcombe Road and a 'Daily Express' in Chelsey Road. The Watcombe Road is just on a Saturday but the other one is every morning from today, except Sunday."

Philip nodded as he placed the papers inside his bag before exiting the shop. As he stepped outside, Paul McBride was crouched down admiring Philip's bike.

"Done a good job Phil," Paul said as Philip approached.

Paul stood up, still looking over the finer details of the bike. He removed a piece of paper from the pocket of his Parka coat. "Here you go," he said as he passed the piece of paper to Philip. "I've written them down in order of importance," he added.

Philip took the piece of paper and opened it up.

"You could sell this if you wanted to Phil, make a bit of profit on it. I know of a couple of interested buyers."

"It's okay, I'll keep it thanks," Philip replied as he began looking at the items on the list.

"I could get four pounds for it, I reckon. We could split it."

"You mean two quid each," Philip replied with a scowling look upon his face. "But I owe you two quid for it as it is. So, you sell it for four quid, you get two quid and I get two quid. Then I give you the two quid I owe you. You get four quid, I get nothing and I no longer have a bike."

"Oh yeah, see your point," Paul replied. "But I'll need the two quid soon. Listen, if you can get hold of a few of these items, especially the ones near the top of the list that may well cover it."

Philip looked at the list again, only this time around, he paid more attention to it.

Transistor Radio
Car Radio

"If you can get your hands on a good car radio," Paul said as Philip continued to look at the list, "something like an Elpico or a Motorola, well they're the best part of fifteen quid brand new. I can sell it for seven or eight, take out the couple of quid you owe me and you are still a couple of quid to the good."

Leather Foot Stool
Brass Wall Mounts
Ronson Hair Dryer (Ladies) / Heated Curlers
Cigarette Lighter (Good Quality, no cheap shit)
Watches Men's and Ladies Ingersol Simba
Travel Alarm Clock

"And watches Phil, nothing specific except for the Ingersol one. I have a customer requesting that particular model, but other watches always come in handy. I can always find a buyer for a watch."

Philip continued to look at the list.

Set of Spanners
Foot Pump
Ford Capri Wing Mirrors
Child's Inflatable Dinghy
Merry Milkman Game
Spice Rack
Fondue Set
Tonka Toy Snorkle Truck
Matchbox Giant Station Maker
Slippers Size 9

"Bit of a strange list," Philip muttered as he reached the final item. "Who wants these things?"

"It's Christmas." Paul replied. "People thinking ahead. The list will get even bigger over the next few weeks."

"How on earth am I supposed to steal a leather foot stool?"

"Just get what you can. It's half-term next week, so more opportunity. Look, I gotta go. Just let me know if you manage to get anything. I need weighing in for that bike soon though." Paul turned away and headed into the shop to collect his papers. Philip folded up the list and put it in his pocket before grabbing his bike and setting off on his round.

It was another twenty minutes or so before he eventually reached the blocks of flats on Clennon Rise. Philip had spent virtually every single second of that time thinking about what he was going to say to his sister. He had put it off all week but couldn't avoid it any longer. He went over it and over what he was going to say but at no point did his imaginary conversation end well.

He wheeled his bike inside his sister's block and positioned it in such a way that he was able see it from the floors above with a quick glance down the centre of the stairwell. He then climbed the stairs to the first floor and knocked on the door to his sister's flat. As he waited for a response, he took a step back and peered over the rails to the floor below. Keeping a watchful eye on his bike, he listened out for the sound of the door behind him opening. After waiting in the early morning silence for longer than he was comfortable with, he turned around and knocked on the door again, only this time a little louder so that the sound seemed to bounce off the walls and echo within the empty space. He was approximately halfway through his rotation back around, so he could check on his bike, when the door to the flat swung open. Standing in the doorway in her dressing gown and slippers with a piece of toast in her hand was Philip's sister.

"What's up, what's happened?" Grace immediately asked upon catching sight of her younger brother.

"Nothing's the matter." Philip replied as he rotated back in the direction of his sister.

"Is mum okay?" Grace said.

"Yes, she's fine," Philip replied.

"Fine is she, just shows how much you know. I thought you were supposed to be keeping an eye on her." Grace stepped into the hallway and pulled the door to behind her, leaving it open a fraction. She stepped closer to Philip.

Philip immediately noticed the shift in both mood and tone as if they were calling out his name and waving at him from the other side of the street.

"What are you on about?" he asked his sister.

"I'm on about you not keeping an eye on her."

"It's a bit difficult when she spends virtually all of her time in her room."

"She still needs your help Philip, your support. I take it you don't even know about this diary that she has been asked to keep?"

"What diary?"

Silence entered stage left and filled the limited space between them for a few seconds whilst Grace adopted a stare of disappointment and sent it in the direction of her brother, rolling her eyes like dice in a craps game for good measure.

"What?" Philip said, growing annoyed by the silence, the stare and the rolling eyes.

"I called round yesterday Philp, whilst you were at school. Thankfully dad wasn't about. Mum says that he has got some extra work in the depot, trying to recoup some of the deficit whist he's on this three-day week. The hospital have asked mum to keep a diary."

"What for?" Philip asked.

"It's to do with her moods. They are trying to establish or identify what triggers her feelings at different times. Is there a pattern or a catalyst? Problem is when she's feeling at her lowest points, she doesn't feel like writing about it and when she is feeling a bit better, she doesn't want to sit and think about what was making her feel so low in the first place. So, you need to help her, you need to encourage her to write it down or talk about it and you can write it for her. Don't mention it to dad though, he doesn't know about it and anyway, he's hardly going to want to help is he."

As Grace stepped back a little, Philip took the opportunity to glance over his shoulder and down the stairwell at his bike.

"What are you looking at?" Grace asked before pushing the door to the flat open with her outstretched leg.

"My bike," Philip replied. "Just checking it was still there."

"Where did you get a bike from?"

"Paul McBride."

Grace shook her head. "How much?" she asked.

"I owe him two quid," Philip replied.

"Wait there," Grace said as she went back into the flat. She returned almost immediately, minus her piece of toast. She handed Philip a one-pound note. "Give him that and tell him you'll pay him the rest next Friday."

Philip took the money from his sister and shoved it into the pocket of his jeans.

"look, I'm gonna be late for work if I don't get a move on," Grace said before adding "Did we find out what it was you actually wanted?"

Philip took a deep breath and looked directly at Grace. "It's about Karen," he said.

"Karen? What about Karen?" Grace replied with an ominous tone in her voice.

"Do you know?" Philip asked.

"Do I know what?"

Philip could detect a nervous tension beginning to pour out of him like water through a sieve. "What she does," he said.

"Philip, what are you going on about. I'm going to be late for work, she doesn't do anything."

Philip looked around, just in case several people had suddenly exited their flats and were now listening to his conversation. Still unsure if they were alone, he stepped closer to Grace and whispered. "She's a prossy."

"Of course she's not, you idiot. Who on earth told you that."

"Well I heard some rumours a little while back, but I didn't say anything. I can't remember who said it. But last week Michael told me when I saw him in Birmingham."

"You mean that your little schoolboy pal told you. And how would he know? Does he save up his pocket money does he, ten pence a week and when he's saved up enough, he comes round for a hand job?"

Not realising that it would be needed again so soon, silence hurriedly re-emerged and made its way centre stage. It squeezed between Grace and Philip, looked them both in the eye and patiently waited.

An alarmed expression suddenly appeared upon Grace's face. "Oh god, you haven't told this stupid story to dad have you?"

"No, of course not," Philip replied.

"Make sure you don't. Don't tell anybody. Just go and finish your paper round and keep your eye on mum."

Grace turned away and stepped back inside the flat, slamming the door behind her as she did so, leaving Philip standing alone in the hallway. He wasn't sure what to do. He just stood there for a moment with his hands shoved deep inside his coat pockets. He had played out this discussion with his sister several times during the past week, but not one of them had ended like that. However after careful consideration, he decided that now wasn't the best time to pursue the matter and he set off to complete his round.

Chapter 47

Woolworth's in the town centre, on a busy Saturday afternoon. Endless opportunities, endless possibilities, just as long as you are thinking straight and with a mind that is as clear as a mountain stream, you have your wits about you and you are focused on the job in hand. Even entering the shop unnoticed was important. It gave you a bit more time, time that could be put to good use, time to become lost amongst the crowd.

Philip knew what to look for when it came to trying to spot the floor walkers. The foe; those employed to identify and catch the shoplifter. It was all about the eyes…well that and the fact that they always shopped alone. But first and foremost it was about the eyes. Whilst the typical innocent shopper would be looking at the items hanging from the rails, the floor walker would always be looking just above the rails. Their heads may be bowed slightly but their eyes weren't looking at any shirts or blouses or jumpers or slacks.

Philip also knew that once he was sighted, he would immediately attract suspicion. All teenage boys, except for those dressed like Lord Snooty and holding their mother's hand whilst she carried a handkerchief in the other hand, attracted suspicion when spotted inside department stores.

Philip entered the store and as customary when entering Woolworth's, he headed straight for the pick 'n' mix sweet section located in the centre. There were good points, bad points and good points for making such a decision. Good point: there was a wide selection of sweets on offer and due to poor thinking within the design department, it was easy pickings. Even a rookie, a rank amateur at the game, could successfully gather up a pocket full of sweets in a very short space of time, undetected. Bad point: the pick 'n' mix section was a magnet, an unavoidable lure for those readily identified by floor walkers as problematic. Good point: volume, number of problems in relation to floor walkers. Although the problems may well be condensed within a small area, sooner or later they are going to scatter. You can watch some of the problems all of the time, you can watch all of the problems some of the time, but you can't watch all of the problems all of the time.

As Philip arrived at the crowded pick 'n' mix stand, hands were busily reaching out and grabbing sweets. Some sweets were being dropped into small paper bags for legitimate purchase, others were finding their way into bulging coat pockets. Philip collected a paper bag so as not to attract any unwanted attention and began surveying the surrounding area whilst walking around the circumference of the pick 'n' mix section. He then approached the counter and purchased a small amount of sweets before setting off deeper into the store with an unpaid lemon sherbet in his mouth and several more sweets in his pockets.

He headed for the electricals section of the store and casually walked along the isles and glanced at some of the products that were located behind the counters. Several of the items on the list were located here; it was just a matter of working out a strategy. He paused at a display of cigarette lighters and patiently waited for a sales assistant to notice him. It didn't take long. A tall, thin, middle aged lady on the other side of the counter walked the short distance required and stopped in front of Philip.

"Can I assist you?" the lady asked.

"Yes please, can I have a look at some of these lighters? Nothing too expensive. It's a present for my grandad."

Unfortunately for Philip, the experienced shop assistant only removed the lighters from the display cabinet one lighter at a time, thus thwarting his opportunity to palm one. After deciding that none of the lighters were quite right for his grandad, he thanked the sales assistant and went on his way. However, he was much more successful in obtaining a travel alarm clock, a pair of brass wall mounts and a pair of men's slippers, size nine, by using the stack and return method.

There are two possible options when using this method. Firstly, you walk around the store, stopping and looking at products. You then proceed to gather up a random selection of items, including the one item that you plan to steal, this is known as the stack. You then start to have doubts about your intended purchases, you look unsure, you ponder. You then proceed to walk back around the store, carefully returning the items, the return. It is during this phase of the operation that you have your two options. You can palm and conceal the item you are planning to steal whilst returning the other items or you can strategically leave it somewhere on route, preferably well hidden in a certain location, ready to be retrieved and concealed a little later.

As well as the items he managed to steal from Woolworth's, he was also able to acquire the Tonka toy snorkel truck from Barnbys Children's Store in the Precinct and quite unbelievably he was also able to walk out of a small furniture store at the far end of the city arcade with an equally small brown leather footstool under his arm. Out of the corner of his eye, whilst serving a customer, a junior sales assistant on the ground floor of the store had noticed Philip coming down the stairs from the first floor, carrying the foot stool. But didn't suspect, not even for a moment, that he would not have paid for the item on the first floor.

After successfully exiting the furniture store, Philip felt that it would be best to head for home, as the sight of a fourteen-year-old boy in flared jeans and a Parka coat carrying a brown leather foot stool under his arm would immediately attract attention in any other shop he cared to enter. After calculating the prices of the items he had managed to lift, he felt sure that he had enough to pay off the rest of his bike debt and also get his school trip payments up to date once he was back at school. He was also conscious of the fact that the football would have kicked off by the time he got home.

Upon returning home, he headed straight for the garden shed. He hid the foot stool and the other items under a plastic sheet he found at the back of the shed and some old newspapers that were lying on the floor, before locking the shed and going into the house. As he entered he was met with sight, sound and smell that completely took him by surprise, as if they had just leapt out of a wardrobe wearing a werewolf mask.

The smell of home baking hanging in the air was instantly recognisable. He was sure that somewhere in the kitchen was a tray of freshly baked jam tarts. Golden, melt in the mouth, pastry and rich sweet strawberry jam, cooling ever so slowly. As the comforting aroma gently caressed him, he glanced down the living room at the sight of James and his mother playing a game of Operation. The sound of the pair laughing whilst they played also hung sweetly in the air as James attempted to remove the patient's ankle bone connected to the leg bone. As Philip stepped back and closed the door behind him, his mother looked up.

"Hello sweetheart, would you like to play?" his mother asked before adding, "there's some jam tarts in the kitchen, they should be cooled by now. Can you bring some in?"

Philip didn't need a second invitation, and as he returned from the kitchen with the plate of jam tarts he already had one stuffed in his mouth.

"Are you playing?" his mother asked again as he placed the tarts on the table.

Currently unable to speak, Philip shook his head and pointed towards the television. He stood and chewed for a few more seconds before eventually being able to announce "I'll play in a bit, I just want to watch T.V. first." He took another tart from the plate and headed for the T.V just as the patient's nose lit up and the buzzer sounded to confirm James's failed attempt at removing the ankle bone connected to the leg bone.

Philip switched on the T.V. and took a large bite out of his second jam tart. He sat down just as the runners and riders for the Riverdale Novice Hurdle over two miles at Kempton Park were entering the stalls. After the race was over, the attention turned to ice-hockey. An extremely contented Philip sat back with the sweet taste of jam tarts on his lips and a head full of laughter and smiles, watching the London Lions take on the Austrian Internationals. As the ice-hockey came to its conclusion with a five-four victory to the London Lions, Philip turned the T.V over to 'World of Sport' for the half-time scores before joining his mother and his brother for a game of Operation.

To Philip's delight, Leeds United were winning 1-0. He did not know it at the time and he had to wait until Match of the Day later that evening to see it for himself, but it was a well worked goal scored by Mick Jones in the thirty third minute. A ball from the left, midway inside the Liverpool half. A cheeky stepover from the referee allowed the ball to reach Billy Bremner on the edge of the centre circle. With his back to goal, he swept the ball out to Peter Lorimer on the right wing. Lorimer collected the ball in his stride, sprinted forward and crossed it into the danger area from just outside the eighteen-yard box. Mick Jones leapt highest, in between Tommy Smith and Ray Clemence, heading home from just three yards out.

It was to remain 1-0 until the final whistle. The result left Leeds United with nine wins and three draws from their first twelve games. They were now four points clear of Burnley and Derby County at the top of the table. Burnley had lost away at Everton whilst Derby County had beaten local rivals Leicester City by two goals to one.

The football results, and the fact that Philip won two games of Operation, contributed greatly to his warm glow as he set off for his evening paper round. Learning that it was faggots for tea, as his dad had earnt some extra cash for working in the depot that week also added a little more fuel and a little more heat as he stepped outside on a chilly October evening.

"Wow, you got a foot stool!" Paul Mc Bride exclaimed with clear surprise in his voice, when he saw the object itself resting upon the handle bars of Philip's bike. "Even fat Bobby didn't manage that one. I'll easily be able to get a couple of quid for that. What else you got?"

As Paul took hold of the foot stool, Philip opened his paper bag and removed the travel alarm clock, the Tonka toy, the brass wall fittings and the pair of slippers.

"Quick, chuck them in here," Paul said as he held open his paper bag. "Done well there Phil, done real well. I'll weigh in in a few days, that alright?"

Philip nodded. "Yeah, that will be fine," he said.

With the foot stool now resting on the handle bars of his bike and the other items secured inside his paper bag, Paul turned away and set off on his paper round. After taking a few steps, he paused and turned his head to look back at Philip. "Do you know what a barometer is?" Paul asked.

"Yes." Philip replied.

"Well if you can get hold of one, I know somebody who wants one," Paul said before turning away again and getting on his bike.

Philip nodded his head and watched as Paul cycled away, before entering the shop.

Chapter 48

My Dear Friend Philip,

May I say how sorry I was to read that you were unable to compete in your first swimming meet due to illness. The timing could not have been worse and I know that it must have been very disappointing for you but I also think that your coach probably made the right decision and acted in your best interests and the interests of the team as a whole. I know that at times decisions can be very hard to take personally but the needs of the team must always come before those of the individual. Thankfully though, your next meet is just around the corner. That is the beauty of sport and competing, another opportunity to do well is never that far away.

It is a similar story here. Whenever we lose, it plays on my mind. I mull it over for days sometimes. What did we do wrong? How could we have prevented the loss? Thankfully though, the next game is never that far away and with it comes the opportunity to perform better and to move on.

As you know, with our latest results, I have yet to deal with a defeat in the league this season and as yet have not had to deal with or question a poor performance. Although we feel that it was probably a point dropped at Leicester, we did well to come back from two behind and gain a draw. We were all delighted with both the performance and the result against Liverpool on Saturday. It is always satisfying to beat a rival team and to claim a victory after three draws from the previous four games was also very pleasing.

We have some tough games ahead, not least the trip to Manchester City on Saturday, always a tough place to go. But as a group, we are all determined to try and keep this unbeaten run going. The pressure builds just that little bit more with each passing game but with that pressure comes a desire, a willingness, a determination within the whole team to do well. We are all upbeat at present, (well all except for Sniffer, as it is now five games since he last hit the back of the net). However, as I have already mentioned, it is the team that is the most important thing and his contributions and determination on the field cannot be faulted.

How are things at home? You did not mention your mother in your last letter. I am hoping that this means that she is feeling a bit better. Try and remain positive and try to be there for her at every opportunity. What about Grace? Is her flat-share still running smoothly? And what about her job? I think that independence is a good thing but it can also be quite a scary thing. I know the circumstances were very different for me when I came to Leeds as a sixteen year-old, but I can still remember the suitcase full of nerves that I brought with me, the butterflies in my stomach, the anxiety. You never forget those moments; certain points in your life when big changes come into view upon the horizon.

Say hello to James. As always, thank you for your continued support and for keeping in touch, it means a lot. It also means a lot to have the opportunity to help and support a young fan through difficult times. Keep me posted on the swimming and let me know how you get on, if you are able to compete at the next meet.

All the best, your friend Billy.

With calm and calculated precision, Philip carefully folded the letter and gently placed it back inside the envelope, before laying it down flat upon the kitchen table. It was Thursday morning of half-term week and thankfully for Philip, the letter had arrived after his dad had gone to bed after his nightshift. James had yet to get out of his bed. Philip and his mother were in the kitchen.

"From your footballer friend, I take it?" his mother said as she checked on her toast that was slowly browning under the grill.

Philip picked up his now empty breakfast bowl, stood up and placed it on the draining board. "What?" He said.

"Your letter, from your footballer?" his mother said again as she motioned towards the letter lying on the table.

"Oh right, yes," Philip said before adding. "Don't mention it to dad, will you mum."

"Why not?" his mother asked as she removed her toast from beneath the grill and turned it over.

"I just don't think he's very happy about it," Philip said.

"Oh, I see, do I need to add it to the list?"

"What list?"

"The list of things your father is not happy about. When he finds out about this swimming thing of yours, that will need to go on the list as well. I take it that is where you were last night?"

Philip nodded.

"Do you want a piece of toast?" his mother asked as she made another quick check of the two slices beneath the grill.

"No thanks mum," Philip replied.

"Well don't go disappearing," his mum said. "I need you to run a few errands for me this morning. Your dad says he is needed in the depot again this afternoon, so it will keep you out of the way whilst he's asleep."

"But I was gonna go out."

"You can go out, you can go out and run some errands and then you can go out wherever you please."

Philip tutted and attempted to exit the kitchen in search of a more comfortable seat in the living room, collecting his letter as he did so. He had one foot on the living room carpet and the other one still in the kitchen, when his mother said "In fact James can go with you. Can you go and tell him to come and get some breakfast. And tell him quietly, so that you don't wake your father up."

"Will you be alright by yourself?" Philip asked as he paused in the doorway, a question that immediately caused his mother to turn away from her toast and look directly at Philip. "What kind of question is that to be asking?" she asked.

"I just thought that you might prefer to have some company," Philip quickly replied.

"What I want is for you to run some errands for me and to take your brother with you, so that he is not getting under my feet."

Deciding it would be better not to say anything else, Philip managed to remove both of his feet from the kitchen. The rest of his body went along as well. He headed upstairs to get his brother, his letter firmly grasped in his hand.

Waiting for James to leave the room, he sat on the edge of his bed. He hurried James along by explaining that his mother had instructed him to go and get some breakfast. Once Philip was alone, he hid his latest letter with the letters that he had previously received, in his usual hiding place. Due to previous unsettling misdemeanours this particular hiding place now also housed his red plastic piggy bank. Once he was satisfied that all items were safely concealed, he headed back downstairs.

He switched on the television, making sure that the volume was a safe level and not so loud that it might wake up his father. Immediately discovering that there was nothing worth watching, he switched it off again. As he sat and stared at the blank screen, he could hear voices coming from the kitchen; his mother informing James of the fact that he would be spending the majority of the morning running errands. He could also hear James's futile attempt at resistance to this news. A minute or so later a disgruntled James exited the kitchen and flopped himself down on the settee next to Philip.

By the time their mother appeared in front of them, James had put his disappointment to one side and was once again reading a comic. Blocking Philip's view of the blank screen, he looked up at his mother.

"I need you to go to the council office at the top of Old Church Road. Do you know where it is?"

Philip nodded.

"Good." His mother replied as she passed him a green council house rent book. "You need to pay two weeks rent, that will be sixteen pounds, and make sure that the lady stamps and signs two weeks. Then you need to go to the electricity board shop in Riley Square. You need to go upstairs to the bill payment window and pay the electricity bill. Make sure that they stamp and give you the receipt." Passing Philip the electricity bill and a shopping list, his mother continued to give instructions. "Then I need you to go and do some shopping for me, everything you need to get is on the list. You also need to take the paraffin can with you and fill it up at the garage. The cold nights are coming; we will need the paraffin heaters on soon."

She opened her purse and removed three ten-pound notes before passing them to Philip. "And don't just shove them in the pocket of your coat," she said before adding "Don't you dare lose any of that."

Philip took hold of the money, folded it carefully and put it in the pocket of his jeans as he stood up. "Come on James," he said. "Let's go."

"Oh and one more thing. Call in and see your sister in Woolworth's and ask her if she wants to come for Sunday dinner. You can take thirty pence out of the change. That should be enough to share a bag of chips and a can of pop with enough left over to get a small cake each from Gladding's."

Chapter 49

The living room door swung open and was quickly followed by the appearance of Francis's head and shoulders as he looked towards the opposite end of the room.

"Boys. Boys, come and give me a hand," he called out whilst holding on to the door handle. Francis waited for about as long as it took for his request to reach the other end of the room, before calling out again, "Come on, come on." He stepped into the living room and clapped his hands together. "I've got to get the truck back by four o'clock."

This final piece of information immediately aroused the boy's curiosity. 'Grandstand', or rather the Commonwealth Games trial marathon from Harlow instantly lost their interest as they both got up off the sofa and headed outside. By the time they reached the front door and looked out onto the street, Francis had already reached the back doors of the Wilkinson Transport DA-21 Leyland Boxer van with a Rochdale phone number blazoned on the side.

With curiosity now gripping them tighter than a wrestler's leotard on 'World of Sport', they sprinted up the path to the garden gate and around to the back of the lorry. The boys eagerly peered inside. Standing in the and striking a pose that was reminiscent of a big game hunter majestically looking into the camera with a foot raised and placed upon the carcass of his kill, Francis looked at his sons.

Scattered across the floor of the lorry (it was difficult to surmise exactly how many there were) lay a large number of broken pallets. Some were more broken than others. With blank expressions duly applied, Philip and James looked at their dad, then at the pallets and then at their dad once again.

"Come on then," Francis said as he picked up a pallet and slid it towards the back of the lorry. "Don't just stand there, help me get these unloaded."

"Where are we taking them?" Philip asked as Francis lowered the first pallet to the ground.

"Round the back of course. Bonfire night, they're for bonfire night! You want to have a bonfire, don't you?"

Suddenly the penny dropped, and the boys' eyes lit up like sparklers.

"And be careful of splinters and nails," Francis added as the boys picked up and made off with the first pallet.

From that moment on the whole operation was completed with military precision and less than twenty minutes later three, as neat as could be expected, stacks of pallets were sitting at the bottom of the garden. No nail injuries occurred, and both boys were splinter free.

"I need a cup of tea," Francis said as he closed the back doors of the lorry, before carrying the final and largest pallet into the back garden. "Go put the kettle on Phil."

Philip was just putting the tea leaves into the pot when Francis entered the kitchen. Francis sat down at the table and glanced at his watch. "Plenty of time," he muttered to nobody in particular, before looking at Philip. "Who have you got today?" he asked.

"Man City away," Philip replied.

"A tough one," Francis said. "Do you know who we've got?"

"You're at home to Lincoln City."

"We need to win that one," Francis said as the kettle came to the boil.

Philip poured the hot water into the pot, gave it a stir and placed the lid on top before getting the tea strainer out of the drawer and placing it on one of the three cups that were lined up on the table.

Hartlepool United had made a poor start to the season and found themselves perilously close to the foot of the fourth division table with only two wins from their first fourteen games. Their record, going in to the Lincoln game, read two wins, five draws and seven defeats. The club was in real danger of dropping out of the football league.

Philip finished making the tea. He placed a cup in front of Francis before carrying his and James's cups into the living room. He had just sat down in time for the 'Tote Roll-Up Stakes' one mile handicap from Newbury, when Francis called him from the kitchen. By the time Philip re-entered the kitchen, Francis had lit a cigarette and was enjoying it along with his cup of tea.

"I needed this," Francis said as he pointed to a chair for Philip to sit down.

Philip pulled the chair from beneath the table and sat down.

"I've some sheets on the back of the lorry," Francis began. "I'll get them for you. You need to cover those pallets in case it rains. We need to keep them dry for bonfire night."

Philip nodded.

"What's on the T.V?" Francis asked.

"Just some horse racing," Philip replied. "The football hasn't started yet."

"I hope you haven't been down that bookies in Wood End. I've told you before to keep out of there." Francis took a drag of his cigarette before asking. "Have you heard from your pen pal recently?"

Philip felt aggrieved as the time allocated for a response clearly wasn't sufficient enough for him to weigh up the two options available. He opted to tell the truth but with as little information as possible. "Yes," he said.

"And what did he have to say?"

"Nothing much dad, he just talked about the last few games, the win against Liverpool and how pleased he was with the draw at Leicester after going two goals behind."

Francis took a noticeably longer drag of his cigarette. He exhaled and the plume of smoke filled the space between them. "If there was anything troubling you, you know you can always talk to me don't you," he muttered as the smoke continued to tumble from his lips.

"I'm fine dad," Philip replied as he pushed his chair back and stood up. "I'm gonna get my tea before it goes cold."

"Hang on a minute," Francis said as he reached into his back pocket and took out his wallet. He opened the wallet and removed two one-pound notes. He placed them gently on the table before closing his wallet again. "Nip up Bell Green and get some fireworks, a couple of boxes and some sparklers. You can't have bonfire night without fireworks and sparklers."

Francis stubbed his cigarette out, stood up, put his wallet back in his pocket and finished his cup of tea. "Right, I'd better get that lorry back. We'll break those pallets up tomorrow, and don't forget to go and get the fireworks."

Francis headed through the scullery and out of the side door, Philip scooped up the money from the kitchen table and headed back into the living room to speak to James.

"Wanna go and get some fireworks?" Philip asked as he waved the money in front of James.

With a response more certain than fish on a Friday in the Pope's house, James closed his comic and leapt from his seat. "Yeah!" he said.

"Just let me drink my tea and we can walk up to Bell Green," Philip replied.

It took Philip three minutes and seventeen seconds to drink his tea. As far as James was concerned, this was three minutes and seventeen seconds too long. They were soon on their way to Bell Green, much to James's relief. He set off at a blistering pace, as if he was in a marching band or a walking race. He was constantly looking over his shoulder, only to see Philip falling further and further behind. By the time Philip entered the newsagents at the top of Riley Square, James had been impatiently waiting by the counter for a full three minutes and seventeen seconds.

"Where have you been?" James asked as Philip entered.

"I told you, I had to post my letter."

Reminiscent of the scene in 'The Good, The Bad and The Ugly', where Eli Wallach constructs his own gun, the shop assistant had laid out a selection of fireworks on the counter for James and Philip to look at. Their eyes were soon darting from box to box and packet to packet.

"What's in that one?" James said to Philip as he pointed at a selection box.

Philip looked at the serial number on the side of the box, and then he attempted to locate the box in the catalogue that had also been placed on the counter.

"Here it is." Philip said. "It's got a Flying Saucer, a Mount Vesuvius, a Coloured Niagara, a Spitfire, a Harlequin, two Crystal Frolics, a Volcano, two Chrysanthemum Fountains, a Jack in the Box, two Roman Candles, a Silver Tree, a Golden Rain and two Pin Wheels."

"How much is it?" James asked.

"Seventy five pence." The assistant replied.

The next box up from this one had a few more fireworks but was priced at ninety five pence. Two of the larger boxes would only leave enough left over for some sparklers, but more importantly would not leave enough for the boys to purchase any bangers.

As everybody knows, boys aged between eleven and fifteen and growing up on council estates up and down the land had to have at least one packet of bangers. Such an opportunity for mischief only presented itself within a narrow window, once a year, and simply could not be squandered. It was like a snowball fight in winter, a water fight in summer; it was to be expected.

A few minutes later the boys left the shop after purchasing one box of fireworks for seventy five pence, one box of fireworks for ninety five pence, one packet of large sparklers for ten pence and two packets of bangers priced at ten pence each. Total cost of sale; two pounds exactly.

Upon returning home, Philip placed the boxes of fireworks and the packet of sparklers on the table in the living room before heading upstairs and stashing the two packets of bangers in a safe concealed place. James had enquired about when they could use the bangers on at least seven separate occasions on the journey home. Each occasion had been met with exactly the same response; 'wait until Monday when dad is at work'.

Philip peered into his mother's bedroom on his way back to the living room, only to find her asleep. Once downstairs and plastic cups of lemonade poured, he settled down in readiness for final score to begin. James was sitting at the table, looking at the boxes of fireworks when the scores began to filter through. As they began to appear, Philip gripped his cup a little tighter. No need to worry; it was another good result. Manchester City 0 Leeds United 1. However it was another bad day for Hartlepool as they suffered yet another defeat, a 0-2 loss at home to Lincoln City.

'The Pink Panther Show' had just started when Philip set off for his paper round. As he approached the shop, he could make out the figure of Paul McBride waiting for him in the fading light.

"Any luck with that barometer?" Paul asked once Philip was within range.

Philip shook his head. "I haven't been able to get into town for the past few days." He said.

"Never mind." Paul replied. "Proving a bit tricky that one. Even fat Bobby Cowley couldn't get one," he added as he reached inside his flared trouser pocket. "Here you go;" he said as he handed Philip three pounds. "I've taken out what you owe me for the bike, so we're all square."

Philip took the money and went to go into the shop.

"Hang on, hang on," Paul said as he removed a folded piece of paper from the left side patch pocket of his three buttoned waistband flares. "See if you can get us any of that."

Philip took the piece of paper and stuffed it into the pocket of his Parka coat.

"See your team got another good result." Paul said

Philip just nodded his head and smiled.

"Better than us. Can't believe we lost to Stoke, they're shit! Three-nil as well: not even close." Paul shrugged his shoulders as he spoke and then set off on his round.

Philip returned home to find his dad and James sitting at the dining room table.

"There's a sausage and chips in the oven for ya," Francis said. "They should still be hot."

As Philip entered the kitchen, he heard Francis call out. "There's one for your mother as well but I'm not sure if she's awake. If you remember, look in on her later and see if she wants it."

The recent change in his mother's behaviour was the only downside to an otherwise good day. The earlier part of the week had felt pleasant, almost normal, but the last forty eight hours or so had seen her drift away again as if she had been carried off on the tide whilst he had been sleeping, and waking in the early hours to discover that she was once again out of reach, still visible upon the horizon but contact now unobtainable.

Chapter 50

"Sunday," Mr Spencer said, believing that this was all he needed to say for Philip to understand what it was he was referring to.

Philip however, just stood on the other side of the desk with an expression on his face that was as blank as a classroom blackboard in the summer holidays. The silence, though only brief, was still as uncomfortable as a pair of wet socks in tight fitting shoes.

"Sunday." Mr Spencer said again. "You have a competition this Sunday."

"It's called a meet," Philip replied with a certain amount of relief in his voice, now he knew what Mr Spencer was actually talking about.

"Sorry?"

"It's not called a competition in swimming sir, it's called a meet."

"As long as you are there to compete at the meet Philip, you can call it whatever you want, a Soiree, a shindig, a knees-up. Just as long as you do not let Mr Kennedy or myself down like last time, understand."

Philip nodded, in an attempt to clarify that he did understand with as little fuss as possible.

"Good." Mr Spencer said as he opened a drawer of his desk and removed a folder. "Do you have any money for me?"

Philip nodded again as his hand disappeared into the inside pocket of his school blazer and removed three pounds. He handed the money over to Mr Spencer.

"Thank you." Mr Spencer said as he opened the folder and removed a sheet of paper. He noted down the payment that Philip had just made.

"You've another two pounds fifty to pay. Will you have it paid by the end of term?"

"Yes sir." Philip said. "That shouldn't be a problem."

Mr Spencer smiled as he returned to sheet of paper to the folder and then the folder to the drawer of the desk. "Better get off to your lesson. Don't want you being late, do we?" he said, as he removed a small metal cash box from the same drawer.

It was about five minutes before the end of morning break when Philip found himself back at Mr Spencer's office. He was sitting outside, waiting. His blazer was a little dishevelled and dirty. He had a small graze on the side of his left cheek and splatters of blood down the front of his shirt.

On the bench opposite sat a boy in his final year at school called Daniel McKenzie, a tall, thin boy with short greasy black hair and acne that was reaching just shy of eight on the out of ten severity scale. Under any set of circumstances, he certainly wasn't pleasant to look at and his current appearance only seemed to make matters worse. Daniel was leaning forward. He had a piece of tissue paper inserted into each nostril. His shirt was heavily bloodstained and the badge on his blazer pocket was hanging off. Standing between them both with his arms tightly folded was Mr Bhanot the maths teacher.

"Oh it's you," Karen said as she opened the door to her flat. Francis Knott was standing in the hallway. "What do you want?"

As sure as every coach driver in the land would give their fellow coach drivers what looked like a Nazi salute when they passed each other on the open road, Karen already knew the answer to her question. Francis also knew that Karen knew the answer to the question, so he said nothing and attempted to step inside. However Karen kept a firm grip on the door and did not move aside.

"I'm busy," she said. "You'll have to call back later."

"Of course you are," Francis replied. "I'm sure that you have plenty to do."

A brief stand-off ensued, not long enough to require an Italian composer and a wild west setting, but still long enough for Karen to move nervously from side to side as the cold air from the stairwell rested upon her neck. Karen eventually moved aside and allowed the door to swing open.

"You'll have to be quick," Karen said as Francis stepped past her, walked down the corridor and into the bedroom. Leisurely would not be the best way to describe it but Karen closed the door and followed slowly. By the time she entered the bedroom and closed the door, Francis was already half undressed.

"It will cost you three pounds," Karen said as Francis began to undo the belt of his trousers.

Francis paused and stood upright with his trousers slowly slipping down towards his knees. "Three pounds?" He repeated.

"That's right," Karen said. "Three pounds, two pounds for sex and one pound for keeping your dirty secret quiet. Obviously if you are not happy with the arrangement, you can always go home and sleep with your wife for free. And it's cash up front."

By the time the price rise had hit home, Francis's trousers had sunk all the way down his legs and were now resting on his ankles. He rather awkwardly bent down and attempted to retrieve his wallet for the back pocket.

'How pathetic do you look?' Karen silently asked him and allowed herself a little smile.

Francis returned to an upright position, with wallet in hand. Karen's facial expression changed as she turned away and started to undress. Once naked and still with her back to Francis, Karen pulled the bed covers back and quickly slipped beneath them. A moment or two later she felt Francis climb in. She immediately felt his body as it pressed against hers and his warm breath crashing into her bare neck. As his arm rested upon her side and his hand firmly grasped her breast, she took a deep breath and closed her eyes tightly.

Mr Spencer stood in the small space outside his office and shook his head. He looked at Philip then at Daniel McKenzie and finally at Mr Bhanot.

"You'd better come in," he said as he entered his office.

Mr Bhanot followed and closed the door behind him as he entered, leaving the two boys sitting outside.

Approximately five minutes later both men reappeared, and Mr Bhanot set off to deliver another inspiring maths lesson.

"Right, in you come Knott," Mr Spencer said.

Philip got up from his seat and walked into the office. Mr Spencer followed.

Mr Spencer sat down, removed his watch and placed it very carefully on the desk in front of him. He raised his hand and pointed an outstretched finger in Philip's direction, before looking back at his watch.

"You have one minute, in your own words. I strongly suggest that you use them wisely," he said. He paused, still looking at his watch. "And your time starts........ now."

"He just kept pushing it Sir, kept saying things, things about my sister."

Philip stopped talking. Mr Spencer continued to stare at his watch. Philip felt as if he could hear the second hand ticking, as if its long bony finger was tapping him on the nose as it continued its journey.

"He had no right to say those things Sir, not about somebody's sister. You cannot expect to be able to say such things and then think you can just walk away."

Philip stopped again and leant forward a little in an attempt to see the watch. He still had twenty-three seconds left. The time seemed to sit in the corner with a disappointed expression upon its face at not being used to its fullest. Philip said nothing else.

"Times up," Mr Spencer eventually said as he picked up the watch and put it back on his wrist. "So let me see if I follow this. McKenzie called your sister a few names and you felt that was enough justification for you to push his face into the wall outside the art block?"

"I must have done," Philip replied as he shrugged his shoulders.

Mr Spencer's facial expression instantly changed and a sterner one duly arrived. "Being smart is a suit that doesn't fit you Knott," he said.

Philip had already taken stock of the shift in facial expression. The message had been sent to his brain that the ice beneath his feet was paper thin and any sudden movements at this moment in time were not advisable.

"So what exactly did he call your sister?" Mr Spencer asked.

"I'd rather not say," Philip replied as he felt the ice beneath his feet start to crack with a sharp, crisp sound.

"I cannot help you if you are not prepared to help me," Mr Spencer said.

Taking a short breath before he answered and taking the opportunity to glance down at his feet, Philip eventually replied. "It's done now sir, it doesn't matter what he said. Can I just have my punishment Sir?" Philip felt the weight of his words push down upon the surface of the ice, and another crack appeared.

Mr Spencer shook his head. "I'll have to contact your parents; school policy I'm afraid. In the future, if somebody says something about your relatives that you find objectionable, I suggest you resist the temptation to plant their face into the nearest wall and report the incident to a member of staff."

Philip nodded his head, gently, so as not to send any additional shock waves towards the ice.

"Well it is up to you, you can have a two-week conduct card or you can get it over with and have two on each."

For Philip it was an easy decision to make. It was like Brazil against Zaire, no contest. There was no such thing as a two week conduct card. This was the punishment equivalent to borrowing money from a loan shark. Once you are on the rack, you never get off it. The chances of going two whole weeks without an 'Unsatisfactory' and therefore avoiding starting the process all over again were slimmer than a slice of cucumber in a vicar's sandwich.

"I'll take the two on each please Sir," Philip replied.

"You'd better go and wait outside then lad," Mr Spencer said. As Philip turned and opened the door, Mr Spencer shouted. "Come on McKenzie, let's have you."

The two boys briefly passed each other in the empty space, before McKenzie disappeared into the office. It was less than three minutes before the office door swung open again and McKenzie stepped out, followed by Mr Spencer, carrying his trusty strip of finely tuned wood.

"Okay then Knott, you first," Mr Spencer said as McKenzie sat down to witness the spectacle and await a similar fate.

Philip stood in the usual spot and held out his left hand. Mr Spencer rested the smooth thin cane upon the smooth soft flesh of Philip's palm. Like a golfer lining up a match winning putt, a rugby player lining up a conversion, a darts player lining up his arrow, Mr Spencer lined up his cane and took aim. He raised the cane steadily towards the ceiling. Philip braced himself for impact like a nervous passenger on a flight coming in to land at Heraklion Airport on a windy day. The downward trajectory gathered pace at a phenomenal rate as the thin strip of wood crashed into the soft white palm. The pain delay was short-lived. The stinging, burning sensation arrived almost immediately. Within the blink of an eye the cane was once again airborne. The eye in question was already starting to fill when the second swipe duly arrived and certainly didn't do anything to help matters. Philip slowly lowered his left hand before equally slowly raising his right. Mr Spencer adjusted his stance accordingly and the whole hideous process was played out again.

With hands throbbing as if they were in a 'Tom & Jerry' cartoon and an anvil had been dropped upon them from a great height, Philip stepped away and sat back down. McKenzie didn't move, instead he just looked across at the anguish written upon Philip's face.

"Come on lad, I haven't got all day," Mr Spencer said as he gently tapped the cane against his leg.

McKenzie slowly got to his feet and made the short journey from his seat to the centre of the space. Philip sat with his hands pressed together and his knees pressing his hands together. He didn't look up. Instead he listened for the sound of the rattan cane moving through the air and crashing into the outstretched palm. Four strokes later and with eyes still watering, he looked up to witness one solitary tear role down the bright red cheek of McKenzie's face. A moment or two later, McKenzie began to sniffle.

"Right you two, that is the matter closed. Now get off to your lessons, you're already late." Mr Spencer paused as he looked at McKenzie. "And go and smarten yourself up McKenzie, you're an awful sight lad," he added as he walked back into his office.

The two boys left together, McKenzie wiping his nose on the sleeve of his shirt as they exited the block. They apologised to each other and had a brief discussion about football, before heading in different directions towards their respective lessons.

At the same time, Francis exited the block of flats, tucking his shirt in as he did so, before setting off for the Green Man public house. Karen lay in her bed, naked and lying on her side. A solitary tear ran along her cheek and dropped onto the pillow below.

Chapter 51

Although joined together and located at the far end of Monkswood Crescent, The three storey block of flats had three separate entrances. Each of the two end blocks had an entrance to the side, and the middle block, unsurprisingly, had an entrance in the middle, located directly behind the small brick construction that housed the large rubbish bins. There were three flats on each of the first and second floors and two flats on the ground floor.

When a flat became vacant for whatever reason, the council came along and boarded up the front door and the windows. However, it was merely a matter of days or even hours, before the board covering the front door and the front door itself had been prized open and a new den was born. The den remained until the time came when the property was reclaimed for its original purpose and new tenants moved in. Once this happened, the search for a new den began and so the cycle went on.

The flat that was currently being used as a den was on the middle floor of the left hand block, a two bedroom flat at the top of the stairs. It had been empty since its last occupant, an elderly gentleman, had passed away in early June. It hadn't been used that much during the summer months. There had been the occasional attempt by Craig Swinburn to improve their base reaching score with Claire Chase, whilst her mother served out her ban from the 'Live and Let Live'. On one balmy evening a few weeks ago, with the help of some No6 cigarettes and two bottles of Babycham, he actually managed to get his hand under her bra. However, mainly due to flat being icy cold, he didn't have the same good fortune when it came to getting his hand inside any other item of Claire's underwear.

On this particular Monday evening in late October, two days after the clocks had changed, Craig Swinburn, Paul Jones, Martin Matthews, Philip and James were sitting in a circle in the centre of the empty living room. Lighting was provided by two small torches on the floor and a small selection of candles on the sills of the boarded-up windows. Once again heating was a different matter all-together.

The boys sat hunched up with Parka coats on and hood over their heads. They looked like a Hereford United supporters club coven, meeting in secret to worship and pay homage to the legendary Ronnie Radford.

"So, what you got?" Craig asked as he looked across at Philip.

Philip shoved his hand inside his coat pocket. He retrieved the two packets of bangers and then placed them inside a shaft of light coming from one of the torches on the floor.

Craig looked down at the red, yellow and white box of bangers and started to laugh. "Astra bangers, bangers for babies," he scoffed. He placed his hand inside his coat pocket and pulled out a small carrier bag. He opened it and delved inside.

In the flickering light from the candles and the shafts of light from the torches, the rest of the boys waited with anticipation. With an expression of sheer pleasure upon his face, Craig placed two packets of bangers on the floor, next to Philips offering. '3-2-1 Zero' bangers'. Craig didn't say a word. He let his bangers make the noise. It was the equivalent of placing a Butlins holiday brochure next to a Pontins holiday brochure, no fun-fair no contest.

"Are they loud?" James asked with eyes bright and flickering like the candles on the window sill.

"Are they loud!" Craig replied. "Are they loud? There's only one way to find out."

Craig reached for one of the packets of bangers, opened it up and removed a single banger. He stood up, took a step and pointed the fuse towards a candle on the window sill. The fuse burst into life and began to fizz. Craig let the banger fall to the floor, as he did so a mad scramble ensued, a blur, a flash of Parkas, fur lined hoods, scooped up their possessions, scrambled to their feet and bolted towards the front door. They were a long way short, a mass of excitement in the hallway when the banger exploded. The noise reverberated throughout the flat and came gambling down the hallway after them, bouncing off the walls of the confined space as it went. Immediately after the explosion of the banger came the sound of glass shattering as one of the boarded-up windows burst out of its frame. However, nobody looked back and nobody hung around to survey the damage. The boys just kept running through the front door, out of the flat, down the stairs, out of the block and back into the close. As they slowed down and stopped running, Craig turned and looked at James.

"Does that answer your question?" he asked.

As laughter filled the night air, not one of the boys seemed to notice that droplets of rain had started to tumble from the evening sky.

"What shall we do now?" Martin Matthews asked.

Shoulders were shrugged for a moment or two, until Paul Jones said. "Let's go and get 'Old Man Butcher' to come out."

Old Man Butcher lived in the first house as you had exited the crescent in the direction of Winston Avenue. His back garden and more importantly his back wall ran along the side of the crescent. The all-important wall was about eight feet high. Old Man Butcher didn't get his name because of any previous occupation. In fact none of the boys had any idea what his name actually was or for that matter what he had done for a living during his working years. He was known as 'Old Man Butcher' because of the folk tale that had been attached to him by the local community. The short version of the tale was that Old Man Butcher had, in an uncontrollable fit of rage, murdered his nagging wife in the middle of the night with a large meat cleaver, chopped up her body and disposed of the remains.

The reality was that his wife and son had died in a house fire some forty odd years ago. Since moving to Monkswood Crescent, he had kept himself to himself, becoming more reclusive, more bitter, more lonely and more and more disconnected with the world around him, thus unwittingly providing the fertile ground needed to allow such folk tales to grow.

When it came to the rules of the game, and the objective, it was about as simple as could be. Very much like Hide and Seek, the objective of the game was explained within its title. Quite simply, you had to get Old Man Butcher to come out of his house and chase you. The wall running along the side of the back garden was a key component, a key device within the fabric of the game. The idea was that the boys would climb up and sit upon it. You then needed to goad or encourage Old Man Butcher to come out of his house. When Old Man Butcher appeared at his back door and entered his back garden, usually with a long stick or something more threatening in his hand, the last person to hold their nerve and leap from the wall before being struck was the winner. Of course Old Man Butcher might approach the problem from a different angle and come out of his front door and along the side of his house. This presented the player of the game with two options, either you jumped from the wall and ran away or you jumped into Old Man Butcher's garden. Once in the garden you then had to wait it out until you spotted Old Man Butcher approaching his back door, then and only then could you safely clamber back over the wall. One slip at this stage though did not bear thinking about and this was an option only considered by the bravest of competitors. Once Old Man Butcher was back inside his house and all the players had regrouped, the whole process would start all over again. However, tonight was different, because tonight there was an added ingredient in the mix.

"Pass us one of your little sissy bangers Phil," Craig said as he held out his hand, a cigarette lighter firmly grasped in the other hand.

Philip opened up the box and passed over an Astra banger.

Craig lit the shiny, thin blue touch paper, waited for the banger to fizz and tossed it over the wall into the garden. A few seconds later it exploded with all the force and fury of a sandbag being dropped onto a muddy footpath. With bodies pressed up against the garden wall, the boys listened. All remained quiet and still. The only sound audible and increasing in volume was the sound of the rain tumbling out of the dark blue sky.

"Come here James," Paul said as he bent forward a little and cupped his hands together, to give James a leg up.

James put his foot in Paul's cupped hands and Paul lifted him up slowly, so that he could grab hold of the top of the wall and peer over.

"Anything?" Craig said.

James shook his head.

"Giz another banger," Craig said.

Philip facilitated the request after a brief amount of rummaging and passed over another banger. As with the previous one, Craig lit it, waited for it to start fizzing and then tossed it over the wall. However, this time around, and fractionally before it exploded, everybody except Martin had leapt up, grabbed hold of the top of the wall, pulled themselves up and were peering into the garden. The banger popped, and the soft grey smoke drifted away into the night air. With their noses almost resting upon the top of the wall, the boys waited and watched. But as before, nothing happened; all remained undisturbed inside the house. One by one the boys released their grip of the wall and landed back onto the ground below. Craig was the last to drop as he held out for a few more seconds before landing with a thud and an extremely disgruntled expression on his face.

"Right, that's it," he said. "This calls for the big guns." He shoved a hand firmly inside his coat pocket and pulled out the packet of 3-2-1 Zero bangers. He removed a banger and then returned the packet to the safety of his coat pocket. With the banger firmly gripped in one hand and the lighter poised in the other, he muttered, "this will get him out, the old bastard."

He rolled his thumb over the wheel of the lighter, releasing a flame into the night. He lit the fuse, waited for the silver and gold sparks to erupt, raised his arm and went to throw the banger over the wall. It was just as he went to propel his arm forward and flick his wrist to release the banger that he was struck full in the face by a ferocious jet of water coming from an upstairs window of the house.

The force of the water, coupled with the shock, made Craig topple backwards and tumble to the ground, thus causing the banger to spill out from his grasp, coming to rest just a few inches away. The jet of water stopped just as abruptly as it had started, giving everybody but Craig enough time to turn away from the banger before it exploded. Who could say for sure, the actual order of events? Did the flash come before the bang or did the bang come before the flash? The noise appeared to pass through the boys where they were standing, bounce off the wall and slap them across the arse on its way back. Once all had again fallen silent, the boys turned to look at Craig. He was lying on the floor, staring up at the sky and blinking continuously.

"What? What? I can't hear anything!" He shouted. Completely dazed, he could see several more faces than the ones that were now peering down at him, though as yet, none of them were in focus. "Help me up," he shouted.

The rest of the boys burst into life and with wide smiles across their faces, they helped Craig to his feet and lent him up against the wall.

"I think it came from the bathroom window," Paul said as he looked up at the house. "He's probably still in there watching and listening."

It took a further minute or two for Craig to begin feeling a little more like his usual self. There was still a faint ringing inside his left ear and a hazy bright white ball of light hovered within the peripheral arena of his sight. The anger etched upon his face was coming through loud and clear. Still blinking with a pace in line with his heartbeat and turning his head from side to side in the hope of causing the ringing sound to tumble from his ear, Craig eventually muttered, "I'm havin him for that."

"What you gonna do?" the boys asked.

With anger still etched and teeth gritted firmly, Craig replied. "I'll show you what I'm gonna do." He quickly removed another banger from his pocket and silently moved along the garden wall and then the side of the house. Except for Matthew, the rest of the boys followed. He had been assigned the task of lookout and was to keep an eye out for any signs of movement from inside the house.

Craig bent down and on his hands and knees crawled beneath the front room window until he reached the front doorstep. With Paul, Philip and James all watching from the side of the house, Craig stood upright and lit the banger. It began to fizz and crackle. Craig waited a little longer this time around, before pushing open the letterbox and tossing the banger into the house. As soon as he let go of the letterbox, he sprinted away like a greyhound that had just caught site of a rabbit. The rest of the group had already set sail and were several feet in front of him. However, they all heard the explosion as they ran back into the crescent and headed for the relative safety of the flats at the far end.

Once four of them were inside the building and attempting to capture their breath (Martin Matthews still had some way to go) Craig muttered "Everybody needs to go home and if anybody asks, you haven't been out all night, okay."

Everybody nodded and exited the flats just as Martin was about to enter.

"Where you going?" he asked.

"Home," Philip replied. "See you tomorrow."

Chapter 52

It wasn't one isolated incident, one specific moment, that resulted in Philip being late for school the following morning, but rather a culmination of a series of minor incidents. On their own and occurring across several different mornings, none of these incidents would have resulted in Philip failing to be ready in time. However, stacked one after the other on this particular Tuesday morning, the impact was unavoidable.

Firstly, upon arriving at the newsagents Philip found a gaggle of paperboys waiting inside. This was due to the delivery driver not being familiar with the route as he was covering for a colleague who was off sick that day.

Mr Underwood himself was also feeling a little under the weather that morning and as a result of both of these factors, Philip, along with the rest of the paperboys, set off on their rounds a good fifteen minutes later than usual.

A further delay was incurred when a dog which had managed to separate itself from its owner's leash, proceeded to chase Philip out of Watcombe Close, across the green, over the road and along Broad Park Road. The dog, a black and tan mongrel with a dopey expression on its face, barked, wagged its tail and lolloped alongside Philip on his bike. It did not take too long for him to realise that he had no choice but to stop riding, grab hold of the dog by its collar and walk himself, the dog and his bike back along Broad Park Road in search of its owner.

He eventually found the owner, a little old lady in her seventies, calling for and searching for her dog 'Bilko' on the open field that ran opposite Chelsey Road and Kingsley Terrace. By the time he had reunited dog and owner, completed his paper round and arrived home, he was running approximately twenty five minutes behind schedule.

Arriving home so late resulted in Philip attempting to prepare his breakfast and get his school bag ready at the same time. This in turn resulted in the milk in the saucepan boiling over and spilling out onto the cooker. Upon failing to reach the saucepan in time and seeing the milk spill over, he accepted his fate. He now knew that after clearing up the mess, heating some fresh milk, eating his breakfast and then finishing getting ready for school, both the 26 bus and the 8a bus would be long gone. Philip paused for a moment to make sure that James was ready and out of the door on time, before returning to the kitchen to clear up the spilt milk.

Now that he had a little time to spare until the next bus, he heated some more milk, ate his breakfast, tidied up the kitchen and finished getting himself and his bag ready, before leaving the house and setting off to catch the next 26 which departed the terminus at 8.40am. He left the house at exactly 8.30am. He headed across the green and out of the crescent, cutting the corner off 'Old Man Butcher's' front garden and round the outside edge of the big old sycamore tree that sat in the centre of the lawn. As he gave a sideways glance towards the house, he noticed that the front door was ever so slightly open. On closer inspection he could just make out a figure lying in the hallway. He could clearly see the soles of the shoes and the outline of a pair of legs as they disappeared into the darkness. Philip stopped and waited for any signs of movement. After feeling that he had waited long enough, he began to slowly walk towards the front door and the figure still lying motionless in the hallway.

"Hello." He called out. "Are you alright?"

He got closer still. He stepped up the step, pushed the door open a little further and looked down at the figure lying in the hallway. He could now see that it was indeed Old Man Butcher. His legs were flat on the floor, his feet sticking upwards and his torso was slightly turned to one side. His head was resting on his outstretched arm. His eyes were closed and lying next to him was a plastic bucket, full of soapy water. Philip then noticed that he was still holding a yellow sponge in his hand.

He stepped further into the hallway. He called again. "Are you alright?" But once more he failed to get a response. Philip laid his schoolbag on the floor, leant over Old Man Butcher and attempted to lift him up. He placed his hands under the old man's armpits and pulled him as best he could so that he was now leaning against the wall. The old man's head was sloped forward and his arms hung down as if they were made of paper.

Philip stepped past and went into the kitchen to fetch a glass of water. As he entered the kitchen, he searched for a clean glass amongst the dirty plates and bowls that were sitting on the work surfaces. He fought his way to a cupboard and was able to locate an unused glass. After giving it a quick rinse, he filled it and returned to the hallway.

He hadn't noticed before, but upon returning to the hallway, He spotted the big black mark on the carpet and the scorch marks caused by the banger. He could also see the dark grey streaks on the wall. He could now ascertain that these were the streaks Old Man Butcher had been attempting to remove as the surface of the wall was still wet.

It was then that he noticed the picture hanging from the wall, almost directly above the blackened, damaged paintwork. It wasn't a big picture; including the frame it was about the size of an A4 piece of paper. The frame was a thin bevelled strip of dark stained wood. There was a crack in the glass running from the top left hand corner to the bottom right corner.

Philip stood staring at and absorbing every aspect of the image. In the centre and dominating the picture was a tall figure of a young man. He was wearing a black and white striped jersey with a white collar. Just by looking at the picture, the viewer could feel the weight of the jersey. The material was thicker than the marzipan on the outside of a Battenberg cake. He was also wearing a pair of black shorts, black and white socks and a pair of football boots that looked like two small submarines attached to his feet. The football in the picture looked rain sodden, along with the heavy bog of a pitch that the figure was playing on. Small dots were crammed into the blurred stand in the background. The footballer sported jet black hair and his eyes were focused upon the ball at his feet. Beneath the image it read 'November 5th 1927, Notts County 2 Leeds United 2'.

"What you doing in my house you little bastard?"

The booming sound of Old Man Butcher's voice filled the hallway, rushed past Philip and out of the open door. Philip felt the old man grab him by the leg. Philip looked down and instantly saw the anger etched across the old man's face. Philip stepped backwards and freed his leg from the old man's grip, dropping the glass of water as he did so.

"Get out of my house! I'll kill ya!" the old man shouted as he attempted to raise himself off the floor.

"I was just tryin to…" Philip attempted to mutter.

"Get out! Get out!"

Philip grabbed his school bag off the hallway floor and quickly backed out through the front door. The old man got to his feet, stepped forward and slammed the door shut. Philip stood for a moment and looked at the house, before realising that he had precisely two minutes to reach the bus stop or he would be later still.

For the rest of the day, he couldn't get the photograph out of his head. Even when he was lying to Mr Spencer about why he was so late for school, he could not shake the image from his mind. During his Religious Education lesson, whilst looking at an illustration of the 'Sermon on the Mount' in his text book, Jesus was wearing a Notts County strip and the crowd were all holding a black and white striped scarf above their heads. On the bus journey home and every time he looked out of the window, he could see a black and white figure from a bygone age, waiting for a bus, getting on a bus, getting off a bus, walking along the street, entering a shop, exiting a shop. Finally and with some relief, he was able to get off the bus and head for home.

As both Philip and James turned the corner into the crescent, they immediately spotted the police car parked outside their house. They quickly sprinted along the pavement, down the side of the house, into the garden and entered the house through the back door. The relief of seeing their mother sitting on the sofa next to a policeman was indescribable. However, curiosity followed closely behind in double quick time. Francis was standing in front of the fireplace, talking to a second policeman.

No sooner had Philip closed the door behind him, than his dad lurched forward and grabbed him firmly by the lapel of his blazer and proceeded to lift him almost fully off the ground.

"What the hell are you doing, breaking into old people's houses?" Francis yelled.

Philip could see that the veins in his dad's neck were swollen, his face was bright red and beads of spit rested upon his lower lip and his chin.

"What? I haven't!" Philip replied.

"Don't lie to me boy, you were caught, the old man caught you, the old boy on the corner, caught you in his house."

"But I didn't break in."

"Oh, got a key have ya?" Francis replied.

"No, the door was open."

"Oh, I see. So you just thought you would pop in and help yourself, did you. I haven't raised you to go around stealing from old people."

One of the policemen stepped forward and helped Francis to release his grip of Philip's blazer. "Now let's all calm down for a minute," he said before turning to look directly at Philip. "So you admit you were in his house." he added.

"Well yes," Philip replied, "but I didn't go in to steal anything."

"So what did you go in for, to borrow a cup of sugar?" Francis blurted.

Philip's mother interrupted. "Let the boy speak Francis."

"Yes, let him speak," the policeman added. "Now go on lad, tell us what happened."

"I just went to see if he was alright," Philip began. "He was lying on the floor."

"I see," the policeman said. "How did you know he was lying on the floor?"

"The front door was open. I could see him; well partly. I was late for school. When I went past, the front door was open. I could see him lying on the floor. So I went over. He wasn't moving. I went inside and propped him up against the wall, then I went to get him a glass of water from the kitchen. When I got back into the hallway, he came to and started shouting at me to get out. I tried to explain but he just kept shouting at me to get out, so I did. Then he slammed the door shut and I went to school."

"So let me get this straight," Francis said to the policeman standing next to him. "There are no signs of forced entry, nothing has been stolen but you are in my house and accusing my son of burglary," he added with a tone in his voice that was as rigid as a vicar's collar.

"He was found to be in the house Mr Knott, uninvited. That amounts to trespassing."

"He wasn't trespassing, he was trying to help the stupid old twat, now get out of my house."

"What we shall do Mr Knott, is go and speak with the old boy and see if we can clarify if your son may be telling the truth. In the meantime, he stays here."

"But I've got my paper round to do," Philip said.

"He's got his paper round to do," Francis repeated.

"He stays here," The officer said again.

"What do you think he is going to do, cross the border into Mexico?"

"HE STAYS HERE!" The officer reiterated with a larger degree of force before he and his colleague left the house.

A full twenty minutes passed. Philip had changed out of his school uniform and was now sitting on the sofa next to James, watching an episode of 'Animal Magic'. His mum was in the kitchen preparing dinner. The chip pan was on, the potatoes had been peeled and cut. Francis was sitting at the dining table. Every so often he leant back in his chair and peered out of the living room window. Upon spotting the two police officers making their way back across the green and towards the house, he got up and went to greet them at the front door.

"Well?" he said as the officers walked towards him.

"Can we come in?" one of the officers asked.

Francis didn't reply. He didn't step aside either.

"Then can we please speak to the boy?"

Francis called for Philip to come to the door. The three men stood in the silence until Philip arrived and stood next to his father.

"We're not going to be taking the matter further at this moment in time," the officer said.

"Why is that?" Francis asked. "Discovered that my son is telling the truth?"

"It appears that there could be some element of truth in the boy's story. It does appear that he may have had a glass of water in his hand and the old gentleman does recollect losing his bearings a little whilst cleaning up the damage in his hallway."

"Fine," Francis said as he stepped back and went to close the front door.

"Just a moment," the officer said. "One last question for the lad."

"Now what?" Francis said.

"Do you know anything about a firework being pushed through the old boy's letterbox last night?"

"Of course he doesn't."

"I'm asking the lad, not you."

Philip looked at the officer, then at his dad and then at the officer again. "I was home all night, last night," he finally said.

"I didn't ask you what you were doing last night, I asked you if you knew anything about fireworks being shoved through letter boxes?"

"No." Philip replied.

"You see, that was the damage the old boy was clearing up and I was just wondering if you went in out of guilt or just wanted to have a look at your handy work."

"The lad has answered your questions. He was at home all night last night and he doesn't know anything."

"Okay, we'll leave it there for now," the officer said before adding, as he turned away, "You can get off and do your paper round now son."

Chapter 53

It had been quite a while since a Saturday morning had been greeted with such anticipation. Although important in its own way, this anticipation had nothing to do with Leeds United's thirteen game unbeaten start to the season and the home fixture against West Ham United, later that day.

This particular bout of anticipation had been born out of claims made by Craig Swinburn on the bus home from school the day before. 'This is it', Craig had claimed. This was going to be the night, the night that he would finally go all the way with Claire Chase. It had been planned with all the precision of a military campaign.

As they all knew, the ban on Claire's drunken lush of a mother, as Craig had described her, had now been lifted. So by seven thirty, she would already be safely seated in the 'Live and Let Live', swaying from side to side with a large gin and tonic in her hand.

The other long standing stumbling block, Claire's younger brother, would also be out of the house by 7pm. He was attending a Cubs activity badge challenge at the Deedmore Road school. It was an opportunity for all the cubs attending to attempt to earn three activity badges in one evening. Claire's younger brother had his heart set on gaining his 'book reader' activity badge, his 'Animal Care' activity badge and his 'Home Safety' activity badge. Craig Swinburn was hoping for an altogether different activity badge.

The Cubs evening started at 7pm and did not conclude until 9.30pm. As he was being escorted to the event by a parent of a fellow Cubs pal, the pathway was clear; the house would be empty for the best part of three hours.

Craig had indeed planned ahead and had managed to swipe three bottles of Snowball from the drinks cabinet at home over the course of a few weeks. They had been carefully hidden away for a moment, an opportunity such as this. He had also borrowed Barry White's debut album from the library in Bell Green, the aptly titled 'I've Got So Much to Give'. How could he possibly fail, he had asked his captive audience on the number 26 bus. What girl could resist three bottles of snowball and a Barry White L.P.? Even the rest of the boys on the bus that Friday afternoon had to admit that all the signs were favourable ones.

Philip was up and dressed within a couple of minutes of the alarm ringing out. By the time he was ready to leave the room, James had already fallen back to sleep. Thankfully breakfast was a solitary, brief affair and Philip had eaten, gathered up his paper bag and collected his bike before anybody else had even got out of bed. To Philip's surprise, Paul McBride was waiting outside the shop when he arrived.

"Here you go," Paul said as he passed over the updated shoplifting list. "Some good ones on there," he added as he also handed over some cash.

Philip took hold of both the list and the money and shoved them into his coat pocket.

"You not gonna have a look?" Paul asked.

"I will when I get home," Philip replied.

"I've raised the bar on the barometer," Paul said without spotting in any way, shape or form the irony in his comment. "I'm willing to go seventy / thirty if you can get one. I just want it off my list."

Philip smiled.

"It's not funny Phil man, it's a friend of me Nan's. I went and told me Nan I could get one and now she keeps going on about it," Paul said as he turned away and entered the shop. Philip followed closely behind.

Although the boys were not meeting up until 10.00am, Philip was operating on the flawed logic of 'the faster I complete my paper round, the faster ten o'clock will arrive'. As he stood in the shop, ten o' clock was two and a half hours away and by the time he finished his paper round it would still be approximately one hour and forty minutes away. No matter the game plan, for every minute it took him to complete a task, he would only find himself one minute closer to ten o'clock.

Philip completed his paper round, went home, got James out of bed, made him some breakfast, washed up, and gathered up his and James's swimming kits along with a carrier bag to put them in. He made two mugs of tea, one for his dad who was now sitting in the kitchen smoking a cigarette, and one for his mother, who was still in bed. He then filled in his team fixture sheet as best he could in his comic whilst watching an episode of 'Barnaby', followed by an episode of the 'Hair Bear Bunch', entitled Love Bug Bungle.

It was now 9.35am, close enough. By 9.45 both Philip and James were sitting on the wall outside the 'Live and Let Live' pub, waiting for the others to arrive. Martin Matthews and Paul Jones turned up a few minutes later but as the time approached ten o'clock, there was still no sign of Craig.

"Where is he?" Paul asked. "Has anybody seen him?"

The boys all shook their heads as one, as if they were all watching an extremely fast tennis rally. Then just after 10am and in unison, the bus appeared in the distance heading towards the roundabout, and Craig exited Dering Close onto Deedmore Road, heading for the roundabout from the opposite direction.

The boys all jumped down from the pub wall and headed off the meet Craig. As they got closer, they could see that his demeanour was that of a dejected, solemn figure. He looked like a small boy who had just discovered Santa Claus face down in the local river and his sleigh lying ransacked and barren on the riverbank.

"How did you get on?" Paul asked as the boys reached Craig.

"Piss off," Craig replied. "I don't want to talk about it." The disappointment etched upon his face was as clear as the sky on a freezing cold winter's night.

It wasn't until he was sitting at the back of the bus with an Embassy Regal cigarette between his lips before a second question presented itself. Again Paul had opted to be the question master.

"So did you get caught in the act?"

Craig shook his head whilst attempting to blow smoke rings as a way of cheering himself up. "No," he muttered.

Desperate for more information and with an increasingly noticeable amount of frustration in his voice, Paul asked, "Then what happened?"

"Nothing, nothing happened." Craig replied.

Still taking the lead on interrogation duty, Paul said, "What do you mean, nothing happened?"

"I mean, nothing happened. I was all set, ready to go, stripped off, except for my socks. I was all set, ready to go and then…" Craig paused. "If any of you breathe a word about this, I mean it, just one word," he added.

As the bus pulled away from the stop and set off on its journey into town, Craig took an extra-long drag of his cigarette, before passing what was left of it to Paul. He exhaled, the grey wispy strands of smoke colliding with the bus window before drifting upwards. Craig turned to face the boys, who were all staring intently at him.

"It was horrible," he began. "I was there, I was set, you know what I'm saying, I was ready to go." He paused again, clearly struggling to re-live the events of the previous evening. "You know those long thin balloons," he continued. "Well you know what they go like when you have blown them up and deflated them a few times. Well it was like that. I don't know how or why but it just deflated. I couldn't stop it."

"What deflated?" James asked.

Everybody turned to look at James. They waited for the penny to drop. They waited a bit longer and then a bit longer still. Realising that James didn't have the correct change, Philip leant across and whispered in his ear.

"Oh, right," James said whilst still looking slightly unsure.

"I couldn't stop it," Craig said. "The more I tried to stop it, the worse it got. I tried to think about things that would help but I started thinking things like what is the point of algebra and trigonometry or sideburns".

"Sideburns!" Philip said.

"I know. I started picturing Malcolm McDonald, Derek Dougan and Neil Martin. How the hell was that going to help? Even Barry White couldn't save me. All I could think was that he needed to take something for his sore throat."

The boys were all staring at Craig with their mouths open and their jaws firmly located in the dropped region.

"It gets worse," he continued. "Then Claire looked down at it and burst into tears."

A collective snigger was released from the group.

"It's not funny. She jumped off the bed crying. Months, months, months it took me to get her undressed and she was dressed again in a flash. Thought it was her fault, thought I thought she was unattractive, disgusting, ugly even. Then she caught sight of it again when I went to put my pants back on. By now it looked even worse, like a runner bean stuck onto a conker. I tried to put my arm around her and she just lost it. Balling her eyes out."

"What did you do?" Paul asked.

"I left," Craig replied. "I finished getting dressed and left."

"You left?"

"Yes, I left. What else could I do."

There was a moment's silence, before Paul asked. "So, you saw her naked then?"

"Yes," Craig said. "She was awesome, she looked beautiful. Everything was smooth and soft and…" Craig's thoughts drifted back to the silver lining of the night before as he gazed out of the bus window. "I've got to fix it, I've got to get her something, I've got to get her a gift."

It was at this point that the rest of the boys realised that he didn't have his swimming stuff with him and he was wearing a long, oversized coat.

"You not coming swimming then?"

Craig didn't reply, partly because he had other things on his mind and partly because he was distracted by the sound of Martin opening a packet of cheese and onion crisps.

Other than the sound of Martin munching on his crisps, the rest of the journey passed by in relative silence. No sooner had the bus arrived at the top of Hales Street, than Craig was off and away into the centre of town. The rest of the boys had already alighted outside Sainsbury's and were now heading for the swimming baths.

They spent the day swimming, splashing about, messing about, looking at girls without actually speaking to them, messing about some more and finally doing their best to get ejected from the pool. Martin was this week's winner with a perfectly timed and perfectly executed belly flop into the middle of a group of young girls. The lifeguard's whistle blew but the sound was almost lost amongst the sound of Martin's big fleshy belly slapping against the surface of the water and the shrieks of the young girls in question.

Once all the boys had been ejected from the pool and had exited the building, it was off to Fishy Moore's for a cone of chips before taking the bus back home.

On the journey home, nobody said a word about it, but everybody was thinking about it. However, nobody was thinking about what happened to Craig; they were all thinking what Claire looked like without any clothes on. Upon arriving home, Philip put his mental picture of Claire in a safe place and turned his attention to the football scores. The vidiprinter was about to start rolling any minute. His mother was in the kitchen, preparing dinner, whilst his dad was in bed, sleeping off a lunchtime session in the Bell Inn.

The Hartlepool score was one of the first to come through. A one-nil defeat away at Northampton Town left them rooted to the foot of division four. Philip sat and waited impatiently for the Leeds United score. Eventually it appeared on the screen, a comfortable four-one home victory, a result that extended their unbeaten start to fourteen games. Eleven wins and three draws left them still sitting at the top of the table.

Content with the result, Philip decided to stay at home a little longer than usual, before setting off for his paper round, in the hope of avoiding bumping into Paul McBride. His plan was successful, even if Mr Underwood had a moan about him being late. Philip got home just as his mother was serving up stew and dumplings, served with crusty bread rolls. This was followed by a mini Swiss roll and a glass of lemonade.

Francis left for the pub soon after dinner but his mother stayed downstairs and after the washing up had been done, sat at the dining table with Philip and James and played several games of Rummy. She even allowed herself the small luxury of a glass of Pernod and the occasional smile whilst they played, calling it a night and going to bed just before 'Match of the Day' started.

Philip had his fingers crossed that highlights of the Leeds game would be on. As luck would have it, it was the second game after Derby County's surprise two-one home defeat to Queens Park Rangers.

Chapter 54

Philip woke up a full thirty minutes before his alarm clock was set to go off. Without hesitation or even considering for a moment the prospect of falling back to sleep, he was up, dressed, breakfast eaten, paper bag collected, swimming kit collected, house departed and bike collected in record time. He arrived at the newsagents as Mr Underwood was still carrying bundles of newspapers inside.

"You're early today lad," Mr Underwood exclaimed whilst a bundle of papers dangled from each hand.

"I've got a swimming competition. Don't want to be late."

"Well in that case, we had better get you loaded up. Don't want to stand in the way of the next Johnny Weissmuller do we?"

"Who?" Philip replied.

"Johnny Weissmuller."

"I thought he was Tarzan," Philip said.

"He was." Mr Underwood replied as he cut the string off a bundle of newspapers. "But before that he was an Olympic swimmer. He was also the first man to swim under a minute for the hundred metres freestyle. A wet Roger Bannister, you might say. I suppose you don't know who he is either."

A slightly annoyed Philip quickly replied, "Yes, I know who he is. I also know who Johnny Weissmuller was, I just didn't know he used to be a swimmer."

A few minutes later Philip's large and heavy bundle of Sunday papers was ready to go. Philip opened his paper bag and took a deep breath in anticipation of the colossal amount of weight that was about to be inserted. It was at this point as he glanced inside, that he suddenly realised he had neglected to bring his padlock and chain with him.

"Shit," he muttered as Mr Underwood filled his bag with the obscene mass of newspapers.

"Problem?"

"No, it's nothing. I just need to go back home before I can go to the swimming baths, I've forgotten something." Philip replied as the weight of the paper bag pulled him towards the ground.

With another deep breath, some gusto and a splash of vigour, Philip lifted the bag and placed the strap on his shoulder. He immediately felt it pressing on his clothes and cutting into his flesh. With his customary Sunday morning lean, he turned to exit the shop.

"Here you go," Mr Underwood said as he held out a Cadbury's Oranges and Lemons chocolate bar. "Some energy for your competition," he added.

Philip thanked Mr Underwood, took the bar of chocolate and set off on his round. By the time he reached Clennon Rise, he was finally in a more upright position. As soon as he entered the block that housed his sister's flat, he heard Grace call out.

"Philip! Philip!" Grace shouted into the space in front of her as she peered over the balcony and down the stairwell. "Quick, come here."

"I can't Grace, I haven't got time."

"What do you mean, you haven't got time."

Philip replied as he made his way up the first flight of stairs. "I know you understood that sentence Grace and I know that you understand the concept of time and how it works. I do not have any time to spare right now." He looked up at Grace, who was still peering over the balcony, before folding up and squeezing a News of the World through a letterbox on the first floor.

"Ha ha Philip, this is important."

"So is the reason why I haven't got time," Philip replied with obvious annoyance and through gritted teeth. "I'll call back later."

"Now Philip, I need to speak to you now."

The constant use of the word Philip told Philip that whatever Grace wanted was clearly important to her. He sighed and begrudgingly made his way up the second flight of stairs. "Two minutes Grace. I mean it; two minutes."

"What's your rush?" Grace asked as Philip approached.

"I've got a swimming meet and I can't be late."

"Oh, silly swimming, you can go later."

"Are you not listening, I'm not going swimming, I have a swimming competition, I am competing."

"This is far more important," Grace said as she bundled Philip into the flat.

"Where's Karen?" Philip asked.

"She's not here, she spent the night at her mum and dad's, I think. But look." Grace replied as she pointed into the living room.

"At what?" Philip asked.

"What do you mean, at what? Look, new T.V, new sofa, new pram." Grace pointed at the shiny new pram that was positioned in front of the window on the other side of the room. "And that's not all, the kitchen, new toaster, new kettle and a new cot in her bedroom."

"So?" Philip said.

"So, I think you may be right, how else is she going to get the money to pay for all this stuff?"

"Look Grace, I really have to go. Can we talk about this later?"

"No wait, that's not the worse bit," Grace said as she grabbed Philip by the shoulder. "Remember a while back, when I saw dad coming towards me on Roseland's Avenue and he ignored me and turned and walked the other way?"

"No."

"Yes you do, and Martin Matthews dad's car parked outside that day. "I think that dad…" Grace paused and looked directly at Philip.

"What you think dad…"

"Yes," Grace interrupted.

"Have you said anything to Karen?"

"Oh yes, of course I have. I said hello Karen, would you like a cup of tea. Oh and by the way, are you a prostitute and does my dad pay you for sex? Two sugars, isn't it?"

Not wanting to hear any more, Philip turned to walk towards the front door. "Look Grace, I really have to go. If I'm late, I'm off the team. I'm sure that you have this all wrong. I'm sure there's a reasonable explanation. Maybe she used your rent money."

Grace glared at her brother, a cold disapproving stare that only resulted in Philip wanting to leave even quicker.

"I'll call back later," he said as he stepped into the hallway.

"We can't talk here," Grace replied.

"We're having the bonfire tomorrow night and fireworks. I'll see you then," Philip replied before darting back down the stairs, grabbing his bike and exiting the building. He was halfway down the stairs when he heard the door to the flat slam shut and the sound echo through the interior of the building.

He set off to complete the rest of his round with Grace's revelation firmly in the forefront of his mind. All attempts to shift it and relocate it to a less obtrusive area were met with the stubbornness of a verruca on a small child's foot. By the time he'd shoved the final paper through the last letterbox, he'd lost count of how many times Grace's words had played over and dominated his thoughts. However, as he turned into Monkswood Crescent from Winston Avenue, the puzzle of how he could get in and out of the house to retrieve his lock and chain undetected put itself forward with the offer of taking centre stage in his brain for a short while. As he approached the close, he caught sight of Old Man Butcher standing in his living room window. The curtains were wide open and he was looking up and down the street. As soon as Old Man Butcher caught sight of Philip, he frantically started waving at him and beckoning him to come over to the house.

Philip was caught in two minds and at first he was tempted to carry on riding past, but curiosity was his downfall, getting the better of him as if he was the baddy on 'World of Sport' Wrestling and Kendo Nagasaki had him in a half-nelson. He leant his bike against the sycamore tree in the front garden and approached the front door, arriving at his destination just as the door swung open.

"In you come lad, in you come."

"I'd rather not," Philip replied.

"Why on earth not?"

"Er, two reasons really. Firstly, as soon as I leave again, you'll probably phone the police and tell them I've broke in and tried to steal your false teeth or something and secondly, I haven't got the time."

"Oh don't make a fuss, that was just a misunderstanding lad and what do you mean, you haven't got the time?"

Philip rolled his eyes and shook his head. "Do you know my sister?" He asked.

"No, I don't. Should I?" Old Man Butcher replied.

"No, I suppose not," Philip said before adding, "It doesn't matter."

"Look lad, this is important, it won't take long."

Curiosity still had him gripped tight and pinned to the canvas. The referee was about to start counting at any moment. Just as the ref's hand was about to collide with the floor of the ring for the third and final time, he managed to break free and leave Kendo frustrated.

"Honest, I really haven't got the time right now but I'll call back later today, if I get the chance," Philip said as he turned away and deliberately avoided making any further eye contact with the old man. As he climbed onto his bike, to make what was left of his journey home, he heard the front door close behind him.

He left his bike outside the house, made his way quickly down the side and into the shed in the back garden. He retrieved his padlock and chain before exiting the shed as quickly as he had entered it. On his way back along the side of the house, he caught sight of his father sitting in the kitchen, smoking a cigarette. Thankfully for Philip, he passed the window undetected. Once back on his bike, he set off for the swimming baths. However, he now had more than one thought vying for his attention. His sister's revelation, what Old Man Butcher wanted and the swim meet itself all tossed and turned and sloshed about in his mind like broken branches on a fast moving river.

Chapter 55

"You're late!"

Philip looked down at his watch, then up at Mr Kennedy as he mounted the steps to the entrance of the swimming baths.

"No need to go looking at your watch lad. If I tell you you're late, you're late."

"But…" Philip attempted to respond after confirming for himself that he was on time.

"Don't question, don't interrupt and don't answer back. Here." Mr Kennedy removed a sheet of paper from the clipboard he was holding and passed it to Philip. "You're down for the fifty metre freestyle, hundred metre butterfly and the medley relay, butterfly again third leg."

Philip nodded as he looked at the piece of paper.

Mr Kennedy looked at the paper bag draped over Philip's shoulder. "I guess your swimming kit is in there."

Philip nodded again whilst still looking at the piece of paper.

"You'll need a cap. I'll bring one down to the changing room. We are in the section at the far end, closest to the pool. Now pay attention. It is your responsibility to be poolside in time for your races, ten minutes before each race. Your first race is ten past ten, the times are on the sheet." He paused for a few seconds until Philip was looking directly at him. "Don't be late."

"You're late!" Mr Kennedy bellowed as he looked past Philip and at another boy who was just coming up the steps. "And don't bother looking at your watch either."

As he headed for the changing rooms Philip could hear the conversation going on behind him slowly fade away. Once inside, as instructed, he made his way to the section at the far end and past the competitors from the other swimming clubs. Most of his teammates (for want of a better word) were already there and at different stages of the changing process. Flared trousers, tank tops and gaudy patterned jumpers were visible in every direction one cared to look. It was just the boys in the communal area whilst the cubicles were occupied by the female members of the team. Philip sat down and looked at his watch. It was almost an hour until his first race. He leant back against the changing room wall before delving into his paper bag and retrieving his copy of 'Shoot'. He noticed a few fleeting glances from some of his teammates, though no attempt at verbal contact was made. The literal and figurative distance was also maintained when the back slapping and motivational cheering erupted just before the call for the competitors in the opening race.

Prior to the rousing, team building chorus, Mr Kennedy arrived and tossed a swimming cap in Philip's direction.

"Getting changed?" he asked as the swimming cap sailed through the air.

"Yes, in a minute," Philip replied.

By the time Philip plucked the cap out of the air, Mr Kennedy was already on his way poolside.

The meet commenced. Philip could hear the faint sound of cheering and the muffled sounds of encouragement coming from the pool. All of a sudden, and appearing with such haste they could have been delivered by Billy Whizz, the nerves arrived. They ambushed him, reminiscent of Indians in a scene from a John Ford western. They raced around and danced about inside him like giggling Morris dancers at a summer fair. All attempts to harness them proved futile. Deep breaths ran out of puff and a time out, timed out.

Once changed into his trunks, he sat back down and stared directly at the floor. Leaning forward, he attempted to put his swimming cap on, but it seemed to have shrunk to the size of a Kippah and his fingers had grown to the size of small French baguettes. The third failed attempt to fit the cap on his head saw it spring off his head, fly into the air and come to rest on the changing room floor a few feet away. He didn't move. He just sat and stared at the cap, now resting upon the floor. Suddenly, in his line of vision, he noticed two bare feet appear. A younger female teammate bent down and picked up the cap.

"Talc," she said as she walked towards Philip.

The bare feet were now directly in front of him. Philip looked up. "What," he replied.

"It's easier to put on if you put some talc in it first," the girl said before passing him the cap. "Here, hold it open," she added.

Philip inserted his now sweaty fingers into the cap and stretched it open. The girl pointed a bottle of talcum powder into the cap and gently shook it a couple of times before removing it again and placing it on the bench next to Philip. She then carefully rubbed the talc around the inside of the cap.

"Now try it," she said.

Philip attempted to put the cap on his head. This time around, he had much more success. Despite clipping an eyebrow on the way past, the cap was now securely positioned upon his head. The young girl smiled at Philip and then turned and walked away.

"Thanks," Philip muttered as she put the talc back in her bag and left the changing room.

With only fifteen minutes until his first race, Philip stood up and made another attempt to shake the nerves out of his body with a few exercises and stretches. Once he had accepted that he was as warmed up as he was going to get, he picked up his goggles and towel before making his way out of the changing rooms towards the pool. With each step, the noise coming from the pool increased. As he walked into the bright light of the pool area itself, he was immediately met by an official with a clipboard firmly grasped in his hand.

"Event?" the official said.

Instantly flustered, Philip struggled to find an answer before eventually replying "Butterfly, I think."

The official looked down at his clipboard, tapped it a couple of times and scrolled down with his pencil, before stopping at the appropriate point. "Take a seat on one of the benches over there." As he spoke he pointed with his pencil, towards the line of benches behind the starting blocks. "You're the race after next."

With head still spinning, palms still sweating and stomach still churning, Philip followed the official's instructions and walked over to the row of benches. He sat down and placed his towel across his lap before putting his goggles on his head. He looked at the tiled floor and gently tapped his feet on the cold surface. As the competitors for the next race were called, he glanced upwards and noticed the young girl who had kindly helped him with his hat. The girl smiled at Philip as she approached her starting block.

"Good luck," Philip mouthed before smiling back. He watched as she climbed on to her starting block and prepared to race. As the claxon sounded and the swimmers dived forward, Philip looked up towards the seating area and the cheering crowd. No sooner had his eye line reached the required level, than he instantly spotted his dad sitting amongst the crowd. Even his nerves took stock of the situation and paused for a moment in a state of shock, but only for a moment. It was like lighting a Catherine Wheel, then stepping back, stepping into that quiet space just before the firework started to ferociously spin and spin and spin, golden sparks filling the dark nights sky.

Nerves had now seized total control of both his body and his thoughts. He was back in a John Ford film and the Indians had circled the wagons. There was no way out, no visible means of escape. His eyes were locked onto his dad, transfixed. Everything else in his area of vision seemed to dissolve as if it was part of a watercolour on canvas. His dad had yet to look in his direction. Philip had no idea what he was going to do when his dad did look at him. Would he smile? Wave? Run?

Philip hadn't noticed the previous race finish and the swimmers exit the pool. He didn't notice the young girl smile at him as she climbed out of the water and collect her towel. He also failed to notice the rest of his competitors approach their starting blocks after being called by the starter. Again undetected, an official approached Philip, only becoming visible once he was directly in the flight path of Philip and his father's location in the seating area.

"I think this is your race lad," the official said before adding. "Butterfly."

Philip stood up rather ponderously and glanced over at the other competitors, standing in front of their blocks, before noticing the empty space that had been allocated to him. He walked over with all the finesse and grace of Robby the Robot from 'The Forbidden Planet'.

With one final glance towards his father, he stepped onto his starting block and lowered his goggles. He curled his toes over the edge of the starting block, bent forward and gripped the block with his hands. He waited, he listened. The starter called out, the claxon sounded. With adrenalin racing through him and nerves jangling like a charm bracelet on a disco dancer, he propelled himself forward and hit the water with a thud.

"What the hell happened out there son?" Mr Kennedy asked as he stood in front of Philip with his arms tightly folded and an expression upon his face that suggested he had just grabbed hold of a rotten tangerine at the bottom of the fruit bowl. "That was awful," Mr Kennedy continued. "Fifth place, 1.37.13. My granny can swim faster than that and she's dead. You've swum 1.26 in training, a full eight seconds inside the qualifying time for your age group and then you go and swim like that. No coordination, no synchronisation, have you stopped watching telly or something?"

Philip, with eyes still fixed on the floor in front of him, replied. "I don't know what happened. It felt like I was trying to swim with somebody else's body."

"Well whoever's body it is that you've brought with you today, I'm taking it out of the freestyle swim. Collins will have to do it. He'll swim a few seconds slower than what you can swim but at least I know he'll do it."

This time Philip looked up before he replied. "No, no, don't. I'll be fine," he muttered.

"I can't take the chance," Mr Kennedy replied. "I'll leave you in the medley though. You can still swim the butterfly leg and see if you can do any better."

Philip remained in the changing room for the rest of the meet, until it was time for the medley relay. As he reached the top of the stairs and was about to return to the pool area, he was met by his three relay teammates.

"You'd better not mess this up."

Philip looked up at the boy who had just spoken to him. It was the boy who had taken his place in the freestyle race. Philip ignored the comment and made his way to the correct end of the pool, accompanied by the boy who would start the race swimming the backstroke leg. Philip was to swim the third leg, fifty metres, one length of the pool.

His teammate's comments seemed to resonate, to galvanise, to focus his mind on the job in hand. To avoid the risk of damage to his current mind-set, he in turn avoided looking up at the stands and simply prepared for his swim and the third leg of the race. The claxon sounded, the swimmers set off, the crowd cheered. Philip didn't hear a thing. He watched the backstroke swimmers get smaller and smaller as they worked their way down the pool, then he calmly walked over and stood in front of his starting block.

As the breaststroke swimmers at the other end of the pool set off on their leg of the race, Philip stepped onto his starting block. He stared intently down the pool as the swimmers came ever closer towards him. With approximately fifteen metres left for them to swim, Philip edged himself fractionally forward. He curled his toes over the edge of the block and gripped it tightly with his hands. He looked up. His teammate had a few metres left to swim. The swimmer representing the Warwickshire swimming club had already set off, along with the swimmers from a few other teams. By the time his teammate touched the wall and he was able to set off, he was about five metres behind the leader and in fifth place.

Philip pushed himself forward off the starting block and dived into the water. The moment he was fully submerged, he felt a wave of excitement rush through him. The water encased him, caressed him and seemed to fit him once more, like the well-tailored suit he was used to. The moment that the top of his head emerged from beneath the waterline, his arms quickly followed. They rotated in almost perfect unison, as if they were being rotated by a cog. His body shape on the surface of the water was crisp and clean. There was hardly a ripple or a splash as he propelled himself down the pool. By the thirty metre mark, he was already drawing alongside the leader, and with two further majestic strokes he was in front. By the time he handed over to the last leg swimmer, City of Coventry Swimming Club were two full metres to the good. Unfortunately the last leg swimmer could not maintain the lead he had been given and they eventually finished a close third behind Warwickshire and Wolverhampton.

By the time the race ended, Philip had already climbed out of the pool and was walking back around to collect his towel. As he approached the benches behind the starting blocks, he passed his three fellow teammates. Nobody uttered a word, not even Philip. He collected his towel and headed silently back to the changing rooms. As he climbed down the stairs and entered his team's designated area of the changing room, Mr Kennedy was already there to meet him. As Philip approached, he clapped his hands and rubbed them together.

"What a swim! What a swim!" He bellowed with a grin across his face that was wider than a Cheshire cat on his birthday. He was holding a stopwatch in his hand and he waved it in Philip's direction as he continued, "Not got the official time yet, but the time I clocked is a club record, I'm sure of it. There are a couple of races left and then I want everybody poolside for a swim down."

"I've got to go," Philip said.

"Why, what's up?" Mr Kennedy replied.

"My dad will be waiting."

"Oh, I see."

"No, I'm afraid you don't." Philip muttered.

"Sorry son, what did you say?"

"It doesn't matter; it wasn't anything important."

"Okay. In light of that fantastic swim, I'll excuse you from the swim down, just this once though. In future you'll dad will have to wait. See you at training on Wednesday."

Mr Kennedy headed back to the pool to watch the remaining relay races. Philip got dried and dressed before slinging his paper bag over his shoulder and heading for the exit. As he walked through the first set of glass doors at the front of the building, he could see his dad standing at the bottom of the steps, smoking a cigarette. Philip took a deep breath, pushed open the second set of doors, and stepped outside into the chilly November air.

As Francis saw Philip approaching, he stubbed his cigarette out on the floor and raised his eyebrows at the same time. "What the hell happened in that first race son?" he asked.

During the walk from the changing room to the front of the building, Philip had considered a whole range of possible questions his father was going to ask him once he was outside. However, not for an instant had he considered this particular question to be the first one Francis would ask. It was a question that caught him completely off guard.

"Nerves," Philip eventually muttered before adding, "especially when I saw you sitting in the crowd."

"Oh, I see. It was my fault that you swam like a fat kid in a pool full of treacle," Francis replied as he smiled at Philip.

"You're not angry?" Philip asked with a bemused expression on his face.

"Well it wasn't a great swim but it's nothing to get angry about, is it?"

"I don't mean the swim. I mean about me joining the club when you said I couldn't and that we couldn't afford it."

"Oh that!" Francis replied. "No, I'm not overjoyed about it and I certainly wasn't overjoyed to learn that you have been leaving James on his own on a Wednesday night."

"But he's not on his own; mum's there."

"Is she?" Francis replied before moving the discussion on as quickly as possible. "I take it your sister is helping you pay the fees?"

"And my paper round," Philip said. He paused a moment, took another deep breath, and then asked. "How did you find out?"

"You had a phone call yesterday, whilst you were out."

"Who from?"

"Mr Spencer. He wanted to make sure that you got here on time today. I admit I was fuming at first and I very nearly said a few things you would regret. But then I got to thinking how much this must mean to you, for you to go behind my back."

"Sorry dad," Philip said.

"I guess you came on your bike?" Francis asked.

"Yes, it's over there," Philip replied as he pointed to his bike in the bike rack.

"Then you had better get yourself home. Bonfire night tomorrow night and we need to finish building the bonfire. I've got to pop in and see Snowy Vest on my way home. Hopefully your mum might be cooking a Sunday dinner."

"Are you not working tomorrow night?"

"No, I've got the night off. Snowy owes me a favour. I'm doing an extra run to Bristol on Thursday. Get yourself off; I'll see you at home. Oh and by the way, that last swim you did, very impressive."

Chapter 56

"Very impressive."

Philip looked across the desk at Mr Spencer. He had an idea what Mr Spencer was referring to, but he couldn't be sure. He could have been referring to the number of lates Philip had incurred so far this term, or the fact that he had avoided a work or conduct card for a number of weeks. So Philip decided it would be in his best interests to remain both silent and stationary a little while longer.

"I'm referring to your relay leg yesterday; very impressive. Mr Kennedy thinks that it could even be a club record. However, what happened in your individual race? How Mr Kennedy described it, you were about as effective as a sticking plaster on a severed arm."

Philip rolled his eyes before adding the negative comment about his first race to the growing collection.

"You appear to have turned a corner," Mr Spencer continued. "Figuratively speaking that is. Obviously not in the pool; in the pool you tend to go in a straight line. Other than your little altercation regarding your sister-and I accept that you may have been provoked; other than that, you appear to have knuckled down, staying on the right path."

Mr Spencer paused for a moment to give Philip time to digest what he had just said and to take a folder out of one of his desk drawers. He placed the folder in front of him on the desk. "I spoke to your father on Saturday."

"I know Sir," Philip replied.

"How's your mother?"

"The same," Philip said.

"And your father?"

"The same."

"And things in general, at home I mean?"

"The same."

"So everything is the same then?"

"Yes Sir."

"You will let me know if anything changes, won't you?"

"Yes Sir."

"Right, well. Have you got any money for me?" Mr Spencer asked as he opened the folder and took out a sheet of paper.

Philip placed his hand inside his trouser pocket, removed a fifty pence piece and handed it over.

"Okay Philip. Better be on your way. Don't be late, and remember what I said, stay on the path."

Philip bent down a little, picked up his bag that had been resting against his leg, and left the office. As he left, he caught sight of a group of boys nervously waiting for a rather more painful interaction with Mr Spencer. As he reached the top of the stairwell that led to the exit from the block, he heard Mr Spencer summon the first victim into his office.

The remainder of the school day was both uneventful and trouble free. It also appeared to last an eternity. A fortnight's holiday in Barrow-in-Furness seemed to have the ability to pass by more quickly. Philip felt as if he was dragging the end of the day towards him like a stubborn dog to a vet's appointment, and claws were firmly dug in. Finally the bell sounded to confirm that he had arrived at the end of the last lesson. The excitement had been bubbling and simmering just below the surface for most of the afternoon. By the time he met James at the school gates and they set off along Arch Road, the anticipation had built up to such a level that it was extremely difficult to peer over the top.

Upon arriving home, the boys spotted Francis putting the finishing touches to the bonfire; the triangular-shaped structure stood tall and proud in the centre of the garden. Philip and James stared at it, as if they were gazing at a beautifully constructed work of art for the very first time. To them it was everything it could possibly be and a bit more thrown in for good measure, like raspberry sauce on the top of an ice-cream.

"When can we light it?" James asked as he hopped from one foot to the other with excitement.

"Not yet," Francis replied. "We need to wait until it gets dark. Anyway, Philip needs to do his paper round first."

"Can some of our friends come?" Philip asked.

"Don't see why not, better check with your mother though, see that we have enough baked spuds to go round."

Philip quickly delegated that particular task to James before heading into the house to get changed out of his school uniform. He returned a few minutes later with his paper bag draped over his shoulder. James and Francis were both still tinkering with the large wooden structure.

"Don't forget to speak to mum," Philip called out as he collected his bike from the garden shed and set off to complete his paper round.

Entering the shop, Philip was surprised to find it devoid of human life, although he could hear activity coming from the back. Despite this clear and obvious opportunity to help himself to a chocolate bar or two, Philip simply gathered up his bundle of 'Evening Telegraphs' put them in his bag and left.

When his round was complete, he arrived home to find his mother wrapping baked potatoes in tin foil and placing them on a metal tray. "Where's dad and James?" Philip asked.

"They've gone to the garage to get some paraffin," his mother replied. "Make yourself useful and butter those finger rolls for me. You can chop some onions as well."

Four packets of finger rolls were sitting on the kitchen table. Philip was only too happy to help. Firstly because it added to the excitement of the evening ahead and secondly it was preferable to watching 'Nationwide' whilst he waited for James and his dad to return. He took a packet of margarine from the fridge, a knife from the cutlery drawer and began to butter the rolls. He was halfway through the third packet when his dad returned, carrying a can of paraffin.

"Are we all set?" Francis said as he poked his head around the kitchen door.

"Almost," His wife replied. "Philip is just finishing off these rolls and then he can come out. Can you take these outside?" she added before holding up a tray of wrapped up baked potatoes.

Philip immediately picked up the pace and quickly finished buttering the finger rolls before following his dad and James outside. As he entered the garden, Francis was busily sloshing paraffin around the base of the bonfire. He then began twisting and twirling strips of newspaper and tucking them under his arm. Once he had about six or seven strips, he called the boys over. He handed them a strip of paper each.

"Hold them up," he said as he took a lighter from his coat pocket. "Now be sure to shove them between the wood just above the ground," he added as he released a flame from the lighter.

The two boys held up the strips of paper firmly grasped in their hands. Once lit, they proceeded to lean forward and push them into the bonfire, instantly igniting the paraffin-soaked wood at the base of the bonfire. A roaring sound filled the air and the light yellow glow of the flames burst forward, lapping at the pieces of wood and climbing up the tower. The boys repeated the process around the other side of the bonfire and within a couple of minutes the majority of the structure was ablaze. The flames danced and swayed in the gentle breeze as they climbed towards the summit, casting shadows on the ground and up the back of the house. With a bright orange glow reflecting in their eyes, Philip, James and Francis stood and watched.

"Once it dies down, we'll be able to chuck the spuds on," Francis said.

"When can we have the fireworks?" James eagerly enquired.

"Once your mother has finished in the kitchen and we all have a hot dog or two inside us," Francis replied.

By the time a small section of the fire had been levelled and the baked potatoes had been placed amongst the burning embers, Paul, Craig, Martin and Grace had arrived and were standing in the back garden. Philip's mum appeared, carrying a plate in each hand overflowing with sausage-filled finger rolls. She asked Philip to go and collect the bowl of fried onions from the kitchen as she circulated amongst the guests like a silver service waitress at a prestigious company gala. Finally, before the excitement got the better of James and he exploded like a firework, it was time for the fireworks.

Everybody apart from Grace, who just leant against the back wall with her hands shoved tightly into her coat pockets, took it in turns to choose a firework. And everybody, apart from Grace, became increasingly frustrated with James, as when it was his turn to choose, he simply couldn't make up his mind.

There were fountains that crackled and spurted out a river of silver sparks. Roman candles that fired glowing balls of colour into the darkened night. Rockets that roared towards the heavens before exploding in a spectacle of gold.

Once the final firework had taken its final bow and the last remnant of colour had faded away, it was time to retrieve the baked potatoes from the collapsed embers of the once majestic bonfire.

Grace could wait no longer and with her hands still shoved firmly inside her coat pockets, she marched over to Philip. "We need to talk," she said upon arrival.

It was rather difficult for Philip to offer an immediate response, due to his mouth being otherwise occupied with hot, soft, fluffy baked potato and melted butter. Eventually he muttered. "Not now Grace, not tonight."

"Why not?" Grace answered rather crossly.

"Have a look Grace." Philip said. "When was the last time we did something like this, all together I mean? Even mum is here, don't spoil it."

"But I think you're right about Karen."

"But what if I'm not? You even said yourself that I was wrong."

The warmth from the bonfire began to subside and lose the battle with the cold November night air. James stared at the charred pieces of wood that had now turned a grey-white colour from the heat. Tiny orange flickers seemed to scurry beneath the ashen surface.

Grace leant a little closer to Philip and whispered in his ear. "We need to find out, need to be sure."

"What good would it do Grace?" Philip replied before adding, "This isn't about Karen is it? This is about dad."

"Well yes, I suppose it is. But what if mum was to find out?"

"How is she gonna do that?" Philip said as he grabbed hold of his sister's now exposed hand and squeezed it tight.

Grace took a step back and pulled herself free from Philip's grasp before attempting to leave. Philip blocked her path.

"If you are not happy then move out. Move back here or somewhere else. But you can't say anything Grace, it will only make things worse."

Grace barged Philip out of the way and marched out of the garden.

"Where's she off to?" Francis asked.

"Home," Philip replied.

Chapter 57

Hello Philip,

How are you? I must confess, I am really looking forward to hearing all about your swim meet. I hope that, in equal measure, it went well and you enjoyed the experience of competition. There is nothing more rewarding or exhilarating than being in the arena of competition. The opportunities it offers are endless and help so much in developing skills for the future challenges that lay ahead.

A bad performance inspires you to do better, a defeat pushes you to try harder, and victories encourage you to keep achieving. Hurdles to overcome, setbacks to be faced, all of these things build character and offer the chance to grow, show commitment and achieve maturity. Without truly understanding this environment and this process, it becomes difficult, virtually impossible, for a sportsman to ever reach his full potential. I can guarantee that everybody in our team would endorse this.

Speaking of the team, it is nice to be able to write to you after securing two more very good victories. When you find yourself on a football field against the likes of Colin Bell, Francis Lee and Denis Law of Manchester City or Billy Bonds, Trevor Brooking and the great Bobby Moore for West Ham, you know that you have achieved something magical, tangible, worthwhile. Then you look around at your teammates and you get a sense of what can be achieved when you have such people with you; it is truly inspiring in any sport or in any walk of life, for that matter.

This is what you must aim for Philip. Don't allow your background or your environment to hold you back and don't use it as an excuse either. I know that things at home are not easy and I am sorry to hear that your mother is still struggling with the more difficult aspects of her life. All you can do is be there for her and try your best not to add to her concerns.

However, look at the footballers playing the game today, most of them grew up during difficult times in tired and rough neighbourhoods. Hotshot grew up in the backstreets of Dundee. Sniffer is the same; he grew up in a big family in the Midlands. Even the great Bobby Moore grew up playing in the grim streets of London's East End. I am not suggesting for an instance that your problems at home are in some way trivial and don't have an impact on you. It is very much the opposite and that is why you need to hang on to your sport. It is so you have something positive, something to hang on to, something to give you hope and strength.

Your kind words help to give me strength, especially during this unbeaten start to the season as the pressure builds a little bit more with each undefeated game. Fourteen unbeaten now and our recent performances have us all believing we can continue to do well. A tricky game ahead on Saturday, away to Burnley. Turf Moor is always a tough place to go and they have been playing some attractive football since being promoted last season. They may not be a team full of internationals but with young players like Brian Flynn and Leighton James coming through and experienced players like Noble and Casper up front, we will need to be at our best.

Well I had better close now. I do not want to be late for training. Pass on my best to all of your family. I hope that school is going well and you are working hard. I look forward to hearing all about the swim meet.

Your Friend

Billy.

Philip had manged to get halfway between the end of Monkswood Crescent and the newsagents by the time he had finished his second reading. He carefully folded the letter before returning it to the envelope and placing it inside his paperbag. He crossed the Henley Road and proceeded to head for the shop. As he approached, Paul McBride was there to meet him.

"Where's your bike?" Paul asked.

"At home," Philip replied. "I wanted to walk today."

"Have you still got the list? I was hoping that you may have got one or two things."

"Sorry Paul. I haven't had a chance to get into town recently. I'll go in on Saturday," Philip said.

"Yeah okay, I'll bring you an updated list on Saturday morning," Paul replied before adding. "I'll see you then," as he set off on his paper round.

Darkness had firmly established itself by the time Philip turned off Winston Avenue and back into the top of Monkswood Crescent. Upon passing Old Man Butcher's house, he saw the front door swing open and the old man in question step out.

"Where you been lad?" he called out. "I thought you were gonna stop by?"

Philip walked over. As he did so, the old man turned and went back inside. By the time Philip reached the doorstep, the door was wide open and the hallway was empty. Philip slowly walked down the hallway, before turning left and entering the living room. As he did so he noticed that the photograph was no longer hanging in the hall. Looking left upon entering the living room was a brown settee and a brown armchair, a wooden coffee table and a television set. Sitting on top of the television set were two framed photographs. Philip walked over and looked at the photographs. One was of a young woman with dark hair, holding a small child in her arms. The second photograph was of a young boy, older than the child in the first photograph. He was about five or six years old with a broad smile across his face and short black hair.

At the other end of the living room sat a dining table and three wooden chairs. Old Man Butcher entered the room, carrying a tray. Upon the tray was a teapot, two mugs, a sugar bowl and a small plate of Lincoln biscuits.

"Come and sit down lad," the old man said as he placed the tray on the table.

As Philip approached, he noticed the photograph from the hallway was lying on the table. He also noticed that the broken glass had been replaced.

"I can't stop long," Philip said as he sat down. "My dad is working an extra shift tonight because he took Monday off."

"You can spare an old man ten minutes can't you? Do you want sugar?"

Philip nodded. "Two please," he said.

The old man finished making the tea before passing a mug over to Philip. This was quickly followed by the plate of Lincoln biscuits. "Help yourself," he said.

"What do you want?" Philip asked as he reached over and took two biscuits from the plate.

"I want you to do something for me," the old man replied as he stirred the remainder of the tea in the pot before replacing the lid.

"What?" Philip asked.

"This picture, the one you were looking at the other day, when I collapsed in the hallway." The old man picked up the picture and glanced at it before continuing. "Do you like football?" He asked.

"It's you isn't it?" Philip said. "In the picture."

"Yes, it is." The old man replied. "It was the last game I ever played."

"How come?"

The old man didn't answer. Instead he asked "Will you do something for me lad? Philip isn't it? The police told me your name the other day."

"What do you want me to do?" Philip asked for the second time as he nodded his head to confirm the old man had his got his name right.

"I want you to take this picture and put it up somewhere in your house, somewhere where you will see it every day."

"Why?" Philip asked.

"I don't expect you to understand but I need to know I am still out there, I need to know before I go, that I existed. I don't have anybody to give it to. I don't have any family to give it to."

"Where are you going?" Philip asked.

"Away lad. I'm moving away."

"And you don't want to take it with you?"

"Not that one, no".

"And you don't have anybody, no family at all?"

"Other than the wife and child I brutally butchered, you mean."

Philip's eyes widened as he stared at the old man. A dunked Lincoln biscuit's journey from mug to mouth was halted in its tracks.

"Eat your biscuit lad. I know what people say about me."

Philip's biscuit set off once more on its journey and thankfully reached his mouth before the dunked half collapsed onto the table.

"Don't worry, you are quite safe. But it is true…" Old Man Butcher paused. He savoured the moment. He could sense Philip's heart skip a beat as it had been lured into the silent gap. He continued. "I did once have a wife and child."

Once Philip was happy that his heart was functioning normally again, he asked. "What happened to them?"

The old man got up and walked across the room. He collected the two photographs from on top of the television set, before walking back and sitting down at the table again. He held on to the photograph of the woman and child, and passed the photograph of the young boy to Philip.

"We called him Alfred. He was such a beautiful boy. His eyes, he had beautiful eyes. So full of warmth, so full of life. And his smile, I don't think I ever saw him without a smile on his face."

"What happened?" Philip asked again.

"I lost them lad, that's what happened. I lost them both, him and his mother. The night after that match." The old man replied as he pointed to the picture of him playing his last game of football for Notts County. "In a fire," he continued. "A house fire. I knew he was dead. I carried him out in my arms. His eyes were open, but I knew. There was no shimmer, no sparkle, they were empty. I knew he was dead. I failed. I couldn't save him or his mother. I was badly burnt myself. My back, shoulders, back of my head and the backs of my legs. I was in hospital for a while. But I had no desire to get out, nothing to get out for. Whilst I was in there about two weeks later, this newspaper chappie came to visit me. He'd been at the game, he took the picture. He'd heard about the fire and he came to see me."

Without realising, Philip found himself gripped and glued to every word that fell from the old man's lips. In turn, Old Man Butcher had found himself an audience who was eager to listen. Just like millions of times past and in every location around the globe, the perfect ingredients were present. A boy who wanted to listen and an old man who wanted to talk found themselves in the same place at the same time. The old man continued.

"It was new back then. Back then people only took photographs of movie stars like Charlie Chaplin, Rudolph Valentino, Greta Garbo and Lillian Gish. He was learning his craft, the lad said. He was younger than I was, his first job for the paper. They put one of his other pictures in the paper. I remember him saying that it was the best one he'd taken and when he heard what had happened, he felt compelled, he just felt that I should have it. It was years before I could look at it and these two." He paused for a moment and motioned towards the photographs. "The pictures didn't perish in the fire because they hadn't been put up yet, we'd not long moved in and they were still in a tin, under the stairs."

He picked up the picture of his son. Philip could see the pain in his eyes, a pain that had never left him, not even for a moment. Even after all these years, it was clear to see that heartache had been his constant companion. As the old man gazed at the picture, Philip scrambled around for something to say.

"What happened when you left hospital?" Philip eventually asked.

"Not a lot really lad. People tried to help, they meant well, good intentions and all that but deep inside, I was out of reach, I was as dead as they were. Well-wishers, friends, whatever you want to call them, they eventually drifted away. You can't blame them really, I wasn't much fun to be around. They started to visit less and less. To be honest I was glad. They only reminded me of what I'd lost. So, did the streets, the places I went to, the park where we'd go as a family, the corner shop, the country lanes. I would find myself walking past his school and hear the noise coming from inside or see them all playing in the playground. I'd bump into people, old friends. They'd ask me how I was keeping, promise to call by but like I say, I was glad when they didn't. The wife's family disappeared as well. I never really thought about it at the time but I guess it was the same for her mum and dad. I probably only reminded them of what they had lost, a daughter and a grandson. And then of course there's the guilt that you have to try and live with. It wastes no time at all in making itself at home, along with the anguish. They certainly make for uncomfortable bedfellows. Eventually I couldn't cope with it any longer, all the reminders, so I moved away, obviously my guilt and anguish moved with me and have done ever since."

In an attempt to pull the old man free from the darkness that had engulfed him, Philip asked. "So how did you come to play for Notts County?"

"It's where I'm from. Well Nottinghamshire at any rate. I was born in a small village called East Bridgford. I don't suppose you've ever heard of it."

Philip shook his head.

"It's famous for its windmills but not a lot else. I was born in 1900. My dad enlisted in 1914, when war broke out, at the age of thirty six. He died in April 1918 during the spring offensive in Arras. My older brother also saw some active action towards the end of the conflict but he survived and came home. My mother never recovered from the loss of my father. She passed away in 1922. She was forty seven. That was the year I started playing for Rainworth Miners Welfare F.C. I, like most young men from the area worked in the pits. Before I played for

Rainworth, I played for Worksop Town F.C. Then after a few years at Rainworth, a chap from Notts County had heard I was quite decent and he came to watch me play. They didn't have these scouting types, like they have today but I guess that is what he was. County had just been relegated to division two. I signed for them and got a weekly wage. We had to move into Nottingham itself but at least it got me out of the pit. That was the start of the 26-27 season. I can remember my first game as if it was yesterday."

Philip could sense the positive shift in the old man's tone as he recalled happier, brighter moments from his past. It was as if the words shone and sparkled as they tumbled from his lips.

"It's a game most county players that day would want to forget. 28th August 1926, away to South Shields F.C. We lost five-nil. I hardly touched the ball all game," he said with a half-smile across his face. "I think nerves certainly played a part in those first few games. I'd never played in front of crowds like that before. Nearly ten thousand came to our first home game that season. Before that, the most I had ever played in front of were about three hundred. That was our first win of the season as well. I scored my first league goal on the 13th September 1926. We were home to Chelsea. We won five-nil and I scored the fourth goal. They had beaten us the week before two-nil. Five days after the Chelsea game we were home again to Nottingham Forest. I'd never known anything like it. The noise, the crowd, the atmosphere was…" He paused, he continued. "I can't describe it really. It is something that you have to experience for yourself to fully understand what a local derby means, the intensity, the expectation. Nearly twenty thousand were there, squeezed into Meadow Lane. We lost two-one. We played well though. We finished sixteenth that season."

"Was your brother there?" Philip asked.

"What?"

"Your brother, you mentioned you had a brother. Did he go to the Forest game, did he go and watch you play?"

"I've no idea."

"Is he still alive?"

"I couldn't tell you. Do you want a fresh cup?" the old man replied as lifted up the teapot.

"No thanks, I'd better not. I need to go soon," Philip replied before asking again about the old man's brother and what became of him.

"I couldn't tell you lad, not a clue. The last time I saw him was at our mother's funeral. He was lording it in front of everybody as usual. Claiming how he was her favourite son and how much he cared about her, all lies of course. You only saw him when he was on the take. He was a waste of space, worthless. A petty, small time criminal who rather bizarrely thought he was important. He abandoned his wife and children. Used those closest to him for his own ends and anyone else he could reach for that matter. Stole from his friends and his enemies. Our mother was devastated, ashamed, especially when he walked out on his wife and three small children. As soon as things got tough, he ran away, left them destitute, left his children to go hungry. Before you ask, I've no idea what became of them. I believe they moved away, the south coast I heard. As for him, the piece of rubbish that he was, I told him when we laid our mother to rest that I never expected to see or hear from him again. That was over fifty years ago and I've never set eyes on him since."

"What, even after what happened to you, after the fire and all, he didn't visit?"

"Why would he, he didn't care about his own family, so why on earth would he care about mine. So you see, I don't have anybody. That is why I want you to take the photograph, why I need you to take the photograph. You see I cannot cope with the notion of it simply being thrown away, it would be like throwing me away, throwing my life away, throwing them away."

Philip picked the photograph up with one hand and a final Lincoln biscuit up with the other hand. "Okay," he said as he took a bite of the biscuit and slipped the photograph into his paperbag. "What about your other photographs?" Philip asked.

"They're coming with me." The old man replied as he stood up and began to clear the table.

Philip finished eating his biscuit and stood up. "What's that?" he said as he pointed to an object hanging from the wall directly opposite his seat.

"A barometer." The old man replied. "It measures air pressure and the atmosphere. It predicts the weather."

The barometer was encased in a dark red wood and was shaped like a giant wrist watch.

The old man placed the tray he was holding back onto the table and stepped towards the barometer. "Would you like it?" he asked Philip as he reached up and took it from the wall.

"Yes please!" Philip replied. "If you don't mind that is and if you don't want it."

The old man smiled before carefully placing the barometer inside the paperbag. As he did so Philip asked.

"Do you have the box it came in?"

"Sorry lad, I don't think so."

"It doesn't matter." Philip replied as he placed the strap of the bag onto his shoulder and headed towards the hallway. "I'd better go," he added.

The old man walked Philip to the front door.

"Goodnight," Philip said as he stepped outside.

"Goodbye," The old man replied. "Take care of yourself and of me."

Philip turned to look at the old man but as he did so he saw the front door close.

Chapter 58

Philip paced nervously up and down inside the confined space of the newsagents. No sooner had he gone up, than he had to turn again and come back down. He was like a groom outside a registry office whose bride was already twenty minutes late and all the guests were waiting inside, with the best man standing in the doorway, sweat tumbling from his brow as he anxiously looked out onto the street.

On each occasion that Philip completed the up, he glanced over at Mr Underwood, who was busily sorting out the Sunday papers, before he turned and set off once more upon the down section. Eventually, as he completed another lap, Philip asked, "Is he here today?"

"Who?" Mr Underwood replied.

"Paul."

"I hope so. Are you able to do his round again if he doesn't show up?"

"Not today, no," Philip replied before adding "I've got swimming training today."

Within a few minutes, Philip's stack of Sunday papers was ready to go. During this time, two other paper boys had arrived, which curtailed Philip's pacing, so he was quite glad to collect his papers and step outside. He heaved his bag onto his shoulder and accompanied by his customary Sunday morning lean, attempted to weave his way out of the shop. Once outside he removed the bag from his already aching shoulder and stooped down to remove the padlock from his bike. As he did so, he felt a tap on his shoulder and a voice from behind him say "Alright Phil."

Philip stood up and turned around. A relieved expression instantly appeared across his face. "Alright Paul, where you bin?"

"Oh I've had a few things going on, family stuff and that."

"Is your nan alright?" Philip asked.

"Yeah, fine, why?"

"Oh no reason. I thought you were ill."

"No, that is just what I told old underpants, just didn't want him asking any questions. It has been a shit few days and on top of everything else we got battered 3-0 by bloody Q.P.R. "

"I've got some good news for you," Philip said with a smile across his face.

"I could certainly do with some," Paul replied. "What is it?"

"A barometer, I've got one but you'll have to come and collect it today."

This particular piece of news delivered on its promise and a broad smile immediately appeared upon Paul's face. "Wow, you're joking. You've got one? Did you rob it? Where did you get it?"

"It's not important where I got it from but it is important that you come and collect it today. It's hidden under my bed and it will cost you five pounds."

Upon hearing the price, Paul's smile went into retreat mode until it was almost unrecognisable. "Five pounds!" he gasped. Where did you rob it from, Arbury Hall?"

"Where's that?" Philip replied.

"Nuneaton. We went there on some poxy school trip last year, some stupid history thing."

"Oh right, well it's not from there but it's still a fiver. I had a look in Owen Owen yesterday and they've got one that is not as good as this one for twelve pounds. And my mum's Gratton catalogue's got a few, there's one that's tiny in the shape of a ship's wheel for nearly a tenner. This one has got to be worth fifteen new."

"Can you do it for three quid?" Paul asked.

"No, I need a fiver. You won't get another one as good as this and your Nan will be well chuffed. I need to pay my swimming subs and pay off my school trip."

"I'll come and have a look at it after my paper round."

"No, it will have to be later today, after my swimming and when my dad is down the pub. Come round about one o' clock." Philip picked up his paperbag and climbed onto his bike. "And be sure to bring the money." He added as he set off on his paper round.

Paul arrived at Philip's house just before one o' clock. He knocked on the door just as Francis Knott was exiting the Bell Inn and walking in the direction of Hall Green Road, heading for the Green Man public house. Already located within a secluded corner of the Green Man bar sat an anxious-looking Lousy and a far less anxious-looking Snowy Vest.

"He's late," Lousy muttered whilst raising his glass to his lips.

"I know," Snowy replied. "I know this because I have a watch, I can tell the time and also because you have said he is late at least five times in the last ten minutes."

"Yes but…"

Lousy was interrupted immediately. "Relax lousy, he'll be here, he has money to collect."

There was a brief silence. However, Snowy knew that it wasn't going to last. He still tried to make the most of it though by taking a sip of his drink and lighting a cigarette. Before the smoke from the spent match had drifted away, Lousy said "Are you sure about this?"

"About what?"

"About cutting him in."

"We've been over and over this Lousy. I thought we agreed. It's better to have him in than out."

"Yeah but we don't have to cut him in if he's out."

Snowy sighed and exhaled before looking directly at Lousy. "If he's out then things can go wrong. What if he fights back, what if he gets seriously hurt? If he believes it is genuine, he's gonna be more likely to talk to the law. If he's in, he keeps quiet."

"But what if he doesn't want in after you tell him?"

"I'm not an idiot Lousy. I'll tell him what he needs to know when he needs to know it."

"Yeah but he will still be able to figure it out when it happens."

"You're probably right Lousy, he's not an idiot either. But he's hardly gonna want to tell the law is he. Even if he suspects, he knows that opening his mouth and letting too much fall out could put him in the frame when they start asking questions and poking around, he's not gonna want that."

"He's still late."

"I know he's late lousy, I know."

As Francis entered the Green Man pub with a Sunday newspaper under his arm, Paul McBride exited Philip's house with a barometer under his. Paul had made every attempt to haggle and reduce the asking price but Philip had stood firm. He almost flinched a couple of times but he held out and got the whole five pounds. Once the money had been safely hidden away, Philip headed outside. He had considered watching 'Star Soccer' but he knew that the likelihood of the Leeds game being one of the two matches shown was very slim. They hadn't played a Midlands team, so that ruled them out of being the main attraction and a goalless draw at Burnley suggested that they wouldn't be the supporting game either, especially when considering the other results. He was right; the first game was Birmingham City's one-one draw with Southampton, and it was followed by Arsenal's two-one win away at Man City.

"You're late," Lousy said as Francis carefully placed his pint of bitter and his newspaper on the table before sitting down.

"Am I?" Francis replied as he adjusted a little in his seat before moving it and himself a little closer to his drink.

"Yes," Lousy said with obvious annoyance in his voice, adding, "You should have been here at half twelve."

"Why, what happened?" Francis asked as he reached for his drink.

Lousy was about to respond when Snowy leant across and gently grabbed hold of him by the arm, just above the wrist.

"He's here now Lousy, that's all that matters," Snowy said before looking across the table at Francis. "How are you Francis?" he asked.

"Fine thanks." Francis replied.

"And our friend in Rochdale, how is he?"

Francis didn't reply, he just raised his eyebrows as he reached for and took another sip of his drink.

"Certainly a colourful character, isn't he?" Snowy said.

"That's one way of describing him," Francis replied before adding. "An arsehole would be another way."

"Don't get on the wrong side of him Francis. We need him and we'll need him even more if this current situation gets worse," Lousy said.

"What current situation?" Francis asked.

"He's referring to this Middle East situation and this impending fuel crisis that's looming large upon the horizon. Don't you watch the news Francis?"

Francis simply shrugged his shoulders and carried on drinking his pint of bitter. "I have my own issues thanks," he muttered.

"Typical as well, just as work was beginning to pick up and we were hopeful of getting everybody back on a five day week. Now we could find ourselves with no fuel!" Snowy concluded.

"Do you think it will come to that?"

"It might Francis, it might."

There was a brief pause in the conversation, just long enough for Lousy to look at Snowy and for Snowy to look at lousy before looking past Francis to check that their meeting wasn't attracting any unwanted attention. He then carefully removed his wallet, took out three ten pound notes, folded them neatly in half and placed them on the table in front of Francis. Francis went to pick up the money but Snowy left his fingers resting on top and looked at Francis.

"Would you be interested in making some real money Francis?" he asked.

"How do you mean?" Francis asked as he manoeuvred the money from beneath Snowy's fingers before placing it in his pocket.

"I mean some real money, money with purpose instead of ten pounds here and twenty pounds there."

"How much?"

Snowy shuffled his chair a few inches closer to the table before leaning forward. "Five hundred pounds," he whispered. "You could do a lot with that. Get yourself a decent motor for a start, a good Christmas, a nice summer holiday. One job, no risk."

"There's always a risk Snowy, always a risk," Francis replied.

"That's why we are offering you five hundred pounds," Lousy interrupted. "Take a risk and earn five hundred pounds, don't take the risk and earn nothing."

"You can't weigh up five hundred pounds against the risk Lousy, you have to weigh it up against the consequences. It is whether the money is worth the consequences, not the risk."

"A most valid point Francis," Snowy replied.

"Yes well, seeing as I don't know what the job is, or the risks, which would in turn allow me to calculate the consequences, I can't really determine whether the job is value for money can I?"

"Another valid and reasonable point Francis, but you would not be averse to being interested in making some real money if the opportunity was to present itself?"

"Yes, of course I would."

"You would be averse or you would be interested?"

"Interested," Francis replied.

"Then meet us here the same time next week and I will be able to enlighten you further on the job, the risks and the possible consequences."

"And when he says the same time, he means half twelve, not the time you turned up today," Lousy muttered.

"Relax Lousy," Snowy said. "Anyway it's your round. I'm sure Francis will stay for another."

Chapter 59

On the face of it, on the surface, so to speak, it was a normal, typical Thursday morning. Perhaps it was a little chilly as Philip stood in the bathroom and relieved himself before heading downstairs. It was even a little chillier when he set off on his paper round, despite having a bowl of cornflakes and hot milk inside him. However, it was nothing too extreme or out of the ordinary for mid-November.

By the time Philip had completed his normal ordinary paper round and arrived back home daylight had started to appear, like a nervous stage director peeking out from behind the thick black stage curtain, to get a glimpse of the audience on opening night. Once back at home, he prepared a normal, ordinary bowl of cereal for James, made his father a normal, ordinary cup of tea and had a normal and ordinary experience as he got ready for school. In fact when he and James left the house if there had been an award ceremony for the most normal and ordinary start to the day, then this particular start to the day would certainly have been shortlisted.

It wasn't until the boys were halfway across the green before normal and ordinary were unceremoniously stopped in their tracks. Almost within the blink of an eye, normal and ordinary hurriedly tossed a few items of necessity into their duffle bags and vanished without a trace. As the boys looked up, they noticed a small crowd of people standing not too far away from Old Man Butcher's house. A couple of local residents and a small number of school children looked on. Outside the house sat three police cars and an ambulance. Two police officers were standing on the pavement, next to one of the police cars. Inside the vehicle, one could just make out a third police officer, talking on his radio. A fourth police officer was preventing the growing crowd from getting any closer to the edge of the green.

"What's going on?" Philip asked as he reached the edge of the crowd and tapped Craig on the shoulder.

"Dunno." Craig replied. "There was one car at first, then about five minutes ago another two turned up and the ambulance arrived about two minutes ago."

"He's done it again." Paul muttered as he turned to look at Philip and James.

"Done what again?" James asked.

"You know. He's butchered somebody. Probably dragged them in off the street and chopped them up."

"Oh right," Philip replied with a tone in his voice that appeared to have been marinated in sarcasm overnight. "So, after they discovered the chopped up remains of his victim, they thought that they should ring for an ambulance, just in case they can find a pulse in one of the severed limbs."

"Yeah, well, maybe there's more than one," Paul replied.

"Oh right. All scattered around the living room floor like a mosaic and they are trying to piece all the bits together, see which bits belongs to who."

"No, I mean that he may have been caught in the act and one of his victims is still alive."

Philip shook his head by way of a protest at Paul's theory of possible events. As he did so, Martin turned and asked, "What's a mosaic?"

Philip was just about to reply and enlighten Martin when the policeman called out. "Come on now people, haven't you all got better things to do? And shouldn't you boys be getting to school? Come on now, on your way!"

The crowd failed to disperse. In fact as if it were part of an exhibit in Madame Tussauds, nobody moved a muscle. By the time the 26 bus was spotted flashing past the top of Monkswood Crescent, the crowd had grown bigger and was up to around twenty six people. They were all muttering amongst themselves and attempting to second guess the scenario that was being played out inside the house.

Philip stood and looked towards the house. He attempted to replay the conversation he had had with the old man the week before. However, each replay seemed to lose a bit of detail or gain a hazy, slightly unsure piece of information. After several further minutes of limited activity, apart from the crowd growing a bit bigger and the boys accepting that the inevitable detention for being late would be waiting for them when they finally arrived at school, the ambulance men exited the house. A policeman flanked the first ambulance man and approximately seven feet behind came the second. The distance between the two accounted for the handles on the stretcher they were wheeling out of the house. Upon the stretcher and concealed beneath a dark grey blanket was the clear outline of a body.

The volume of the chatter amongst the crowd increased as more of the stretcher came into view. Philip remained silent, his eyes locked upon the shape as it was wheeled around the back of the ambulance. The sound of the ambulance doors closing echoed in the cold empty space of the morning, and the crowd slowly began to disperse. Philip just stood and stared at the ambulance as it pulled away, escorted by two of the three police cars.

He was struggling to grab hold of how he was feeling. It was as if he was trying to unhook a fish in the dark, whilst wearing a pair of boxing gloves. He couldn't make sense of the thoughts that were racing through his mind, or even manage to stitch two of them together at any one time. For a few moments, he felt that everything around him and connected to him no longer fitted.

"Phil man!" Paul called out. "Shows over, let's go."

Philip suddenly realised that he was now standing all alone at the edge of the green, whilst the rest of the boys, including James, had already passed the parked police car and were heading towards Winston Avenue. He slowly jogged towards the group and past Old Man Butcher's house but chose to remain a few feet behind them. He could still hear the group discussing the possible scenarios as they walked to the bus stop. He heard Paul mention that the old man had probably died in his sleep or had a heart attack and on this occasion he hoped that Paul was right, but he couldn't shift the nagging feeling that Paul was wrong. The nagging feeling stuck to him like scrunched up snow on a child's mitten and every attempt to shake it off failed.

He spent the rest of the school day trying his best to avoid his friends. But by lunchtime it seemed that virtually the whole school had heard about the old man's death and the Chinese whisper mill had already created imaginative versions of events. At some point during the day he even heard a boy he had never met before telling another boy he had never met before that the old man had been murdered by another schoolboy who was being held prisoner in the house. It was a very disjointed but ultimately relieved Philip that finally arrived home after his paper round later that day.

He got back just in time to watch the second part of a two-part 'Scooby-Doo' adventure entitled Guess Whose Knott Coming to Dinner. The mystery had been solved with the villain revealed and placed into custody thanks to those pesky kids and the credits were rolling when there was a knock at the front door. Francis, who happened to be sitting at the dining table reading the morning newspaper, got up to answer the door.

Philip and James could hear voices but could not make out any clear passages of dialogue, even after they had turned down the volume on the television. Their mother appeared from the kitchen just as Francis returned to the living room with two policemen.

"These officers would like a word with you Philip," Francis said as he ushered the officers forward enough to close the living room door behind them.

"Nothing to worry about lad, you are not in any trouble," the first officer said.

"What's this about?" Philip's mother asked.

"It's about the elderly gentleman who lived across the green, in the house on the corner."

"Did you just say lived?" Francis asked.

"Yes sir, sadly he was discovered this morning. A neighbour raised the alarm. It appears that he has been dead a few days, possibly even a week."

"And what on earth has this got to do with my son?" Philip's mother asked with a certain amount of anxiety in her voice.

"Well it seems that the elderly gentleman left your son a note," the second officer said as he held out a small brown envelope.

Philip stood up, looked at the officer, then the note, his mother, his father, and the officer again before giving his eyes a well earnt rest by focusing for a while longer on the envelope still in the officer's hand.

"Switch that TV off," Francis said to James as Philip stepped forward and took hold of the envelope. Francis was still busily processing the information from the officer. Eventually the process reached a question. "This wasn't natural causes then?" he asked.

"What brings you to that assumption?" the officer replied.

"I am assuming this on the basis that people don't usually leave other people notes then drop down dead."

"Yes well, we don't know what the note says yet, do we."

"No, you don't know what the note says but you do know how he died," Francis replied.

Still holding the envelope, Philip looked at his dad.

"Well go on son, open it," Francis said.

The room fell almost silent, except for the sound of the envelope being opened. As he opened it, Philip noticed that on the front of the envelope, the old man had written 'Philip, 107 Monkswood'. Philip removed and unfolded the single piece of paper that was inside.

"Read it out," Francis said.

It certainly did not constitute a letter, more a brief note. Philip read it out.

'I've taken them with me, like I said I would. I just needed to be with them again. I've been on my own for far too long. I needed to see them again, hold my boy in my arms, and see his smile. Don't forget now will you, put me where you can see me. I know there will not be any tears shed at the news of my passing but it is not about me and where I've been anymore but about where I've gone. I just hope that where I've gone is filled with joy. God bless you and thank you. P.S. You can keep the frames if you like'.

Philip folded the piece of paper and wiped away a tear that had fallen onto his cheek. He glanced over and caught sight of his mother doing the same.

"Frames," the one officer said as he turned to face his colleague. He then turned his attention back to Philip. "There were two picture frames on his T.V but they were empty. I guess you know what was in them?" he asked.

Philip nodded. "That's what he meant by taking them with him," he replied.

"So it was suicide then; he did himself in," Francis stated.

The officers chose not to reply. Instead they waited for Philip to continue. After coming to the conclusion that Philip wasn't about to offer any further information, they quickly realised some sort of prompt was required.

"So what was in the frames?" they asked.

"One was of his wife and his son when he was a baby. The other one was of his son when he was six. They'll be in his pocket I guess. Please don't remove them, he wouldn't want that to happen."

"How do you know all this son?" the officer asked.

"He told me," Philip began. "He told me all about them and all about his life. He used to be a footballer."

"Did he?" Francis said.

"Yeah. He played for Notts County. That's what he meant by putting him where I can see him. He gave me a photograph of him playing football. I think he just wanted somebody to remember him after he'd gone, even if it was me."

"Did he give you anything else?" the officer asked.

"No." Philip replied.

"Are you sure? It's just that there was something hanging from his living room wall, that's not there anymore, just an outline of where it used to be."

Philip shook his head.

The officer was just about to ask another question when he noticed smoke drifting out from the kitchen. "I think something may be burning." he said.

The expression upon Philip's mum's face instantly confirmed the officer's suspicions were correct and she turned and bolted towards the kitchen door. As she pushed the door open a wall of grey smoke bellowed out, into the living room, engulfing her, swallowing her up like the car in front vanishing into a heavy blanket of fog. She returned to the living room, carrying a grill pan with eight smouldering sausages upon it. "Dinner's ruined," she muttered.

Francis wafted away the smoke with his outstretched hand before glancing down at the sad looking sticks of charcoal that were once sausages.

"We'll be off," one of the officers said. "If we need anything else, we can call back."

They headed towards the front door with Philip following closely behind. As they stepped outside, Philip said "Please don't let anybody take his photos from him."

"It's really important to you, isn't it lad?" the officer said.

"Yes," Philip replied. "But it's more important to him."

Philip closed the door and returned to the living room just as Francis had removed a one-pound note from his pocket and was holding it aloft. "Looks like it's a chippy tea," Francis said. "Who's going?"

Chapter 60

"Sit down Francis, sit down, you're late," Snowy Vest snapped as he glanced down at his watch.

Francis immediately got the impression that Snowy wasn't his normal relaxed self. The facial expression, body language and tone of voice were all big giveaways. The only things missing were a drum roll and a spotlight. "Where's Lousy?" Francis asked as he placed his drink on the table and sat down.

"Gents; he'll be here in a minute," Snowy quickly replied.

"Everything alright Snowy?" Francis asked. "Have you got to go and visit the in-laws this afternoon?"

"Always got a joke or a wise crack up your sleeve, eh Francis. A sense of humour, all the ladies like a man with a sense of humour."

"So they say Snowy, so they say."

"Yeah well, right now Francis, I haven't got a lot to laugh about. Right now, I am deeply troubled. Right now…" Snowy paused mid-sentence as he caught sight of Lousy exiting the gents. "Here's Lousy," he said before finishing his drink, standing up and heading towards the bar.

Francis and Lousy acknowledged each other's presence, before sitting in silence and patiently waiting for Snowy to return from the bar. Precariously carrying three full pint glasses, Snowy arrived back at the table and gently placed the drinks down.

"Have you told him?" Lousy immediately asked.

"Not yet Lousy, no."

"Told me what?" Francis asked.

Snowy sat down and positioned the drinks so that each respective drink was placed in front of its intended consumer. "We have a problem Francis," Snowy said.

"What?" Francis replied.

"More of a who, than a what," Lousy interrupted.

"George Meadows," Snowy said.

"George Meadows? What has he got to do with anything? I thought he'd gone in to business with his brother-in-law."

"So did he Francis, so did he."

"What's happened?" Francis asked.

"It all went sour Francis, that's what. The brother-in-law ripped them off. How can you do such a thing to your own sister? He's taken everything, every last penny, cleaned them out, took every penny and scarpered. He sold the company from behind their backs and vanished."

"You what?" Francis said, clearly struggling to make sense of the news he had just received.

"That's not the best bit. Tell him the best bit," Lousy said.

"There's a best bit?" Francis asked.

"Depends on your point of view, I guess, but the best bit that Lousy is referring to is the fact that the brother–in–law hasn't scarpered on his own. It appears that he's upped sticks and run off with the best part of two hundred thousand pounds and a twenty two year old secretary called Gaynor." Snowy paused before adding, "Welsh, I think."

The three men took refuge in their drinks and contemplated for a moment or two before Francis said, "But I thought it was all above board, documents, contracts and all that."

"The fucker tricked them, didn't he?" Snowy began. "Convinced them to wait until they had purchased the other yard or depot and all that. Said it would save them paying twice to have all the paperwork drawn up. Then he sent them some pre-agreement documents to sign from some bogus solicitor's office. Fake of course; the solicitor didn't exist. All the time he was negotiating with some bigger firm to buy him out. The other depot was legit though. The asking price went up if he had an extra depot and extra transport. Almost thirty grand George put in, his wife's inheritance and the money from re-mortgaging the house."

"Thirty grand and all he's got to show for it is a bloody nose," Lousy said.

"A bloody nose?" Francis asked with one eyebrow suitably raised.

Lousy put him in the picture. "Yes, well he hadn't heard from the brother-in-law for a few days. Phone out of order at the house or so they thought. So George drove to the depot only to find the new owners' manager sitting behind the desk and obviously a new secretary. When that manager had filled in the blanks, undoubtedly George got a bit upset. The police had to be called and in the ensuing melee George took a whack on the nose."

"So where's he gone?" Francis asked.

"If you are referring to the brother-in-law, nobody knows. The speculation is that he's in Spain, Australia, America or Mexico. As for George, he's left his Mrs and the house is up for sale, but they owe it all to the bank anyway. The daughter has had to postpone her wedding and George has moved into a grubby little one bed flat in Barras Heath, above a chip shop," Snowy said. "He's working six nights a week in the chippy below. I get the impression that he is one more kick in the teeth away from pouring whisky on his cornflakes."

The Green Man bar was as crowded as usual for a Sunday lunchtime. The card games, darts games and general discussions within the room were in full swing, thus allowing for a lack of concern about being overheard. The three men continued to discuss George Meadow's recent misfortunes.

"Sorry for sounding unsympathetic to George's plight but how does it impact upon us exactly?" Francis asked.

"Well you see George wants to be reinstated. He wants his old job back and the arrangements that went with it," Snowy began. "The problem is, he's threatened to go to the police if he doesn't get what he wants. We can't take this threat lightly as I don't think he has got a lot left to lose, unless he's concerned about blowing his promotion to fish fryer in the chip shop. The second problem, and the one that I cannot get through to George at the moment, is there isn't a job available for him to come back to. We are struggling to find enough work for those who are here, never mind those who are not."

"So what are you going to do?" Francis asked.

"It's not what I'm going to do, it's more of a case of what we are going to do. We are going to get the job done as quickly as possible, then shut things down for a while. I'll take care of George. I've already chucked him fifty quid. But we need to be ready to act, as soon as we get the right load."

"Apologies for being the one chucking all the spanners here," Francis said, "but what exactly are you talking about? Any chance of putting me in the picture?"

It was at this point that Snowy Vest realised that Francis still hadn't agreed to participate in his plan. Or for that matter, even know what the plan was or what his role in the plan would be. He was plan-free.

Snowy again looked around at the activities taking place in the crowded bar. At each table sat a selection of middle aged men, all washing down the blood, sweat and tears of the previous week's labour whilst preparing for the next. Games of cribbage, dominoes and seven card brag were in full swing, with ashtrays clinking to the sound of coins being tossed into them. In the far left corner a darts game was also gaining momentum as the two players involved got ever closer to a double finish. Plumes of smoke from cigarettes tightly squeezed between fingers or delicately balanced between lips drifted towards the ceiling. Over to the right, a group of elderly gentlemen sat and read the Sunday papers. A middle-aged barmaid was weaving her way between the tables, a book of raffle tickets in one hand and a pint tankard full of change in the other. Once the barmaid had visited their table and fully satisfied that all was as it should be, Snowy turned his attention back to Francis.

"We can't keep messing about with a few boxes here and a few boxes there Francis. It's okay I guess, it keeps us ticking over in difficult times but the reality is the risks far outweigh the rewards."

"So?" Francis said.

"So, we are going to take a whole lorry load in one hit. We are just waiting for the right load, one with plenty of value."

"Aren't they going to notice?" Francis said.

"Who?"

"Well, Rochdale. I appreciate they may not be the brightest but when I roll up-I assume I will be driving or I wouldn't be here having this conversation- When I roll up and swing open the back doors to reveal an empty trailer, I think there is a good chance somebody is going to notice."

"But you won't be arriving at the depot Francis. Your empty lorry and you will be discovered where you normally offload the odd box or two."

"Discovered? Discovered by who?"

"The police of course," Snowy replied.

"Oh and I suppose I just tell them I didn't notice my lorry being robbed."

"Ah..." Snowy said before pausing for a moment and glancing over at Lousy.

"Ah,' what?" Francis said as he stared hard at Lousy, who avoided his gaze long enough for him to turn his attention back to Snowy.

"Yes, well, we can't exactly have you sitting in your cab eating a ham sandwich and a bag of crisps with a wagon wheel on your lap when the police arrive and discover your empty trailer."

"So?" Francis said.

"So, Francis, when you arrive at the lorry park..."

Francis interrupted. "Why am I stopping at a lorry park which is only twenty minutes away from the depot?"

"Because you always do, that's why. This is where you take a break. You like the peace and quiet. You stop for thirty minutes or so before you carry on to the depot." Snowy paused, took a drink from his glass and quickly checked that the rest of the bar was still engaged in their own activities. He continued. "When you arrive, you will see two transit vans parked up at the far end of the park. You drive over and park up next to them, spin yourself around so that the back of the trailer is facing the bushes. Have your flask open and a sandwich half eaten. You then go and explore a suspicious noise coming from the back of the trailer. Upon going to investigate, you receive a blow to the head. Not too hard, not so hard that it knocks you out, just hard enough to leave evidence that you received a blow to the head which would suggest you were knocked out. They will then tie you up, gag you and put you in the back of the trailer. Then you just need to sit tight or rather lie tight until the police discover you."

The amazed look upon Francis's face had made itself comfortable a few sentences ago, at about the point of discovering he received a blow to the head. "You are joking?" he said.

"No Francis, I am not. You're the joker remember. I'm very serious."

"And what if it goes wrong, what if we get caught?"

"You won't get caught, you'll have evidence to back up your story. As you said yourself Francis, it's about weighing it up, risk against reward. Is the reward of five hundred pounds worth the risk? A whack on the head, a few uncomfortable hours in the back of a lorry, a brief statement to the police, you can't tell them much as you didn't see who struck you. A trip to the local hospital to get checked over, probably get a cup of tea and a biscuit. If you are lucky, a young nurse's firm breasts pressed against you as she cleans your wound, then its job done."

Francis finished his drink. His amazed expression had been replaced by a more thoughtful one. He got up to go to the bar.

"Hang on Francis," Snowy said before removing a one pound note from his wallet. "Get a round out of this and I'll have a whisky chaser as well."

By the time Francis had completed his second trip back from the bar carrying his pint, Snowy's whisky chaser and thirty six pence in change, he had a list of questions. He asked the first one as he sat down. "What happens when the police start asking questions?"

"We'll answer them."

"What if they discover all the other stuff that has gone missing?"

"They won't. Lousy has taken care of that."

Francis stood up again and took a large drink from his glass.

"Where are you going now?" Lousy asked.

"Toilet," Francis replied.

"So what do you think?" Lousy said as he leant across towards Snowy whilst watching Francis weave his way between tables and head for the toilets.

"About what Lousy?"

"About the job of course! Do you think he'll do it?"

"Of course he'll do it, he needs the money," Snowy replied.

Chapter 61

Since learning about Old Man Butcher's suicide Philip had spent the best part of a week attempting to unravel how he felt about the event itself and his own mortality. His biggest concern stemmed from not being able to understand why he felt the way he did. Numbness had taken root, pitched a tent and set up camp and as yet, nothing was getting through.

The detention he had received on Friday morning in his history lesson for failing to do his work or to put it another way, for staring aimlessly out of the window, had itself failed to provoke any sort of emotion. When this detention was coupled with the one he had received the previous morning for being late, he would have expected some sort of emotional response. However, Philip remained unmoved. The two detentions had resulted in Philip receiving a conduct card for the week ahead and a lecture from Mr Spencer on Monday morning, yet the numbness remained and batted away every word of Mr Spencer's speech.

Most surprisingly, Saturday's 3-0 victory over Coventry City, with goals from Billy Bremner, Allan Clarke and Joe Jordan had also failed to break through the barricades. Paul McBride had been left quite stunned, shell-shocked even, when Philip appeared to pass up the chance to gloat and rub his nose in the dirt of defeat as they had collected their papers on Saturday evening. The goal fest that same evening on 'Match of the Day', with Liverpool's four-two victory over Ipswich Town and Newcastle United's three-two victory over Manchester United, had also failed to fire a flaming arrow into the camp. A Leeds United victory along with a Manchester United defeat would normally result in an extremely iced cake, figuratively speaking, but not on this occasion. It was a similar story when watching 'Star Soccer' the following day. Even his favourite Sunday evening treat of cold Yorkshire pudding smothered with strawberry jam only produced the briefest of smiles in his mother's direction.

More football matches were forced to lick their wounds in defeat on Tuesday evening when 'Sportsnight' aired highlights of the evening's league cup fourth round fixtures. Coventry City had bounced back from their weekend defeat with a two-one victory over Stoke City and Plymouth Argyle had secured a surprise win at Queens Park Rangers by three goals to nil.

By the time Philip sat down on Wednesday evening to watch an episode of 'Steptoe & Son', he had already collected two unsatisfactory signatures on his conduct card. This was enough for another card and a caning when he came to hand it in the following Monday morning. One more unsatisfactory signature and the card would have to go in the wash or the dog, if he had one. He had also skipped swimming training on Wednesday evening. He had decided after completing his paper round that he just simply couldn't face it. However towards the end of Wednesday evening there was a slight chink of light that was just about visible to the naked eye. It only lasted a short while but he found himself paying full attention to an interview with Ray Harryhausen on 'Film 73' as the animator discussed such films as 'Jason and the Argonauts' and 'The Golden Voyage of Sinbad'.

The letter that was waiting for him when he arrived home on Thursday seized upon the opportunity, seized upon this slightly positive upturn, chink of light, gap in the circle and managed to punctuate the numbness. With warmth now flowing through his body like the boy in the Ready Brek commercial, he took the letter upstairs and placed in on the dresser, next to Old Man Butcher's picture in readiness for when he returned from his round.

As he approached the newsagents some twenty minutes later, Paul Mc Bride was there to meet him. Once Philip was within range, Paul thrust a folded piece of paper in his direction.

"Here you go," Paul said. "Plenty on there, some good earners too, if you're brave enough."

Philip took hold of the piece of paper and dropped it into his paper bag. "I'll look later," he said.

"Can you get hold of another one of those barometers?" Paul asked. "My Nan's friend really likes it and now she wants one."

"Shouldn't think so," Philip replied. "That was a bit of a one off."

"Yeah okay," Paul replied with an air of disappointment in his voice before he added, "Yeah, you need to be careful this time of year, the floor walkers are out in force as Bobby Cowley found out on Saturday. The fat twat."

"Why, what happened?"

"Got caught didn't he. His own fault, trying to steal some ladies leather gloves in Owen Owen. Everybody knows a fourteen year old boy cannot hang about for too long in the ladies section of a store like that. To make matters worse, he got greedy. He had the gloves but went in for another pair and some sort of make-up thing with a mirror in it. As he tried to leave, two floor walkers bundled him back into the store. Twenty minutes later the police were carting him off to Little Park Street. Took a statement then chucked him in the cells for three hours until his mum came to collect him."

"I bet she was happy," Philip said.

"Not really, the gloves were for her."

For the first time since the death of Old Man Butcher, Philip found himself laughing. "I take it the gloves are still on the list," he said as he wiped a tear from his eye.

"No, they were never on it. It was a purely private arrangement. His dad had given him two pounds to buy his mum something for her birthday and fat Bobby saw an opportunity to pocket the cash and spend it on getting even fatter in the Wimpy. Anyway, I'd better get going. Let me know when you have something for me."

Paul set off on his round, leaving Philip to push open the newsagent's door, head inside and collect his papers. Philip left the shop a few minutes later with his papers securely placed inside his bag and a Cadbury's Amazin Raisin Bar securely placed in his coat pocket. He made his way from street to street, close to close and house to house as darkness set in.

Due to entering Monkswood Crescent from Henley Road when he came home from school, he hadn't noticed what had happened at Old Man Butcher's house, had only been visible from the side. But upon returning from the opposite end, off Winston Avenue, he was now able to see that all the windows and the front door had been boarded up. He stood and stared at the house whilst eating his stolen bar of chocolate. As he did so, he slowly came to realise what it was that had been troubling him, what the feeling was that he had been unable to shift or explain for the past week. It was guilt, guilt about his own contribution, however small or insignificant, towards the old man's unhappiness. He started to think about the times he and his friends had tormented the old man, played tricks on him, called him names and accused him of terrible crimes. He didn't just think about his actions but he thought about the kids that had gone before him and the kids that had gone before them.

He stared to fumble inside the pockets of his coat until he was able to retrieve a small pencil that he had acquired during a recent visit to the betting shop on Hilmorton Road. He walked up to the front door and upon the protective wooden barrier, he simply wrote the word 'sorry'. He returned the pencil to one of his coat pockets and went home. He immediately went upstairs to his room and picked up his letter. He also picked up the photograph as he climbed onto his bed. Using his feet as levers, he removed his shoes and let them fall to the floor. He opened his letter.

My Good Friend Philip,

Oh my! Your first competition and you have manged to achieve a club record swim! Well done. Although your swim was part of a relay swim and therefore does not count as an individual club record, it is certainly a fine platform to launch yourself from, in readiness for your next meet. I think it was a great achievement, especially when you take into consideration how you actually performed in your individual event. It just goes to show that an athlete cannot always perform to their best. As with football, it really can be a game of two halves and you will always get the opportunity to put a bad performance behind you. Remember though, poor performances are equally important and valid in the development of an athlete. It is these performances that push us to work harder and to strive to do better.

I am sure that your parents were immensely proud of your achievements and I look forward to hearing about further successes. Winston Churchill once said 'Success is not final, failure is not fatal. It is the courage to continue that counts', and you certainly showed that you had the courage to continue.

A sportsman always remembers their first competition or their first game, their first fight or their first race and for it to be a triumph makes it taste so much sweeter. When you look back on your life it is something that stays with you, like your first date or your first kiss. I certainly remember my first game for Leeds, 23rd January 1960. I hadn't long turned seventeen. We were away at Stamford Bridge against Chelsea. I think I did well. It was a heavy pitch, cut up and full of divots as you would expect at that time of year. It certainly wasn't a good pitch for passing which as you know, is a big part of my game. However, we managed to win the match three-one.

I still have the cutting from the Yorkshire Evening Post. The reporter, Phil Brown, wrote that I showed enthusiasm, guts and intelligence. My mother, as I recall, had a tear in her eye as she read the article. My first goal came against Birmingham City, on the 9th March 1960. We were at home and it was a three-three draw. My goal was a bit scrappy and certainly wouldn't live long in anybody else's memory but they all count and that is what counts. But it wasn't all plain sailing. It was difficult to hold down a regular first team place.

I was still quite raw and still learning the game. We were relegated that season, which hurt. It hurt a lot, if I am truly honest, as I am sure it hurts for every player who has experienced relegation. However, I remembered the words of Winston Churchill and Maya Angelou, an American poet who wrote, 'You will face many defeats in life but never let yourself be defeated'.

Hibs put an offer in for me the following season. At the time I would have been happy to go, as it would have meant returning to Scotland, something I would have been happy to do. But the new boss, Don, rejected the offer. He also moved me from outside right to the centre of midfield and by the time I was twenty, I had found my place in the team. We were promoted the following season and now here we are. Sixteen games played, twelve wins, four draws and two clean sheets in a row. I have to say, I agree with your analysis and feel that the nil-nil result at Burnley was indeed a good result and as you pointed out, they are unbeaten at home this season and have only lost twice on their travels. However, although no game is easy and we don't have the right to simply turn up to win, we would have been disappointed to drop points against Coventry City. Though they do have some good players in their team, including a few fellow Scots, like Tommy Hutchinson and Colin Stein, we were pleased with both the performance and the result. Your letters continue to be a great help to me and a source of inspiration as the pressure continues to build. Each undefeated game allows us to stay ahead of the other teams but also adds a bit more pressure, but with it an incentive to take into the next game. Talking of our next game, it is another tricky away fixture against Derby County, another team with a pair of tough tackling Scots in midfield in Archie Gemmell and John McGovern. Then we have Q.P.R, Ipswich Town and Chelsea, all before Christmas. If we are still unbeaten by the time Santa gets here, then we will be in great shape.

I notice that your next swim meet is not until the New Year. Keep working hard though Philip and be prepared to go for that individual record. Hopefully I will hear from you again soon; as I said, your letters do mean a lot. Give my best to all your family, especially your mother.

Your Friend,
Billy.

After a second reading of the letter, Philip carefully folded it, put it back in the envelope and slipped it equally as carefully, under his pillow. He then removed from the back pocket of his flared jeans the folded piece of paper Paul Mc Bride had handed to him outside the newsagents. It was the longest list to date and it read, in no particular logical order;

Spice rack, oven gloves, fondue set, Charlie perfume, Kodak instant camera, Remington shaver, Boxes of chocolates (any will do), men's slippers (size nine), Alba radio, horse brass, glass fruit bowl, brass candlesticks, Morphy Richards door chime kit, Roy Orbison L.P., Elvis Presley L.P., Country and Western L.P., Phillips cassette player, Watches (men's, ladies, kids), Lighters (good quality), Sparklets beer tap, kitchen wall clocks, kitchen utensils, tool kits, foot pumps, torches, air-bed (single), Tonka toys, Yahtzee, Risk, Merry Milkman, Subuteo.

Philip shook his head and let out a deep breath as he finally reached the end of the list. He folded the piece of paper and placed it carefully under his pillow. As he did so, he heard his mother call up from the bottom of the stairs, informing him that his tea was ready. With a final check that the items under his pillow were still there, he climbed off his bed, placed the photograph back in its location and made his way downstairs.

Chapter 62

As he stood in Mr Spencer's office on a grey and overcast Monday morning, and despite the fact that he had just handed over a conduct card with two unsatisfactory signatures displayed upon it, Philip could not help but embrace the warm glow of normality he was currently feeling and the ups and downs that went with it. He had accepted that the two unsatisfactory signatures were merely par for the course and although he knew only too well, the implications of such a card, he was more than happy to accept and even embrace this normal state of affairs.

The weekend had had its fair share of highs and lows as well as some non-descript moments that had landed somewhere in-between. Leeds remained unbeaten and kept their third clean sheet in a row but had only managed a goalless draw at Derby County. Hartlepool were knocked out of the F.A.Cup in the first round, away to non-league Altringham, by a score of two goals to nil. Francis however appeared not to be too perturbed by the loss, due to being pickled in beer and having a small win on the horses earlier in the afternoon. That evening, he had happily removed a pound note from his pocket and sent Philip to the chip shop.

The downside to this was the fact that Philip's mother had not felt strong enough to cook tea. Her mood had unfortunately spiralled downwards late on Friday afternoon and when Philip and James had left for school on Monday morning, their mother was still a victim of her depression and still in her bed. As Francis could not cook even the most basic of meals and as he was also quite inebriated, the chip shop was the only solution.

The highs and lows of normality continued to roll in and out like an ocean tide for the rest of the weekend. A chippy tea had been followed by a bowl of rice pudding with a fine amount of sugar sprinkled on the top. The lowest point had occurred around midnight on Saturday evening. Philip was just drifting towards the land of nod when he realised that the loud voices he could hear were coming from his parents' bedroom and were not part of his dream. As he lay in the darkness with his eyes wide open, he could feel the anger in his father's voice as it seeped through the wall and into the room. He could also sense through the tone and pace of the voice that it was predominantly the alcohol that was doing most of the talking.

Although the heated exchange seemed quite short, it certainly didn't demonstrate any aspects that could be considered sweet. It concluded with a loud shout from Philp's mother of, 'get out, you're drunk, get away from me'. This was followed by a brief commotion and then the sound of a door slamming and footsteps descending the stairs. The slamming had also stirred James from his sleep.

"What was that?" he asked.

"It was nothing James, go back to sleep," Philip replied.

Sunday had been a similar sort of day, a pick 'n' mix affair with another random selection of ups and downs. After advising James to stay in bed, Philip had tip-toed around the house, getting ready for his paper round and swimming training, so as not to wake his dad, who was still sleeping off the night before on the sofa. The swimming session went reasonably well and he spent the majority of it working on his turns, with his coach continually reminding him that they were just as important as the swim itself.

Upon returning home, he discovered that the sofa was empty but the all too familiar odour remained. He left the back door open in an attempt to coax some more acceptable air into the room. He didn't see

Francis again until the following morning, when he discovered him back on the sofa, as he entered the living room to get ready for his paper round.

The rest of Sunday had been spent mostly outside. Both Philip and James played with the usual group of friends. A few games of headers and volleys, kerby and hot rice filled the majority of the afternoon. He took care of James; made them both some tea, made sure that they both had a bath, and made his mother a few cups of coffee which were left to go cold at the side of her bed. The cheese and pickle sandwich also remained untouched. However the weekend did finish with a positive note. As there wasn't anybody around to pack them off to bed, Philip and James stayed up a bit later than they would normally have been allowed to and watched 'Morecambe and Wise' on 'BBC2'.

"Two unsatisfactory signatures," Mr Spencer began. "One more and it would have been either the washing machine or the dog," he added as he looked over the top of the card and directly at Philip.

"We still haven't got a dog," Philip replied.

"Oh yes. I recall you sharing that piece of information on a previous visit."

Philip chose not to reply.

"We seem to be on a downward trajectory here, slipping back into old ways, don't we Knott?"

Philip knew that Mr Spencer wasn't really referring to both parties in the room but again he opted to choose the fifth and remain silent, hoping that if a statement could be rhetorical, then this was such a statement. Philip appeared to be correct in his assumption that the statement was indeed rhetorical; however the follow up question, or rather questions, were clearly designed to require some sort of answer.

"Any reason for this? Anything specific that has resulted in you opting to make such bad decisions? Anything at all that can go some way towards explaining why we are back here again?"

"It was just a bad week sir," Philip muttered.

"Oh, I see, a bad week. So you are claiming that this is nothing more than a blip, a one off, rather than a return to normal."

Philip looked at Mr Spencer, and then he tilted his head to look at the floor. "I'm not sure I know what normal is at the moment sir. One day I think I do, then the next day..." Philip stopped talking and shrugged his shoulders in an attempt to visually explain how he felt.

Mr Spencer handed Philip a fresh, unblemished conduct card. "Is everything okay at home?" He asked as Philip took hold of the card.

Philip shrugged his shoulders again. "The same as normal, I guess," he replied as he placed the card in his blazer pocket.

"The swimming going okay?"

Philip nodded. "Fine," he replied.

"Good. Then if there is nothing else you want to discuss, I suggest that you wait outside and send the next one in."

Philip picked up his bag and stepped outside of the office. He tapped a boy on the shoulder and signalled for him to go inside. He didn't recognise the boy but he looked at least one, maybe two years younger. The boy had a deeply troubled expression on his face and through his body language and pace of movement gave the impression that this was his first such visit.

"I bet he wets himself," one of the boys sitting opposite said as the younger boy disappeared inside the office.

Philip sat in the space that had just been created and looked across at the boys sitting opposite. Together in a row were Brian Mason, Chris Burns and Tank. They acknowledged each other with a brief nod of the head and simultaneous raising of the eyebrows.

"I bet he wets himself," Brian Mason said again. "Any takers?" he added.

Due to the faint sound of sobbing that could now be heard coming from Mr Spencer's office, surprisingly enough, there were no takers.

"Haven't seen you for a while," Brian said.

"No," Philip replied. "A run of good fortune, I guess."

"I heard that it was because you were teacher's pet, even got your own private swimming pool."

"Not exactly," Philip replied. Eager to try and change the subject, he looked at Chris Burns. "What you in for Chris? Singing again?"

Chris nodded.

"What song this time?"

"Crocodile Rock," Chris replied. "In general science."

"What about you Tank?"

"He's going for the record," Brian interrupted. "Ain't ya Tank?"

Tank smiled.

"Five Unsatisfactorie's last week."

"Five! That's three on each for sure!" Philip replied.

"And four the week before and four the week before that. At this rate he'll be on a conduct card until he's thirty-four, won't ya Tank?"

Tank just laughed.

"What about you?" Philip asked Brian.

"Fit up, absolute fit up. Old Bennet reckons he caught me extracting dinner money from some first years. Just because the kid was upside down in the toilets with money falling out of his pockets."

Tank laughed again.

As the laughter subsided, the office door swung open. The younger boy, still sobbing, stepped out, followed by Mr Spencer, carrying his cane. The young boy looked directly at Brian and winked at him as he wiped his nose with the back of his hand. To the amazement of the other boys present, he then turned and left.

"Come on then. I haven't got all day, whose first?" Mr Spencer said with a voice that filled the whole space.

Tank stood up and stepped forward.

"Full house for you, isn't it lad?"

"I guess so," Tank replied.

"Knowing you lad, by the time you get your first Unsatisfactory signature of the week, your hands will still be throbbing. And before you say anything Mason, it is nothing to be proud of."

Tank held out his hand. Mr Spencer gently rested his cane across the palm of tank's hand. Lining it up, Mr Spencer adjusted his position a little, like a new batsman that had just arrived at the crease. Once happy with his starting position, Mr Spencer raised his arm and the cane went with it. Then with much more ferocity came the descent as the thin strip of wood crashed into Tank's soft white palm.

For valour, for honour, for the sake of schoolchildren across the land, Tank tried to stand firm, stand tall, but as the fourth stroke struck, he buckled. As the fifth stroke came crashing down upon its target, Tank began to sniff and sob gently. There was no shame to be found here, just a defeated boy. Once it was over and with tears rolling down his cheeks, Tank sat down, his hands tightly clasped together.

Philip went next. As he was only receiving one stroke on each hand and after witnessing what happened to tank, he knew that he had to stand firm. He didn't flinch. In fact, rather perversely, it felt quite normal. Once all of the punishment had been dished out to all of the recipients and Mr Spencer had delivered his well-trodden speech about lessons being learnt, the boys were allowed to leave.

"Same time next week Sir," Brian Mason said as he stood up.

"Although I am quite sure you can, I however, fail to find any humour in that statement. The sad fact of the matter is you are probably correct," Mr Spencer replied as he returned to his office.

Both Philip and his conduct card managed to reach the end of the school day unscathed. A perfect set of satisfactory signatures had been emblazed upon day one of the gleaming white piece of card. Unfortunately the same could not be said for Tank, who was already halfway towards having a treat for his dog.

Philip and James arrived home to find Francis sitting at the dining table smoking a cigarette. As the boys entered, he stubbed his cigarette out, stood up and walked towards them. He asked them both to sit down on the sofa.

"Nothing to worry about," Francis began. "But your mum won't be around for a few days."

"What's up?" Philip asked.

"Like I say, it is nothing for you to worry about but your granddad is a bit poorly and your mum has just gone to look after him for a while. She left straight after her hospital appointment this morning."

Upon hearing this news, James got up from the sofa and made his way upstairs.

"You alright son?" Francis called out.

James didn't reply.

"He'll be alright dad, he just likes having mum around."

When it came to extended family, Philip, Grace and James had only really known their grandad on their mother's side. Francis's parents had both passed away within the space of eight months when Philip was quite young and James was just a baby. They never knew their mother's mother as she left when their mother was a young girl. They had some relatives up north but very rarely heard from them or of them.

"When you get back from your paper round, make you and your brother something to eat," Francis said. "There is plenty in the kitchen and some fish fingers and burgers in the freezer. Call in and see your sister on your round and let her know. Ask her to come and keep an eye on you from time to time when I'm at work, and no staying up late."

Philip nodded.

"Right, I need to get ready for work." Francis concluded as he disappeared into the kitchen.

Before setting off for his paper round, Philip changed out of his school uniform and checked that James was okay. By the time he left the house, James had come downstairs and was watching Blue Peter.

Approximately thirty minutes later Philip entered Clennon Rise and headed up the stairs, towards Grace's flat. As he approached the door, he discovered Grace standing in the hallway, waiting to meet him.

"Grandad's not well," Philip said.

"Grandad's fine," Grace replied.

"But dad just told us that mum has gone to look after him."

"Is that what he said?"

"Yes," Philip replied with a confused expression clearly visible upon his face.

"What happened on Saturday night?" Grace asked. "You are supposed to be looking out for mum."

"I do my best," Philip replied after first swapping his confused expression for an annoyed one.

"Yeah well, mum came to see me at Woolworth's this morning. She had a swollen lip with a small cut on it. She wouldn't tell me how it happened exactly but how many guesses would you like? Anyway, she did mention a row on Saturday night and that she needed to get away for a while and was going to stay with grandad. She told me to give you this." Grace handed three one-pound notes over to Philip. "I guess she didn't trust dad to give it to you. It's for emergencies. If you need any more, you will have to let me know."

"No, I should be okay, Paul McBride owes me a bit."

"Mum also asked me to come and help you out but I don't want to bump in to dad. What time does he leave for work?"

"About six. The same time as he has always done," Philip replied.

Grace glanced at her watch. "Yeah okay, I'll come over about six thirty."

Grace turned away and went to go back inside. Philip descended the stairs. Just as he was about to exit the building he heard Grace call out.

"And tell James to keep out of his way, but don't tell him the truth."

Chapter 63

"We're on," Snowy said as Francis reached the table and placed his drink down.

"Say again?"

"We're on Francis; the job, it's this week."

"Oh right," Francis replied as he nodded his head. "That will explain it."

"Explain what?"

"Explain why Lousy is sitting there looking like a chicken that has just walked into a foxes' convention."

Lousy was perched on the edge of his seat with his palms busily sliding up and down the top of his thighs. His eyes were equally busy, as they darted around the room, pausing every now and again if they landed on something that didn't seem quite right.

"Do you write your own material Francis?" Snowy asked before adding as Francis sat down, "He wants to see you tomorrow night."

"Who wants to see me?"

"Our man in Rochdale, who do you think. It appears that you make him nervous Francis. He doesn't like you."

"He doesn't like anybody Snowy."

"Yeah well, that may be so but for whatever reason, he especially doesn't like you."

"What can I say?" Francis replied with a grin on his face as he reached for his drink.

"You can say all the right things Francis, that's what you can say.

You can smile when you need to smile. Laugh at the man's jokes. Do whatever you need to do to keep him happy and keep him sweet."

"I'll take him to the pictures if you like."

"Can't help yourself, can you Francis?" Lousy said. "You're making a lot of people nervous, a lot of people, people who have a lot riding on this and have a lot more to lose than you."

"Oh is that right. And exactly what have you got to lose Lousy? I thought you had already lost it all when the wife pissed off and left you with no more than a souvenir mug and a deck chair."

Snowy grabbed hold of his silver Rowenta lighter and slammed it down on the table with enough force to grab a room full of attention that he didn't want. After patiently waiting for the rest of the crowded bar to return to their own affairs, he glared at Francis, then at Lousy. "Gentlemen, may I remind you both that if this goes belly up, it goes belly up for all of us, we'll all be out of work and guess what, that will be the least of our worries."

"I was under the impression I had an alibi," Francis said before taking a rather large gulp pf beer from his glass.

Snowy smiled. "You have a story to tell the police," he replied. "But if they tumble that this was an inside job and they start digging around, then your story will fall apart quicker than a Liz Taylor marriage."

"Oh right, now you tell me."

"Tell you what Francis? What have I just told you that you didn't already know? We have already been down this well-trodden path. You weighed it all up yourself, risk on one side, reward on the other side, remember. Nobody's forced you into this, nothing's changed."

"And when exactly will I get my reward?" Francis asked.

"When we get paid, you get paid." Right now however, your only concern is making sure you are in that lorry park by 10pm tomorrow night." Snowy finished his drink before standing up, still clutching his now empty glass. "Let's drink to more productive times." he said. "Francis, bitter?"

Francis nodded.

"Same again Lousy?"

Lousy nodded.

"A whisky chaser on the side, eh lads. A toast to future success," Snowy added as he set off towards the bar.

By the time Francis arrived for work on a soggy Monday evening, the alcohol he had consumed during the two sessions on Sunday was still sloshing around in his system, like the ocean on a stormy day. His head felt as clogged as a disused drain and his mouth was as dry as a bag of bird seed. He clambered into his cab and placed a small bag containing his flask of tea and cheese sandwiches on the passenger seat before he closed the cab door. As he reached inside his overalls pocket for his cigarettes the passenger door swung open and Snowy climbed inside.

"Not looking good," Snowy muttered as he shook the glistening drops of rainwater from his hair.

"What's not?" Francis replied with an obvious amount of concern in his voice.

"The country Francis, the country. These soddin miners know when to put a spanner in the works don't they? An oil crisis, fuel prices rising, economy on its knees, we are all struggling to make ends meet and the bloody miners want a seven percent pay rise. Mark my words Francis, it won't be long before the whole bloody country is forced out of business."

Due to a combination of not giving a damn about the current political landscape or the state of the country and not feeling anywhere near his best, Francis immediately acquired an uninterested expression which, for effect, was accompanied by an equally uninterested shake of the head.

"Listen Francis, for whatever reason, you may not choose to notice and you may be happy to live in your own little world but there's a lot of discontent in this green and pleasant land at present and it's going to get a lot worse before it gets better. There are dark days ahead. That is why we need this job. Without it, without the opportunity to have something in reserve, there could be several long months ahead of us."

Snowy removed a sealed brown envelope from his pocket and placed it down next to Francis.

"What's this?" Francis asked.

"An inventory, a list of what will be on the back of the lorry on Wednesday night. Give it to our man in the north when you get there tonight. It is so he can keep an eye on things, check that nothing goes missing."

"I thought it was all going missing."

"Yeah well, we just want to make sure that what goes missing doesn't go missing after it has gone missing."

"Are you sure we can trust him?" Francis asked as he picked up the envelope, folded it carefully in his lap and slipped it into his overalls pocket.

"No, I'm not," Snowy replied as he reached for the handle to open the door. "But that makes no difference either way, because, A, we are stuck with him and B, I don't trust anybody. Don't be late Francis and don't do anything to upset Bradbury, okay?"

Snowy clambered down from the cab and slammed the door shut. Francis calmly lit a cigarette and casually sat in his cab and smoked it. This was partly because he needed it in the hope that it would make him feel a bit better but a slightly bigger part of him just wanted to annoy Snowy. A few minutes later, after finishing his cigarette and with Snowy watching from the entrance to the depot building, he started his engine and drove the lorry out of the yard.

The Journey north was trouble free and uneventful. Realising that he was making good time and with an irresistible desire to arrive late, Francis pulled off the M6 and into Knutsford Services just after 8.30pm. Francis parked up, stepped down from the cab and stretched. He was greeted by the cold evening air, which happened to feel very refreshing as it rested upon his skin and journeyed through his hair. He walked across the lorry park and into the main services building. Once inside he headed in the direction of the cafeteria.

"What can I get you love?" The lady said as Francis reached the cafeteria counter.

"A bacon sandwich and a mug of tea please love," Francis replied.

"That will be thirty pence sweetheart. I'll bring it over when it's ready."

Francis smiled, said thank you, handed over the correct amount of money and went to find a seat. His mug of tea arrived first, quickly followed by a hot bacon sandwich. After calculating what time he needed to leave in order to be around twenty minutes late, he ate his sandwich, drank his tea and smoked a cigarette. He made a quick visit to the gents on his way out. He climbed back into his cab and exited the services at exactly twenty past nine. An hour later he arrived at the lorry park. He followed his instructions and drove over to the far corner, swung the lorry around, reversed into position, stopped and switched off the engine. No sooner had the engine fallen silent than the passenger door swung open and Douglas Bradbury attempted to clamber inside.

"You should have been here at 10 o' clock." He said upon finally reaching the passenger seat.

"Why, what happened?" Francis replied.

A response that was rewarded with an immediate cold stare. "Don't try and get smart with me. Who do you think you are?" Bradbury said.

"I know exactly who I am and I don't recall inviting you into my cab."

"What?" Bradbury replied with an anger in his voice that was more apparent than flees on a stray dog. "Do you know who you are talking to?"

Francis sighed. "Bloody twenty questions now," he said before adding, "I know exactly who I am talking to. I'm talking to a fat, greedy, northern asshole who thinks he has the right to treat people like shit. Now say what you have to say, then get your fat ugly arse out of my cab."

Bradbury was momentarily lost for words. The rage within him rushed to the surface. His face turned red, beads of sweat formed within the creases on his forehead as if to order. "You what?" he roared. "You're a nothing, a nobody, if it wasn't for me, you'd be in the gutter somewhere. You ever speak to me like that again and I'll kill ya."

"No you won't, you'll get somebody else to do it," Francis replied. "People like you don't get their own hands dirty."

"You need to tread carefully, wouldn't want that blow to the head causing any lasting damage."

"Yes, I see your point. It might affect my ability to think straight when I'm giving a statement to the police."

"Providing you are able to give a statement that is."

"All I've heard since you climbed into my cab, uninvited may I add, is empty threats and a load of hot air. Say what you need to say," Francis said as he handed over the brown envelope.

Bradbury reached for the envelope. "You just make sure that you are here on time on Wednesday night."

"And how do you propose I do that?"

"I don't care how you do it. You just make sure you are here by 10pm. Park in the same spot as tonight. They'll be a space between two transits. Then sit and wait for the signal."

"What's the signal?"

"You'll hear somebody bang on the back of the trailer. That will be your signal to go and investigate. Make sure that you leave your flask open and a sandwich half eaten in the cab. It will look more believable when the law arrives."

"Is that it?" Francis asked.

"Yeah, that is about it."

"Okay, great, thanks for telling me everything I already knew."

"Oh well there is one more thing, one more thing that I am sure you didn't know. Once this job is over, I can assure you that you will be looking for a different employer."

Francis reached for his cigarettes as he turned to look directly at Bradbury. "And I can assure you that if you are not out of my cab in ten seconds flat, I'm going to drag you out. Now piss off," he replied.

Chapter 64

"You have got to be joking, tell me you're joking. Tell me it didn't happen, Tell me I had a bad dream. Tell me you didn't call Douglas Bradbury a fat greedy asshole. Tell me I didn't get a phone call this morning." Snowy was looking up at the heavens and frantically waving his arms in the air as he spoke, as if he was re-enacting a scene from 'The Birds'. He had been waiting by the entrance to the yard for Francis to arrive, pacing up and down like an expectant father outside a delivery room. The moment Francis had driven past and into the yard, Snowy had marched over to the car, swinging the driver's door open as soon as the car had come to a stop. He had launched into his angry rant even before Francis had managed to switch the engine off. As Snowy continued, Francis simply sat in the driver's seat and stared straight ahead.

"Why? Why? All you had to do was be nice, smile, shake his hand, nod your head. But no, not you Francis, not you. Lousy went ballistic! I thought he was going to have a heart attack."

"In that case Snowy, I strongly advise that you make sure he's sitting down the next time you speak to him."

"Why is that Francis?" Snowy asked with a tone in his voice that indicated both intrigue and concern.

Francis tilted his head forward a little and peered through his windscreen at the nights sky just as soft white flecks of snow began to tumble gently towards the ground. "Because the deal is off unless I get half the money up front," he said.

Snowy stepped forward and filled the empty space created by the car door being open, leaning inches away from Francis as he spoke. "Now I know you are joking. You must be joking. I think your act needs some more work though; cannot see that particular gag getting many laughs."

Francis spun around in his seat, causing Snowy to momentarily stumble backwards. Francis climbed out of the car, slammed the door shut and stared hard at Snowy. "You've got it wrong. This will bring the house down Snowy. This is my big finish. You've got until tomorrow night. Either I get two hundred and fifty quid or I drive the lorry straight to the depot. And you can tell that piece of shit in Rochdale he'll be looking for more than gainful employment if he threatens me again. He'll be looking for his head, which he'll find shoved up his arse."

"I can't get hold of that kind of money by tomorrow night! Be reasonable Francis. I told you; you get paid when we get paid."

"Not anymore Snowy. Of course you can always find somebody else to drive the lorry. Perhaps Lousy can do it. That will be just fine with me. And if I get anymore shit from you or that arsehole in Rochdale, the price goes up."

The two men stood toe to toe in the yard, leaving just enough space between them for a snowflake or two to dissolve. The flakes themselves were now picking up pace and were falling thicker and faster.

"Why now Francis? I don't get it. Why cause all this trouble now, when we are so close? We get the job done, we wait a short while, everybody gets paid and everybody has a merry Christmas."

"I'll tell you why Snowy. Because I don't trust that twat in Rochdale. I don't trust him to pay up. I don't trust you either. I don't trust you to do something about it when he doesn't pay up. You haven't got a backbone. I'm amazed that you can even stand up. And what exactly do you mean by 'we get the job done'. What exactly will you be doing tomorrow night? I'll tell you what you'll be doing. You'll be sitting at home watching the football highlights on 'Sportsnight', sitting nice and cosy in your slippers, patting the dog on the head whilst the Mrs fetches you a nice ham sandwich and a couple of pickled onions for your supper. Meanwhile, I'm getting a blow to the head and several long hours in the back of a freezing lorry, followed by a trip to the hospital and a grilling from the law. So here's your options, you drive the lorry and I'll phone in sick, or somebody else drives the lorry and I still phone in sick, or you can be here this time tomorrow night with two hundred and fifty pounds in your pocket. And if Lousy ain't happy, then it will save me the trouble of having to wipe the smile off his face. If I haven't heard from you by 6pm tomorrow night, I won't be here."

"This isn't going to go down well Francis." Snowy replied before adding, "You are going to make a lot of people unhappy and what happens if none of these options are acceptable?"

Francis turned away, opened the back door of his car and reached inside to retrieve his flask and his sandwiches. He closed the door, locked his car and turned back to face Snowy. "Six o'clock tomorrow," he repeated.

"Francis! Be reasonable! What if I can't get the money?"

"Then somebody else drives the lorry."

"But I cannot get somebody else to drive the lorry, not just like that."

"Then you drive the lorry."

"I'll tell you something for nothing Francis, this is the end of the road for you. Once this is done, you are out of a job."

"What, you are going to sack an employee who has just been hijacked, assaulted and left to rot in the back of a freezing lorry. That's not going to paint a nice pretty picture for the law to stick on their fridge."

"I think you will find that you have unfortunately been made redundant Francis; economic climate and all that."

Francis smiled, he knew that Snowy's threat lacked bite. "Not before we have discussed severance pay. They'll be a price to pay for me to go away Snowy and if you refuse to pay it, then we all go away."

Francis turned away and walked towards his lorry, leaving Snowy standing in the yard, with the snow tumbling down and resting gently upon his exposed head and rigid torso.

Chapter 65

Philip and James arrived home from school on Wednesday afternoon just in time to watch an episode of 'Pixie and Dixie'. Whenever Philip watched 'Pixie and Dixie', he always wondered why Pixie chose to wear nothing but a blue bow tie and why Dixie had opted for a small red waistcoat without buttons. As the episode burst into life the boys could hear movement coming from upstairs. A short time later, as the show was reaching its climax, Francis could be heard descending the stairs. Moments later, he entered the living room.

"Good you're both here," Francis said. "Listen Philip, no swimming tonight, okay. I want you straight back here after you have done your paper round."

Philip attempted to muster up a protest to his father's request but he only got as far as 'but'.

"No buts, not tonight. I've asked your sister to come and stay tonight. Not sure what time I'll be back. If anybody comes calling for any reason, you just say that I went to work as normal okay, nothing more. I've asked your sister to come straight from work, she'll bring some fish and chips with her. Oh and there's a letter for you somewhere Philip, not sure where I put it, try the kitchen."

Francis turned away and headed back upstairs. "I'm going for a bath," he muttered as he disappeared out of the room.

Philip went in search of his letter. He found it lying on the kitchen table with a crisp golden brown ring from the bottom of a mug incrusted upon it. He took the letter upstairs, making a futile attempt to remove the debris from its surface as he went. He placed it under his pillow, changed out of his school uniform and then set off to complete his paper round.

Philip arrived home again just as the national news was starting on BBC1. His dad was in the kitchen, preparing his flask and sandwiches. James was lying on the settee, ignoring the television and reading 'Stig of the Dump'.

"Right, I'm away," Francis said as he appeared in the kitchen doorway. "Remember what I said, no swimming and don't leave the house. Your sister should be here with the fish and chips any time now. I'll see you both later."

As Francis departed via the scullery, Philip headed eagerly up the stairs and into his room, his paperbag still draped over his shoulder. He allowed the bag to fall onto the bedroom floor, climbed onto his bed and retrieved his letter from beneath his pillow. Still smarting and struggling to see past the tea stained ring on the front of the envelope, he carefully opened it and removed the contents.

My Dear Friend Philip,

How are you? A rather strange thing to ask you under the circumstances and to be honest, I probably know the answer already. It really is quite difficult to know what to say, what the right thing is to say? We are all different and we all deal with the issue of death in different ways. Death at the best of times, if there can be such a thing as the best of times, is never easy. But when it is under such sad and tragic circumstances, it becomes that much harder to address or comprehend. For a man in the twilight of his years to feel compelled to take his own life is truly a sad indictment of us all as a society. To feel so isolated, so lonely and in such depths of despair that taking your own life appears to be the more favourable option, is genuinely tragic.

However Philip, this is not of your doing; you mustn't feel bad or blame yourself for this. You say that you only knew your friend for a short amount of time. His reasoning and his decision to end his life would not have happened on the spur of the moment, or on a whim. This would have developed and formed over a much longer period of time, over many years of feeling isolated and alone, becoming more and more withdrawn and disconnected from the world around him.

You mentioned that he had no family, nobody close. Well, over the years this would surely take its toll and will have certainly affected his ability to think rationally. Yet to him, his final act, his final decision, would have felt entirely rational. You said that you have adhered to your friend's request and honoured his last wishes. Then I think lad that is all you can do now. You have done the right thing, you now need to let it go, learn from it, then file it away and move on. Just as we have to do as sportsmen, just as we had to do in the dressing room on Saturday after the game against QPR. We should have won but we were lucky not to lose. The playing conditions were certainly a leveller and the snow covering the pitch made it very difficult to execute the quick passing game that we like to adopt at home. When the pitch is both frozen and covered in snow, it becomes extremely difficult to predict what the ball is going to do. So upon reflection, if you had offered me a 2-2 draw at the start of the game, I would have been foolhardy not to accept it.

We were incredibly fortunate with the disallowed goal just before half-time. The Rangers players were incensed when they left the field of play and headed down the tunnel and I could understand why. Their mood certainly didn't improve much when I managed to find an equaliser right at the start of the second half. It is a big psychological hurdle to overcome when you feel you should be two-nil in front and you find yourself at one-one. To be honest with you, although we were fortunate to take the lead, when they went behind, I thought the job was done and we would see the game out. But when you have players of Stan Bowles's quality in your team, then you always have a chance and you always have hope of getting something from the game, as it proved when Stan himself grabbed the equaliser.

I have to admit, the atmosphere in the dressing room after the game wasn't the best. But we don't point fingers in this team, we don't apportion blame or highlight individual errors. We all make mistakes; we try to learn from them and move on as a group, as a team, towards the next game. However, we are still unbeaten after eighteen games and with no disrespect intended, we feel that we now have a run of winnable games upon the horizon, up to and including the Boxing Day fixture away at Newcastle.

You neglected to mention your swimming or your family in your letter. I hope that they are all well, especially your mother and your sister, as I know life has continued to be a struggle for them both lately. Is your sister still working at Woolworth's? Is she still looking to move out of her flat? And how is your mother coping at the moment? Returning to sport, how is the training going? Are your turns showing signs of improvement? I know that it is still a few weeks until your next important meet but the time between events can be the most crucial for any athlete. As we have discussed in the past, you will never meet a successful sportsman who hasn't prepared, then prepared, and then prepared some more. So do your best to make it to all of your sessions. I fully appreciate that at this time of year, due to the weather, this may not always be possible. But try to remember that a training session missed is an opportunity missed; an opportunity to improve has been missed.

Well, I had better sign off now Philip. Stay positive and stay strong for yourself and for your family. I look forward to hearing from you again soon.

Your friend,

Billy

Philip carefully folded the letter, returned it to its envelope and placed it under his pillow in preparation for a second read later. He headed back downstairs and set off for his paper round. He returned home just as Grace entered through the front door, carrying a bag of fish and chips.

"Is dad here?" Grace asked as she closed the door behind her.

"No, he's gone to work," Philip replied.

"Good," Grace said, before adding, "What's going on?"

"What do you mean?" Philip asked as they both made their way through the living room and into the kitchen.

Grace placed the bag down on the table and began to remove the individually wrapped bundles as Philip gathered up the plates, cutlery and other essential items such as the bread, butter and tomato sauce. The aroma from the fish and chips had filled the living room as the bag had passed through, causing James to raise his head out of his book and follow the trail into the kitchen. No sooner had James managed to get all of his body inside the kitchen than Philip thrust a selection of items in his direction.

"Here James, go and put these on the table."

Eager to eat his fish and chips, James did an immediate about turn and exited the kitchen carrying the items Philip had given him.

"Shut the door a minute," Grace said once satisfied that James was out of range to hear.

Philip closed the door as Grace continued.

"Something's up," Grace began. "Dad came to Woolies today, all on edge, like. I've never seen him like that before. You could tell something wasn't right. He was insisting I came and stayed tonight. Told me I had no choice, wouldn't leave until I agreed, even gave me the money for tea, wouldn't say why though, just said I needed to be here in case he wasn't back from work in the morning. Has he said anything to you?"

"No," Philip replied as he shook his head. "Just said that you were bringing tea and that you were staying the night. He did say I couldn't go swimming though and we had to stay in."

Grace continued to plate up the food whilst sporting a deeply troubled expression. Her concerns had caused Philip to revisit the conversation he had had with his father earlier that evening. This was a process that resulted in him inheriting his own uneasy feeling and as they left the kitchen, carrying three plates of fish, chips and mushy peas between them, they did so in silence.

Chapter 66

"I know it's not the full amount," Snowy muttered quietly, despite the fact that he and Francis were sitting at a secluded table in a deserted works canteen. He placed the envelope in front of Francis. "There's two hundred pounds there. As I said it's not quite half, not quite what you asked for but it was the best I could do. So it is up to you Francis, you can either take the money, get in your cab and do the job, or you can leave the money, go home and never show your face around here again."

"I thought I was going to be sacked anyway," Francis replied.

"Made redundant Francis, not sacked."

"Yeah well, we'll cross that out of court settlement when we get to it Snowy," Francis replied as he picked up the envelope and peered inside.

"I'm a bit lost Francis and before I get another one of your famous, oh so witty remarks, I am not speaking geographically. I am lost because I can't work out why. I can't work out why you have chosen this course of action, why you have chosen to go down this road and I'm speaking metaphorically. Everything was fine, all was going well, everybody benefitted and we looked out for each other."

Francis squeezed the envelope tightly in his hand as he glared intently at Snowy. "You what," he began. "Looking out for each other. You, people like you make me want to throw up. You don't look out for people, you do nothing of the sort. You use people. You, that arsehole in Rochdale and as for Lousy, he's the worst of all, he hides behind people, uses them to use others. As soon as George Meadows left, you had a vacancy to fill. 'We are looking for somebody to use', that's what the advert should have said. Lousy had everything and because of that, he thinks he can look down at people. Thinks he is more important, better than them. His miserable wife was just as bad as he is, sat on her fat arse all day, sipping sherry, painting her nails with her hair in curlers and flicking through the pages of a holiday brochure. Then as soon as she got tired of him, up sticks and takes the lot. Yeah we all know what she left behind. Now he's got his hand in the till, stealing from the company as if it was their fault that she left him." Francis took a short breath and attempted to continue but Snowy had heard enough.

"Oh I get it now. This isn't about Lousy or me, this is about you. This is a hard luck story. Wish you had said, I would have bought a clean hankie to wipe away the tears. Poor working class Francis, bottom rung of the ladder, feeling bitter because everybody else is higher up, achieved more, worth more, a better car, flock wallpaper in the hallway, a downstairs toilet. If your wife left you and took everything, it would probably take you the best part of a week to notice. I've had enough of this."

Snowy stood up and stepped towards Francis with his hand held out. "So what's it to be Francis, are you going home or are you driving the lorry?"

Despite only being inches apart, the silence between them reinforced the ever growing distance. Francis stood up and placed the envelope in his pocket.

"I thought as much," Snowy said. "You despise us but not quite enough to turn down the money. Or are you just being used but the offer was too good to turn down? Choose whatever one helps you to sleep better Francis but right now you're already running late and that lorry needs to be in Rochdale by 10pm."

Grace began to clear away the empty plates from the table. James had already returned to the settee and immersed himself in his book as Grace walked past, on her way to the kitchen.

"What you reading?" Grace asked.

"Stig of the Dump," James replied.

Grace stopped dead in her tracks. "Really?" she exclaimed. "That's one of my favourite books. Hold it up, let me see."

As requested, James held up the book.

"It is as well. It's my old copy. I pinched it from school. Where have you got to?"

"Stig and Barney have just stopped the robbers from getting away with the silver," James replied as he lowered the book again and carried on reading.

As Philip entered the kitchen, Grace was already running the water into the sink. I'll wash, you dry," Grace said.

Philip picked up the tea towel from the back of the chair and waited for the first soap sodden item to be sent in his direction.

"I know what you are going to say but I've decided I have to tell mum," Grace said as she dipped the first plate into the hot soapy water. As she removed it, she caught sight of a rigid, motionless Philip staring at her, as if he had just looked into the deep black eyes of a gorgon. Still holding the plate, Grace looked back at her brother. "What?" she exclaimed.

"What do you mean what? You know what."

Grace motioned forward a fraction and held the plate closer to Philip. "She's got a right to know."

"A right to know what exactly?" Philip replied as he finally relocated the ability to move and took hold of the plate.

"You know what," Grace said immediately. "About dad and about him and Karen."

Philip froze for the second time in as many minutes, causing a plate traffic jam as Grace removed the next gleaming, clean plate from the bowl and held it out. "And you have evidence of this, I take it? It wasn't that long ago that you didn't even believe me about Karen and now you want to tell mum that dad is one of her customers. Do you have any idea what this might do to mum? And have you stopped to think what dad might do? Have you actually stopped to think about this at all or are you just focused on dad and how much you hate him?"

"And have you stopped to think that dad might actually be the problem, the cause, the reason that mum is the way she is?"

"Oh I see," Philip replied as they both stood in the kitchen, holding a plate each. "That's your professional opinion is it, your diagnosis. So how long have you been Dr Upton?"

"Dr who?" Grace replied.

"No, not Dr Who, that's a different programme altogether. Dr Upton is from 'Doctor in the House.'"

Grace was still none the wiser and the expression on her face only helped to confirm her lack of knowledge of fictional television doctors.

"It doesn't matter," Philip said.

"Good. Then perhaps you can get on with the drying up or are you hoping that if I hold this plate for long enough it will dry itself?"

With serious annoyance now racing through his body, Philip finished drying the first plate before snatching the second one out of Grace's hand.

"Don't worry," Grace said. "I am not going to say anything until I have moved out."

"Oh that makes me feel so much better, waiting for you to decide when the bomb goes off".

"Stop being so melodramatic."

"Of course I am, there's nothing to worry about, I am sure it's an everyday conversation between mother and daughter. Hello mum, fancy a cup of tea, oh, by the way, your husband is paying for sex with a teenage prostitute, two sugars."

Grace was just about to reply when James peered around the kitchen door. "Can we play a game?" he said.

"What do you want to play?" Grace replied.

"I don't mind, Monopoly or Escalado," James said.

"Escalado," Philip replied. "I hate Monopoly, but I'm only playing until 'Sportsnight' starts."

Just off the M62 between Drub and Hightown is the small village of Cleckheaton. On the outskirts of Cleckheaton sits a small patch of land, attempting to disguise itself as a lorry park. Francis pulled in, parked up and switched the engine off. His lorry was the only lorry in the park. As all fell silent around him, he stared into the darkness for a moment before glancing down at his watch. He couldn't quite make out the time, so he switched the small cab light on. It was nine forty five. He was still twenty miles and thirty minutes away from the lorry park he was expected to be in by 10pm. 'Looks like I'm gonna be late' he muttered to himself as he lit a cigarette, before reaching up and switching the small cab light off again.

A cup of coffee, a cheese and onion sandwich, a curly wurly, a deep breath and another cigarette later, Francis restarted the engine and exited the lorry park. With every passing minute and with every passing mile, the tension in the cab edged a little bit closer to him, like a nervous teenager sitting on the sofa next to his date. As he approached the entrance to the lorry park, the tension had gripped so tightly he felt as if Kendo Nagasaki had got him in a headlock and was reaching out to tag Big Daddy, to finish him off. As he entered, a crumb of comfort was gleamed from the fact that the park was virtually deserted. He immediately spotted the two transit vans in the far right corner and swung the lorry in that direction. No sooner had the lorry come to a stop than his cigarette packet was once again in his hand. However, before he was able to light a cigarette, the driver's door of the cab swung open.

"Out fly boy."

With his unlit cigarette pressed firmly between his fingers, Francis turned his head and looked downwards. A thick set, tall, middle aged man with a bald head and well-formed moustache glared back at him.

"If you look at me for much longer, I'm gonna get the idea that you want to take me home to meet your mother. Now I know you heard what I said so why are you still sitting in that cab?"

Francis climbed down. As he did so, he heard the sound of the trailer doors opening.

"Turn around and put your hands up against the trailer."

"What?" Francis replied.

"Do I need to be writing this down? Just turn around and put your hands on the trailer."

"Why?"

"Because I'm going to search you, that's why."

Francis stepped a little closer to the man. "Are you sure you have enough light?" he said.

"You what, why should I need more light to search you?"

"You don't, but you'll need it to pick up your teeth when you've finished."

The man chuckled and a wry smile appeared upon his face. "Is that so?" he muttered, before turning towards the back of the lorry and calling out, into the darkness. No sooner had his words disappeared into the night than two even larger gentlemen appeared from behind the trailer and began to approach the pair.

"Oh I see," Francis muttered whilst he clenched his fists in preparation. "Need your little playmates do you?" He paused, and then he added once the two men were now to a scale of one to one. "What exactly are you looking for?"

"The money of course," the man replied.

"What money?"

"What money?" The man laughed a little and shrugged his shoulders. "What money?" he repeated. "I'll tell you what money. The two hundred pounds you inherited earlier this evening."

"What two hundred pounds?" Francis replied.

"Yes, I think I have had just about enough of you. Either you hand over the money or it will be you that's keeping his teeth in his pocket. Do you have any idea what the police would think when they find you all tied up with two hundred quid stuffed inside your overalls?"

"I don't have it," Francis said.

"What do you mean. Where is it?"

"I posted it."

"You what?" the man replied before turning to the slightly larger of his two accomplices. "Search the cab," he said.

"You won't find anything. I put it in the post before I left Hinckley."

The accomplice hesitated. Francis continued. "I didn't want it going missing after I was dumped in the back of the lorry or if it was discovered by a copper who decided to help himself. I could hardly put my hand in the air and complain about my missing two hundred pounds or report it stolen as I was sitting in the police station."

Convinced that he was being sold a tale too tall to keep in his garage, the man turned to his accomplice for the second time. "Search it anyway," he said as he stepped a little closer to Francis.

He was just about to reach out and grab Francis by the collar when out of the darkness, a cavalcade of police vehicles came screeching through the entrance of the lorry park with headlights glaring and blue lights whirling. Before Francis was able to gather his thoughts and bring into focus the entourage heading in his direction, he found himself standing alone by the open door of his cab. The three gentlemen and their colleagues in the back of the lorry had raced through the undergrowth at the edge of the lorry park and vanished into the woodland beyond.

Francis attempted to shield his eyes from the overwhelming silvery white glow of the headlights that engulfed him as the vehicles screeched to a halt and doors flew open. Police officers emerged, coming from every possible direction, at least a dozen or more. The first three officers darted past Francis, as he stood motionless, their dark uniforms quickly disappearing into the night. The next two officers that approached greeted Francis in quite a forceful manner by slamming him into the side of the trailer and holding him firmly.

"What's going on?" Francis muttered.

Another officer, whose seniority was given away by the shape of his hat, was the next to approach.

"Cuff him," the senior officer said as still more officers raced by and headed into the woodland.

Francis immediately reacted and protested by attempting to break free. "What? I haven't done anything. They were robbing me. I was being held prisoner whilst they emptied the lorry." he said as the officers spun him around and cuffed his hands behind his back. Once cuffed he was instantly turned around again. "Look, I haven't done anything, I'm telling you, they were robbing me."

"Yes, I'm sure they were and I'm having a late supper with Googie Withers and Anna Neagle. Why don't you save your story until we are all sitting comfortably?" The senior officer turned to his junior colleagues. "Stick him in the back of the van," he said.

Francis was marched towards and placed in the back of the police van, then the door was slammed shut behind him. He leant forward, sweat forming upon his brow. He looked through the small square window at the blue flashing lights, beams of bright white light and the furtive activity of a number of uniformed men, before slumping back in his seat again and looking up at the roof of the van.

Chapter 67

It was just past seven o' clock on Friday evening when the back door suddenly swung open and Francis, accompanied by an icy wind and swirling flakes of snow, stepped inside. The chilly blast of air quickly greeted Philip and James, who were both sitting on the settee. Philip was attempting to locate the little man hidden on the cover of 'The Weekend' magazine. James was still engrossed in the adventures of Stig and Barney.

After closing the door with the same force he used to open it and without any hint of acknowledgement in the direction of the two boys, Francis quickly covered the distance from one end of the living room to the other. Crisp white flakes of snow tumbled from his shoulders and translucent clumps of ice detached themselves from his boots and rested upon the carpet like a trail of clues in a winter's version of Hansel and Gretel, as he raced through the room and left it again at the other end.

Grace appeared in the kitchen doorway. "Where's he gone?" she asked.

"Upstairs," Philip replied just as he located the little man peering behind the capital letter 'N' of the magazine's masthead.

"Mum!" Grace immediately responded with an extremely concerned expression on her face.

Their mother, who herself had returned to the family home earlier that day, was resting upstairs.

Grace vanished for a moment, into the scullery, returning almost at once carrying both Philip and James's coats. "Take James and go out and play for a while," Grace said.

"What?" Philip replied with surprise as his coat was launched into the air and headed in his direction. "Have you seen the weather out there."

"Oh yes, that will be right, because you and your friends never play out in the snow," Grace replied as she fumbled around in the pockets of her own coat, which was lying over the back of the settee. With frustration clearly mounting, Grace yanked her purse free from one of the pockets, turning the lining of the pocket inside out as she did so. She opened the purse and removed a small amount of coins. "Here, take this and go to the off-sales at the Livvy or the chippy or whatever, just don't come back for an hour or so. "JAMES!" Grace shouted, "Put your coat on."

Even before Philip and James were ready to leave the house, raised voices could be heard from upstairs and the familiar ritual of shouting at each other at the same time was already gathering pace.

Once outside, the two boys headed for the relative shelter of the 'Live and Let Live' off-sales. The thirty four pence given to them by their sister, was well spent. They left the off-sales clutching two small bottles of lemonade, a Curly Wurly each and a small white paper bag, containing an assortment of chewy and chocolatey sweets, including Blackjacks, Fruit Salads, Sherbet Dips and Drumsticks. Although James was slightly confused by the purchase, Philip also bought a box of matches. The reason for the purchase became apparent a short time after, once they were back in the close and inside the empty flat on the middle floor, at the far end of the block.

This was the first time they had been back to the flat since just before bonfire night. However Philip was sure that there would still be a couple of candles inside.

"Watch out for the broken glass," Philip said as he struck a match and attempted to peer into the living room.

Somebody, perhaps a neighbour or a council employee, had clearly been in the flat since their last visit as all of the shattered glass from the window had been swept neatly into a corner of the room. Thankfully two candles were still attached to the windowsill, or they had been reattached. Either way Philip was pleased to see them. As he struck another match and lit the candles, he noticed that one of the wooden panels on the outside of the window had come away from the frame in the bottom corner. He was able to slide it over a little and peer out, onto the empty close. The snow was still tumbling down. Thick white flecks seemed to appear out of a dark blue sky as if they were tiny lights being switched on.

The flames from the two candles flickered within the semi-darkness as the boys sat down beneath the broken window and opened up the bag of sweets.

"Can we go home soon? I'm cold." James muttered as he reached for a Fruit Salad.

"Soon." Philip replied as he ripped open his Curly Wurly before taking a large and satisfying bite.

"Why did we have to leave in the first place?"

"Because mum and dad were gonna start fighting again and Grace wanted you out of the way."

"Why?" James asked.

"Because you get upset when they fight."

"No I don't," James snapped. "Anyway, I didn't mean that, I meant why are they fighting?"

"Habit," Philip replied.

"But what about mum? Doesn't dad care about mum being poorly?"

"I don't think it is that exactly. I don't think dad understands."

"Understand what?"

"What's wrong with mum."

James paused for a moment as he finished his Fruit Salad and scooped up a Blackjack from the bag. "What is wrong with mum?" he finally asked as the Blackjack reached his lips.

"I don't know," Philip replied.

James looked at his brother and screwed up his face before muttering, "I'm cold, can we go home soon."

"Soon," Philip replied.

Still working his way through his Curly Wurly, Philip stood up, pushed aside the semi-detached wooden slat and peered out of the window once more.

"Is it still snowing?" James asked.

"Yeah. It's really coming down and it's settling," Philip replied.

James smiled to himself as he reached for another sweet.

Philip was just about to do the same and bend down towards the bag, when he heard the sound of a door slamming, coming from somewhere within the close. He watched and waited for a sign of life. A few moments later Francis appeared on the pathway at the front of the house. He marched off as best he could under the conditions, doing his coat up as he went and a few seconds later, he disappeared out of view.

Philip released his grip of the wooden slat and allowed it to fall back into place. "We can go home now if you want." he said as he turned away from the window.

James immediately got to his feet, grabbing his unopened bottle of lemonade and what was left of the bag of sweets. Philip blew out the candles before striking a match for guidance purposes and they both tentatively made their way out of the empty flat. Upon exiting the block, they were met by a stiffening evening breeze and swirling flakes of snow. Thankfully the journey home was short and within a minute or so they were opening the back door and stepping into the living room. However, the sight that greeted them certainly wasn't as warm and welcoming as the room itself.

As they entered, their mother quickly attempted to compose herself, brushing away tears with the back of her hand and wiping her nose with what was left of a paper handkerchief, before slipping the handkerchief up the sleeve of her dressing gown. Grace was sitting next to her mother on the settee, arms folded tightly and with a face made of granite. She glared at her brothers to suggest that they had arrived back home too soon.

"Oh my, where have you two been? You look frozen. What you need is a hot drink," their mother said as she stood up.

As she did so, Philip immediately noticed the vibrant red mark across her cheek and the swelling in the corner of her bottom lip. As his mother entered the kitchen, Philip caught sight of Grace's cold hard stare. It was a stare that was easier to translate than a rude hand gesture. It said don't say anything and don't ask any questions. Most of the time in the kitchen was spent attempting to find a brave face to put on. Once applied and with an added smile, their mother returned, carrying a tray of hot milky Horlicks drinks. She placed the tray of drinks on the dining table, and asked what was on the T.V.

After getting up from the settee and quickly flicking through the three channels, Philip shrugged his shoulders and replied, "Nothing much, the 'Black and White Minstrel Show' or…"

He was about to relay the information regarding the other two viewing options, when his mother interrupted.

"Oh I don't like that programme, why don't we have a game of Monopoly."

To his surprise and despite trailing in a remote third, Philip found the next hour and a half a thoroughly joyous and wondrous experience. Mum came last but seemed to get her enjoyment from watching her children play whist taking over the duties as banker. James almost bubbled over with excitement like a couple of eggs boiling in a pan as he sensed a victory was within reach. However defeat was waiting just around the corner and unfortunately arrived within a blink of an eye, or rather a throw of a dice. After landing on The Strand with four houses on it, he followed this up by arriving at Bond Street with a bright red hotel standing majestically upon it, both properties belonging to Grace. After watching his sister dodge a bullet by missing both Mayfair and Park Lane before visiting an empty jail, James's fate was ultimately sealed two throws later, when virtually bankrupt, he landed on Northumberland Avenue with a hotel on it. Moments earlier the property had belonged to Philip, but he himself had to relinquish ownership of the property in order to pay off his own debts, his final act. A victorious Grace was left to sit back in her chair and admire her property empire.

The two boys began to pack the game away whilst their mother cleared away the rest of the debris from the dining table and headed for the kitchen. Upon returning, she announced her departure for bed. As she passed through the living room, she stopped to kiss James on the cheek and to ruffle Philip's hair before reminding them not to stay up too late.

After reaching an agreement with James to go and get ready for bed, in return for him being allowed to stay up a little longer, Grace turned to Philip.

"He's gone," Grace said with a smile on her face that was wider than a full back's volley.

"What do you mean?" Philip asked.

"Dad, he's gone. Mum told him to get out and not come back."

"And you're pleased about that, I see."

"Yes, of course."

"And what about me? What about James? Are you going to be the one to tell him his dad's left?"

"He hit her Philip."

"I know Grace, I can see. I can't see why you are so happy about it though." Philip paused before slipping back in his chair. "And how are we going to manage?"

"We'll be okay," Grace replied as she walked over to the settee and sat down. "I can move back in, my wage will help out."

Philip was stunned. He felt as if he had just received a blow to the head from a boxer's right hook and was just about to topple over. "Now I know why you are so happy. You just want to move back in so you don't have to deal with Karen. Why don't you go and pack your bags now?"

"No fear," Grace replied. "I'm not going anywhere tonight, in case he comes back after the pubs are shut."

"But you admit it."

"Admit what?"

Philip's response was curtailed by James's return to the room. In his cotton pyjamas and with a comic in his hand, James walked across the room and sat down next to his sister. Shaking his head at nobody in particular Philip got up and went to bed, leaving James to read his comic and Grace to stare at an episode of 'Ironside' with an ear cocked in the direction of the front door.

Chapter 68

Philip had been awake for over two hours when the sound from his alarm clock filled the room. He had had what can only be described as an extremely restless night's sleep. He had spent most of the night staring into the darkness and trying to fall asleep whilst one big wave after another came rolling in. He tossed and turned and with each passing wave his thoughts jumped from his dad leaving to his dad turning up at any moment. He pushed back the blankets and climbed out of bed with a mood that had been setting all night and with a dark rain cloud above his head. It was as if he was the new driver of the Creepy Coupe in an episode of the 'Wacky Races' and the Gruesome Twosome was now a threesome. Little did he know as he got dressed and headed downstairs that he was only a few short hours away from the great Monkswood Crescent snowball fight of 1973.

As Philip opened the scullery door to set off on his paper round, it immediately became apparent that travelling by bicycle was out of the question. The snow now resting on top of the wall that ran between his house and the house next door was a good seven or eight inch thick. Due to drifts, the snow along the side of the house was especially deep. As he stepped outside, his feet disappeared and the snow came to rest well above his ankle. He attempted to close the scullery door behind him, a task that proved more difficult than one would have imagined due to the amount of snow that had tumbled inwards and was now resting upon the scullery floor. Once the snow had been cleared and the door had been shut, it took a few more steps out into the crescent itself before walking became a little easier and the depth of the snow was a little less challenging. The crescent looked beautiful. As yet, no vehicles had come in or out, so all he could see was unspoilt snow, not a mark upon it. It glistened beneath the dark morning sky as the reflection from the moon seemed to gently rest upon the surface. A white as vibrant and as smooth as a sheet of paper stretched out before him.

It wasn't until he approached the end of Monkswood Crescent and caught sight of Henley Road that the winter wonderland scene began to dissipate a little. The occasional animal and bird footprint was now replaced by tyre marks. In turn the soft white snow had also been replaced by a murky grey sludge that stretched all the way along the road like a heavy smoker's clogged artery.

By the time he reached the shop both his cheeks were a flaming red colour, along with his nose. His hands were stubbornly refusing to come out of his pockets and he had a plimsoll line on both legs of his jeans, a few inches below the knee.

As he stood in the shop with his arms pressed tightly against his torso and wearing his shoulders as earrings, Mr Underwood looked him up and down. "Are you alright lad?" he asked.

Slightly surprised by the question, Philip replied. "Sort of, have you seen what it is like outside?"

Equally surprised by the response Mr Underwood started to chuckle. "That's just a bit of snow lad, a light flurry. Nothing compared to the winter of 63. Do you remember the winter of 63?"

"Not really," Philip replied as he finally managed to free his hands from inside his coat pockets. "I was only little."

"That was a proper winter that one, the coldest for over two hundred years. I remember not being able to get to the shop at first. I'd not had it long, if I recall it was my first winter. Just before Christmas it started and went on for about three whole months. Snow drifts so big they swallowed houses whole. Waterfalls froze, even the sea froze, it was that cold."

Philip looked up at Mr Underwood. "I usually have history on a Thursday," he muttered.

Mr Underwood either didn't hear Philip or chose to ignore him. He continued. "Bitterly cold artic winds for weeks on end. The temperature dropped to minus twenty. I remember when I finally reached the shop, I ended up being trapped for about three weeks. Thankfully I had a few supplies, a small heater and a camping stove that stopped me from starving or freezing to death. It snowed virtually every day for the best part of three months. Whole communities cut off, roads blocked, railways unusable, power lines down." Mr Underwood looked at Philip and quickly realised that he was losing his audience, if he ever had him in the first place. "Yes, well," he concluded. "Time to get on, your papers are ready to go."

Upon exiting the shop, Philip's hands once more submerged themselves inside his coat pockets, only coming out again when he arrived at his first delivery. As he continued on his round, the damp patches on his jeans seemed to be getting ever closer to the knee. His white with orange stripes, plastic trainers were unable to resist the conditions any longer, resulting in his feet being both cold and wet by the time he reached Broad Park Road. The round proved to be a very tough and arduous slog. Two things however, kept him going; the stolen bar of chocolate he managed to acquire whilst Mr Underwood went for his stroll down memory lane and the thought of making a snowman when he eventually returned home. Other than the round itself, another dark cloud came in the form of thinking how he was going to break the news to James about their father leaving home. At least it helped to keep his mind off the condition of his feet. When he finally opened the back door and stepped back into the house, James was already up and sitting on the settee in his pyjamas, eating a bowl of Rice Krispies with warm milk.

Philip offered James an equally warm smile. "Wanna build a snowman after I've had my breakfast?" he asked.

"After the Hair Bear Bunch," James replied.

"Sure," Philip said. "Here, I've got you this," he added as he put his hand inside his paper bag and took out this week's copy of 'Whizzer and Chips', before tossing it on to the settee.

James's eyes sparkled like the fuse on a firework. "Thanks!" he said with a mouthful of spoon and Rice Krispies. He picked the comic up and placed it on his lap, reading the adventures of Sid's Snake as he finished his breakfast.

Philip left James to enjoy his comic and headed upstairs in search of some dry clothes. Once the dry clothes had been sourced, breakfast had been eaten and the 'Hair Bear Bunch' had been watched, the boys headed outside. To their surprise, upon reaching the green in the centre of the crescent, they found that it was already a hive of activity. A smattering of younger children, some accompanied by a parent or older sibling, were running amok through the soft white snow. Snowmen of differing shapes, sizes and, to be fair, quality were also beginning to take shape.

Philip and James were about twenty minutes into their own snowman build when the first snowball was thrown. Nobody knows for sure who took aim and fired the first shot, except of course the person that threw it. The snowball itself caught a young boy called Daniel Allen a glancing blow on the back of the head, just to the side of the bobble on his hat. The young boy's smaller brother took the next hit as a snowball crashed into his shoulder, releasing small fragments of snow that caught him on his cheek. On this occasion the culprit was identified and swift retribution from both the boys and their father quickly followed. One snowball flying across the green led to another, then another, then another. The history book will show that a six year old boy, Barry Banks, was the first to fall. A snowball just above the left eye was immediately followed by a second strike to the back of his head as he attempted to turn away. Off balance, he stumbled forward and then plummeted to the ground.

Soon, more and more people began to appear on the green, young and old, including a grandparent or two. Thirty people now began to break away and form themselves into tight knit regimented units. Some went for a chaotic approach whilst others formed a chain of command. Craig, Paul and Martin had arrived in search of something to do and joined forces with Philip and James. They were in mid-battle with a group of younger boys who were being ably assisted by a couple of grown-ups, when out of the corner of his eye, Philip spotted his mother standing on the path in front of the house. She had a radiant smile, a sparkle in her eyes and an expression on her face that Philip had almost forgotten existed. However, her expression quickly changed when James took a flurry of blows in quick succession. Running on to the green, scooping up a handful of snow as she did so, she took aim almost immediately, releasing the snowball and taking her place within the ranks. Philip couldn't believe what he was seeing. If he had the time to do so, he would have stopped and pinched himself. With snowballs flying in every direction, raining down from all angles, there he stood, next to his mother, both of them giving as good as they got. The battle continued for another thirty minutes or so. When it was over, nobody could claim that they came away unscathed, although it is fair to say that some took more blows than others.

Philip hadn't enjoyed himself so much since bonfire night. By and large and putting aside his failed ten pence each way ITV7, which sank without trace in the third leg when a 9/2 second favourite trailed in seventh, the rest of the day was equally pleasing. He and James built a fine looking snowman in the back garden. They had a bowl of hot chicken soup each for lunch. They played Super Striker and watched 'Grandstand' in the afternoon, whilst their mother made a batch of jam tarts in the kitchen. They had bacon burgers, egg and chips for tea, followed by the afore-mentioned jam tarts, with custard. Grace had returned home from her shift at Woolworth's carrying two bags of pick'n'mix and the cherry on the top was Leeds United's comfortable three-nil win away at Ipswich

Town. All four of them spent the evening watching television whilst sitting in front of a roaring coal fire. They watched 'Bruce Forsyth's Generation Game' and an episode of 'The Goodies' amongst other things before their mother went to bed and Grace went for a bath, before bed. Philip waited for 'Match of the Day' in hope rather than expectation and despite highlights of the Leeds game not being included, he didn't allow this slight disappointment to spoil his very enjoyable day. Instead he settled down and watched Derby Country's one-one draw with Arsenal and West Ham's two-one win against Manchester City. He then watched 'Parkinson' but gave up on the late night film on 'BBC 2' and headed for bed a little after midnight. James was already asleep and also playing on Philip's mind when he climbed into bed. Despite an extremely pleasant day, Philip drifted off to sleep knowing that he still had to break the news to James about their dad leaving.

Chapter 69

The opening throes of Sunday morning were pretty much a carbon copy of Saturday morning. Philip had been awake for some time and had already switched off the alarm clock long before it had the opportunity to ring out and signal the official start to the day. On this occasion however, his thoughts were not yo-yoing as they were the morning before. Instead they were firmly fixed on how to break the news to James. Perhaps if he left it long enough, James would work it out for himself, or somebody else would tell him…

Philip climbed out of bed and got dressed. He had become quite skilled in the art of getting dressed in the dark. In fact he was better at it than Donald Pleasence was at spotting small pins on the floor of his prison camp cell from over twelve feet away.

The temperature had dropped considerably overnight and as he ventured outside, the soft white snow from the day before was now a more translucent, solid and crunchy consistency. The green field showed the scars of battle and the roads, though passable, were slippery at best and treacherous in parts. He cycled to the shop with the care and precision of a tightrope walker in a big top circus.

The precarious weather conditions, coupled with the excess weight of his paperbag, once filled, meant it became very difficult for him to ride his bike for the majority of his round. Once finished, he cycled into town on thankfully more passable roads and made his way to training. Under the circumstances, arriving only eleven minutes late was quite impressive.

He locked his bike outside the swimming baths and made his way to the changing rooms. Little had changed regarding his acceptance within the team and the majority of his fellow swimmers still made him feel about as welcome as a calypso band at a Ku Klux Klan family fun day. Philip arrived poolside just as Mr Kennedy was issuing his first set of instructions for the session.

"Okay people, let's get started. Three swimmers to a lane, set off at ten metre intervals. You know the drill; gentle strokes please, maintain the distance between you and the swimmer in front. Freestyle or front crawl for those of you who don't know what I mean by freestyle. Four lengths of the pool; away you go."

Philip slipped silently into the water. It was a snug fit; it wrapped around him like the arms of a close friend. In fact it was a close friend. The training session flowed seamlessly from one aspect to the next, except for working on his turns, which were still a concern, though they were showing signs of improvement, like a patient that had been taken out of intensive care and placed on a general ward.

It was as he returned to the main pool for his warm down, end of session swim that he noticed his dad sitting on the back row of the spectator seating area. After a quick final swim, Philip got out of the pool, showered, changed as quickly as possible and left the building still rubbing his hair with his rolled up towel. As he pushed through the glass doors, he caught sight of his dad standing next to his bike, his coat buttoned, hands shoved in pockets, a folded newspaper under his arm and a cigarette hanging from his lips.

"Dad," Philip said as he approached.

As Francis removed his hand from his pocket, to then remove the cigarette from between his lips, Philip caught a glimpse of the bruises and scratches across his knuckles and working towards his wrists.

"I need you to do something for me," Francis said as he exhaled his smoke into what was left of the morning air.

Philip didn't reply. He just stood and waited for his dad to continue.

"In your sister's room, on top of the wardrobe is an old brown suitcase. It's just got some old car manuals, some newspapers and some old magazines in it."

Philip felt his whole body become tense. Even his hair felt as if it was momentarily getting shorter. He knew what was coming.

"I need you to empty it and pack it for me. Get as much in as you can, shirts, trousers, my shoes, they are in the scullery and don't forget my shaving stuff from the bathroom," he said as he stroked the stubble on his chin.

"So it's true what Grace said; you're leaving."

"Listen son, I'll explain later. Right now, I need you to do this for me. I've got to go and see Snowy Vest, okay. I need you to bring the suitcase to the carpark at the Bell." Francis glanced at his watch. "Two o'clock, I need you there by two o'clock. If the suitcase is too heavy to manage then jump on the bus but I need you to do this for me son and I need you there by two o'clock."

This was an extremely unusual situation for Philip. He had never seen his father act in this way before. He felt as if he could reach out and actually grab hold of the desperation in his father's voice. There was a lot that he wanted to say but all he could do was stand there and nod his head.

"Good lad," his dad said. "I'll see you at two," he added as he turned away and headed in the direction of the carpark across the road.

Less than twenty five minutes later, Francis flung open the doors to the bar of the Green Man with such force that his actions attracted far more attention than the already agitated Snowy was happy about. With equal amounts of vigour and determination Francis marched over to where Snowy was located. He pulled out a stool from beneath the table and sat down.

"I'm not happy Francis," Snowy muttered. "Let me tell you right now, I'm not happy."

"You're not happy? You're not happy! Let me ask you Snowy, do you see a big beaming smile upon my face?"

"Listen Francis, I'm only here because you threatened to turn up on my doorstep. I don't like being threatened Francis, I don't like it."

"And I don't like being sold down the river I certainly don't like being set up."

"What do you mean, set up?"

"I mean set up Snowy. Do you think those coppers turned up on a whim. A lucky dip? Chanced their arm? I don't think so. They knew the whole operation." Francis paused before asking, "Where's Lousy?"

Snowy Vest hesitated before answering, taking a sip of his drink in order to buy a little more time. He finally muttered, "Your guess is as good as mine. My guess, for what it's worth, is he's currently staying at Lord Lucan's holiday lodge."

"Oh funny, very funny Snowy. I'm glad you are still able to raise a smile and crack a little joke. It's just a shame I don't have the time to sit back and enjoy the whole routine but unfortunately I haven't got the patience for any more of your shit Snowy. However, I have got enough time to shove your head up your arse."

Snowy leant forward a little and with a stare as cold as the bottom of a frozen lake and with a clenched jaw, replied, "Don't threaten me Francis, I've already told you, I don't like being threatened."

"At first, whilst I was being questioned for two days, at first I thought it was George Meadows. But he didn't know did he, not enough, not the exact details and whoever it was that grassed knew the full script."

"You've not been charged with anything then?"

"Not yet Snowy but it's on its way. 'Further enquiries' they say."

"Yeah, I know. They've been to the depot and taken away a whole stash of paperwork."

"So you've not been charged yet, either?"

"No Francis."

"Questioned?"

"No Francis."

"So you're not in the frame then?"

"Not at this exact moment in time, no Francis."

"Well I am. Smack bang in the middle of the picture. Standing there with a big beaming smile, sombrero on my head, castanets in one hand and a souvenir donkey under my arm and if you don't want to join me Snowy, I need that money."

Snowy looked down at his glass, before lifting it slowly towards his lips, pausing around halfway into the journey. "You've got to stop threatening me Francis. It's not going to resolve your situation." He finished his drink and placed his empty glass on the table. "I'll get the drinks in," he added as he stood up and manoeuvred himself past Francis.

The trip to the bar and the subsequent return journey helped to put Snowy a bit more at ease. He was able to observe that the other Sunday lunchtime patrons were all busy with their own agendas and he didn't seem to be attracting any unwanted attention. As he placed the drinks on the table and sat down again, he felt as if he had the upper hand.

"So Francis, if you don't mind me asking, where do you think I can get £300 from and why exactly do you feel I owe you this money in the first place?"

"You hired me to do a job. You told me what the job paid. I did the job, so I want paying."

"But you didn't do the job Francis."

"How do you come to that conclusion Snowy? You asked me to drive the lorry, you told me where to drive it to. It may not have worked out as you planned or as you expected but you cannot deny, I did my part."

A break in play, possibly to introduce the new ball, allowed each man to raise their glass and take a drink whilst still maintaining eye contact at all times. Once glasses had been returned to the table, it was Francis who continued to bat.

"Perhaps you need to realise that you are not giving the money away. You are getting something in return."

"And what exactly am I buying for £300?"

"Freedom," Francis replied. "A get out of jail card, or rather, a stay out of jail card. I appreciate that it is not exactly free but the end result, the outcome is the same."

"Another threat Francis?"

"You can look at it any way you want but if I get charged, which is pretty much guaranteed, I will be telling them a different story to the one I've told them so far. It's a story that will put you firmly in the frame. Would you like to hear it? It might help you to work out its value."

Snowy picked up his drink and sat back in his seat. "Will it take long?" he asked.

"No, it shouldn't take too long, after all I don't think we need to waste time setting the scene, or offering much of a back story to the main characters, or describing the locations. The storyline is fairly straightforward too."

Snowy slowly took another sip of his drink. He looked over Francis's shoulder and surveyed the rest of the bar before replying, "I'm all ears Francis, all ears."

"It goes like this," Francis began. "I had no choice officer. I was told one day that redundancies were in the pipeline and if I wanted to avoid being one of the ones made redundant, it was only possible if I agreed to take on a new role. If you check the books you'll see for yourself. I used to drive to the depot in Bristol. The previous occupier of the position had left and I could either fill the vacancy or move on as well. It was just a few boxes here, the odd item there and of course it would mean an extra few pounds in my pocket. I admit, I was happy to take the money but I only agreed in the first place because I couldn't afford to lose my job. Then they said they were going for it, a big job, the whole lorry. I didn't want anything to do with it but Snowy said I had no choice. I said I wanted out but they threatened to shop me, said they could make it look like I'd been stealing and make it look like it was just me, said they'd go to the bosses and the police. It was Snowy Vest and Lousy but Snowy was calling the shots; he was definitely the ringmaster." Francis leant forward and picked up his glass. "So what do you think of it so far?" he asked before taking a drink.

"Fascinating Francis, fascinating," Snowy replied. "If they make it into a film, who do you think will play me? Michael Caine perhaps, or Kenneth More? No, no, I know. Alec Guinness!" Snowy added as he nodded his head. "Yes, definitely Alec Guinness."

Snowy knew that he was backed into a corner, deep in a hole. Unfortunately, he didn't have an ace up his sleeve or a utility belt and he had completely run out of shark repellent spray but he was determined to do his utmost not to let it show.

Francis finished his drink and placed the empty glass gently but precisely upon the table. "Well I'll be off." he said as he reached inside his coat pocket for his cigarettes.

"Where you off to?" Snowy asked.

"I'm going home Snowy, to wait for the police to arrive."

"What's the rush? Why don't you stop and have another?" Snowy replied in an attempt to buy a little more time.

"No thanks Snowy. I want to work on my story, make sure I can inject the right amount of emotion when it is needed, and to be honest with you, I'm not really enjoying the company all that much."

"What guarantee do I have?" Snowy asked as Francis stood up and lit a cigarette.

"How do you mean?"

"I mean, if I give you £300, what guarantee do I have that you still won't tell your story?"

"You don't, you just have my word. That's if they manage to find me of course."

"I don't follow."

"I'm kind of hoping you're not alone."

Snowy looked puzzled and just stared at Francis, waiting for some sort of clarification.

"Sorry Snowy, did I forget to mention that minor detail. For your money, you also get me disappearing, not staying around to tell my story, on the run if you like, just like your good friend Lousy."

"You've been watching 'The Fugitive' again, haven't you? Where you gonna go?"

"I am afraid you don't get that bit of information for your money. Just think though, if the police do come knocking at your door, I am sure you will be able to tell a convincing story of your own and blame it all on Lousy and me."

There was a silence, not long enough to be rented out but long enough for Francis to feel that the conversation was at an end. He turned to leave.

"Wait, wait, WAIT!" Snowy said, too loud for his own comfort but not loud enough to attract any long lasting attention. Just a couple of short sideways glances were tossed in his direction.

"I don't have the time Snowy."

As Francis spoke, Snowy removed a brown envelope from his pocket and placed it on the table. His hand remained firmly pressed on top. With his cigarette pressed firmly between his lips, Francis sat down again.

"Before you take this money Francis, there is something that you need to be aware of. If you take it, I never see or hear from you again. When you do get caught, you never mention my name. If you do and the police do come calling, you'll pay a much bigger price than £300."

"Are you threatening me Snowy?"

"I just want to make sure you understand exactly what I'm buying."

"Fair enough Snowy, fair enough," Francis replied as he pulled the envelope from beneath Snowy's hand. "Oh and one more thing, not that it is worth all that much, in fact you can have this for free. If you want my opinion on who set us up, then look no further than your pal in Rochdale. Goodbye Snowy, take care."

"Goodbye Francis," Snowy replied.

Chapter 70

Philip slowly and oh so carefully weaved his way through the slushy remnants of snow and ice and with dedicated focus upon the road in front of him, he turned into the crescent. As he happened to glance upwards, he noticed a small crowd of people, about eight or nine, milling around on the opposite side of the green. His attention however was quickly diverted to the three police cars that were parked along the road in close proximity to the small gathering. Due to the distance between the vehicles, it was impossible to say with any certainty which house the occupants of the cars were actually visiting.

As he dismounted his bike on safety grounds, he was able to take a closer, longer look at the crowd. He observed that two or three of them were sobbing. Consoling arms and shoulders were being presented by way of offering some form of comfort and support. One or two individuals were rubbing their chins at the same time as shaking their heads, whilst others were simply standing motionless and staring at the ground. Philip processed the information before quickly filing it away for later consideration. He then turned his attention back to the task in hand and the packing of his dad's suitcase.

Philip made his way past the kitchen window. The condensation on the inside could mean only one thing; the cooking of a roast dinner was in full swing. However as he pushed his bike past, he could also hear a strange sound, an alien sound, a sound that for some time now had been long forgotten. It was the sound of music. When he reached and swung open the back door, he was immediately greeted by Roy Orbison, who was halfway through one of his mother's favourite tracks, 'Leah'.

The steamed up kitchen window, Roy Orbison's singing and a deserted living room had allowed Philip to enter the house undetected. He quickly moved from one end of the room to the other, past the record player, resting on the dining table, and out of the door towards the stairs. The only evidence of the journey actually taking place were some slightly soggy footprints on the living room carpet but just like the falling tree analogy, nobody was there to see them.

Philip quickly and silently made his way up the stairs, moving like a well-nourished vampire sneaking out of a trainee nurses' dormitory just before sunrise. He entered his sister's bedroom, retrieved the suitcase from the top of the wardrobe, emptied the contents onto the bed and took the now empty case into his parents' bedroom. Using the volume of Roy's singing as an alert system for somebody coming up the stairs, he started to fill the case.

Unbeknown to Philip, his brother had been lying on his bed, enthralled in the climatic conclusion of Stig of the Dump. Therefore he failed to hear James as he approached and appeared in the doorway.

"What are you doing?" James asked as he observed Philip opening drawers and scooping up items of clothing before tossing them into the empty suitcase.

"Packing," Philip snapped in response before adding, in an attempt to change the subject and to divert James's attention, "Do you know what's going on over the road?" It didn't work.

"But that's dad's stuff," James replied.

Philip paused and whilst holding an armful of clothes, he looked across the room at his younger brother. "Dad's going away for a while," he muttered before dropping the latest bundle into the suitcase.

"Where?" James asked.

"I don't know."

"Why?"

"I don't know that either. You just won't see him for a while, okay."

"How long for?"

"I don't know James. I'm taking him this suitcase. You can come with me if you want to."

James didn't reply, instead he chose to just watch as Philip continued to pack the suitcase.

"Will you go and get Dad's razor and shaving brush from the bathroom?" Philip asked, "and grab a towel from out of the airing cupboard."

After completing Philip's request, James continued to stand in the doorway and observe. As Philip shut the suitcase and dragged it off the bed, he heard the volume of the music from downstairs increase as the living room door opened.

"Dinner in five minutes," Grace called out into the empty space at the bottom of the stairs, before going back into the living room.

"So, are you coming with me?" Philip asked.

Although extremely unlikely that the prospect of a roast dinner was the deciding factor, the thing that tipped the balance, James shook his head in response.

"Okay," Philip said as he lifted the suitcase and ushered James out of the doorway, before adding as he went past, "It will be alright James. I promise."

Philip struggled down the stairs, trying to rein in the momentum that was being generated by the weight of the suitcase, before heading out of the front door. As he headed for the far-right corner of the flats and out of the crescent, he noticed that both the number of police cars and the number of people standing about had been reduced to two of each. Looking at the two police cars alone, it was still somewhat difficult to ascertain which house was receiving the authority's attention. But the two women that remained were standing and talking outside Claire Chase's house.

Due to the aforementioned weight of the suitcase and the conditions underfoot, Philip had to stop and swap over from one hand to the other every twenty yards or so. By the time he reached the Live and Let Live, he knew that walking all the way to Bell Green and on to the Bell Inn was out of the question. Instead he arrived at the bus terminus opposite the pub, let go of the suitcase, blew on his hands and waited for the next number twenty-one bus to arrive.

Thirty-five minutes later and almost fifteen minutes late but with hands he could once again feel, Philip dragged the suitcase off the platform at the back of the bus. He crossed over the junction between Bell Green Road and Old Church Road and shortly after dropped the suitcase at the entrance to the Bell Inn car park. He looked up and immediately spotted his dad, pacing up and down at the far end of the car park.

Upon spotting his son, Francis quickly sprinted over and took hold of the suitcase. "I thought you weren't gonna make it," he said with a wave of relief clearly evident in his voice. "Did you pack everything I asked?"

Not sure if he had done so, Philip simply replied, "I got as much in as I could."

"Come and get in the car and out of the cold, I need to talk to you."

They walked towards the car, which was located at the far end of the car park, without saying a word. Francis put the suitcase in the boot before they both climbed in to the car. Once he was seated, Philip lowered his head, looked down at the floor and muttered, "Do you really have to go?"

Francis didn't rush into a response. He lit a cigarette first, he removed his coat, placed it on the back seat and then replied. "I'm afraid so."

"But can't you and mum work it out?"

"It's not that easy son. You see for your mother and me, love has finally died. This is no happy home but god knows how I tried."

Philip turned and looked straight at his dad. Francis looked straight ahead. "That's a song, they're lines from a song, an Elvis song," Philip said.

"Does it matter? You know I'm no good at expressing myself I just thought that Elvis could do it better. What I said was true. It could have been worse I could have told you that Saturday night was alright for fighting or that I had a long haired lover from Liverpool."

"Is that where you're going?"

"What?"

"Liverpool, is that where you're going?"

"Of course not. I was just trying to make a joke, raise a smile."

"Where are you going?"

"I'm not sure and anyway it's better you don't know. The less you know the better it will be for the both of us." Francis turned to look at his son. "Listen Phil, this isn't just about your mum and me. You see, I've made some wrong decisions recently, some bad mistakes, some errors of judgement, you might say. There are lots of reasons why I can't stay. Like I say, it's best that you don't know too much. But there is one thing I can tell you with my hand on my heart. Leaving you behind and leaving your brother is the hardest thing I have ever had to do."

"Then don't leave, stay. Stay and try and sort it out."

"I can't Phil. I wish I could but the price I'll have to pay, it's too much, I can't afford it. And anyway, Elvis aside, I can't turn the clock back and I cannot change the future, there's no way forward for your mother and me."

Philip couldn't fight it any longer. He started to sob gently and the tears began to roll down his cheeks. He turned away from his dad and looked out of the passenger window, wiping his nose on the sleeve of his Parka coat as he did so.

"Come on Phil, don't make this any harder than it needs to be. I need you to be strong, I need to know that you can be strong. I need to know that you are capable of looking after your mum and your brother. He's gonna need you in the days ahead." Francis reached out and placed his hand on Philip's shoulder. "The only thing in my life that doesn't hurt when I think about it, is you and your brother. I wish you could come with me but that wouldn't be fair. You need to stay here, you need to stay at home, stay in school."

Francis reached over and grabbed his coat from the back seat. After a short amount of fumbling, he retrieved the item he was searching for before dropping the coat onto the back seat again.

"Look at me son," he said as he adjusted his position and fidgeted a little in his seat.

Philip attempted to stop sniffing and wiped his eyes with the palms of his hands as he turned to face his dad.

Francis handed Philip the item he had just removed from his coat pocket. "Give this to your mum," he said. "Whatever you do, don't lose it. There's £300 in there. Should get you through Christmas at least."

Philip took hold of the envelope. He'd never seen that much money before, so he couldn't resist a quick look inside.

"Put it in your pocket," Francis said as he removed his wallet from his own pocket and removed a five pound note. "This is for you. A little while ago I was caught a bit short so I borrowed a few quid out of that old plastic piggy bank of yours. This should make us even."

Philip took the money as Francis delved into his pocket once more, on this occasion to retrieve his car keys.

"Listen Philip, I have to go. I'll drop you off at the bottom of the crescent," he said as he started the engine and drove slowly out of the car park. Less than a minute later, he pulled the car over at the bottom of Monkswood Crescent. He left the engine running and looked across at his son.

"Philip, you will probably hear some things about me in the coming days or weeks. Just promise me you'll make up your own mind and not choose to believe all that you hear. Life's not always that simple. You'll discover this for yourself as you get older. I did try though son I tried my best."

Francis leant across and held his son one last time. The embrace was short but it meant everything to him. Once released, Philip clambered slowly out of the car before turning around and looking at his dad. Fighting as hard as he could not to start crying again, he nodded and said goodbye, before asking.

"When will I see you again?"

Francis smiled. "Now you're the one doing the song lyrics."

They both laughed.

"I'm sorry son but I have to go. Look after yourself."

Philip closed the passenger door and watched as his dad slowly pulled away. He continued to watch as the car moved silently along the Henley Road. He waited until it was out of sight before turning away from the road and walking home. He couldn't fight back the tears any longer and as he walked home he gently sobbed.

Chapter 71

Philip sat in the armchair next to the fireplace, a fireplace filled with the soft grey ash of what was once a roaring coal fire from the night before. He was folding up a sheet of newspaper, several folds, before attempting to insert it into one of his school shoes. He then took a few more sheets of newspaper, folded them a couple of times and put them in his school bag, ready to be used for the same purpose as the sheets now tightly nestled in his shoe, later in the day.

Due to not feeling too well during the night and convincing his mother that he was still poorly, James had manged to wangle a day off school and was lying on the settee with a blanket resting over the top of him. Philip was sure that his brother's failure to complete his science and geography homework had something to do with his feeling unwell but due to the present circumstances he was more than happy to keep his opinion to himself.

Once the hole in his shoe had been sufficiently filled, Philip finished getting ready and set off for school. As he approached the number 26 bus stop he could see that Paul, Craig and Martin were deep in conversation. When he got within range, he heard Paul ask Craig,

"Have you spoken to her yet?"

Craig shook his head by way of a response, took a big drag of his Embassy Regal cigarette and released a sigh disguised as an exhale.

"Not at all?" Paul asked, just for clarification purposes.

"NO!" Craig exclaimed.

"Spoken to who?" Philip asked in an attempt to find a way into the conversation.

"Claire of course," Paul replied.

"Why?" Philip asked.

Paul, Craig and Martin froze on the spot. Even the smoke drifting upwards from Craig's cigarette seemed to come to a sudden halt.

"Are you for real Phil?" Martin asked. "Have you spent the whole weekend hiding under your bed or something?"

"No, he fell down a mineshaft and has been waiting all weekend for Skippy to come and rescue him," Paul added.

Both puzzled and annoyed, and hoping that his facial expression was able to convey both emotions to his friends, Philip abruptly enquired, "What are you talking about?"

This time around Craig put him in the picture. "I can't believe you don't know but Claire's mum's dead."

"What do you mean dead?" Philip replied.

"I mean no longer alive, the opposite of alive: dead."

"I bet you he doesn't know about Karen Fairchild either," Paul said.

Puzzlement and annoyance had been replaced by bewilderment and confusion. Philip shook his head.

The number 26 bus came into view as it made its way up Winston Avenue.

"I'll tell you on the bus," Craig said as he began the process of finding his soon-to-be required bus fare.

Everybody else began the same process as they watched the bus trundle past on the opposite side of the road, enter and exit the roundabout and travel back towards them before pulling in to the terminus. By the time the boys had paid their fare, climbed to the upper deck and sat down at the front of the bus, Philip had already asked three questions. At the point of a certain part of his anatomy making contact with the seat however, none of them had been answered. So, desperate for more information, Philip asked his first question for the second time.

This time around, he got a response.

"The stupid cow froze to death," Craig replied.

Philip could have been given the opportunity to make several guesses as to what Craig was going to say but the chances of him still trying to guess, by the time they had to get off the bus, were too high. "She what?" He asked in disbelief.

As the driver started the engine and the bus pulled away from the terminus, Craig offered up a fuller response.

"Saturday night, what do you expect, as usual she was hammered, drunk as a lord in the Livvy. She staggered out, so drunk she forgot her coat. By all accounts, she lost her bearings and staggered over the fields." Craig pointed towards the small blocks of flats that ran along the top of Winston Avenue, as the bus rolled past. Behind the flats and situated between them and the Wood End Junior and Infants school was an old dirt track and a patch of overgrown wasteland. Craig continued. "You can imagine what she was dressed like, and without her coat. They reckon it wouldn't have taken long before she became disorientated. They reckon that she collapsed or passed out in the long grass. With all the snow on the ground and the freezing temperatures, she lay there all night. Some old boy walking his dog found her the following morning, her house keys in one hand and her shoes in the other."

"Dead?" Philip asked.

"No, of course not," Paul said. "She was sitting there doing her nails."

The boys sat in relative silence, and apart from the cigarette being passed between Craig and Paul, activity was also limited, until the bus turned off Wyken Croft and onto Torcross Avenue. As it did so Martin asked anyone who cared to offer an answer,

"What's going to happen to Claire and her little brother?"

"Not sure," Craig replied. "Her dad's not been around for years and he was just as big a drunk as her mum. Her older brother is still in borstal after what happened when he was in that stolen Austin Allegro," Craig paused. "Or was it a Vauxhall Viva?"

"She's got her grandparents though, hasn't she?" Paul said as he passed what was left of the cigarette to Craig.

"Yes." Craig said. "They live on Ellacombe Road. She's got an aunt as well but I doubt she'll want to know. She's all well to do and posh, got her own house with a driveway somewhere, not sure where she lives but it's not round here."

Due to now having certain things on his mind, it wasn't until they had clambered off the bus and were closing in on the school gates that Philip remembered Paul mentioning something about Karen Fairchild.

"What did you say about Karen Fairchild?" Philip asked as he tapped Paul on the shoulder.

"I was joking," Paul said as he spun around and walked backwards for a stride or two.

"Oh right, so nothing's happened then?" Philip asked.

"No," Paul replied. "I was joking about you not knowing. Your sister lives with her, how can you not know."

"Well if my sister does know something, she hasn't said anything to me, so what happened?"

"All I can tell you is at some point on Saturday night, probably whilst Claire's mum was freezing to death, Karen stumbled across what is believed to be a burglar in her flat and upon being discovered he proceeded to give her a kick-in, put her in hospital."

"How do you know it was a burglar?" Philip asked.

"I don't. I'm just going on what I heard."

"Who from?"

"Her mum told the nosy cow that lives two doors up from us, she told the woman next door and she told my mum."

"Is she badly hurt?" Philip asked as the school gates honed into view.

"I don't think so, I'm not sure," Paul replied as the boys walked through the gates and headed off in different directions. "Catch you later."

By the time Philip arrived at his blocks' morning assembly, his brain had reached bursting point with the amount of information it had received on the journey to school. He busily tried to move things around in an attempt to create space for any new information that was likely to come his way during the rest of the day. With his thoughts clearly on other things, the majority of the content of the morning assembly passed by unnoticed. However, he did manage to hear his name being called out along with the instruction to remain seated once the assembly had reached its conclusion. Any possible reason for him having to stay behind failed to make an appearance at the forefront of his mind. To be honest, it failed to make any appearance at all.

Still nonplussed about why he needed to remain seated, Philip took hold of the letter Mr Spencer handed to him. He did try to pay attention whilst the content of the letter was explained to him and the other pupils in the room but he failed dismally. The letter explained in detail the forthcoming outward bounds trip he had paid to go on and importantly gave clear instructions about the inventory of items each pupil need to bring with them. As soon as Philip realised that Mr Spencer had stopped talking and people were now leaving the room, he folded the letter, put it in his pocket, and headed for his first lesson of the week. No matter how hard he tried to shake it off, the news about Karen Fairchild clung to him like a sloth in a treetop on a breezy day.

The day itself dragged along at an alarmingly slow rate, like an arthritic tortoise attempting to climb a flight of stairs. Even the usually short lunchtime trip to the chip shop on Ansty Road for a tray of chips and gravy seemed to stretch out so far into the distance that he was unable to see its conclusion. On any normal day this would have been fine but on this particular day, it simply prolonged the agony. With his mind still firmly fixed upon the events of Saturday night, he collected a detention in his maths lesson that afternoon for not paying attention. He didn't notice.

When he got home from school, he was hoping that his sister would be home from work but she wasn't. When he got home from his paper round however, his sister was there to meet him, standing by the back door with a finger of one hand pressed against her lips and her other hand pointing towards the garden shed. As Philip put his bike away, his sister followed him inside.

"Have you heard about Karen?" Philip asked as he sensed Grace's presence on his shoulder.

"How do you know about that?" Grace replied.

"Paul told me on the way to school. I guess you know then."

"Karen's mum came into Woolies earlier today and told me. She was quite nasty to be honest. Wanted to know if I knew anything and where I was when it happened." Grace paused before asking, "Do you think it was dad?"

"What?" Philip replied as he spun himself around to face his sister. Due to the darkness within the shed, he was unable to present the full force of his facial expression so was forced to rely on the tone of his response. "You didn't tell her mum that did you?"

"No, of course not," Grace replied. "But she said the police would want to talk to me. Why do they want to talk to me? What do I do then?"

"Were you there? Did you see who it was?"

"No, of course not."

"Then that's what you tell them."

"But they'll ask me if I know who might have done it."

"Then you say no. If it was a burglar, then it wasn't dad was it? Why would dad want to burgle your flat?"

"But what about what you said about his hand when you saw him yesterday? And and you said that he said the reason he couldn't stay wasn't just to do with mum; there was something else."

"Listen Grace, whatever dad may or may not have done, you can't say anything, you can't just guess that it may have been him. Mum said that he lost his job and the scratches on his hand could have come from anywhere, an argument at work that turned nasty, which might be why he lost his job. Or he could have just fallen over drunk. Anyway if it was dad then leave it to Karen to tell the police."

Philip stepped forward and attempted to usher Grace out of the shed.

"But…" Grace began.

"No Grace, you've got what you wanted; dad's gone. Just leave it at that. I'm hungry. I want my tea."

Chapter 72

"Are you sure you don't want to come swimming?" Philip asked again.

"NO!" James replied with a face like a scrunched up crisp packet.

Philip was actually more than happy with his younger brother's response. He only asked him again because his mother had requested that he did so. Philip didn't want his brother tagging along on this occasion as he didn't plan to spend a great deal of time in the pool. Just that morning, he had received a shoplifting list from Paul McBride that was longer than a post office queue on pension day. The night before, as well as finding three detention slips in his blazer, his mother had also found his itinerary letter for his forthcoming school trip. So with Paul's requests and the items he needed to buy for the trip; Philip planned to spend the majority of Saturday in town. Having his brother tagging along would only make things awkward.

It was fair to say, based upon the evidence in his blazer, that it had not been the best of weeks at school. Due to events at home and his current state of mind, his concentration levels were severely impaired in the early part of the week, This resulted in him collecting another detention on Tuesday and another on Wednesday, to go with the one he picked up on Monday afternoon.

The police did turn up, twice in fact: once on the Monday evening to speak to Grace, then again the following evening to arrest and formally charge Francis. They left, pretty much empty handed, on both occasions.

Grace fielded the first visit and the first set of questions very well, giving extremely short, unhelpful answers at virtually every opportunity. She did ask if Karen had any idea who had attacked her, a question that caused Philip to gasp quietly as he stood and listened from the kitchen. However the question was ignored, or simply went unanswered, depending on how you chose to look at it. When Grace was asked if she had any idea who the intruder might have been, she responded by categorically asserting that she did not associate with burglars. She also highlighted the fact that, based upon where they lived, the number of suspects would be quite high.

The following evening, when two other police officers arrived in search of Francis, it was their mother that went into bat, doing equally as well, if not better than Grace. She simply informed the officers that Francis had packed a suitcase and left the house on Friday evening. He hadn't been back since and they had no idea where he had gone, nor for that matter did they care where he had gone. When the officers attempted to question the children of the house, they were quickly shown the door along with the instruction not to waste their time by coming back again. Attempting to impress the seriousness of the matter upon all the residents of the house proved a futile exercise for the two officers and the door was closed in their face.

Upon James's second confirmation that he did not want to go swimming, Philip got ready as quickly as possible, before his mother attempted to make other suggestions such as Saturday morning cinema or staying at home and playing games. He left the house a little after 10am, just as James and his mum were cuddling up on the settee to watch 'Laurel and Hardy'.

At ten minutes past ten, he arrived at the bus stop to find Craig pointing at his watch, whilst Paul and Martin were pointing at their imaginary watches.

"Where you been man? You're late!" Craig muttered.

"You should have been here twenty minutes ago," Martin chipped in.

Unable to resist the set-up he had just been presented with, Philip replied with a broad smile across his face. "Why, what happened?"

Annoyed at falling for such an old gag, Martin quickly replied, "We missed a bus waiting for you."

Thankfully another bus wasn't that long in coming and only a few minutes later they were all seated at the back of the top deck.

"How's Claire?" Philip asked.

"Okay I guess," Craig replied.

"You guess? You have seen her, right?"

"Yes, a couple of times but I don't know what to say and even before I do say anything, she starts crying. Her grandad's being a spaz as well. Won't leave us alone. But to be fair, he sent the old man packing pretty sharpish when he showed up."

"Did he?" Paul asked.

"Yeah, he turned up Thursday night with some skin and bones lush in tow, as the grandad called her. The old boy saw through him like a window. Tried to claim he'd come to look after the kids, like some knight in shining armour, when all he was really after was a place to live. Him and this bird are living in some hostel in Foleshill and he thought he could wangle himself a council house. Her grandad said it would be like replacing a dog that bites with a dog that bites."

"So what's gonna happen?" Paul asked.

"I think they are going to move. The grandad reckons that once the funeral was over, they'll go to the council and see about a four bedroomed house."

"Four?" Philip asked.

"Yeah, they need one for her brother when he comes out of borstal. Reckons they won't need to wait too long cus of the circumstances and they will give up two houses for one in return."

As the bus passed the police station on the Stoney Stanton Road, Craig seized upon the opportunity to change the topic. "Your dad still on the run then Phil?" he asked.

Philip was equally determined not to hang about in the conversation any longer than was necessary. "He's not on the run," he replied. "He's just left."

"Are you sure?" Martin asked.

"Are you fat?" Philip replied.

"Piss off," Martin said as he removed a packet of bon-bons from his coat pocket and turned away.

"Okay ladies, no falling out now. If Philip doesn't want to talk about his dad being a fugitive from justice, he doesn't have to. Has he got a poster in the Post Office yet?" Craig smiled. "I'm only joking Phil. Who have Leeds got today?"

Under normal circumstances, this particular fixture would be vying for centre stage, pole position, in Philip's thoughts. However, as the current circumstances were an extremely long way from normal, the fixture was firmly fixed on the periphery of his mind. It was left to jump up and down whilst waving its arms in the air, as if it was standing on a deserted island trying to catch the eye of a passing vessel upon the horizon.

Along with the rarely mentioned Manchester United, today's opponents, Chelsea were about as big a rival as Leeds United could get. It was a rivalry that had been elevated to the next level following the 1970 F.A Cup final.

The chemistry within the teams was very similar. Both were solid at the back; Chelsea had Peter Bonetti, 'The Cat', in goal. They were equally impressive in defence with David Webb and Ron 'Chopper' Harris. The midfield boasted three very strong players in John Hollins, Peter Houseman and Alan Hudson, with the goal scoring threat of Peter Osgood up front.

The rivalry was born out of similar players but very different styles and philosophies concerning how the game should be played. Chelsea were the stylish and sometimes flamboyant southerners, whilst Leeds United were the dogged, hardworking northerners. It had taken three attempts for Leeds to get past Manchester United in the semi-final, eventually winning the second replay one-nil. After the final, a game that finished two-two after extra time, the state of the Wembley pitch meant that the replay was relocated to Old Trafford. If the first game at Wembley was seen as an excellent game of football, the replay was anything but. It was more of a battle than a football match with personal skirmishes breaking out all over the pitch. It was one bad tackle and one swinging punch away from the infamous Italy vs Chile World Cup encounter of 1962. Ever since that F.A Cup final, which Chelsea won two-one after extra time, the fixture now had an extra dash of spice to it as football fans' memories are very much on a par with elephants'.

Philip still could not offer an explanation for it, nor was he prepared to spend any time searching for one but the moment he entered the water, everything around him simply fell away. His sister, his dad, his mum, his three detentions melted like a lump of lard in a well heated frying pan.

Philip lay on his back, looking up at the roof of the pool and serenely floated along. It was a bright winter's day and the sun poured through the panes of glass, leaving a golden light flickering upon the surface of the water. As he gently bobbed up and down, staring up and arms outstretched, he briefly thought about the shoplifting list nestled in his coat pocket. After weighing things up and taking into consideration his current healthy financial situation, he changed his mind and decided against leaving the pool early as originally intended; instead he opted to stay and play with his friends and legitimately purchase the items for his school trip with the money his mother had given him.

The pool remained surprisingly quiet throughout the course of the day. The positive side of this was that there was plenty of room to swim and to play. On the negative side it meant that the final 'last person to be ejected' game was a whole lot trickier. Martin won by default, having waited for the others to be told to leave, before he executed his trademark belly flop off the first diving board. The rest of the boys watched and laughed from just inside the pool exit before they all headed for the showers and then the changing rooms.

As Philip left the building, the nerves were there to greet him, like a big kiss on the cheek from a grandmother, that you would wipe away with the back of your hand as soon as she turned her head.

It was too late to walk into town and peer through the Redifusion shop window at the half-time scores but he should just about make it home before the vidiprinter started to roll. Philip made it with minutes to spare. On ITV, Mick Mc Manus had just slammed Catweazle onto the canvas of the ring at the Bedworth Civic Hall, whilst over on BBC1 Eddie Waring was seeing out the last few minutes of Warrington versus Castleford in a Rugby League Cup Second round tie. Philip didn't notice the score but Warrington won 18-9.

Eddie said goodbye, we returned to the Grandstand studio and the vidiprinter started rolling. The first batch of results always seemed to be from the Scottish leagues; perhaps the Scottish referees were keen to get to the bar. Eventually English scores began to filter through, including results from the second round of the F.A.Cup. Merthyr Tydfil's heroic cup run had come to an end, beaten three-nil by Hendon F.C. Blyth Spartans drew at Grimsby but Kings Lynn got thumped six-one. In League Two Bristol City beat Cardiff City one-nil away. The first First Division score to come through was confirmation of Coventry City beating Manchester United three-two at Old Trafford. Philip made a mental note that he now needed to avoid Paul Mc Bride later on, for two reasons. The vidiprinter was now busily clicking away as if it was at a castanet convention. Philip sat with hands clasped tightly together as score after score rolled into view. Then the score he was waiting for finally began to appear. Chelsea 1, Leeds Utd 2. Philip leapt from his seat with his arms in the air.

"Yes!" he called out.

It turned out to be a good day all around. Other than Derby County the other teams directly below them in the table dropped points. Ipswich lost, Stoke City lost and Liverpool drew at Norwich.

Philip arrived at the newsagents deliberately late, hoping not to bump into Paul McBride. His plan bore fruit. He quickly collected his papers and went on his way. Upon arriving back home however, he immediately bumped into Grace.

"I've got to go to Karen's. Come with me?" Grace asked.

"What now?" Philip replied with his face in the protest position.

"Yes now."

"Can't we do it later?"

"No, I need to get it over with. I need to get my stuff and I haven't told her I'm moving out yet."

Philip's demeanour changed in acceptance of his fate. His head and shoulders dropped in unison. "Come on then, let's get it over with."

Just as they were approaching the entrance to Clennon Rise, Grace turned to Philip and said. "Don't mention dad."

They entered the flat to find Karen sitting on the sofa watching 'Bruce Forsyth's Generation Game'. Her bottom lip was still swollen and there was evidence that it had also been cut. Her cheek was also swollen and her left eye was still heavily bruised and partially closed. Karen chose not to acknowledge Grace and Philip's arrival at first.

"Hello," Grace said.

Whilst doing her best to remember the items on the conveyer belt, Karen replied, "I thought you'd moved out."

"I have," Grace nervously replied. "I didn't want to but our dad has left and mum can't manage on her own."

"Yes well, it's probably for the best," Karen said.

"Will you be okay after what happened?" Grace asked.

"Why wouldn't I be?" Karen said as she watched the doors to the conveyer belt close.

"I just thought that after the burglary…"

"It wasn't a burglary," Karen interrupted. "That's just what I told the police."

"Do you know who it was then?"

Philip, standing just behind his sister and slightly to the left, felt his whole body tense up as if a thick plank of wood had been inserted up the back of his shirt, as he braced himself in readiness for Karen's response.

"Of course I do," Karen said as she reached for her cigarette packet on the coffee table in front of her.

"Why didn't you tell the police?" Philip asked, a question that received a hard stare and an accompanying nudge to the ribs from his sister.

"Because I didn't want to. I just wanted him out of my flat and out of my life."

"Who was it?" Grace asked as a second, even sturdier, plank of wood was inserted under Philip's shirt.

"It doesn't matter who it was."

"But what happened, why did he…"

Karen interrupted again. "Look Grace, it's not anybody's business but I told him something he either didn't want to hear or he didn't want to believe, I don't know which, then he just lashed out. To save you the trouble of asking your next question, I told him that he was my boy's father."

"But I thought…"

"Yes, so did he for a while. That's why he left when I told him he wasn't. So now you see why I lied to the police. I don't want everybody to know the truth and now I'm sure that he will stay away. It would be more trouble than it is worth for him." Karen stood up and switched off the television set. "Listen Grace, I'm off to my mum and dad's to collect my son. Just put the keys through the letterbox when you're done and don't say a word about this to anyone."

Karen stepped past Grace and Philip, collected her coat from the hallway and left. No sooner had the door to the flat closed than the broadest of smiles appeared across Grace's face.

"What are you so happy about?" Philip asked.

"Don't you see, you heard what she said, it means that it wasn't dad that did it, it was her boy's dad."

"Can we just get your stuff and go?" Philip replied. "I'm hungry."

Chapter 73

Philip woke up on Wednesday morning with mixed emotions and like the lime cordial and lemonade in a homemade snowball they couldn't be separated. It was the last day of school before the Christmas holiday, a reason to rejoice. However, it was also the day of Claire Chase's mother's funeral.

It was another bitterly cold and dark winter's morning with the threat of snow no more than an exhaled breath away when Philip left the house and headed for his paper round. As he delivered his papers, his thoughts leapt between which game to take to school and Mrs Chase's funeral with the precision of a figure skater completing a triple salchow. By the time he got back home he had at least reached a decision on which game to take to school, he had decided on 'Rebound'. James had already opted for 'Kerplunk'.

As Philip headed upstairs to get his brother up for breakfast, he could hear a commotion, including a few choice words, getting louder as he climbed. He reached the landing to find Grace standing next to a set of stepladders. He could hear his mother's voice coming from inside the attic.

"What's going on?" he asked.

"Mum can't find the Christmas tree," Grace replied.

"Is that Philip?" their mother called out. "Philip, do you know where the bloody Christmas tree is? I've found the decorations but not the tree! Why isn't the tree with the decorations?"

James appeared in the doorway to his bedroom at the same time as their mother's head appeared from within the attic. "Dad threw it away," he muttered.

"He what?"

"Dad threw it away last year, said that it was past its best and we needed a new one."

"Are you sure?"

"Yes," James replied.

"Right, wait there and grab hold of these boxes," their mother said as she disappeared inside the attic again.

"So that's a tin of Quality Street, a tree and some chocolates for the tree," their mother said once she was safely out of the attic and the boxes of decorations were nestled on the table in the living room.

Philip and James got ready for school. Grace got ready for work. They all ate their breakfast on the settee whilst their mother emptied the contents of the decorations boxes onto the dining table. Tinsel of various lengths and colours, shiny baubles, a silver star, a fairy in a silver dress and a selection of paper streamers amongst other items were being strategically placed upon the table by the time the boys set of for school with their respective choice of game placed in a carrier bag and wedged under an arm.

After a brief discussion about their choices, the bus journey to school was a relatively silent one. All four boys tended to gaze out of the window at a cloudless off-white sky. Just as they were getting closer to their stop, Philip looked across at Paul.

"What time is the funeral?" he asked.

"One o'clock," Paul replied.

"Craig's going then?"

"Yes, Claire wanted him to go." There was a pause before Paul added, "The only half decent day of the year to go to school and he has to go to a funeral."

"I've never been to a funeral," James said as they all prepared to get off the bus.

"I have," Martin replied as they began to make their way down the stairs. "Horrible, miserable it was and boring. It was like watching Songs of Praise only with lots of people crying."

Martin's view of funerals did little to lift the mood and although both lessons that morning were spent playing games or taking part in allegedly fun filled Christmas quizzes, Philip was unable to find much to smile about, especially when it got closer to one o' clock.

Lunch (which consisted of a tray of chips and gravy), the afternoon lessons (which consisted more quizzes and the playing of games) and the journey home (on foot) were as equally downbeat and sombre as the morning's activities. It was when he arrived home that his mood began to shift in an upward trajectory. There were two reasons for this sudden skywards surge. Firstly, as the two boys stepped into the living room, they were met with a dazzling display of colour from all of the Christmas decorations that had been put up. Strips of gold, red, silver and green tinsel set off from the corners of the ceiling, all meeting in the centre of the room. Fairy lights were draped around the living room window and a plastic Santa Claus sat proudly on top of the television set. A Christmas tree sat next to the fireplace with an angel perched upon the top. The rest of the tree was bare.

"I thought we could decorate it together," their mother said as she smiled at the boys. "After tea and when your sister gets home." She walked over to the dining table and picked up an envelope. "This came for you today," she said to Philip as she handed him the second reason for the positive turn in his mood.

The envelope wasn't the usual size or shape and it felt much more rigid. Philip quickly took it upstairs and slid it under his pillow, ready to be opened once he had completed his paper round. At least that was the intended plan but it didn't quite work out that way. Upon arriving home, his tea was ready and after tea, once the washing up was finished, it was time to decorate the tree, something that he didn't mind doing at all. He also didn't mind when their mother opened the tin of Quality Street.

One penny toffee and one strawberry cream later, a little after eight o' clock, Philip finally climbed onto his bed and retrieved the letter from beneath his pillow.

He carefully opened the envelope, breaking the seal with a crisp snapping sound. Inside was a Christmas card and a neatly folded inside the Christmas card was a letter. The inscription inside the card read, 'To Philip. Wishing you a wonderful Christmas, Billy'. Philip gently laid the card down on the bed and unfolded the letter.

Dear Philip,

I have to be honest and confess that I was deeply troubled by the content of your most recent letter and to hear the news that your father has chosen to leave the family home and move away. It is equally concerning that neither you nor the rest of your family know where he has gone. I can only begin to imagine how difficult this must be for both you and your younger brother, especially at this time of the year. If there is a small crumb of comfort to be gleaned from this awful situation, then it must be found in the fact that your letter hinted at your mother feeling more positive since your father departed.

In respect of the choice your father has made, I personally feel that running away from one's problems is never the answer. No matter how far you run, you eventually have to stop running and then your problems will inevitably catch up with you. However it is not for me to sit here and pass judgement, especially when I do not understand the situation in its entirety or how your father was feeling. One thing I do know though and it is, as the saying goes, as certain as death and taxes and that is we all have to stand by the choices we make in life. Whether they are proven to be the right choices or the wrong choices is somewhat academic. It is also not for others to judge you on the choices you make or to judge whether you have made the right or wrong decision. Only the individual can decide that. All of us as individuals have to live with our decisions and your father will ultimately have to live with his. I just hope that given some time and some space in which to think, your father reconsiders his actions and gets in touch with you soon. No matter what has happened, you and your brother are still his children and he still needs to do as much as he can to support and care for you.

It is at times like this when other aspects of your life can appear to have little importance, or value. This, I assure you, is not the case. You must continue to work hard at school and you must continue to remain focused on your swimming. What is currently happening in your life will undoubtedly impact upon the now, upon the present. It is vitally important that you do not allow it to impact upon the future as well.

It may seem a little insensitive or out of place to discuss football at a time like this but maintaining a sense of normality during difficult times is very important. Thank you as always for your kind words and also for the advice on how to remain calm whilst the pressure around me continues to build; wise and supportive words for somebody so young. I think your swimming is helping you to understand the complexities of competition. After the draws against Derby County and Q.P.R. it was especially pleasing to record back to back wins in our last two matches. The victory over Chelsea on Saturday was a delight for a number of reasons. Winning away from home is always pleasing but to beat one of your fierce rivals away for home is even more satisfying.

We nearly let them back into the game and it could have been a very different result. For a twenty minute spell in the second half, ten minutes either side of their equalising goal, they certainly had the upper hand. But it was pleasing to see that our heads didn't drop and we slowly wrestled the initiative back. Retaking the lead took the wind out of their sails somewhat and we were then able to see the game out quite comfortably after that. Most games in football are about winning but some games are about something more than that and beating Chelsea away from home is such a game. I also believe that by not losing on Saturday, we have set a record of remaining unbeaten for the first twenty games of a season.

With the Christmas schedule now upon us, we will have played at least four more league games by the time I have the opportunity to write again. Games against Norwich, Newcastle, Birmingham and Tottenham are all upon the horizon and potentially they are all tough games. Although they are all in the bottom half of the table, form takes a back seat at this time of year and we mustn't get complacent. The atmosphere in the dressing room becomes a little more intense and serious with each passing game. We still try to raise a few laughs before kick-off and Jack always has a couple of jokes to tell. But as captain, I can sense that tension is always just beneath the surface as we prepare to step out on the pitch. From a captain's point of view this is not a bad thing as I know that everybody is focused on the task in hand and everybody will work tirelessly in their quest to gain a positive result. In a small way, the pressure can actually make my job just that little bit easier.

I will sign off now Philip but I will be sure to write again very soon to see how things are going for you at home. Do your best to remain positive and I hope that you all manage to have an enjoyable Christmas. Try to stay strong and be there for your mother and your siblings, especially your younger brother.

Your friend, Billy.

Thursday morning appeared as if by magic, as if it had just been extracted from a magician's hat. Philip couldn't remember how many times he had read the letter or when he fell asleep. He didn't hear James come to bed or anybody else for that matter. Thankfully he was only a little late for his paper round and if he skipped his breakfast until he got home again, he would be back on schedule, especially as he was already dressed. At least there was no need to rush to complete his round, no bus to catch and no school awaiting.

Philip was back home and halfway through his bowl of Weetabix when suddenly there was a loud and rather frantic-sounding knock at the front door.

"Who's that?" James asked.

"I tell you what, after I've answered it, I'll let you know." Philip replied as he got up and went to the door.

He returned almost immediately. "Quick James, get your coat," he said.

"Why, what's going on?" James replied.

"Just get your coat and hurry up," Philip said as he grabbed hold of his coat from the back of the dining chair. They both stepped outside to see Paul Jones impatiently waiting at the end of the path. They followed him towards the flats, into the flats, up the stairs and into the empty flat on the first floor. Upon entering the living room, they found Craig and Martin already waiting. Martin was sitting beneath the partially boarded up window and within the dim light in the centre of the room stood Craig. Craig was wearing a fake leather jacket with the collar turned up, looking like a council estate James Dean and with a smile upon his face as wide as the flares on his jeans.

"Well, we're all here now," Paul said as he shrugged his shoulders and looked at Craig. "So, what's the big news."

"I did it!" Craig said.

"Did what?" Martin asked.

"IT!" Craig replied with eyebrows raised, although it was too dark to see them. He continued. "With Claire, yesterday at the funeral, she was all upset and wanted comforting, so I comforted her."

"At the funeral?" Philip said in disbelief. "You comforted her at the funeral?"

"Not at the actual funeral, obviously, might have been a bit off-putting for the vicar. Afterwards there was a wake at the Livvy."

"You comforted her in the Livvy?"

"No, no, not in the Livvy. If you just shut up, I'll tell you."

"Can I just ask?" James interrupted. "When you say you comforted her, do you mean that you…"

"YES!" everybody shouted.

Silence reigned for the briefest of moments as they all waited for Craig to continue.

"There was a wake in the Livvy, after the funeral like. They were all getting drunk and talking shit about what a lovely lady the old soak was. Claire couldn't stand it, got all upset and didn't want to stay. So she asked me to walk her home. When we got there, the house was empty. She suggested that we went upstairs. So we went upstairs to her room and well we were sitting on her bed, she was still upset, so I comforted her."

Clearly dissatisfied by the lack of details, the boys formed an orderly queue to ask questions. Paul went first.

"What was it like?" he said.

"Quick," Craig replied.

"How quick?"

"About three minutes," Craig said.

"What, everything?" Philip asked. "From the moment you went upstairs?"

"Oh no," Craig replied. "From the moment we went upstairs, all of it from start to finish must have lasted at least eleven minutes." Craig paused before asking, "Is that normal, is it supposed to last that long."

Everybody shook their heads and shrugged their shoulders before Paul said, "I guess so. It doesn't last that long when you see it on the telly."

Craig was visibly reassured by this and his smile, which had begun to fade a little, was restored to its former glory. "Any of you virgins fancy going swimming?" he said. "Meet you at the bus stop in fifteen minutes," he added as he took a cigarette from behind his ear, placed it between his lips, lit it, discarded the spent match, tugged at the leather collar of his jacket and left.

Chapter 74

It doesn't matter whether they are a boy or a girl: ask any child of school age what they believe is the longest day of the year and there is one thing you can be certain of, not one of them will give June 21st as their answer. Each and every child will undoubtedly respond by telling you that the longest day of the year is Christmas Eve. This is followed a long way behind by the day before your birthday, and making it onto the rostrum in third place is the day before you go on holiday. Admittedly and by default, second and third place could well fall on June 21st but it would not be the day itself that was specifically mentioned. However there can be no confusion surrounding the date of the longest day of the year and no possible chance of mixing up June 21st with December 24th.

On this particular Christmas Eve, Philip and James were sitting on the settee. They were staring at the 'Magic Roundabout' on the television and waiting for the 'Wonderful World of Disney' to start. Philip glanced at his watch; it read six minutes past ten. Philip sighed. He was convinced that it had been at least fifteen minutes since he last looked at it, and the last time he looked at it it had read four minutes past ten.

They could both hear the activity coming from upstairs and they both assumed it was their mother busily wrapping presents that would allegedly be delivered by Santa Claus in the early hours of Christmas morning. Philip had given up on the existence of Santa some years ago. A part of James however was still clinging onto the faint hope that the myth was more than just a myth and there was an outside chance that an overweight pensioner and eight reindeer could feasibly deliver presents to every child on earth in just one night.

'Disney Time' too seemed to last twice as long as usual, which resulted in a rather puzzling scenario. On the one hand, it was a very enjoyable programme, so why should there be an issue if it lasted twice as long? However, on the other hand, the painfully slow passing of time was weighing heavier than a collapsed scrum on skinny schoolboy.

"What's on now?" James asked.

"Dunno, where's the Radio Times?" Philip replied.

Without saying anything, James pointed towards the floor by the side of the television. Philip got up, scooped up the aforementioned item from the living room floor and then sat back in his seat.

"Right, let's have a look," he said as he searched for the correct page. "On 'BBC1' it's 'Tom and Jerry', a double bill, followed by a Marx Brothers film. Forget 'BBC2' unless you really want to watch 'Play School'. There's an Abbot and Costello film on 'ITV'; let's watch that?"

Philip closed the magazine before switching the T.V. over to the appropriate channel. The boys settled down and watched the last hour of the film. To buy into the narrative, a huge leap of faith was required in order to believe how two wrestling promoters from Brooklyn found themselves in the French Foreign Legion. The boys however were more than happy to leap.

Upon returning to the Radio Times at the end of the film, Philip quickly realised that the quality of viewing had somewhat diminished. BBC1 had careered downhill with more speed than an Olympic bobsleigh team. A cavalcade of dull viewing ran through the afternoon schedule, kicking off with the 'Perry Como Winter Show' and culminating a few hours later with a wildlife safari in Argentina. 'BBC2' was equally uninspiring, as was ITV, at least until 'Clapperboard' started at 5.20pm.

"I think we will have to find something else to do," Philip said. He tossed the Radio Times to one side just as their mother entered the room.

"If you two have nothing to do, you can run up to Bell Green for me. There are a few things I need, and when you get back you can post some Christmas cards for me."

Faced with the daunting prospect of having to watch Perry Como, the boys were only too happy to go shopping. Their enthusiasm for a trip to the shops even caught their mother off-guard.

"I need two packets of Angel Delight, some custard powder, plain flour, cornflour, a packet of bread sauce mix…" She paused and after realising who she was talking to, she added, "I'll write it down."

Once the boys were sufficiently attired for the conditions, their mother handed Philip the list and some money. "You should be able to get it all in Sainsbury's. You can take twenty pence each from the change and have some lunch in the café opposite Dick Sheppard's, if it's open."

Sainsbury's was as crowded as expected. Each aisle was filled with last minute shoppers, all reaching for items they didn't need, items that would either perish and be chucked away a week or so later or find themselves located at the back of cupboards until the festive season came round again. Most of the annually-purchased treats such as Brazil nuts, Tuc crackers and soft foreign cheeses were sold out. Thankfully Philip was able to get everything on the list except for the bread sauce mix. He tried two other shops that were likely to sell it but there was no joy there either. Upon exiting shop number three, Philip unequivocally accepted defeat and the two boys set off for the café; it was open.

"What can I get you boys?" the waitress asked after they had spent a couple of minutes looking at the rather basic menu.

"Beans on toast twice, a glass of milk and a lemonade please," Philip replied.

As the boys sat and waited for their lunch to arrive, out of the blue James suddenly asked, "Where do you think dad is?"

"I don't know," Philip replied.

"Do you think he'll come and see us tomorrow?"

"No," Philip said. "I shouldn't think so."

"But why?" James asked. "Doesn't he want to be with us on

Christmas Day?"

"I think he wants to but he can't."

"Why not?"

"I've told you before. I don't know for sure. I just know that he didn't want to leave but he had to. We just need to make the best of it and enjoy Christmas."

The waitress returning with the drinks brought the conversation to an end. Although James was clearly upset, Philip was relieved. He smiled at his younger brother as he passed him his glass of milk. "I tell you what," he said. "After this, we'll nip to Woolworth's on the way past and get some sweets."

Once back home and once again positioned on the settee with a paper bag full of assorted chocolate sweets by their side, both boys were still unable to shift the bitter taste from the back of their mouths. The television had very little to offer in the way of comfort and the prospect of delivering Christmas cards around the crescent did very little to lift the mood that had taken root in the café.

Working their way through the contents of the Woolworth's bag and delivering the Christmas cards only seemed to pass a little more time and by 3.30pm they were once again back in front of the television and still a long way from 'Clapperboard' starting. For the second time that afternoon, their mother offered a temporary reprieve.

"Right then, who's going to help me make some jam tarts and a trifle?" she asked.

Both boys were in the kitchen before the word 'trifle' had managed to remove itself from between their mother's lips. Helping their mother to bake tended to require more watching than doing but they helped to weigh and to mix and to tidy up as they went along and the event itself if nothing else, helped to pass some more time. Once the trifle was complete and the jam tarts were cooling, the boys returned to the living room whilst their mother began to cook dinner. They had totally forgotten about 'Clapperboard'.

Dinner was eaten and Grace returned home from work. The evening was spent playing a variety of games; a game of Monopoly, several games of Escalado and to finish, two or three games of Ker-Plunk. The boys were allowed a snowball each whilst playing and Grace had two Babychams. The evening passed quicker than expected and after James had claimed victory by three marbles in the final Ker-Plunk game of the evening, it was time for bed. Trying to sleep on Christmas Eve is like trying to tie your shoe laces whilst wearing an oversized pair of boxing gloves. Eventually however, all in the house were asleep and Christmas day duly arrived.

Christmas day smiled, introduced itself and then raced off into the distance. Every attempt to catch it up proved futile. Philip just about managed to grab hold of its shirt tails around about the time of the Queen's speech but it was only fleeting and failed to slow the day down in any meaningful way.

Whether it was due, in some small way, to being abandoned by their father so close to Christmas, the boys did better than expected in the presents department. They had woken up to find two selection stockings at the foot of their beds. You know it's Christmas day when you are allowed to eat two bars of chocolate before breakfast. Downstairs they discovered a very respectable bundle of gifts waiting for them. They got an annual each; James got the 1973 Beano annual whilst Philip received a copy of Boys World. To share, they got the Matchbox Cascade Marble Game from their grandad and Perfection from Grace, mainly because she was able to get a very reasonable discount from Woolworth's. They also received a Meccano set each, a few more games, some Lego and Airfix kits. James got a Spitfire whilst Philip got a De Havilland Mosquito. James was also chuffed to bits with his Spirograph but for Philip his main present was by far the best. It was a yellow tracksuit with three thin white stripes down the sleeves of the top and the outside of the bottoms. Although an official Leeds United tracksuit was beyond his mother's price range it didn't matter as she had also bought and added an iron on transfer of the club badge. Philip loved it and it was already caked in mud and in the wash basket before James had finished reading his 'Beano' annual and Christmas lunch was on the table, minus the bread sauce of course.

Christmas lunch was out of the way and so was desert (James opted for trifle, Philip went for Jam tarts) by the time the Queen appeared to give her customary speech. Grace washed, Philip dried whilst James helped his mother to tidy up the living room, then everybody settled down to watch 'Billy Smart's Christmas Circus'.

Christmas night arrived with such haste that one would be forgiven in thinking that it was being pursued by the authorities. Philip and James were playing with their Meccano sets until the table was needed for tea; turkey sandwiches and cold Yorkshire pudding covered in strawberry jam. Then it was back to the settee, another snowball each for the boys, the Quality Street tin with the lid left off and the 'Morcambe and Wise Christmas Show' on the T.V. They flipped a coin to decide which film to watch; 'Von Ryan's Express' was the winner although their mother was rooting for 'The Odd Couple'. Their mother called it a day and retired to bed after the film. Grace also opted to turn in shortly after. James fell asleep on the settee, leaving Philip to enjoy 'Quatermass and the Pit' on 'BBC2'. All things considered, it had been a very enjoyable day.

Chapter 75

Although it was by no means a vintage performance, Leeds United had managed to scrape a one-nil win over Norwich City on the Saturday before Christmas. A solitary goal by Terry Yorath had proved to be enough and had extended their unbeaten start to the season to twenty one games, exactly halfway through. The Boxing Day fixture however, was a far more challenging trip to Newcastle United and if the team wanted to keep their unbeaten run going, a much better performance would be needed.

For Philip, Boxing Day also meant a trip to the betting shop in Wood End, the King George VI Chase at Kempton Park being the highlight of the Boxing Day racing calendar. The day itself got off to quite a chilly start. The temperature outside was still below freezing as he set off for his round. He half-expected to bump into a yeti or Scott's ill-fated Antarctic party as he made his way to the shop. He purposefully remembered not to mention his feelings about the cold weather whilst inside the shop as he wanted to avoid another history lesson on the winter of 1963. He was also keen to get home as his De Havilland Mosquito, having been left to dry overnight, was now waiting to have its transfers and its first coat of paint applied.

On a Boxing Day morning there are few things quite as satisfying as prizing the lid off of a pot of Airfix paint and peering at the deep rich colour inside. With three pots prized open, brush in hand and an egg cup full of cold water, Philip set to work. The plane was predominantly light grey, with a dark grey undercarriage, a dark grey stripe on each wing and bright red cones at the front of the propellers. He was midway through painting the undercarriage when the living room door swung open and Grace appeared in her Woolworth's uniform.

"What time is it?" Grace asked as she headed for the kitchen.

"About eight," Philip replied.

Grace paused just as she was about to disappear from view and turned to look at Philip. "Have you had breakfast?" she asked.

Philip shook his head as he dipped his brush into the egg cup of clean cold water. By the time he had completed the bulk of the painting and was about to attempt the dark grey stripes on the wings, some fifteen minutes later, his sister reappeared, carrying two bacon sandwiches.

"Cheers," Philip said upon realising that one of the sandwiches was for him. "Are you going to work?" he asked before taking a bite from his sandwich.

"Whatever gave you that idea?" Grace replied with a broad smile on her face.

"No, seriously, are you going to work?"

"Yes I am, its double time if I go in today and we need the money now he's left us to fend for ourselves. Maybe you should cancel your school trip and get your money back."

"No thanks," Philip replied, almost choking on his sandwich as he did so.

"Yeah, well, I suppose we'll manage. I think mum's even thinking about going back to work and at least he's gone, that's the main thing."

"Yeah, that's the main thing, isn't it Grace?" Philip replied with sarcasm in his voice spread thicker than the butter on his bacon sandwich.

"Are you trying to tell me things aren't better around here since he left? Yesterday was lovely and look at mum, look at how much happier she's been since he left."

"I'm just saying that it's not the same for everyone, that's all."

"Like who?" Grace asked

"Like me and especially James."

With an obvious shift in her mood, Grace slammed her half-eaten sandwich down on her plate. "You saw what he was being like, the drinking and the anger. He's been hitting mum and other stuff that we don't need to discuss here and now and you don't think this is better?" Grace paused before adding as she grabbed her sandwich again, "For all of us, better for all of us."

"I'm just saying that not everybody is as happy as you are about dad leaving, that's all."

"And mum?" Grace replied.

"Mum what?"

"You don't care about mum, about the fact that she's happier?"

"Of course I care."

"It doesn't sound like it."

Philip was annoyed by his sister's suggestion but as he was about to respond, the living room door swung open and James walked in. He looked at Philip and then at his sister. "Are you going to work?" he muttered.

"Yes James," Grace replied with a warmer tone in her voice. "And tonight I'm gonna try and talk mum into coming down the Livvy with me. She could do with a night out, I can't remember the last time she had a night out, can you?"

Just then, the living room door swung open again and their mother walked in. "I thought I could hear voices," she said before looking directly at Grace and asking, "Are you going to work today?"

"Why has everybody asked me that? Doesn't the way I'm dressed give you enough information about my plans for the day?" Grace took the last mouthful of her sandwich and whilst clutching the empty plate in her hand, she added "I'm going to work now."

She stood up and with the demeanour of a disgruntled child being sent to bed early, sloped out of the room.

"And you two, what are your plans for the day?" their mother asked.

"Nothing much," Philip replied whilst James, still in his pyjamas, shrugged his shoulders.

Philip still had several hours to kill before the betting shop would be open and with nothing to watch on the T.V. he returned to his painting before turning his attention back to the Meccano set. He also passed some time by helping James to build his Lego vehicle set, a steam shovel with transport carrier. Just before midday and aware that the first race on 'Grandstand' was the 1.05 from Kempton Park, Philip set off for the betting shop.

The moment that you push open the door and enter the Wood End betting shop, you are greeted by a thick veil of silvery grey smoke. There are even rumours that because of the amount of smoke in such a small space, it fails to disperse overnight when the shop is shut and is still waiting to greet the owner when he comes to open up the following morning. A permanent smog hovers between four and five feet above the floor of the shop. The aforementioned floor is awash with discarded cigarette butts, spent matches and scrunched up betting slips. The shaft of sunlight that races in as the door opens is soon vanquished once the door is closed again, leaving behind a dim yellowish glow, emitted from the small number of exposed light bulbs hanging from the ceiling.

Philip picked up a pencil and a few betting slips before squeezing between two old boys with tobacco-stained teeth and tobacco-stained fingers. He then began to glance over the runners and riders on the Kempton card.

His grandad had taught him how to read the form and what all the numbers and symbols meant next to the horses' names. Around the age of ten or eleven and before the old man's health had deteriorated, whilst visiting him they had had a few day trips to Worcester racecourse. Philip's grandad had been around horses for most of his working life and could tell a good thing simply by watching them walk around the paddock and canter down to the start.

'This doesn't mean they'll win,' he would say. 'That depends on the trainer and the skill of the jockey and if they actually want it to win.'

The smoke in the shop seemed to settle just above the bridge of Philip's nose, leaving the top of his head poking out above, like a Scottish mountain peak on a cloudy afternoon. When you placed your bets at the Wood End betting shop, you did so by sliding the slip beneath a small gap at the bottom of a window, in the direction of a man sitting in what can only be described as a cage, big enough to house, but still annoy, a small baboon.

The man sat with a permanent cigarette hanging from his lips and with a face that went above and beyond the lived in look. In fact his face went as far as suggesting that it had accommodated a variety of squatters over the years and things would on occasion turn ugly when the eviction notices were served. However, he never asked any awkward questions or sought any identification of age. His skin was a shade of grey that matched the thin strands of greasy hair upon his head. He made the occasional sound but only when really necessary would he go to the trouble of forming actual words. His only noticeable sense of movement would occur when he pulled the cord that slid the results board along its tracks and into the cage. He would then wait whilst his assistant, whose appearance was remarkably similar, just less hair and more weight, climbed a small stepladder and wrote the results on the board. Once the task was complete, the cord would be released and the board rolled out again for the patrons to view. Two small speakers, positioned high up in the corners where the walls meet the ceiling, crunched and crackled their way through each race commentary with a constant threat that they were about to slope forward and fall silent, at any moment, like an unsuspecting mafia victim.

Philip approached the cage and slid his bets beneath the gap at the bottom of the window. He had three five pence wins, two five pence each way doubles, one ten pence each way double and his big, somewhat lavish bet, a twenty five pence each way single on a horse in the King George; a grand total of one pound and five pence invested.

He arrived home in time to make himself and his mother a cup of tea and watch the first horse in one of his five pence each way doubles finish third at the disappointing price of four to one. According to the paper in the betting shop, the horse was priced at twelve to one, but at least it got a place and kept the bet alive. Unfortunately the second horse in the double failed to make the frame and it was a similar story for the majority of his other bets. His big investment in the King George only got as far as the third fence before sending his jockey tumbling to the turf. He did manage two winners on his five pence single bets. The first one was a two to one favourite but the other horse won at a far more satisfying price of six to one, a return in total of fifty pence, down fifty five pence on the day.

Although his gambling losses took a bit of the shine off the day, it wasn't all bad. Mum had made egg fritters for lunch. 'It's a Christmas Knockout' was on the television, followed by an hour of the brilliant Les Dawson on the other channel and to lift the mood considerably, Leeds United won one-nil away to Newcastle thanks to a screamer of a goal from outside the box by Paul Madeley.

Grace arrived home a little after 5.30pm, carrying a bag of pick 'n' mix and a bottle of cherryade. "These are for you and Philip later," she said as she held the items in question aloft for James to see. Upon lowering them again, she placed them on the dining table. "Where's mum?" she asked.

"In the kitchen," James replied.

After a relatively short conversation between mother and daughter, about the length of an episode of the 'Perils of Penelope Pitstop', Grace returned to the living room.

"Mum and me are going out tonight," Grace announced. "So I don't want you two being silly and spoiling it, mum needs a night out of this house, okay."

James didn't really take any notice and Philip, not wanting to be distracted from watching 'Disney Time', just nodded.

It was a little after 8pm and the boys were too engrossed in the film on television to notice the effort their mother had put in to getting ready to go out.

"You look lovely mum," Grace said as she gave Philip a kick to attract his attention. "Doesn't she Phil," Grace added.

Philip quickly and happily endorsed his sister's viewpoint without any noticeable attempt to look at his mother before plunging his hand into the paper bag to retrieve another sweet.

Boxing Day was in its final throes and rapidly closing in on midnight when their mum and Grace arrived home. James was asleep on the settee and Philip was trying desperately to stay awake whilst attempting to watch 'The Old Grey Whistle Test'. It was immediately apparent by the raised voices in the hallway and the audible sound of their mother crying that something upsetting had occurred during their night out. Philip then heard footsteps as somebody ran up the stairs. He was quickly able to surmise that they were his mother's when the living room door opened and Grace entered.

"What's going on?" He immediately asked.

"Nothing's going on," Grace replied.

"Oh right, that's why mum has just run upstairs crying. If nothing's going on, you must be great fun to go out with."

"It wasn't me, I didn't do anything."

"Then who did Grace?"

"It doesn't matter okay," Grace snapped before walking into the kitchen to make a cup of tea.

Annoyed by the lack of information he had so far received, Philip immediately followed, closing the door behind him as he entered. "It doesn't matter if it doesn't matter to you Grace but it matters to me, so what happened?"

Grace sighed and lowered her head a little as she stood in front of the sink with the kettle in her hand. "If you must know, a few people said a few things that upset mum, okay?"

"No, it's not okay. A few things about what?"

"Dad," Grace replied as she turned on the tap and filled the kettle.

"Dad?" Philip said in surprise, "What about dad?"

"Just stuff about dad."

"Are you sure it wasn't you?"

"What do you mean me?" Grace said as she switched the tap off and the kettle on.

"You know exactly what I mean Grace, you blame dad for everything. It's a good job he's scared of flying or you'd have him down for that plane hijack in Nepal or being a member of the Black September Group."

"The black what?" Grace asked with an expression as blank as the canvas of an artist who's just had his bowl of fruit stolen.

"September," Philip said as he gazed at Grace's bewildered face. Annoyed with himself for sending the conversation in an unnecessary direction, he quickly attempted to get it back on the correct flight path. "Alright, it wasn't you, so what was said about dad?"

"I don't want you saying anything. I mean it, not a word to mum or James."

"I might be wrong, but I think mum already knows."

"Don't be cleaver Philip, you know what I mean. I don't want you talking to mum about it."

Philip didn't say anything. He pulled out a chair, sat down and waited for Grace to continue.

"It doesn't matter," Grace began. "And it doesn't prove anything but it was about why dad left."

It was now Philip's turn to accommodate the blank expression. "What are you on about? Just tell me what was said".

"Claire's mum," Grace muttered. "The night she died, she was drinking in the Livvy."

"Yes I know, we all know, everybody knows," Philip replied.

"Yes well, what you probably didn't know was that she spent the entire evening drinking with dad, the two of them sat in the corner and got hammered together. They also reckon that they left the pub together."

The room fell silent except for the sound of the kettle coming to the boil. Grace opened the tea caddy and placed a large scoop of tea into the teapot before adding the now boiled water. She gave the pot a stir before replacing the lid, collected two mugs from the cupboard above the table and sat down.

"Now you know," Grace said as she looked directly at a still in shock Philip. "Do you want tea?"

"No", Philip replied as he stood up. "I'm going to bed."

"Not a word Philip, not a word," Grace reiterated as Philip left the kitchen.

Chapter 76

Leeds United completed the busy Christmas period with two one-one draws against Birmingham City and Spurs. Neither result was something to shout about, especially when considering a trip to Birmingham and a home game to Spurs were games that needed to be won if the league title was to be achieved, However, on the positive side of the results, the unbeaten run remained intact and now stretched to an impressive twenty four games.

Philip took what he could from this as it was the one ray of light in an otherwise darker second week of the Christmas holiday. The week had taken this darker turn both literally and figuratively. Firstly, the events in the Live and Let Live, Boxing day evening, had resulted in their mother taking several steps back from her newly found positive outlook, as if a large and hungry looking grizzly bear was heading in her direction, and she spent the majority of the second week in her bed. As sternly requested by Grace, the matter had not been discussed again or divulged to James and figuratively speaking, everything now felt several shades darker.

The literal darkness had kindly been supplied by the British government and was in direct response to the ever-growing fuel crisis that had ushered in the New Year. In a desperate bid to preserve energy, power cuts had been introduced and from New Year's Day at 8pm in the evening on a weekday and 10pm at the weekend the electricity was switched off, plunging those not prepared into darkness. For Philip and James, certain aspects of the situation were quite novel at first, whilst other aspects were less so. If you needed to use the toilet, you took the torch upstairs, so as not to walk about the house with a candle in your hand. Candles however, were used for providing light sources downstairs so the batteries were not wasted in the torches. The lighting arrangements were very much the novel aspect of the power cuts; the loss of the electrical appliances, especially the television and the kettle were definitely on the other side of the coin.

Swimming training had also been impacted by the cuts as Philip discovered on the first Sunday back after the Christmas break. The Sunday session itself was okay but due to the nation's need to conserve energy, they were unable to run the Wednesday evening session for the foreseeable future. This had quite clearly angered Mr Kennedy as it meant that there would only be three more training sessions before the big meet towards the end of the month.

The day before Mr Kennedy's two and a half minute poolside rant about the fuel crisis, the inept conservative government, Edward Heath and just for good measure and possibly as a form of cleansing, his mother-in-law's extended Christmas stay, had been a very important day in the footballing calendar. Every fan, the length and breadth of the country knew that the first Saturday in January was F.A. Cup third round day.

This was a day when legends could emerge, moments could be written into the pages of football folklore; the minnows, the giant killers, the unbeatable being beaten. For the fan of a lower league club or even better a non-league club, reaching the third round was the holy grail of cup football. Only through the magic of the cup were such things possible as Rhyl F.C. playing Swansea City as they did in 1971. This is when and where teams such as Maidenhead, Leatherhead, South Shields, Margate and Blyth Spartans stepped forward to be counted. This was the day of the Ronnie Radford screamer from outside the box, when David might slay Goliath. The third round of the F.A. Cup always promises so much and always lives up to and keeps its promise. Saturday the 5th of January 1974 was no exception.

Non-league Grantham F.C. battled all the way, at home to Middlesbrough, eventually losing two-nil. Grimsby town lost to first division Burnley by the same score. Boston United drew at Derby County, Hendon drew at Newcastle and Hereford United were at it again, a one-one draw away to West Ham. They went on to win the replay as well before eventually losing at home to Bristol City in the fourth round.

For Philip it was a nervous, uncomfortable wait as the vidiprinter began to roll and the scores started to come in. He was still emotionally readjusting and coming to terms with the cup final defeat of the previous season, the now world famous Sunderland victory over Leeds United. He would still, on occasion, some seven months later, wake in the middle of the night, cold beads of sweat rolling around on his chest, as he relived Jim Montgomery stretching out an arm and diverting Peter Lorimer's goal bound strike onto the bar in the seventieth minute.

This season's third round draw had paired Leeds United away to Wolves, a tricky tie against another Division One club. The score eventually appeared at the bottom of the screen; it was their third one-one draw in a row. The game itself was the main game on Match of the Day that evening, along with the Hereford United game and Manchester United's rather fortuitous one-nil victory at home to lowly Plymouth Argyle.

Darkness was clearly establishing its authority on the situation and a stiff cold breeze was gathering pace when Philip arrived home from school on the day of Leeds United's F.A. Cup replay against Wolves. The first three days back in school after the holiday had passed without any major incident and the belated conduct card he had received on Monday morning remained unblemished. He didn't spot the letter straight away, it was only when his mother had briefly appeared in the kitchen doorway and told him of its arrival, that he noticed it lying on the dining table.

"You've a letter from your footballer," she said before vanishing again inside the kitchen.

Due to the adverse weather conditions and equally difficult reading conditions, Philip opted to leave the letter until after he had completed his paper round. He took it upstairs and placed it under his pillow. He changed out of his school uniform and set off for his round. On his way through the scullery, his mother grabbed his attention.

"Will you get a tin of mushy peas on your way past Broad Park?" she said as she passed him a ten pence piece. "It's faggots for tea and I thought I had some to soak but I must have used them up," she added.

As Philip entered the small supermarket at the opposite end of the row of shops to the White Horse pub, he bumped into Paul McBride travelling in the other direction.

"Ah, Phil, result!" Paul said. "I'm glad I bumped into you. I was gonna call round and see ya."

"What's going on Paul?" Philip replied. "Old man Underwood says that you've jacked in your round. He's got a card in the shop window, looking for a replacement."

"Don't need it, do I? I don't need his grief or his poxy money. My operations are doing well, especially on the bike stealing front. I got a couple of lads always on the lookout and a list of customers, especially this time of year. Some good bikes to be had, know what I mean?"

"Oh right." Philip replied before glancing over his shoulder to check that he had locked his bike.

Paul laughed. "My other operation is still in full swing too, that's why I was gonna come and sees ya. People still want stuff even if Christmas is over. You in later? I'll drop the list round."

Philip wasn't given any meaningful amount of time to formulate a response before Paul had headed off in the direction of the Manor Farm estate. "Catch ya later." Paul called out with his back to Philip and momentarily waving a hand in the air.

Philip returned home, placed the tin of peas on the kitchen table, along with the change and then headed upstairs to retrieve the letter from beneath his pillow. With his usual customary carefulness, he separated the letter from the envelope and then lay down on his bed to read it.

Dear Philip

I was glad to receive your last letter as to be honest with you, under the circumstances, I was worried about how your Christmas was going. Reading what you have told me, I needn't had worried too much as your Christmas, on a personal level, seems in fact rather similar to our Christmas on the pitch. Some very pleasing aspects at the start of the holiday period but certain elements of the second half could have been better. I am pleased that your father's absence does not appear to have impacted upon you all too much. Give your mother time; as you said yourself, there are certainly plenty of positives to cling on to and change does not happen overnight. There will always be setbacks in life as in sport, as we have discussed in the past, and some hurdles are tougher than others to overcome.

The beautiful thing about a New Year is that it always brings with it new hope and new opportunities to move forward and on to a better place. I think that it is a good thing for your sister to be living back home again, a good thing for her and for you all as a family. As long as you all continue to be there for each other and support each other, then things can only improve for all of you and not just for your mother.

I noticed that you neglected to mention how your swimming was going in your most recent letter. I do recall however, that your next competition is not that far away. I hope you are doing your best in training and doing all that you can do to prepare for the meet. I know we have talked about preparation and commitment and effort when it comes to sport but it is always worth remembering that there isn't a successful sportsman out there who hasn't had to work hard for their success. If I do not hear from you before the meet, I hope it goes well.

I also hope that your up and coming school trip goes well. It sounds very exciting and completely different to anything you have probably encountered before. Experiences such as this can stay with you for the rest of your life and years later you will find yourself reminiscing upon the events and magical moments that never seem to fade. As always, a big thank you for helping me to stay focused and keep my feet on the ground as this unbeaten run continues to stretch its way through the season. The most pleasing aspect at present, even despite the two rather disappointing draws recently, is that everybody is contributing to the goals scored and everybody is focused upon playing for the team. Six different goal-scorers in recent games is certainly a positive sign. Again though we cannot rest on our laurels, we need to stay focused and keep working hard. We have allowed the chasing pack to close the gap in recent weeks so it is up to us to get back to winning ways, starting with Southampton's visit on Saturday. There are also games against Chelsea and Arsenal looming into view upon the horizon.

I will close now. As mentioned, good luck in the swimming meet if it takes place before I hear from you again. Keep trying your best at everything you do, especially in school. You cannot put a value on a good education, it is one of the things in life that is truly priceless. Look after yourself and those closest to you.

Your friend,
Billy.

Chapter 77

"Have you got everything?"

"Yes."

"Are you sure?"

"Yes."

"Where's the letter gone with the list of what you need to take with you?"

"It's on the table."

Philip's mum stood up and walked towards the dining room table, scanning the surface as she approached in search of the letter. Once sighted, she reached across and picked it up.

"What time do you need to be at the bus station?" she asked as she flipped over the first sheet of the letter to get to the items listed on the second page.

"I have to be at Pool Meadow by quarter past nine," Philip replied before adding, "The coach leaves at nine thirty."

Reading the letter as she went, Philip's mum walked back towards Philip and the open suitcase resting on the settee. "Flannel," she said upon arrival. "Have you packed a flannel?"

"Yes." Philip replied.

"And a bar of soap?"

On this occasion, Philip just nodded.

"Sandwiches!" Philip's mum suddenly called out with enough energy in her voice to cause Philip to drop the jumper he had been folding. "It says that you need a packed lunch for the journey. Wales is a long way. You need to take something to eat. I've got some eggs, do you want me to do you an egg sandwich?"

"No thanks," Philip replied, shaking his head as he attempted for a second time to fold his jumper.

"Paste, I think there's a jar of paste in the cupboard. That will have to do. You can take a packet of crisps as well. Now hurry up, you should have told me this last night," she said as she headed into the kitchen to make the packed lunch.

Philip hadn't had the best night's sleep as a mixture of excitement and apprehension spent the majority of the small hours keeping him company. On the whole however, as he packed the last few items on the list into his suitcase, excitement had, for now at least, won through and taken a firm hold of the situation. He'd never been away on his own before, nor had he ever embarked on an outward bounds activity holiday. The only person who wasn't best pleased about Philip's school trip was Mr Kennedy. Mr Kennedy was not happy at all that Philip would miss the final training session before the big meet at the end of the month and as he had pointed out several times at yesterday's session, 'We still need to work on those turns.'

Right now however, as Philip completed one final check before closing his suitcase, his turns were the last thing on his mind. The main thought that was front and centre as he checked to see if James was ready for school, was how he would find out the Leeds United result on Saturday. The victory over Southampton at the weekend now meant the unbeaten start to the season had reached an impressive twenty five games but he knew the next game, Everton away, was not going to be easy. They had only lost once at home all season and that was the Merseyside derby against Liverpool. Their home record currently stood at won seven, drawn five and lost one. Despite not having a prolific marksman up front they still had the capability to hurt teams and had they had plenty of players who knew exactly where the goals were; players like Mick Lyons,

Joe Harper, Bob Latchford and John Connolly. Their defence, especially at home, was one of the best in the league.

By the time Philip got off the bus at Pool Meadow, he had temporarily put his concerns about the football scores to one side. For the first time since he decided to go on the trip, his thoughts had turned to who else was going to be on the coach, if he would know anybody and more importantly, if he would want to spend the next ten days hanging out with anybody. As he climbed aboard the coach, he began scanning the interior in search of an acceptable companion. At first glance, it didn't look good. All he could see were faces of boys he usually avoided as a matter of principle and boys who avoided him for precisely the same reason. It wasn't until he was over halfway down the coach that he spotted Brian Mason and Derek Windass sitting on the back seat. The relief was instant. A feeling washed over him as if he had just reached the urinal with literally seconds to spare. He immediately picked up the pace and headed for the back seat of the coach.

"Am I glad to see you two," Philip said as he reached the back seat. "I thought I had got on the wrong coach for a minute and I was off to an arse- licking convention."

"Alright Phil?" Brian replied before adding, "Still would have been better than spending the next ten days at school."

"Depends whose arse you're licking," Derek chipped in.

"Yeah, fair point." Brian said as Philip sat down.

They arrived at the Dol-y-Moch outwards bounds centre a little before four o' clock. It may have been situated in Mid-Wales but for Philip and his friends it could have been another planet, another solar system, another galaxy. The only way of knowing for sure that it wasn't any of these things was the amount of time it had taken to get there. Even these boys knew that you couldn't reach another solar system in a little over six hours on a coach.

As they climbed from their non-space travelling coach and looked up the remainder of the driveway, they were met by the sight of a preposterously large stone and slate covered seventeenth century house with equally preposterously large stone steps, leading to an equally preposterously large front door. It looked like a holiday let for the giant in Jack and the Beanstalk. Over to the right hand side of the house and partially hidden by the thick, dense woodland was a winding trail which weaved its way to a long thin outbuilding, which over the years had had many uses and was currently being used as a dormitory.

The boys all gathered around the side of the coach and began collecting their luggage before being instructed to make their way into the house in an orderly fashion. As orderly as possible whilst dragging heavy suitcases up large stone steps, the boys fulfilled the request. However, this actually proved to be a much easier task than the one that followed for these boys who had then to carry their suitcases up a narrow spiral staircase which lead to the large dormitory at the top of the house. The sleeping arrangements had been assigned alphabetically. For Philip and Brian it meant venturing up the spiral staircase. For Derek it meant dragging his suitcase back outside again, as he was sleeping in the dormitory at the end of the narrow path.

Once everybody had settled in, which consisted of dumping their suitcases on top of their allocated beds, it was time to eat. The cuisine was one step up and two steps sideways from their usual school fare, similar in both appearance and texture but with slightly more flavour. Dinner on the first evening was followed by a two hour presentation from the outward bounds team leader, Leonard, and his assistants. The talk was designed to inform the boys of some of the activities that lay ahead over the next ten days. If the talk was also designed to help put the boys at ease, then a roaring success it wasn't. What it did succeed in doing was to send the boys to bed on that first night with a whole host of reasons for having a restless night's sleep, every last one of them firmly placed in the negative camp.

Some boys went to bed feeling anxious, some went to bed feeling apprehensive, some went to bed fearing for their safety, some went to bed fearing for their lives. For some it was a mixture of feelings with thoughts racing from one emotion to the next and then back again. For two boys in the dormitory at the top of the house and three boys in the dormitory in the wooded area a feeling of homesickness was also thrown into the mix and they spent several hours lying in their beds gently sobbing into the darkness.

The following morning a group of very tired and nervous boys sat quietly and ate breakfast before being issued with the equipment needed for the day's activity and handed a packed lunch concealed inside a brown paper bag. Once suitably dressed, prepared and briefed for the activity that lay ahead, the boys were ushered into mini buses and driven the short distance from Dol-y-Moch to the drop off point along the bank of the Afon Dwyryd. Once they were all assembled and the engines of the mini buses had faded away, Leonard pointed towards the snow covered peaks in the distance.

"That's where we are heading boys," he said before adding, "With some activities on route."

He may as well had been standing on the banks of the Amazon or pointing towards Mount Kilimanjaro, as each and every boy was frozen to the spot and it wasn't on account of the cold January weather. They were completely overawed, overwhelmed by the amount of wide open space that surrounded them, an environment that was so far removed, so alien to anything that the majority of them had ever experienced before. They felt incredibly small, incredibly lost. They feared that they would never see a bus stop again, never walk into a crowded room, never find themselves standing on a busy, bustling street. One of the boys thought he had seen something similar once, in an episode of 'Whicker's World', but he couldn't be sure. At this point in time if the boys had been offered a full refund and a coach back home, each and every one of them would have accepted. But that wasn't going to happen; they weren't going home - far from it. So after some positive gestures and words of encouragement from Leonard and his team, they all set off. The boots on their feet now felt several pounds heavier than they did twenty minutes ago and the rucksacks on their backs were stuffed to the top with dread, leaving just enough room for their waterproof coats and their packed lunches.

The next two hours were spent on a slow and steady ascent through forest, across open spaces, over rock formations, more forests, more rocks and more space until the air felt thinner than a coat of paint and they were all convinced that they were now several miles above sea level. Eventually as they came out of a wooded glade and into yet another vast open space, they could hear the sound of rushing water. No sooner had the sound registered than they all caught sight of the waterfall. As far as waterfalls go, obviously it wasn't to be found in the top division. It may not have been Angel Falls or Niagara Falls but for a group of schoolboys growing up in inner city Coventry it was definitely big enough, measuring approximately eight metres wide and twenty five metres to the river below. However, immediately after Leonard announced that they would soon be abseiling down it, it got a whole lot bigger. At that precise point in time, the only consolation was the fact that nobody had brought a barrel with them.

Whilst Leonard's not at all glamorous assistants set up the equipment and positioned themselves at either end of the waterfall, Leonard himself gave the boys a brief abseiling demonstration at the same time as showing how to fit their safety harnesses and attach themselves to the guide rope.

Waiting for his turn to go was like sitting in the tunnel of the 'Great Escape'. It was worse than sitting in the waiting room at the dentist, knowing it was only a matter of time before the door swung open and the nurse called out his name. For Philip, as each nervous boy leant backwards and slowly disappeared over the edge of the waterfall, his stomach churned faster, his heart rate increased, his palms began to sweat, the blood rushed to his feet and the world around him began to sway.

"Okay Philip, your turn," Leonard called out as he stood at the top of the waterfall.

Philip stood up, checked that his helmet was securely fastened beneath his chin and steadily edged forward.

"Come on lad, we haven't got all day."

Upon arrival, Leonard took hold of Philip's harness, checked it and his helmet before attaching him to the rope with the aid of the carabiner around his waist.

"Okay lad you're ready to go. Now listen to your instructor," Leonard said as he encouraged Philip to step forward.

With his heart firmly relocated at the back of his throat, Philip stepped to the edge of the waterfall.

"Take hold of the rope lad, but not too tight," Leonard's assistant said before adding, "Now turn yourself around and step into the water."

Philip did as instructed and looked down at the clear water as it rushed over and past his feet.

"Okay then, when you are ready you just need to step back so that your toes are on the edge."

Philip stepped back.

"Legs nice and straight, now lean back. Keep hold of the rope and gently feed it through your hands, not too quick though."

Gripped by fear, Philip slowly leant back. Staring intently at the rope, he slowly fed a little of it through his hands. The volume of water around him seemed to increase in both sound and quantity.

"Now bend those legs and push yourself away from the rock, feeding the rope through as you go."

The moment he pushed away from the waterfall, the fear left his body quicker than the water rushing past his feet. All of a sudden and whilst in mid-air, he found the experience exhilarating. He swung back towards the waterfall, bent his legs on impact and pushed away again, guiding the rope through his hands as he went. Soon, a very different teenage boy arrived at the bottom of the waterfall to the one who had set off from the top.

From that point onwards, he embraced every activity as a new adventure. He skied for the first time, badly, with all the finesse of a broken shopping trolley on a frozen lake. He abseiled again, better than he skied. He went canoeing, about as well as he skied. He went orienteering; a complete disaster. He and his orienteering partner, a boy called Andrew Toole, ended up at Ffestiniog railway station when they should have been arriving at a small shack in the middle of a forest about two and a half miles away. The telling off they received when they were eventually collected from the station only added to the experience. He didn't even mind having to wait until tea-time on Sunday to find out the football results from the day before, a goalless draw at Everton.

Philip had arrived at Dol-y-Moch, a fish out of water and full of apprehension. Ten days later, he left with a completely new outlook upon the great outdoors and a stack of memories that he knew would stay with him for a very long time.

Chapter 78

"Some boy came looking for you whilst you were away." Philip's mum paused for a moment before continuing. "Twice, I don't think he's very bright. I told him when you would be back but he still called round again. Can't say I was very much taken with him either, quite an unsavoury boy in both appearance and manner. I do hope that he is not a good friend of yours."

Grace leant across the table, closer to Philip. "Paul McBride," she whispered.

"Oh him, no not really," Philip said in an attempt to reassure his mother.

"Then what does he want with you?"

"He has a paper round at the shop. He mentioned being able to get some transfers for my bike, it might have been that or he might have wanted me to do his round."

"Yes well, just make sure that the transfers are his to give and not somebody else's and whilst you're at it, I'd rather he didn't call here again."

Philip nodded. "Okay mum," he replied before taking another bite of his fish finger.

That evening it felt good to be home. Even though he had thoroughly enjoyed his time away, it still felt good to be sitting by a roaring fire and in front of a T.V. screen. The living room seemed to fit around him and fill him with a sense of belonging. The sight of his mother preparing the candles in readiness for the rapidly approaching power cut, an event he had forgotten about, failed to dim the glow within him, a glow that was able to match the one being emitted by the fire. Even when the screen went black, halfway through the first ever episode of 'The Liver Birds', it didn't seem to matter. Card games, mainly Shoot, and a game of Frustration by candlelight followed before calling it a night and listening to Radio Luxembourg fade in and out on his battery powered transistor for an hour or so before drifting off to sleep in the comfort of his own bed.

The sound of the strong wind whistling and swirling and the swollen droplets of rain crashing against the bedroom window woke Philip from his slumber minutes before his alarm clock was able to complete the same task. The weather outside went a long way to dampen down the warm glow that had accompanied him to bed the night before. He kicked off the blankets with his feet and clambered out of bed. The thought of completing his paper round in such inclement weather, followed by a day at school, only succeeded in extinguishing the remaining flickering embers. He went downstairs and into the cold kitchen. As he was a few minutes ahead of schedule, he decided that it was a morning that called for a breakfast with hot milk; he opted for cornflakes.

Once fed and dressed as suitably as possible for the conditions, he collected his bag and his bike before setting off for the shop. By the time he exited Ellacombe Road at the end of his round, the rain had managed to seep through every layer of clothing. He could even feel his vest clinging to his back like a soggy flannel clinging to the side of the bath. As he entered Monkswood Crescent, he heard somebody call out his name. He turned to see Paul McBride cycling towards him.

"Hello Phil," Paul said.

Keen to get out of the rain, Philip just nodded and carried on walking.

"Hang on Phil, hang on. I got this for you, try not to get it wet," Paul said as he thrust a folded piece of paper towards Philip. "Some good stuff on there Phil, money to be made, chance to earn some shekels. I would have brought it round your house but the last time I called round, your mum was a bit weird. I don't think she likes me much."

Philip just smiled and took hold of the piece of paper before stuffing it into his damp coat pocket. As he did so Paul turned his bike around and set off in the opposite direction.

"Catch you in a few days," Paul shouted as he peddled into the distance.

When Philip got home and entered the house through the scullery, his mother was waiting in the doorway to the kitchen, with a towel in her hand. Philip stood in the scullery and stripped down to his vest and pants before drying his hair with the towel. Whilst he dried himself off, his mother went and fetched his pyjamas.

"Put them on for now," she said upon her return. "And come into the living room, I've got something for you."

With curiosity immediately aroused, Philip quickly put on his pyjamas and rushed into the living room. His mother was sitting on the settee with a shoe box in her lap.

"I think these are the ones you wanted," she said as she held up the box.

Quicker than Billy Whizz, Philip took hold of the box, sat down next to his mum, removed the lid and peered inside. In the box was a pair of gleaming, imitation leather, black and burgundy platform shoes, a one inch heel at the front and a three inch heel at the back.

"Shouldn't need any newspaper for a while," his mum said with a smile as he lifted one of the shoes out of the box and rested it in both hands.

"Have you had your breakfast?" his mother asked whilst Philip sat and gazed at the shoe.

"Yes," he replied with a short accompanying nod of the head.

"Then go and get your brother up, don't want you being late for school on your first day back."

Philip set off for school in his new shoes, feeling and looking about three inches taller. His new footwear got the seal of approval from his friends at the bus stop and even Mr Spencer commented on them later that morning when Philip entered his office after being summoned during assembly.

"How was your trip?" Mr Spencer asked immediately after complimenting Philip on his new shoes.

"It was okay," Philip replied with a brief shrug of the shoulders.

"Only okay?" Mr Spencer asked.

This time the shoulders shrugged alongside a nodding of the head. "It was okay." Philip said again.

"Everything set for Saturday?" Mr Spencer asked.

"What?" Philip replied.

"Saturday," Mr Spencer said with a tone in his voice that clearly demonstrated disapproval in Philip's response. "Saturday lad, the competition."

"Oh that, yes," Philip replied.

"What time do you need to be there?"

"Five 'o' clock, I think."

More disapproval came racing towards Philip. "You think, you think. I think you need to make sure that you know. Make sure that you are there on time and ready to swim. Don't forget that you're representing the school as well as the city and the swimming club. You are the first boy in the history of the school to swim for the city so don't let us down."

Mr Spencer's facial expression and the tone of delivery of the speech removed any possible grounds for a misunderstanding and Philip was sent on his way knowing exactly what was expected of him. He was also a little heavier, due the flea he now had in his ear.

Although the wind had eased when Philip woke up on Saturday morning, the persistent rain had now turned to sleet. After completing his paper round, his plans for the rest of the day had been temporarily derailed when his mother had requested that he took James to Saturday morning cinema. With a few minor adjustments however he soon had his schedule back on track. Exit the cinema around twelve noon or just after, back home for 1pm, a quick turnaround consisting of a crisp sandwich and a wagon wheel, out again with swimming kit no later than two o clock, back in town by approximately two thirty, giving him about two hours to see what he could acquire from the list and then be able to make his way to the sports centre in plenty of time for the meet.

All went to plan in the cinema. Even the main feature, 'Snowball Express', was an enjoyable experience, and they departed through the foyer at about ten past twelve. They arrived home just past 1pm. A cheese and onion crisp sandwich and a wagon wheel later, Philip set off again. He had to wait a little longer for the bus than he was hoping to but he remained roughly on schedule. Whilst on the bus, he had another look at the list. He paid particular attention to the smaller, easier to conceal items. He was sure that he could pick up a Prestige wall mounted tin-opener, a men's Phillips shaver with triple floating heads and a Pifco torch from Owen Owens, so upon arrival in Pool Meadow, he headed there first.

Sure enough, within twenty five minutes of entering the department store, he was heading for the side exit with all three items concealed about his person. It was just as he went to push open the glass door and step outside that a very large man suddenly blocked his path. As Philip attempted to manoeuvre around the obstacle in his way, another equally large gentleman suddenly appeared behind him, and between them, they both manoeuvred Philip back into the store, up the small flight of stairs and into a small room just to the left of the stairs. As the door closed behind him, he heard a loud piercing shrill of a voice fill the air.

"Where's my bottle of Charlie, you thieving little bastard?"

All Philip could see was the chest of the man standing in front of him. The man stepped aside and in the centre of the room, all perfectly painted and perfumed, with a face as distorted as a politician's version of events, stood Gwendoline.

"Got you this time, you little shit!" Gwendoline triumphantly exclaimed.

Unknown to Philip, whilst on her way back to her cosmetics counter after a short break, Gwendoline had spotted him entering the store. She had proceeded to follow him until she had been able to pass the responsibility onto the floor walkers. From that point on, he was a sitting duck as they had watched his every move.

Gwendoline turned her attention to the two large gentlemen. "He was in here a few months ago, before Christmas, claiming he wanted to buy a bottle of perfume for his sister's birthday. Wanted it so he could get his leg over some fat girl more like. When my back was turned the little sod swiped a bottle of Charlie."

One of the men walked over to a desk, tapping the surface upon arrival. "Over here son, empty your pockets and your bag."

Philip didn't move.

"Come on son, don't make it difficult, either you do it or I have to do it and I'd rather you do it."

With his palms sweating and his heart going quicker than Woody Woodpecker's beak, Philip walked towards the table. He slowly began to remove the stolen items and place them down as requested. "Can I go now?" Philip asked in hope rather than expectation.

Gwendoline released a short burst of laughter.

"I'm afraid not son," the floor walker replied.

"But I've got to be somewhere. I can't miss it, I've got to go."

"The only place you're going to is Little Park Street," Gwendoline said with glee drenching every word.

"What?" Philip replied.

"I'm afraid so son," the floor walker said as he looked over at his colleague, who was still standing by the door. "Go and get the lad a cup of tea, eh Frank. You know what the police are like, it might take them a while to get here." He turned to face Gwendoline. "Don't you need to be getting back to your counter? We can handle things from here."

"I guess so," Gwendoline replied before looking directly at Philip. "Bye," she said with a smile so wide that her lipstick almost reached her ears.

"Sit yourself down son, you might have a bit of a wait," the floor walker said as Gwendoline left the room.

As they waited for both the drink and the police to arrive, the floor walker took a closer look at the items Philip had placed on the table.

"So when did you start shaving?" the floor walker asked.

Philip didn't reply.

"A rather eclectic bunch of items here. Are they all for you?"

Again, Philip didn't respond.

"Look son, I think you need to have a good think about the direction you are heading. The road you are on doesn't lead to anywhere you want to go. The longer you spend on it, the more isolated it becomes, a bit like the M6." The floor walker offered Philip a smile but Philip had very little to smile about. The floor walker continued. "The longer you stay on the road, the further you travel and the harder it becomes to get off it. You need to trust me on this one, I speak from experience, not my own you understand but of others. The people I come across doing this job. It is the same old faces time and time again. It's all they know, their only purpose, their only way to survive, to get by. When they finally realise the road they're on and try to change direction, it's too late. They've been travelling in the same direction for far too long that there's no other road for them to take."

The police arrived about twenty minutes after a lukewarm, unsweetened, stewed cup of tea that Philip didn't drink had arrived. They gathered up the items that Philip had attempted to steal before one of the officers took a firm grip of Philip's upper arm and after a brief conversation with the floor walker, escorted Philip out of the store and to their waiting vehicle which was parked in a bus stop in Broadgate. An extremely short ride later and he was being led into Little Park Street police station through a rear entrance. After being processed, as the officer behind the desk had referred to the brief interaction, Philip was escorted to and placed inside a cell, where he remained for the best part of an hour before being collected again and escorted to an interview room.

He was asked to sit down next to a gentleman in a brown pinstriped suit and a gaudy designed tie that had no earthly chance of going well with any outfit one cared to choose.

"This is the duty solicitor," one of the officers said before adding, "You need an adult present and we are still trying to contact your parents."

"There's just my mum," Philip replied.

The officer nodded and motioned for Philip to sit down. He then took the stolen items out of a bag and placed them on the table. "Do you recognise these items?" the Officer asked.

Phillip nodded.

"You have to speak son, you need to give a yes or no response."

"Yes," Philip replied.

"An interesting set of items for a fourteen year old boy to be stealing. Is there anything you would like to say about that?"

"No," Philip replied. "Not really."

"Listen son, I'm not really all that interested in why you stole a torch and a tin opener. What I am interested in is whether you are going to make the mistake of becoming a regular visitor to this establishment."

Philip shook his head.

"Listen son, I know that this isn't the first time you've done a bit of shoplifting but it is the first time that you've been caught. You need to think long and hard about the choices you are making. Once you've got a record, once you are in the system, got a label, been taken to court, it's like a grass stain on a pair of white flannel trousers, it never goes away son. Follows you everywhere, like a shadow, in fact it's worse than a shadow because it's always there, even visible in a dark room. Do you understand what I'm trying to say to you?"

Philip nodded.

"You don't want to go down this road son. It only leads to a lot of miserable places and I mean miserable, even more miserable than a weekend in Goole."

"Is that on the M6?" Philip asked.

"No, it's the M62." The officer stood up. "Come on," he said to Philip. "Let's get you back to your cell until your mother gets here."

Upon arriving back at the cell, the officer asked Philip if he was hungry. Philip nodded.

"I'll see if I can find you a sandwich and a cup of tea," the officer said as he proceeded to lock Philip in. Thirty minutes later he returned with a cheese sandwich, a cup of tea and the news that Philip's mother had been contacted and was on her way to collect him.

When Philip arrived again at the custody desk, his mother, with arms folded tightly, was already waiting.

"Okay lad, as I've explained to your mother, you are not going to be charged with any offences today but you will be receiving a caution. See it as an opportunity to avoid that grass stain we talked about earlier. Not so much a get out of jail free card, more a case of an avoid entering the system card. But be warned, if you find yourself back here again, there will be no second chances. You will find yourself in court. Now I suggest you get off home and think about what I have said." The officer approached the door to the station and held it open.

Philip's mother unfolded her arms and gently nudged Philip towards the door. Moments later they both stepped out into the cold early evening air. Philip braced himself for the tongue lashing he thought he was about to receive but to both his surprise and confusion, it never arrived.

"Are you hungry?" his mother asked.

Five minutes later, a still very confused Philip was sitting in a window booth of the Wimpy restaurant on Fairfax Street, opposite his mother. He continued to ask himself why they were there and why was he being treated for being caught shoplifting. Without looking at the menu, when the waitress approached the table, his mother ordered.

"He'll have a cheeseburger, chips and a glass of lemonade. I'll just have a bowl of soup and a cup of tea, thank you."

The waitress scribbled the order down on her pad before turning away.

Philip could feel the question forming in the pit of his stomach. He felt it as it slowly travelled north and moved towards the back of his throat. He tried to fight back, tried to resist but it was futile, a losing battle. The question rolled across his tongue before reaching the back of his lips. He made on last pathetic gesture to try and stop it being released but it was no good. "Aren't you angry?" Philip asked.

"I was," his mother replied. "Especially when there was a policeman on the doorstep and all the neighbours suddenly discovered they had jobs to do in their front gardens. But now I'm just disappointed. The problem is, I don't know who I am more disappointed by, you or me."

Both puzzled and troubled by his mother's response, Philip asked, "Why are you disappointed in you?"

"Because I've failed, I've failed as a mother and I've failed as a parent. I've failed you. I thought I'd taught you right from wrong. Taught you that if you wanted something in life, you had to work for it, you couldn't just help yourself and take it. I know this past year or so hasn't been easy for you. It hasn't been easy for any of us but I didn't realise how bad it had got. I failed to see what was happening to my own child, so I feel responsible for what has happened now."

"But it wasn't about right and wrong, I know it was wrong."

"So why did you do it?"

"I needed the money, I needed to pay for my swimming."

"Oh I see, so every time you need some money you are going to turn to stealing."

"No, I didn't mean it like that mum."

His mother was just about to reply, then paused for a moment as she found herself altering her thoughts and in turn what she was about to say. "Wasn't tonight your swimming competition?"

"Yes," Philip replied.

"Oh Philip, I'm so sorry, I forgot all about it."

"It doesn't really matter now," Philip replied as the waitress arrived with the drinks.

"I guess not son," his mother said.

Mrs Knott spent the next minute or so gazing at her son as he sat and drank his glass of lemonade. She reached across the table and placed her hand on his.

"Listen Philip, do you have any idea where your dad is right now?"

Philip shook his head.

"No, me neither, but I do know one thing, he's somewhere he doesn't want to be. Eventually, whatever it was that he ran away from will catch up with him and he's living every day just waiting for it to arrive. Sleeping with one eye open and having a permanent stiff neck for continuously having to look over your shoulder is no way to be living your life. I don't want that for you or your brother. That is why what happened today must never happen again, understand Philip."

Philip nodded his head as he took another drink of lemonade.

"I also don't want you mentioning any of this to your friends. I have enough to deal with, with your dad and the neighbours curtains twitching and tongues wagging. I don't want them thinking and saying things about you."

Philip nodded again.

"Good. Then we will consider the matter closed."

In the way of a conversation, very little was said after that. They ate their food before heading back home on the bus. They arrived home just as 'The Man from Ironside' had solved another case. However he had to go to bed without knowing how Leeds United had faired in the F.A.Cup. He had to wait until Sunday morning when he was able to see the results in the newspaper. Thankfully they had progressed to the next round with a convincing 4-1 win away to Peterborough United.

Chapter 79

You could put your house on it, if you owned one. You could put your life on it, if you felt you had one, you could even put your shirt on it, if you could spare one. One thing was guaranteed, a dead cert on that Monday morning in assembly. That was, when Mr Spencer read out the roll call of names of the boys that needed to wait outside his office, Philip Knott's name would be on the list. Not only was it on the list but it was the first name to be called. However, he was the last person to be called into the office. He witnessed four boys receive the cane, one boy sobbing before during and after receiving the cane and two further boys being informed that they had been dropped from the school rugby team for the forthcoming fixture against Binley Woods on account of their continued poor behaviour. They too received the cane before being sent on their way. Once Philip was the only boy left, Mr Spencer returned to his office and waited a minute or so before calling him in. Determined not to appear fazed by the situation, Philip got up quickly and entered the office.

"Shut the door lad," Mr Spencer snapped with nostrils flared and brow ruffled, the moment he caught sight of Philip entering.

Mr Spencer's aggressive tone immediately caught Philip off guard and he was instantly ill at ease as he turned and closed the door.

"Well then, let's hear it, I'm all ears."

There was a price tag already attached to the story Philip was about to tell. So far the cost stood at fifty pence. That was the fee James had requested and received when asked to back up Philip's story if he was to be questioned. The story itself was formulated on Sunday afternoon in preparation for this very moment.

"It was my grandad," Philip began. "He wasn't well and my mum needed me to go with her. He lives near Hereford."

"Why did you have to go?"

"My mum needed somebody to help her and somebody to stay at home to look after James as she knew we would be away overnight. She didn't want to leave James and me at home and James was too young to go with her in case the situation was very bad. So my sister looked after James and I went with my mum. My sister had to leave work early."

The part about his sister leaving work early hadn't cost him anything as he felt quite confident that she wouldn't be interrogated or asked to corroborate events.

"So you couldn't let Mr Kennedy know? Instead you just decided to let him down, let the club down, the city down, the school down and me down?"

"I telephoned the baths and left a message," Philip replied. This particular piece of information, like the rest of the story, was utterly false but again Philip was confident that it could not be proved or disproved, so he was more than happy to run with it.

The annoyance on Mr Spencer's face was plain to see. Although he was desperate to summon up the cane as punishment, he knew that he couldn't. Instead he handed Philip a conduct card for the week ahead.

"But Sir!" Philip protested. "I wasn't at school."

"Nothing to do with it." Mr Spencer replied. "You were still representing the school and you let the school down, therefore your conduct was unacceptable."

Philip took hold of the conduct card and as he did so, he thought to himself, instead of being the first person to represent the school at swimming, he became the first person in the history of the school to receive a conduct card for shoplifting in Owen Owens. Philip left the office, managing to clutch his conduct card whilst having his fingers tightly crossed. The one gaping hole in his story was his mother. He now just had to hope that Mr Spencer didn't contact her to validate the weekend's events. Philip had considered asking his mother to cover for him but in light of what really took place over the weekend, he thought better of it.

Philip arrived home from school on Friday afternoon with his conduct card unblemished and his story still intact and undisturbed. Feeling that he was in the clear, his thoughts had turned to Leeds United's next fixture at home to Chelsea, but more pressing was what he was going to write in his next letter to Billy about missing the meet. He didn't want to tell him the same tall tale that he had told Mr Spencer but he didn't want to tell him the truth either. He was however to receive a large slice of guidance on the matter when he arrived at training on Sunday morning.

Saturday had been spent at home. He'd turned down the opportunity to go swimming; he wasn't in the mood. He also didn't fancy the cinema. He did manage to go to the betting shop in Wood End and place a small bet on the 'ITV7', ten pence each way. The bet went down at the first hurdle, quite literally, when his horse succumbed to a crashing fall at the first fence in the first race. Philip spent the first part of the afternoon, after the demise of his bet, helping his mother to make some jam tarts. The aroma coming from the kitchen as they slowly baked in the oven wrapped itself around him as his attention returned to the all-important match. Despite Chelsea hovering precariously just above the relegation zone, it proved to be a very difficult encounter. Leeds United had to come from behind to salvage a one-one draw. A Trevor Cherry header from a Billy Bremner cross levelled the match midway through the second half and that was how it stayed. Despite the result being a bit of a disappointment, the unbeaten run now stretched to an impressive twenty seven games.

Philip made sure that he arrived at the swimming baths on Sunday morning on time. He headed straight for the changing rooms and towards the section where the boys were changing. Upon his arrival, he was met by a wall of silence and an impromptu game of statues as the other boys present all froze and stared at him. Eventually one of them spoke.

"What are you doing here?"

"What?" Philip replied.

A different boy stepped forward and walked towards Philip as he spoke. "You're not in this club anymore. You're not a part of this team. Understand? We don't want you here."

Philip was just about to raise his arms and push the boy away when Mr Kennedy appeared.

"Can you come with me please Philip?" Mr Kennedy said before adding, "The rest of you get in the pool and warm up."

Philip followed Mr Kennedy out of the changing rooms, up a flight of stairs and into his small office.

"Sit down son," Mr Kennedy said as he reached his desk and listened out for the sound of the door closing behind Philip.

Philip sat down and looked across at Mr Kennedy. At first Mr Kennedy struggled to make eye contact with him.

"I'm sorry about this son," Mr Kennedy began whilst still looking at the surface of his desk. He looked upwards and across at Philip, "But you're not on the team anymore."

"But why?" Philip asked with a clear hint of distress in his voice.

"I can't do anything about it, it's out of my hands. If you stay on the team, I no longer have a team, I've just got you."

Philip shook his head. "How do you mean?" he asked with his voice now clearly trembling.

"We finished third on Saturday, behind both Birmingham and Wolverhampton. However, we were only nine points off finishing top. If you had been here and swam the way I know you can swim, we would have won."

"But it wasn't my fault."

"I know, and believe me I did all I could to fight your corner. But you see it's the other parents. There are two reasons why they don't want you on the team. Firstly, I'm afraid your face doesn't fit; you are from the wrong geographical location. Secondly and more importantly, you are a much better swimmer than any of their little darlings. After what happened on Saturday, they have seized upon the opportunity. If you stay they have threatened to take their kids to other clubs. I have to put the club first. To be honest I would be more than happy to see the back of some of these parents but I have to think of the team. I have to do what's best for the club. You are without doubt one of the best young swimmers I've ever seen and maybe when they realise we would be a better club with you in it, they might change their minds. If they do, you will be the first to know but right now, I am afraid you are off the team."

Philip looked towards the bright yellow light hanging from the ceiling, his eyes busily collecting small pools of water as he sniffed and attempted to swallow. Mr Kennedy handed over a one pound note.

"Here, take this back. Make sure that you keep swimming and in a year or so maybe things will be different. I'll let you know." Mr Kennedy stood up, manoeuvred around his desk and opened the door. "I've got to go son. I think you should get yourself home."

Philip stood up, wiped his nose on his sleeve and walked out of the room.

"You're one of the best natural swimmers I have ever seen, remember that," Mr Kennedy said as he turned away and set off to take charge of the training session.

Philip left the building with tears still forming. As he approached his bike, he remembered the pound note now nestled in his pocket. Before cycling home he went to the Wimpy and ate two banana longboats washed down with a glass of lemonade.

Upon returning to his bike and cycling home, and despite having two banana longboats and a glass of lemonade sloshing about in his stomach, Philip felt emptier than a Christmas decorations box on Christmas Eve. His world also felt as dark as the attic that the empty box was now residing in.

It was a little after seven o' clock, Sunday evening. Both Philip and James were in their pyjamas, sitting on the settee and reaping the full benefits of the roaring coal fire. Grace was upstairs after her bath, whilst their mother was completing chores in the kitchen. The monopoly board was set up and ready to go on the dining table. The game was to commence shortly, when there was a gentle tapping sound on the back door. Philip stood up, pulled the curtain across and attempted to peer outside. Looking back at him with his face pressed against the glass stood Craig Swinburn. Not wanting to let any heat out, Philip opened the door just enough for Craig to look inside.

"I need to speak to you," Craig said.

The night air felt colder than an ex-wife's shoulder.

"Give us a minute," Philip replied before closing the door again and heading towards the scullery. He put his coat on and his dad's wellington boots, before heading back through the living room and stepping outside. Craig was waiting.

"You'll have to be quick, we are about to play monopoly. What's up?"

"I've got to tell you something, but you can't tell anybody, you can't tell anybody I've told you. You can't say anything because if they know you know, they will know that I've told you and then they'll know that you know where I've gone."

"What?" Philip replied.

"Understand?"

"No, no I don't understand, what are you on about?"

Craig sighed. "What I'm about to tell you, you can't tell anybody that I've told you, understand."

Philip nodded. "Yes," he muttered. "What is it?" he added as he attempted to fit more snuggly into his coat.

"Claire's pregnant," Craig replied.

Philip just stood and stared at Craig. He desperately tried to think of something to say. Eventually all he managed to mutter was "Pregnant?" That was the best he could do. Then he thought a little more about what Craig had just said to him. "What do you mean, when you've gone? Where are you going?"

"I'm going away. My dad's arranged it all. He says that if I stay here my life will be ruined. My mum's in bits, hasn't stopped crying for two days. She doesn't want me to go but my dad says that it's better for everyone this way."

"Where you going?"

"I'm joining the merchant navy, I'm running away to sea." Craig laughed an empty, hollow laugh that quickly evaporated into the cold dark night.

"You what?" Philip said in utter astonishment at what he had just been told. "But you're still at school."

"I know, but I was gonna leave at Easter and I'm sixteen, so I'm old enough."

"When are you going?"

"Tonight," Craig replied. "My dad was in the merchant navy for nearly fifteen years. He still knows people. A friend of his has got me on to a ship. It leaves Hull at four o' clock tomorrow morning. We're driving up there tonight."

Even with only the dimmest amount of light being emitted from the other side of the curtains, Philip could still see the anguish in Craig's face.

"Do you want to go?"

"Of course I fuckin don't!" Craig snapped. "I'm terrified."

"So why are you going?"

"Because I'm even more terrified of living in a crappy flat in Loxley Close, trying to raise a baby. My dad says it will also be better for Claire this way too. Her grandparents will help her and the baby will be better off. She won't have to manage by herself."

"Won't you get in trouble, not going to school?"

"Don't think that will matter somehow, do you? By the time the truant officer gets wise to it I would have left school anyway. Can't see him searching the oceans for me. Imagine that, some truant officer in a dingy pulling up alongside some big ship to ask me why I'm not at school. I planned on joining the army when I left school, so no big deal."

Philip could tell that it was a big deal and it didn't take much working out to see that Craig was scared stiff of the prospect of what lay ahead.

"So why have you come to tell me?" Philip asked.

"You're good at writing, letters and stuff, you write to that footballer."

"Not for much longer," Philip interjected.

"Yeah well, I want you to write to me. Tell me what's going on."

"How?"

"My dad says that there is a standard address that you write to. You just have to add the name of the vessel. Somebody knows where all these ships are going and the post gets sent to the ports they will call at."

"Oh right."

"It might take a few weeks to get the letters but I'll get them."

Suddenly the back door swung open and Grace's head appeared. "Mum wants to know what you're doing out here," she said. "We're waiting to play Monopoly."

"I'm coming," Philip replied, before waiting for Grace to close the door again. As she did so, Philip noticed that Craig was already walking away.

"I've got to go," Craig said. "I'll write to you and send you the address and the name of the ship. You can't tell anybody, okay Phil. I'll see ya Phil, see ya."

Philip stood and watched as Craig disappeared around the corner and out of sight. He didn't much care for a game of Monopoly any more. But knowing full well he would have to play, he slowly made his way back inside the house.

Chapter 80

It wasn't until the following Sunday lunchtime that Philip finally located the courage required to sit down and write what was to be his final letter to Billy. The main talking point of the week, at the bus stop in the mornings, on the bus, at school and on the way home again, had been what was going on with Craig. True to his word, Philip kept his word and never said a word. Paul had called for Craig on Monday morning, as he did every school morning, only to be told that Craig would not be going to school for a while. When Paul called around again on Tuesday evening, he was informed that Craig would be away for the foreseeable future and he was asked not to call around again.

On that first bus journey of the week on Monday morning, Philip spent most of the time gazing through the window and trying to picture Craig, an insignificant, scared boy on a large steel ship in the middle of the sea.

Philip spent the week at school doing his utmost to keep out of trouble. He was determined not to have to pay a visit to Mr Spencer's office on the following Monday morning. He had half expected to be summoned on the Monday after being removed from the swimming team but to his astonishment and relief, it didn't happen.

Two further minor but notable events that week came in the shape of the police visiting the house on Wednesday evening and Paul McBride waiting for Philip outside the newsagents on Thursday evening. The police came calling, to Philip's mum's obvious annoyance, around teatime and wanted to know if Francis had been in contact. They went to the trouble of pointing out that his current actions were not helping his cause and if he was to get in touch, then they all needed to stress upon him that he was only making matters worse for himself in the long run. However the two officers themselves were given a very short, sharp response and told not to call at the house again.

Paul McBride was a different matter and one that wasn't deterred quite as quickly or easily. He accompanied Philip for over half of his paper round, thrusting a folded piece of paper at him at every opportunity.

"Come on Phil, what gives? Money to be made."

"I can't, I told you I can't. If my mum finds out, she'll go mad."

"How will your mum find out? You're hardly going to tell her."

"She'll find out the same way as last time," Philip replied before disappearing into a block of flats at the end of Ellacombe Road, to deliver his papers.

Upon exiting the block, Paul was still waiting. "What do you mean, last time?" He asked. "What last time?"

"I got caught, that's what," Philip began. "In Owen Owens, I got arrested and taken to Little Park Street. They sent for my mum, she had to come and get me. Try and guess how happy she was about that?"

"You're joking."

"No I'm not," Philip replied with a voice as rigid as the handle bars he was now holding.

"Have you been charged?"

"No, I got a caution."

"Then what are you worried about, you're in the clear. Some easy money to be made here," Paul said as he again waved the piece of paper about in front of Philip. "Lots of easy items on here."

"If they're that easy, then why don't you steal them?" Philip replied.

"Look," Paul said as he leant over and dropped the piece of paper into Philip's bag. "Just have a look, no harm in looking is there. No pressure, I'll come and finds ya sometime next week."

It was just after midday on Sunday when Philip finally sat down in his bedroom with a blank piece of paper and a pen in front of him. 'Economics of the Real World' on 'BBC1' and the fact that his mother wanted to listen to some music whilst cooking Sunday lunch had finally driven him upstairs. A slight, soft snow flurry was drifting past his bedroom window and the smell of a roast dinner and the sound of Elvis Presley were drifting up the stairs as he straightened the piece of paper and lifted up the pen.

Due to an excellent result the day before, he was able to start the letter on a positive note. A very good three-one home win over a strong Arsenal side who were chasing a European spot in the league had stretched the unbeaten run to twenty eight games. A goal down at half-time, Philip had feared the worst, but two second half goals from Joe Jordan and an own goal had rescued both points and the unbeaten run. The letter itself, though not necessarily long, took several attempts to write and the final version, the one he posted, wasn't complete until Thursday evening.

Dear Billy

Congratulations on the excellent result against Arsenal last weekend. Hopefully we will get a similar result against Manchester United this Saturday. I am sorry that I have taken some time to write to you but it has been a bit difficult deciding how best to tell you my news. After a lot of thought, I have decided to give up swimming, for now at least. With my dad leaving, I now have much more responsibility at home and that must come first. There is lots more for me to do now around the house and at weekends, helping both my mother and my younger brother. I want to thank you for writing to me these past few months and for all of your good advice but I think it is now time that I learnt to stand on my own two feet. Good luck with the rest of the season and with the unbeaten run. I hope we win the league.

Philip.

Philip took a while to release his grip but on Friday afternoon, whilst on his paper round, he posted the letter in the post box on Broad Park Road.

Perhaps because it was, Saturday seemed like a fairly normal day, other than the discussions about Craig on the bus into town. Philip, James, Martin and Paul spent the day at the baths. En route to the pool and on the journey home, several possible theories about Craig, ranging from him running away with a teacher from Lyng Hall School, to his joining the foreign legion were discussed. It was Martin who had offered up the foreign legion option on account of him recently watching Laurel and Hardy in the 'Flying Deuces'.

After the swimming and a trip to Fishy Moores for a cone of chips, it was back home in time for the football scores. The horrific thought of losing to relegation-threatened Manchester United had niggled away at him all day and he couldn't quite shake it off, it was like having wet feet on a cold day. He needn't had worried; two second half goals from Joe Jordan and Mick Jones had secured the win. The result kept them at the top of the table and also stretched the unbeaten run to twenty nine games, a victory that was extra sweet.

The following week, Philip narrowly avoided a trip to Mr Spencer's office by only picking up one detention. Once again he couldn't resist the booth scoring game in his French lesson on Wednesday. On this occasion, all four players on the back row of booths received a detention slip. Thankfully, the second detention slip, which would have triggered an office visit and a conduct card, was averted despite coming close a couple of times.

The following week was a similar tale with Thursday being a particularly bad day. Leeds F.A.Cup exit at the hands of second division Bristol City the night before, probably went some way to explaining his lack of effort and disaffected attitude, but thankfully it only resulted in the one detention slip being issued in Geography.

Saturday however was to take disappointment to a whole new level. A depleted Leeds United team took to the field away at Stoke City. Midway through the first half it appeared that it was going to be business as usual with Leeds United already two goals to the good. A deflected free kick in the twenty seventh minute halved the deficit and was a catalyst for a Stoke City revival. By half-time it was all square at two-two. The second half saw ex-Chelsea player, Alan Hudson, pulling the strings in midfield and by full time a headed goal by the colossal defender Denis Smith had inflicted the first defeat of the season. The game finished in a three-two win for Stoke. The unbeaten run was finally over. To rub salt in the open gaping wounds, Peter Lorimer had a thunderous free kick disallowed in the last minute of the game. The following day Philip watched the highlights on Star Soccer. He could almost sense the obvious joy in Hugh John's commentary when the final whistle was blown.

When Philip arrived home from school on Thursday evening, he had just about come to terms with the defeat. He was however surprised to discover a letter waiting for him. He knew straight away that it was from Billy. He grabbed the letter off the dining table, rushed upstairs, kicked off his platform shoes, climbed onto his bed and carefully opened the letter.

Dear Philip

Like you, it has taken me some time to write this letter and just like you, I too have been struggling with how best to say what I want to say. I think that it really is a shame that you have chosen to give up on your swimming and I hope more than anything that it is only a temporary decision. To have something in your life that you enjoy and are also good at is something to cherish and not to be taken lightly. I can speak from experience.

I fully understand your reasons for giving up; family is indeed important. But I hope, in time, you can and will return to the pool. Speaking of things coming to an end, yes the unbeaten run is finally over. I am not entirely sure what exactly happened at Stoke. We started the game very well but from the moment they scored their first goal we seemed to play like a struggling division four side. The last-minute disallowed goal would only have papered over the cracks of a very poor performance.

I am glad that you feel you are ready and that it is time to stand on your own two feet and take on more responsibility. It is just a shame that you feel you cannot write to me any longer. I just want you to know that your letters have really helped. They helped me to stay focused when times were tough during the unbeaten run and they helped me to help the team stay focused. In a strange way, the loss at Stoke has offered some relief and it seems to have lifted the pressure off both me and the rest of the team. Your letters though, as I just mentioned, helped me through this period of games. If you take away with you only one crumb of comfort from this, please always remember, you are the boy who saved Billy Bremner.

Take good care of yourself and your family. Keep working hard at school. You will only

ochieve in life if you are prepared to make the effort. Fingers are tightly crossed for the rest of the season. I know that I will always have your support. If you change your mind and want to drop me a line in the future, you are always welcome.

Your friend.
Billy.

Philip read the letter twice more before folding it up, placing it back in the envelope and putting it with his other letters. He changed out of his school uniform, went downstairs and into the scullery to collect his paperbag. He was just about to set off for his round when his mother appeared in the doorway to the kitchen.

"Hurry back," she said. "I thought we would have fish 'n' chips from the chip shop tonight," she added with a broad warm smile across her face.

Philip smiled back. "Will do," he replied before turning away and stepping out of the door.

The End

www.ingramcontent.com/pod-product-compliance
Lightning Source LLC
Chambersburg PA
CBHW011956150426
43200CB00018B/2923